T3-BEA-345

Inside

Transracial

Adoption

Inside

Transracial

Adoption

Gail Steinberg and Beth Hall

Perspectives Press
Indianapolis, Indiana

Copyright © 2000 by Gail Steinberg and Beth Hall
All rights reserved. No part of this book may be reproduced in any manner or form whatsoever, electrical or mechanical, including photocopying, recording, internet or information storage and retrieval systems, without written permission, except in the case of brief quotations embodied in critical articles and reviews. For information address the publisher:

Perspectives Press
P.O. Box 90318
Indianapolis, IN 46290-0318 USA
(317)872-3055
http://www.perspectivespress.com

Book and cover design and production by Bookwrights, www.bookwrights.com
Manufactured in the United States of America

Hardcover ISBN 0-944934-24-2
Softcover ISBN 0-944934-26-9

Family photos used for the cover and throughout *Inside Transracial Adoption* are of Pact families photographed by Eliot Holtzman

Mi Ok Song Bruiningís poem from the collection *A Ghost at Heart's Edge* edited by Susan Ito and Tina Corvin (North Atlantic Books, l999) has been used in Section 1: The Experts Speak Out, with her permission

Lynna Williams' quote in Section 3: The Experts Speak Out was used by permission from the collection *A Ghost at Heart's Edge* edited by Susan Ito and Tina Corvin, (North Atlantic Books, 1999)

Casi Wildflower's quote in Section 4: The Experts Speak Out was used with permission from *Stories of Adoption: Loss & Reunion* by Eric Blau, M.D. (NewSage Press, 1993.)

Library of Congress Cataloging-in-Publication Data

Steinberg, Gail, 1942-
    Inside transracial adoption / by Gail Steinberg and Beth Hall.
        p. cm.
    Includes bibliographical references and index.
    ISBN 0-944934-24-2 (hardcover : alk. paper) — ISBN 0-944934-26-9 (pbk.: alk. paper)
    1. Interracial adoption—United States. 2. Intercountry adoption—United States. 3. Adopted children—United States—Psychology. 4. Racially mixed children—United States—Psychology. 5. Whites—Race identity—United States. I. Hall, Beth, 1954- II. Title.

HV875.64 .S74 2000
362.73'4'0973—dc21

00-035984

To our children:
Sofia Hall Gallagher, James Hall Gallagher, Liza Triggs,
Seth Steinberg, Jeremy Steinberg and Shira Gale,
in gratitude for the greatest gift—being your mothers.

Contents

Section 1:
The Challenges of Transracial Adoption 1

The I—You Bridge 2
The Experts Speak Out 5
How to Use This Book 7
Our Perspective on Transracial Adoption 8
Identifying the Real Issues 10
Race=Adoption 11
Personality Issues 12
Acknowledging Differences 14
Negative Reactions from Communities of Color 18
Our Working Definitions 21
Useful Books 25

Section 2:
Racial Identity 27

Protecting My Child from Her Mom, A Racist 28
The Experts Speak Out 31
Racial Identity: For People of Color 34
Racial Identity: For White People 36
Facing the Issues: Race 38
Respecting Feelings 51
Strategies: Seeking Diversity 60
Strategies: Concrete Tools for Operating in a Racist World 71
Useful Books 96

Section 3:
Family Matters 99

Together. No Matter What 100
The Experts Speak Out 103
Strengthening Family Identity 105
Parenting in Adoption 128
Birth Family 138
Extended Family 143

Siblings in Adoptive Families 148
"You are soooooo special." One-Child Families 155
Families that Grow through Birth plus Adoption 157
International Adoptive Families 159
Single-Parent Transracial Families 168
Gay and Lesbian Families 170
Religious Choices and Beliefs 172
Providing for Your Childís Future 176
When Family Members Have Special Needs and Issues 177
Useful Books 188

Section 4:
Through Development's Lens 191

All in a Name 192
The Experts Speak Out 195
Sorting Out the Issues 198
Infants 199
Preschoolers 216
School-Agers 232
Teens 253
Our Children Are Our Children Forever 272
Useful books 277

Section 5:
Cultural Specifics in Focus 281

Belonging or Be-Longing? 282
The Experts Speak Out 285
Building a Foundation 287
Who Defines Normal?—White Identity 290
One Drop Rules—African American Identity Issues 301
Racism and Rice—Asian Identity Issues 324
Mi Familia, Mi Corazon—Latino Identity Issues 339
Being Seen—Native American Identity Issues 349
More than a Box—Biracial and Multiracial Identity Issues 355
Claiming Identity—Whatever the Culture 366
Useful Books 370

Section 6:
Parting Thoughts 377

And so it goes 378
A Transracially-Adopted Child's Bill of Rights 379
A Transracial Adoptive Parent's Wish List 380
Conclusions 381
Test Your Knowledge 383

Acknowledgments 385
Index 387
About Pact, An Adoption Alliance 397
About Perspectives Press 401
About the Authors 403

Section One

❖

The Challenges of Transracial Adoption

The I—You Bridge

By Gail Steinberg

I like to imagine that the Traveler's Aid waiting room at Chicago's O'Hare airport has not been remodeled in the last thirty years and has become a shrine to the night when Mel and I spent a century there, waiting to be transformed into a mommy and daddy. Looking back at it now, that room seems like the place where Dorothy first met the Wizard of Oz. She had built up her hopes to be saved by his magic and what saved her instead was a glimpse of the truth.

Decorated in airport impersonal—pale green plasterboard walls, a row of plastic chairs lined up against the walr , and in one corner a desk with nobody at it—the waiting room was too small to hold all of us. "All" means ten sets of anxious parents-to-be from different cities in the Midwest who had never met one another before, all adopting for the first time. We had been told to be there at exactly 9 PM, but we were not told the plane from Korea wouldn't land until midnight. Mel and I got there about four hours early, and we were not the first. This was in the olden days, before they had such a thing as "smoking areas." We sat forever on hard green plastic chairs, blowing smoke rings, exchanging nervous laughter and attempting chitchat in the smoky room we had been cautioned not to leave.

That room was on the "I" side of an invisible bridge. On the "I" side, all one could know was how "I" felt, what "I" wanted, how nervous "I" was, and what "I" needed. In that wary time of waiting, our view of the "you" side of the bridge was so out of focus that not one among us even thought to write down the others' names and addresses, just in case the children might want to get together later.

At one AM ten small, disheveled children got off the plane on the "you" side of the bridge. Lined up with the other parents at the gate without a clue about what to do, I wondered who was going to tell us which child would be our daughter. Straining to recognize her from the wrinkled snapshot we had memorized during the billion impatient years just past, Mel and I silently promised each other that we would love her anyway, even if she turned out to be the ugly one, the one lagging behind to pick her nose. It was incredible to be so pumped up with the hope of getting all I'd ever wanted, yet so scared it wouldn't work out right, I didn't dare breathe.

The Korean workers who had traveled with the children did not help us. They were busy, talking to each other over the kids' heads. Since nobody told us what to do, we parents-to-be began running from child to child, searching the white plastic bracelets each one wore, exactly the kind they graft onto you when you check into the hospital, each of us looking for our child's name. It's beyond belief when you're feeling so crazy to have to invade a child's privacy like that. Exhausted and terrified, the kids just let us do it. Swept up in the frenzy, I felt like I was violating the helpless, but I didn't let that stop me. I was too busy trying to find my daughter, as if someone else might claim her first.

And then we found her! She was exquisite, fragile, three years old, and had our last name on her wristband. I've tried to remember exactly how she looked in that first moment when we first saw her, how she held her head, the look in her eyes, how she moved her hands, that sweet-sour ribbon of her sweaty scent...but honestly I can't be sure. Maybe it's too long ago to remember. I'm afraid I was too flooded with my own feelings to be able to wake up and really see hers.

What I can remember is that it hit me in that moment that it mattered to me in a way I had been sure it wouldn't that she was Korean ("I can love any child. I just want to be someone's mom."). I hated myself for even having that thought. I was afraid to admit I felt so clumsy. I couldn't risk telling my husband; it was so huge, so surprising, such an enormous blank. What did she think we were doing, bundling her into the heavy sweater we had bought that on her little body seemed three sizes too large? Why did she think we were stuffing a teddy bear that was almost as big as she was into her arms? A bear? The Korean group leaders seemed tight lipped and disapproving. All the other parents seemed to know what they were doing and their children were smiling. Someone was telling us all to line up for a photograph. That couldn't be right.

Instead we scooped our daughter up and ran to the car, desperate to get out of that airport and away from all those other people, out of that town, to hold her in our arms and rejoice that she was here, that at last our dream had come true. Was I really suddenly someone's mother? Mel was behind the wheel. Our plan was to keep driving until we got to our home in Ohio, a six to seven hour car trip. We were determined that she should sleep in her own new bed that night, but it was too dark for us to see what she looked like. I had to hold her as tight as I could, because she was too droopy to hold me back.

Finally I had to recognize that she was miserable. I was devastated. It's almost too painful to talk about. I had been so sure that I would be such a wonderful mother and that she would feel nothing but immediate overwhelming love for me that I couldn't believe it. I had thought of myself as good with kids. I'd even won the "Counselor of the Year" award once upon a time. "Let's stop at a motel," I said. "Something's wrong. We need to stop moving."

When Toto pulled back the curtain and revealed to Dorothy that the Wizard of Oz was not a magic force, but a harassed little man, the start of her journey to her real home began. When our little girl sat rigid on my lap, avoiding eye contact, not reacting to anything we said or did, it was the starting point of our noticing what she needed.

Her behavior forced me to challenge my own assumptions about what I needed to do and about the scary transition she was facing. I'm embarrassed that it took me that long to begin the crossing to where she was—out there all alone on some strange planet. It was the first step of moving toward her side of the bridge, the "you" side. On the "you" side, you come first, your needs are more important than mine. I can see you. Inching toward the "you" side was the first dawning of what it really is to become a parent.

The Experts Speak Out

They said
smile for the camera
Open your eyes, they are squinting
But my eyes weren't squinting.
They said
Stop crying, stop feeling bad.
Those kids who call you "Chink"
And "Flat Face"
Don't know anything
Besides, you probably provoked them.
They said
You don't belong here.
Where do you come from?
Do you speak English?
Do you like America?
As if I just landed
From a distant galaxy.
They said
Everything I hoped and dreamed
And prayed they wouldn't.
They still do."

—Mi Ok Song Bruining

"*Before I was adopted, I was separated from two families—my birth mother's and my birth father's. I was also separated from my culture and my race. These losses have been huge. People interpret honest talk about them to mean that I wish I weren't a part of my family. OR that I am not connected. OR maybe even that my mom and dad did something wrong by adopting me. OR that I am not grateful. But you know what, I am not 'grateful' that I had to be adopted. I don't' feel 'wonderfully lucky' that I was raised in a culture different from the one I was born into. What I do feel is that I love my mom and dad very much. I do feel totally connected to them. I wouldn't trade my family for any family in the world—and still I know what I have lost.*"

—Liza Steinberg Triggs

"*It is essential that families who adopt a child from another country acknowledge, accept, and care a great deal about the heritage of the child they are adopting, not in a patronizing or condescending fashion, but in a manner that is genuine and born out of dignity and respect for the child's birth country… All of us who are adopted come to our families with histories behind us. That truth cannot be ignored. Instead, it is important to acknowledge that you are an adopted person forever. That isn't good or bad; it just is. What is essential is to determine the best role of that fact in our lives."*

—Susan Soon Keum Cox

"My name is Roxanne and this is the story of my adoption experience: not so sweet, but I survived, which is basically the point of my telling it. For anyone who is in fear of the unforeseen monsters that may be lurking around the corners of adoption: yes, as with anything, there are monsters to be conquered and there is that potential that they could gobble us up, which makes our actions so much more important. But please, for a moment consider that as you are reading this, there is a child who is battling very real monsters alone. And imagine that when you make the commitment to take up arms, side by side with the child, how many unnecessary scars you can, as a family, prevent."

—Roxanne Agur

The Challenges of Transracial Adoption

How to Use This Book

Covering all of the issues for multiracial families formed by adoption or fostering is an impossible task. Each family is unique. Our goal is to provide information on issues common to these uncommon families, to offer concrete strategies, and to allow you a variety of ways to use the material.

Inside Transracial Adoption is organized by three general categories: racial identity, family life, and adoption. It focuses on the challenges families face; the development of racial identity for people of color and for white people; family issues common to all transracial families and specific to families of particular construction; and also looks at these issues from a developmental perspective, as they affect infants, preschoolers, school-aged children, teens, and young adults.

Audience

We have written this book for parents of transracially adopted kids. We include among this group international and domestic adopters, infant and older child adopters, adopters of special needs kids and kids who are "normal." Between us, we ourselves are parents to children in all of the above categories. Although each subgroup has its own unique experiences, we believe that the adventures we share in common far outweigh the differences. We know that the majority of parents who adopt across racial lines are white. This book speaks to white parents in particular, focusing on differences between white perceptions of the world and the experiences of individuals of color. In spite of this, we believe this material will be important to any adoptive parent whose child is of a different race or ethnicity than him or herself. Our focus is on children of color and so we are not specifically addressing issues for children adopted across ethnic or cultural lines who are the same race as their adoptive parents. We have chosen to write about adoptive parenting rather than foster parenting, but we hope this book will be useful to those that find themselves in fostering and other roles with children across racial and cultural lines.

Language

Terminology is more than personal style in a book like this. It's very political. We use the terms *transracial* and *transcultural* interchangeably although we understand that they each have different meanings. We have chosen to use what we hope are respectful terms to describe populations of color, people touched by adoption, and family structures. Our information comes largely from what people who are part of the groups described have suggested to us are the terms they would have us use to describe them. Please see the definitions on page 21–24 for a listing of these terms. If the terms we've chosen are not to your liking, we hope that you will still be able to consider our larger message.

Our Perspective on Transracial Adoption

A *problem* may be unsolvable—at the least, perplexing and difficult. An *issue* is a starting point—a matter that results from a cause, can be anticipated, has no blame attached and can provoke growth and expansion to new consciousness.

A *problem* is perceived of as a challenge or obstacle, a dilemma which requires resolution so that it can be laid to rest. An *issue* can be perceived of as an experience or circumstance to move forward from—an opportunity for change whose goal is not single minded or simple.

Transracial adoption is an issue, complex to be sure. When a family adopts members of different races, each person receives the opportunity to understand and experience life from a new point of view never before imagined. The family as a whole has the chance to move forward to develop its own new form.

Let's begin by our sharing with you what we believe to be some indisputable core truths about transracial adoption:

Principles of Transracial Adoption

- Transracial adoption is more complex than same-race adoption.
- Visible differences between parents and children increase challenges to their acceptance as a family unit.
- There are predictable developmental stages for transracial adoptive families which are different from those of same-race families.

- Issues regarding racial or ethnic awareness and development of positive racial identity must be addressed.
- Transracial adoption is an issue, not a problem.

In a larger context, what makes these core principles indisputable are these broader truths…

Adoption is a response to a life crisis. For all whom it touches, adoption is a turning point separating everything that comes before from what happens after. A decision that forces adults to confront the most basic goals of life, adoption fosters change and growth for all who are touched by it.

Race matters. We believe that holding fast to the stance that love can and should be colorblind (of course it should!) ignores the more complex reality of institutional, societal and internalized racism and so is seriously misguided and potentially damaging to children. When parents are raising a child of a race different from their own, the parents' lack of experience with the race or ethnic background of the child's birth heritage creates challenges for all members of the family. When those parents are white and lack first-hand experiences with racial bias and stereotyping directed towards them, their learning curve to understand and anticipate their children's life experience is likely to be a long one.

Transracial adoption issues are not easy or comfortable subjects to discuss. Support from well-meaning friends and family is not enough. This book exists to serve the special needs of adoptive parents of children of color by providing tools for exploring issues and offering suggestions for moving toward resolution. Breaking through the isolation and discovering how others handle similar situations can be a great relief.

Adoptive families need to develop the desire and capacity to help themselves. Asking for help is not an expression of weakness or defeat but a show of strength, even though you may not be feeling particularly strong at the moment. The alternative, to become passive and not to reach out to find a useful action, is a response that will not serve your family. Our hope for this book is to support your positive desire to stretch as far as you can for your family.

Families built by transracial adoption can let challenges beat them down or they can embrace their issues—a process that only builds strength. The chance to face the issues that come with a multicultural life increase opportunities for intimacy and family cooperation. These experiences form families that are closer and stronger than most. We reject the notion that blood is thicker than water, while believing that racial and cultural pride are part of the birthright and legacy that belongs to our children.

Identifying the Real Issues

"Not everything that is faced can be changed, but nothing can be changed until it is faced"

—James Baldwin

Is transracial adoption best for kids?

Regardless of the factors that contribute to the existence of transracial adoption, it is common and will continue. In the context of children's lives, we believe that the more important questions are

How can children gain their new families without losing their birth heritage?

How can adoptive parents address their child's needs without apologizing for being white?

How can we offer support after placement?

Our focus is to look at concrete ways to make positive differences in children's lives, children whose parents are a different race than their own.

The issues are complex

We believe that transracially-adopted kids have an absolute right to their own history and to honest answers, even to questions not yet asked. The issues facing them and their parents are layered, like an onionskin. At the core are the regular, everyday developmental issues that all children experience as they grow from birth to adulthood, no matter how they joined their families. The next layer is comprised of the basic emotional issues of adoption: sensitivities to loss, attachment, intimacy–core needs (including honesty, including love, including good enough parents who are responsive to their needs,) etc. For children adopted transracially, in addition to all of these things, the extra layer is the challenge of growing up feeling comfortable within one's racial and cultural identity of origin. Adults who grew up with parents of races different from their own often say, "Don't make me choose between my race and culture and my family. I want to feel proud to be who and what I am."

The issue, then, is not transracial adoption, but rather the concern that transracial adoption could result in the loss of racial or cultural identity. Though it is a challenge that parents have probably not faced before, they can provide means for their children to embrace and feel confident in the racial identities that are their birthrights. This will require race-conscious parents who can find the courage to change their own lifestyle in order to place their child's identity needs above their own discomfort or fears.

Feeling separated from the culture one would have grown up in by birth because it has no ongoing presence or priority in your family is a loss of major proportions. It is a loss that can be addressed and, to a great extent, mitigated. When parents make the commitment to stretch their environment, values, and circle of friends to balance family life, so that their child's heritage commands as much space in the life of the family as the parents' heritages do, step one has begun. When parents can connect their child to his or her heritage without apologizing for being white and without keeping the child separated in any way from the traditions within their family, step two will have started. Taking action is step three. Living is step four, and the journey is both exciting and ongoing—the very journey of family intimacy that we came to adoption in search of in the first place!

Race=Adoption

Many transracially-adopted adults have told us that they have never been able to think about adoption as an issue separate from race. For children adopted across racial lines, race and adoption often become inextricably connected. Racial differences may serve both appropriately, and at other times inappropriately, as the universal explanation for issues of "not belonging."

(Gail): According to ten-year-old Liza, "All for one, and one for all," and "If you mess with my sista, brother, you be gone," was "How all black families are." Her own mixture of Muhammed Ali meets the Three Musketeers! Accordingly, she believed her two brothers had been put on earth to guard, defend and rescue her, no questions asked. She was adamant it would be that way in any black family and should be that way in ours. So on the horrible day that the sadistic teenager who lived down the way tried to hurt her kitten James and her two brothers refused to go after him, she went into melt-down. James actually hadn't been hurt. Liza had, by her brothers, not the bully.

Wrapping James in a towel like a baby in swaddling, she sat with him alone in the yard under a tree, fiercely rocking him with a grim, empty stare and tears falling down her cheeks. She looked like the last human left on the planet.

"Liza?" I asked, putting my arm around her. "Let me help you... Breathe."

"They don't care about me," she sobbed. "I wish we could be a black family. They don't act like real brothers"....

Was it the powerful black family she didn't have that she was

*crying for or her fear deep inside that our family wasn't real because
her brothers didn't take care of her in accordance with the myth she
wanted to live by—didn't protect her the way she thought all brothers
should?*

Because race is so obvious a marker of difference between members of a
family created through transracial adoption, it is likely that the child finds
race a powerful reminder of his or her unique status within the family and of
his lack of genetic connection to his adoptive parents.

This does not mean that transracially-adopted kids do not experience
adoption-specific issues around loss, rejection, guilt and shame, grief, identity and intimacy (the seven core issues of adoption so well described by
Deborah N. Silverstein and Sharon Kaplan Roszia in their paper of the same
name). It means only that racial concerns often shape the field on which
those issues play out. For children of color with white parents, loss often
looks like separation from other people of color, shame can feel like being
ashamed of being adopted into another race, and identity questions become
focused on racial or ethnic identity.

Too often adults assume we know what kids mean without really listening to them. We keep our own mouths so busy that we fail to hear what's
coming from theirs. But in the end, the child's perception is all that really
matters. Parents need to let their child teach them about his or her unfolding
sense of adoption and race.

Our goal as transracial adoptive parents must be to have our child able to
say, "I'm glad you are my parent because you care about how I feel."

Personality Issues

Are you the kind of person who is temperamentally well suited to meet
the challenges that are inherent in parenting a child of another race? Each of
us is "hard-wired" in particular ways. That means that we are more comfortable in certain circumstances than others and are likely to make life choices
that support our own personality traits. It can be tremendously useful to think
about your own personality patterns and how they mesh with the issues that
come with parenting across racial lines. Although personality traits are not
easy to change, understanding your own temperament will help you assess
the level of challenge you will feel addressing the issues you and your family
are likely to face.

Transracial adoption means that your family becomes "public" because
the differences between family members are obvious to others. As a parent,

you are on display. If you enjoy being different and standing out from the crowd, as a transracial parent you will get chances every day. On the other hand, if you are shy and like to blend in with others, being out and about with your child is bound to be laborious for you because you will always be noticed. Those of us that are natural hams or easy leaders are likely to find this easier than those who like to be followers or prefer to be one of the crowd. If you share with me (Gail) an inner feeling of being different, you may find transracial adoption relieving, because it affirms and celebrates that inner sense of being different by making it visible.

You will need to seek help from adults of your child's racial or ethnic heritage who understand your child's experiences first hand in ways that you cannot. If you are the sort of person who likes to teach yourself and learn on your own, you will be pushed to seek help in ways you might not do naturally. Having never had the patience to read an owner's manual in my life (Beth), not relying solely on myself is one of my great challenges as a parent. If you hate to seek help or dislike contact with strangers, such tasks will likely prove more demanding for you than for someone who enjoys them. Those of us who are stimulated by new people and information can find this contact invigorating.

Are you the kind of person who tends to read more than one book at a time or likes to have many "irons in the fire" at the same time? If you enjoy complexity, then the demands of transracial parenting will be less challenging for you than if you are the sort of person who strives for a life of simplicity. If you do like simplicity then you will need to satisfy those needs within other areas of your life, because this kind of parenting will be more complicated, not less.

You can expect to face challenges ranging from differing hygiene rituals to preparing your child for situations you have never faced. If you believe there is one right way to do most things, it will be harder for you to incorporate the different points of view that will likely evolve from your child's experiences, but if you take pleasure from considering new ways of thinking, you will enjoy the stimulus. If you have strong points of view about how things ought to be done or what is right and wrong, you will need to develop new flexibility to understand that there can be more than one way to get things done and more than one appropriate response to each situation.

If you understand yourself to be a person who faces significant challenges because of the day-to-day experiences of transracial adoption, take the time to develop some workable coping skills. Being prepared for the lady in the grocery store who makes inappropriate remarks and being able to cope with the emotions she brings up makes all the difference.

Parenting should be enjoyed. Look to your strengths. Acknowledge your weaknesses.

Acknowledging Differences

Your child is having a different experience than you are in the world.

I (Beth) remember the day as if it were yesterday. Gail, Marta (Pact's Adoption Coordinator who happens to be African American), and I went to a race awareness training. The program began with an exercise where each of us said how old we were when we first became aware of racial bias.

I had grown up in a neighborhood of Oakland, California, that my parents had chosen specifically because of its diversity. They wanted us to grow up knowing that racial barriers are wrong. They brought us to civil rights marches, and my father was proud to be the banker for the Black Panthers. I thought back with fond memories on the people of my neighborhood. Earl Fatha Hines' daughter and I were in the same class. I only understood years later what an incredible experience it was for me to grow up dancing in our tu-tu's and go-go boots to his accompaniment. The Kangs lived two doors down and Gracie had been my sister's best friend since forever. I recalled the blessings of growing up in a white family who gave my sister and me the chance to experience a childhood world without racial tension or discord. I figured I was about eight or ten when I began to be aware of the Klan and others who opposed racial unity with such vigor.

Imagine my surprise when Gail said she figured herself to be five or six when she realized the world was racist. I questioned her memory and her veracity, because how could she have realized such a travesty at such a young age? When Marta revealed her own awareness at age three or four, I was truly dumbfounded. I fought their reality with every shred of my own memory and experience. I resisted as long as I could, always my parent's daughter, willing to fight the good fight and stand up for what I knew to be true in my deepest core.

I can't remember another word that was spoken by those trainers but I learned from my friends that day that my own experience as a Mayflower decendant was completely different from that of a Jew whose family had been exterminated in the camps and a black woman who had grown up in the days of busing and forced integration. My liberal white world came shattering down and I realized with a depth and profundity that I hadn't experienced before that everything I had known to be true about the world, about myself and most importantly about the experience of my children was not necessarily so. And so the journey began…

Counter-Intuitive Parenting
The super powers of good parents

Most of us grew up accepting certain myths implying that good parents have the wisdom and the will to take care of all of their child's needs. But what if you can't?

You are the expert on your child

Even though you and your child are of different races, your child needs to belong to your family in every way possible. That means that you must share every aspect of your heritage as unquestioningly as you would with any child you'd given birth to. Your child's primary need is to belong to you. Your child's other primary need is to belong to his or her birth culture.

Culture is what you live

Remember the story of the ugly duckling? Could the mother duck that raised a swan have taught her baby to swim like a swan or to sound like a swan or to act like a swan? Of course not—she was a duck. In this children's story we don't question the truth of this. We empathize with and understand the baby swan's dilemma. We are not surprised that when he compares himself to a duck the little swan sees himself as ugly simply because he's not a duck. But as transracial adoptive parents, we sometimes have a hard time understanding how similar comparisons affect our own children. This happens not because we don't love them, but in fact because we love them so much. We are afraid of failing them. Facing the truth—that we cannot provide what we don't know—is not giving up on parenting your child. It is the way in which we become parents who are able to put their children's needs first, to see their children for who they really are, for all that they can be. The duck mother could certainly teach the baby swan everything she knew about how to act like a duck, but she couldn't know how to be a swan. She could read 1000 books about swan history and habits, she could become a duck who knew a great deal about swans, but she couldn't be an authentic swan. Baby swan could learn all of the important bird stuff from mother duck, but he had to learn from other swans how to be a swan.

In the same way, the foremost challenge you face as an adoptive parent is that you will not be able to provide directly for all of your child's essential needs, no matter how hard you try and no matter how much you want to. No matter how many books you've read or how much soul food or chilies or dim sum you eat or how educated you become about the history of her race, you will not be able to provide personally for your child's need to belong to his culture. You will always be acting beyond your own intuition and experience and can never be fully conscious of all the implications of your child's birth identity. Nor can your child ever become the same race as you. Neither should she be reduced to thinking that to join your race would be better because you are her greatest role model and after all you are white. Culture is not something you learn about in books. Culture is something you live. You become part of it by living in the experience. Instead, your role becomes one of giving permission to your children to explore, to learn and to live the cultural heritage that is theirs. This begins by learning and appreciating together, but one day it means being willing and open to letting them waddle alone to the pond of swans, knowing that you have given them the confidence and presence to learn and to grow into the beautiful swan that they are.

Family is where belonging starts

"A rightful place is not one that is granted by the powers that be, not even by parents; this is too shaky a source for a true feeling of belonging. A rightful place is the place we gain for ourselves, first through loving and being loved in the right way, later through one's own efforts. This alone makes the place secure, one's very own."

— Bruno Bettelheim

What this is really about is how you and your own dear swanling can rest securely in the feeling of belonging together when you experience daily life differently because others treat you differently. We're almost certain that, even during the times when confusion prohibits conclusions about such things, we all just know that even though they have so much in common, both being birds and all—a duck is different than a swan…it just is. Think of it this way: if a man and a woman each dressed up and went to a meeting wearing a fabulous satin robe or a football helmet, would you respond the same to each of them? Be honest! So, for reasons we don't need to go into here, we know that one of the important ways we all find out who we are in the world is by the messages we get from others. The question is, in spite of our differences, can members of a family feel that they belong together? We believe that this is possible. No, in truth, we *know* that this is possible. The journey of adoption, and especially transracial adoption, is daily living proof—family is about person-hood, about relationship and knowing. Outside the door other factors matter, we are defined or at least influenced by societal norms and people's reactions and realities, but in the intimacy of our families, when they are healthy and conscious, we are simply known—perhaps the greatest expression of love there is.

"To belong" means "to have a rightful place." Sooner or later, if things go right, no matter whether you join your family by birth or by adoption, no matter your age, or how weird, or boring, or amazing your family is, you come to believe in an absolute way that you have a rightful place in your home and that's where you learn how to love and be loved, to become yourself, to feel safe, and to accept your family members even when they're weird. With the foundation of family life, you have what you need to find your rightful place in your racial group, neighborhood, kindergarten class, church, synagogue, or ashram, etc.

Finding our rightful place may be the work we are put on earth to do. Even though you and your child will never share a racial experience, the roots he grows within your family can be so formative that deep inside they will be the means by which he comes to recognize himself. Adoption exists because most of us agree that if kids don't have a family first and feel secure in their own place within it, their chances of feeling part of the larger world are usually enormously diminished. Family is the beginning for all that is possible beyond.

Be a bridge

But don't make kids choose between family and race! Children can't make such a choice without negating parts of themselves. In order to feel whole, they must feel connected to all of the worlds they inhabit. Every adopted person has a dual identity: one based on genetic heritage, the other shaped by experiences in the family in which he grows up. For those adopted transracially, this duality plays out in the context of race. Your child needs to belong to groups you cannot belong to. So when you can't be the direct provider of culture, be a bridge to the culture your child needs to be a part of. Please don't feel discouraged by his participation in a culture that does not include you. The connecting links you can forge will not only support him, but will expand your family life in ways that will continue to unfold throughout your lives. Nothing could be more positive.

This is a wake-up call

The best tool you can develop as a parent of a child of another race is a healthy ability to challenge your own assumptions about what you need to do and about what your child faces. Even though, in every possible way, you are your child's parents and she is your child, she will be living in a different world than do you. You will not be able to provide for all her needs yourself. Once you give up that expectation, you can begin the process of providing all that you have to offer.

Negative Reactions from Communities of Color

I (Beth) never forgot the look in her eyes. The way she hated me without even knowing me. Couldn't she see I was on her side? Couldn't she tell I didn't believe she should have less and I more, even though there was a difference between the color of our skins?

My friend Carl and I were only fifteen. On a "date" of sorts, going to a statewide high school basketball tournament at the Coliseum where the NBA usually played. We were on our own, no parents. Although we had been unable to drive ourselves, we felt big and at the same time nervous with each other and being amongst such a big crowd on our own. Toward the end of the event, we went out to call my parents for a ride. I remember being on the phone with my mom, when my world changed. Carl was being dragged and kicked by two black boys who were larger and fiercer than we could ever be in the next decade. The girl with the eyes came up to me and started yelling. Somehow I couldn't seem to hear her. I was vaguely aware that my mother was screaming on the phone I had dropped but everything seemed pretty surreal. The girl kept screaming and finally I realized she wanted my money and my watch.

I was so taken aback that I responded with words, the only defense I could seem to find in my panic and disbelief; "Hey, you're making a mistake. I'm on your side. You don't have to do this. Please, we can…" That was when she looked at me with the hate and began to beat me up. She couldn't see who I was—to her I was just another honky, a stupid white girl, and part of the larger conspiracy to ruin her life.

As the gang left, one of the boys who had been part of it all hung back and found a way to look me in the eye. "We can't change the way it is. You gotta accept who you are, who we are. We will never be on the same side. You gotta accept who you are, or you gonna be dead. Don't forget what I'm sayin', and don't ever do it again."

They had beat us up pretty good, especially Carl; taken our stuff and left and all the while my mother hung on the phone screaming for it all to stop. When we finally came out of our daze and spoke to her again, my father was on his way to our rescue. We both had to be hospitalized and treated for our injuries. In the hours and days that followed, Carl moved from scared to angry and we were never really friends again. He hated "them" and would never forgive their injustice. I tried to explain that their whole life experience had made them think we were part of the problem instead of the solution. It sounded weak, even to me. But I couldn't accept the reality that she hated me without even knowing me.

I learned that day that I am a white girl, now and forever. Those black kids were far too consumed with sorting out their own life issues to be concerned with my delicate feelings. Except for that one boy. I have often wondered what became of him. Because in his eyes I saw the sadness of living with the harsh reality of racism but also the knowledge of what might have been. We don't have to like it. And maybe we don't have to accept it all the time, but he was right. We have to accept who we are and who "they" are and know that it makes a difference before we can ever begin to understand or communicate.

Most people understand that the great majority of people who adopt do so because of the yearning to raise a child and live as a family. The same is true for parents who adopt across racial lines. But as the African proverb says, "It takes a village to raise a child." In order for the child to succeed, it is essential that both the child's parents and members of the child's racial or ethnic community see themselves as allies and friends of transracial families. Our children need us all.

Parents must help children feel part of the race with which society will identify them. To learn to connect, these children must have role models within their race. Parents must include adults of their children's race as friends, business partners, and skilled professionals. Picture books, ethnic restaurants and festivals are not enough. But it's a whole lot easier to say "go out and make significant relationships with folks of color" than it is to do it. Building these kinds of relationships requires learning respectful approaches that may be totally new to you, learning how to find common ground, and learning new ways to nurture such friendships once they get going.

And in spite of your best efforts, there will be some people of color who will not accept your family. On a street corner not far from one of our homes is a sign that says,

"STOP STEALING OUR CHILDREN AND CALLING IT
ADOPTION. TAKE BACK OUR OWN!"

Yes, there is work to be done in communities of color to help people understand the devastating fear children can feel if they imagine that they may be forced to choose between the family they feel part of and people of their same race or ethnicity. Suspicion about the motives of white families adopting children of color can appear anywhere along the spectrum, from the grotesque fear that the children will be cut up and their vital organs used as transplants, to the belief that people are stealing children for the pleasure of ownership. In order for our kids to find their rightful places, communities of color must welcome children and allow them to participate, regardless of their parentage. Not to do so is to deny them their birthright.

But members of those communities themselves—leaders whose ideas and voices have earned respect—best accomplish the work of influencing opinion. How grandiose it would be to think that we get to be in charge of how others welcome our children! Who are we to make demands of communities we don't belong to, no matter how right the cause? We see terrible things happening across the planet on a daily basis when one group tries to control another's beliefs and actions. So please let's put our soapboxes back in the attic. We can demand all we want and in the nicest possible ways that our child's community accommodate her needs, but we can't be in charge and will only seem self serving if we mount a political campaign. Acceptance has to be earned one person at a time, like linking prayer beads together end to end.

Our work is on a different plane. It is helping our children to understand the context and history behind the signs in our neighborhoods. It is helping them to feel safe. Despite the fact that many will not understand or accept their situation they don't have to choose. Slowly, slowly, we progress, one person at a time, as we nurture a friendship, opening our lives and our hearts until understanding develops. And it will happen that your new friend of color will hold your child and see her needs, and invite her in. And our children will be seen and our hearts understood.

If we are successful at giving transracially-adopted children all that they need, we will raise adults with a unique ability to understand and interact with white-dominated society, while retaining proud membership in their own racial community.

Our Working Definitions

African American: n.	A person of African heritage who is a native or in American: n habitant of America.
Amerasian: n.	A person whose parents are nationals of both America and one of the Asian/Pacific Island countries
Asian/Pacific Islander: n.	A person whose parents are members of one of the ethnic groups designated Asian, e.g., Chinese, Filipino, Japanese, Asian Indian, Korean, Vietnamese, Laotian, Cambodian, Thai, Hmong, Burmese, Sri Lankan, Bangladeshi, Malayan, Indonesian, Samoan, Fijian, Pakistani. Some also would include Iranians, Turkish, Iraqi, Jordanian, and Palestinian people as Asians
Bicultural: a.	Having or showing competence in two cultures, balancing two cultures
Biracial: a.	Having genetic parents belonging to two different races, e.g. biracial child
Black: n.	A term for a person of African descent. Once used within the African American community as a pejorative, the mid 20th century goal of reclaiming "blackness" as a chosen term of identity was believed to help combat skin color hierarchy by taking the word back and empowering it with positive attributes. "Black is beautiful" was a well-accepted campaign during the Civil Rights movement. Similar reclaiming is currently happening in the open adoption records movement reclaiming the word *bastard* by the group Bastard Nation and in the Gay and Lesbian movement reclaiming the use of the term *queer*
Culture: n.	a. the customary beliefs, social forms and material traits of a racial, religious or social group; depends upon man's capacity for learning and transmitting knowledge to succeeding generations; b. The sum total of ways of living developed by a group of human beings to meet biological and psycho-social needs:

continued

continued from previous page	refers to elements such as values, norms, beliefs, attitudes, folkways, behavior styles and traditions that are linked together to form an integrated whole that functions to preserve the society
Ethnic: a.	Of or relating to races or large groups of people classed according to common traits and customs. *It is important not to confuse the term* minority *with the term* ethnic. *Ethnic groups may be either a minority or a majority in a particular population*
Ethnicity: n.	Connectedness based on commonalties (such as religion, nationality, region etc.) where specific aspects of cultural patterns are shared and where transmission over time creates a common history
European American n.	A term applied to people with ancestry from mostly northern European countries; sometimes southern and eastern European ancestry is also implied
heritage: n.	a. Something transmitted by or acquired from a predecessor: a legacy; b. Something possessed as a result of one's natural situation or birth: a birthright
Hispanic: n	People of Latin American descent living in the U.S., e.g. Cuban, Mexican, Puerto Rican, etc. *Preferred term in the Midwest and on the east coast. Many Hispanics prefer to be referred to according to their nationality. In much of Texas we understand Mexican Americans prefer to be called simply Mexicans even if they have lived in the US for many generations*
Indian: n.	A native or inhabitant of India or of the East Indies
Interracial: a.	A relationship between two people (peers, adults) of different races, e.g., interracial marriage
Latino/ Latina: n.	A person of Latin American descent living in the U.S., e.g. Cuban, Mexican, Puerto Rican, etc. Probably short for the Spanish word *latinoamericano. Preferred term on the West Coast. In California, many*

continued

	Mexican Americans choose to use the term Chicano/ Chicana, terms similar to Latino/Latina with an additional political meaning having to do with involvement in the Civil Rights movement
Mulatto: a.	A person of mixed race, usually derived of black and white ancestry. *Derived from the Spanish word for mule, this is a once derogatory term that is today sometimes used among biracial people about themselves— as explained in the definition of black, above, in this context it is a term this community is choosing to 'take back.' It is not a term we ever use nor recommend that white people should use*
Multiracial: a.	Formed through the coming together of two or more races, e.g. multiracial child, multiracial family
Native American: n	Member of indigenous tribes that live in the United States
Oriental: a	A term that applies to objects like art and rugs derived from Asian cultures or countries, but does not properly apply to Asian people
People of Color: n	Members of those groups in America that are and have been historically targeted by racism. This includes people of African, Asian, Latino and Native American descent
Race: n.	a. A class or kind of people unified by community of interests, habits or physical characteristics; b. Groupings of mankind possessing traits that are transmissible by descent, and sufficient to characterize it as a distinct human type. *The concept of human biological race is based on the false assumption that anatomical traits, such as skin color, hair or facial traits cluster together in single distinct groups of people. They do not. There are no clearly distinct "black," "white," or other races*
Self-concept: n.	The mental image one has of oneself

continued

continued from previous page	
self-esteem: n.	How we feel about our self concept
self-image: n.	How we imagine ourselves to be
Transracial: a.	Connected across races; e.g., transracially adopted children are adopted by parents of a race different from their own, transracial families are multiracial families
White: n.	A group or race of people of European decent who currently hold a dominant role in U.S. society; these are people who often are associated with reduced skin pigmentation although that is not definitive
White privilege: n.	A system of societal benefits received simply be cause one is white, which one may not have asked for or realize that one has. *Examples of these privileges include the expectation of being treated with respect in most situations, having shopping malls and grocery stores with fair prices in your neighborhood and the fact that most positions of power in this country are filled by white people.* Whiteness can be a difficult concept for whites to grasp because the benefits are secured without taking action, for example, when a person's race is unmarked in a written description, the person is normally assumed to be white

Useful Books

Bettelheim, Bruno; *A Good Enough Parent* **(NY: Alfred A. Knopf, 1987.)**
A book of child rearing with an important perspective on identity development and the role of parents in a child's life.

Cox, Susan Soon-Keum; *Voices from Another Place* **(St. Paul, MN: Yeong & Yeong, 1999.)**
A first-person collection of writings by young adults who were adopted from Korea.

Crumbley, Joseph; *Transracial Adoption and Foster Care: Practice Issues for Professionals* **(Washington, D.C.: Child Welfare League, 1999.)**
Joseph Crumbley, a well-respected authority on transracial adoption and foster care, describes specific ways that practitioners can work with transracial families to ensure that children develop positive racial and cultural identities, as well as how professionals can better serve these families. Dr. Crumbley also addresses such professional concerns as cultural competence and recruitment of minority adoptive and foster parents. Case studies and "myths" of transracial adoption provide valuable background.

Edelman, Marian Wright; *Measure of Our Success* **(NY: Harper Collins, 1992.)**
Marian Wright Edelman is a powerful role model. In this inspiring book, written for her own children, who are biracial, she details the lessons for life she hopes to pass along to the next generation. Beautifully written and highly recommended.

Gillespie, Peggy & Kaeser, Gigi; *Of Many Colors* **(Amherst, MA: University of Massachusetts Press, 1997.)**
In this intimate look at multiracial family life, a compelling and revealing photograph of each family is accompanied by illuminating and revealing text culled from interviews with the family members who describe in their own voices some of the joys and challenges of their life. Because the text reflects conversations with the children as well as the adults involved, this book offers the valuable reminder that different members of the same family may have differing points of view about life in a multicultural family. The families include transracial, interracial, same-race blended, adoptive, single-parent, and two-parent families, both heterosexual and homosexual.

Kirk, H. David; *Shared Fate* (Vancouver, BC: Ben-Simon Publications, 1984.)

Delineates the necessity for adoptive families to acknowledge differences. This book had a major impact on contemporary understanding of what healthy adoptions look like.

Register, Cheri; *Are Those Kids Yours?* (NY: Free Press, 1990.)

Books in Print says, "As the adoptive mother of two Korean girls, Register has considered some practical and ethical issues involved in cross-cultural adoption: are the parents in the wealthier nations 'entitled' to raise children left homeless in other parts of the world by poverty or social stigma? Do adoptive parents have a responsibility to their children's birth countries or to other disadvantaged children and their families? What does it mean to 'own' a child, anyway, and who can ultimately make that claim? Register addresses these and other issues and shows how they are played out in the actual, day-to-day experience of her own and other adoptive families.

Van Gulden, Holly & Bartels-Rabb, Lisa M.; *Real Parents, Real Children* (NY: Crossroad-Herder, 1997.)

We think van Gulden offers insights no adoptive parent can do without. Want to know what your kids are thinking/feeling about their adoption? Want great ideas about how to talk to them from infancy on? This is a book about some of adoptive life's essential moments, those instances when, in a split-second of time, you're called upon to tackle some central questions and problems. Holly van Gulden offers tools and insights you need to consider. Highly recommended. A Pact bestseller.

Wolff, Jana; *Secret Thoughts of An Adoptive Mother* (Kansas City, MO: Andrews & McMeel, 1997.)

This book generated some controversy when it first came out in hardcover. We appreciated its candor and well-polished style, but we were concerned that the author's "secret thoughts" actually served to reinforce negative stereotypes about triad members. In this revision, Jana doesn't flinch from describing her ambivalence (about her son's birth mother, for instance), but acknowledges that her reactions stem from fear and ignorance. She addresses the early complexities of transracial parenting in a way that is sure to ring true to many readers. "An eloquent, refreshingly honest memoir, both disturbing in its revelations and hilarious in its smashing of taboos."—*San Francisco Chronicle*.

Section Two
Racial Identity

Protecting My Child from Her Mom, A Racist

By Gail Steinberg

Act One: The Race Drama

My daughter slams the door to her bedroom so hard that my picture falls off the wall upstairs in the living room. Another Disillusioning Parenting Failure is center stage, starring me as the tyrant-without-a-heart, her dad as the savior, and our princess as the child who can't afford to act too white.

We've always encouraged our children to express their feelings freely. This they do with an intensity most other people reserve only for life's largest moments, like being caught on the sinking *Titanic*, for example. If I'd known at the start that no matter what came up she would always blame me and Daddy would get to be the good guy, I might have tried to keep her from learning to talk. Who knew?

"I'm not going to your stupid *&# adoption picnic!" she yells. "You can't pick my friends. Those kids are nerds. You only like them because they have brown skin. Who cares? No Nigger is ever gonna be President."

"Did you say Nigger?" Righteously offended, I allow a stream of thou-shalt-nots worthy of my own mother, the very ones I'd promised in my diary at the age of thirteen never to inflict on my children, to stream from my lips.

Her dad ponders calmly, wondering aloud in a slow, thoughtful tone, if we really do have to go to the support group meeting after all; maybe it isn't a good idea; besides, there are so many things he'd rather be doing and it looks like rain, ho hum.

Predictably, he and I get into it and our child explodes, "Don't always talk about me! Now you're fighting because of me. What do you expect?"

With this the man of the house decides that we *must* go to the picnic after all, launching into a lecture about the dangers of prejudging strangers and the human need to understand one's roots and to have others to talk to who share our experiences.

Without pause, to avert the brewing confrontation between father and daughter which might take me out of the spotlight, heaven forbid, I do what any good mommy would do. I poke my head out of the window and suggest that the support group picnic will probably be called off because of approaching rain, oh dear.

What do you know. We are able to agree not to venture forth. Our little girl, appearing pleased, though antsy, commandeers the phone to report triumph to her best friend, Jennifer. She slams the door of her room once again, out of habit, and just to stay in practice.

Act Two: Remorse

Act Two takes place in my darkest closet. Out of kindness, let's call it wallowing. If racism is a virus, I moan, to what degree have I infected her? The says-it-all truth is that there are few black people among our nearest and dearest. My attempts to deepen friendships with friends of color remains a work in progress, at the baby-step level. Though I am trying, the truth is that I'm not trying hard enough. Blame it on my crazy fears of rejection, but our circle of friends is still majority white after all these years; our neighborhood, and the kid's schools, the same. Is our daughter's reluctance to embrace other black kids somehow provoked by her identification with me or by my own racism?

Act Three: Buying Love versus Living Truth

Our goal has always been to help our kids take pride in their heritage, but my nagging has probably given her the opposite message, the message that says, "You need to connect with people we pick out for you on the basis of race alone, even if we can't do the same thing ourselves." Feeling responsible for her feelings is my way of buying her love. It isn't to help her, but to relieve me. In an attempt to avoid my own discomfort at failing to provide good-enough racial role models, my impulse too often is to push her to master skills I have not been good at mastering myself. Even though I know a lot about the reasons why, this is a hard piece for me to admit.

Our daughter's feelings of being less than have been hard enough for me to admit. My own sense of failing her is harder yet. I stay so busy trying to make her feel okay about herself that I deny her real feelings. What she needs from us is help with clarification of her emotions, not a model for masking them. That little family drama was not about going to a meeting. It was about how hard it is to negotiate the tasks we all know that we must face.

Act Four: Hope

How do you apologize to a headstrong teenager? With trepidation. Nevertheless, I knock softly on her door, manage to get invited in, and find words to deliver the fairly naked truth about my view of what just happened. "I know that you can make your own friends. I trust you to take care of yourself. I know that it's a stupid idea to expect you to make friends with people just because of the color of their skin. But I'm your mommy. I still think it's my job to help you connect to the black community. I just want so much for you. I want you to feel good about yourself."

By the end of the conversation we both feel better. "Be patient, Mom," she says. "God isn't done making me yet."

In a complex family system like ours, where the children are the ones expected by outsiders to have problems, self-disclosure from the adults helps us all deal with the losses we can't fix. When I dare to share the moments of doubt I am not so eager to disclose—like how I know I am a racist—something good happens. Sharing my embarrassing stuff with my child shifts something between us. Part of feeling real is being trusted with others' real selves. To have a good laugh from time to time about the things we can't control gives us hope.

The Experts Speak Out

"Daddy, when I grow up I want to be white, just like you."
        —Aaron, age 3

"When I look back at my experiences as a black kid growing up in a white town, all I can say is, 'It sucks.' My parents believed that a loving family 'makes' the child. I disagree. Many of my issues may not even have existed had I lived in a more appropriate environment. My question is why even deal with this when you have other alternatives. There are many places that a family can live a rural life and still be close enough to a city to provide their children with enriching and firsthand experiences of their culture… when I was a child my life wasn't 'colorless.' It was white. And colorblindness is a luxury black children can't afford. Love does not prepare an African American child for the society we live in. And love does not replace the importance of knowing your own ethnicity and culture. Today, I say I am African American."
        —Rachel Nordlinger

I feel a special connection to mixed-race kids. It's important for me to think I'm mixed-race. I found strength in others who are mixed-race or adopted, like Greg Louganis and Scott Hamilton. At one meet, a father brought over a four-year-old and said, "Look, this is Dan O'Brien. His mom was white and his dad was black and he's okay." I guess his son was being ridiculed for being mixed. I want to try to understand what kids like me are going through. Part of my curiosity is understanding why I am not being accepted: "too black to be white; too white to be black… I call myself a chameleon. I can always give people anything they want."
        —Dan O'Brien, Olympic Decathalon Gold Medalist

"When a white person says to me, 'It doesn't matter if they're black, white, brown or green…' or 'there's only one race, the human race,' a shudder goes down my spine. Those sentences erase a history of oppression and survival against enormous odds, as well as a legacy of courageous resistance and struggle. They also set us up to fail. As we grow into our teens, transracially-adopted children discover that being 'human' is simply not enough."
        —Julia Sudbury-Oparah

"Sometimes I wish I could crawl in a hole. I hate the way people get that look on their face or laugh when I talk. Then they speak extra

slow, or extra loud to me. I know I have an accent— I was born in Vietnam. I'm not retarded and I'm not deaf. I wonder how they think they would sound if they tried to speak Vietnamese. "

—Sam, age 17

More French than Taiwanese?,
More Sioux than Irish?,
More Black?
More Jewish?
More American?
NO! I am 100% of all of the above
And proud
Of all I bring

—Leah, aged 12

Racial Identity

"Not one of us knows how to walk when we get here. Not one of us knows how to open a window, unlock a door. Not one of us can master a staircase. We are absolutely ignorant of the almost certain results of falling out of a five-story window. None of us comes here knowing enough not to play with fire. Nor can one of us drive a tank, fly a jet, hurl a bomb, or plant a tree.

We must all be taught that. We have to learn all that. The irreducible price of learning is realizing that you do not know. One may go further and point out—as any scientist, or artist, will tell you—that the more you learn, the less you know, but that means that you have begun to accept, and are even able to rejoice in the relentless conundrum of your life."

— James Baldwin

Transracial adoption is a lifelong journey, complex and challenging. Transracial adoption can work well for kids and families when parents are prepared to look at things from a new point of view. Most adoptive parents can tell stories about how they fell in love with their own most precious, best-beloved child, the child they love more and better than all the sweetest and most gratifying pleasures of the universe. Most parents raising a child not born to them can recount the wonders of coming to know that their family was destined to belong to each other and discovering for sure that, although blood may be thicker than water, love is thicker than blood.

We know from personal experience that on top of all that, being white adoptive or foster parents of a child of color is as exhilarating and world-altering as is standing on your head for long periods of time. Upside down, everything looks different—is it the world that has changed? Or is it we who are different, glimpsing a new view of the way things are all the time—a view that usually exists outside our frame of reference?

We believe that multiracial families are enhanced by developing the ability to catch a glimpse of each member's unique vision, together deepening and pooling their collective insights, and wondering at the beauty and complexity of the world as seen through the differing prisms each person contributes. Racially aware parents can provide support and access to help their children begin building positive racial identity sooner rather than later.

In learning how best to raise their children, most parents use their intuition, part of their lifetime of personal experiences. It is important to remember that for our children of color, life is like that other world—the one visible when we are standing on our heads, the one in which things differ from our usual view. Our children are viewed and judged and measured by standards and assumptions other than those we're familiar with. That other world and its judgments are not the one we're used to—but they are real, nonetheless. In some ways, the challenges faced by white parents who adopt or foster children of color can be compared to those of a single father trying to raise a daughter on his own, or those of parents of average intelligence trying to raise a child with a sky-high IQ. Because Caucasian parents' direct experiences do not generally encompass racial challenge and prejudice, our sense of the world will significantly differ from that of our children. It's just about a miracle—and a gift to our families—if we can keep that idea consciously in mind.

For People of Color

In his landmark book *Shades of Black* (Philadelphia: Temple University Press, 1991.), William Cross describes several predictable stages in the development of black identity, stages we believe to be similar to the stages of the development of identity for most Asians, Latinos, and Native Americans living in a white-dominated society. There is no particular age range attached to each stage and no expectation that all individuals will move through all stages, though the process typically spans the period from preadolescence to middle adulthood. Building racial identity is an ongoing process that continues over each person's life span. Some may stay at a particular stage without change, depending on temperament and life experiences. Cross suggests that persons traverse the following stages in developing racial identity:

- **I'm a person of color, but who cares (Pre-encounter)** I may have no education about my cultural history, but I am sensitive to discrimination. I believe that white is best, so I experience "spotlight anxiety," or discomfort about being too different from white as the norm. My emphasis is on learning to fit into white culture.
- **Then along comes racism, right between my eyes (Encounter)** An unexpected event occurs that catches me off-guard and forces me to acknowledge racism. It may be a personal event or something that happens in the larger community, such as the conflict in Watts between

Koreans and blacks, or the passage of laws to limit or deny services to my group. The encounter phase has two steps: experiencing an event, and then being "turned around" by it. I begin to think about what it means to be a member of a group assaulted by racism. I feel like a yo-yo swinging between high and low self-esteem. Very personal questions come up which bring on guilt, anger and anxiety. I'm so emotional that it gives me energy to get on to the next stage.

- **Riding the identity roller coaster (Immersion/Emerging)** Now, I kick out my old white-is-right view and decide to change. I don't really know how, only that change is needed. There is nothing subtle about this stage. I surround myself with symbols of my culture and seek out opportunities to learn from same-race peers. White people are boring. I don't have any interest in them. I yearn to learn about me and about where I've come from. My focus is on self-discovery. Confrontation, bluntness, and an either/or point of view are all I have time for. I just don't understand other people of color who don't live Black or Latino or Asian or Native "enough." Sometimes I think "whites are devils," and I want to drop out of the process of getting along with them. Sometimes I get excited about the complex subtleties of racial identity. The last possibility opens the door to stage four.

- **Proud to be me/Inner peace/Fully grown (Internalization)** Ah-ha! I feel fine, but it's hard to describe why, because it sounds phony— too good to be true. Finding inner peace as a person of color in a society that habitually undervalues my personhood is something huge, a transformation as powerful as the heat of the sun at midday. Dignity and deep relief arrive. A flood of energy to embrace my own heritage from the roots and the security to interact with others from different groups have come together during this stage, because the conflict over wishing to be what I am not or blaming myself for being the target has been resolved. Race has high significance in my life every day. I join new groups, change my style of dress, what I read, my opinions about the role of my group in history, what art and music I respond to, the causes that activate me, maybe even my name. Much that is important in my life changes. According to Cross, by this stage the following five positive defensive functions have been developed: 1) awareness that racism exists; 2) anticipation of being targeted; 3) well-developed defenses to use when confronted with racism; 4) awareness that the problem is in the circumstances and does not result from the individual self; 5) spiritual orientation that prevents the need to demonize whites.

- **Commitment** In this final stage, I will become able to look beyond myself to develop an ongoing interest in the well-being of my racial community. Great examples of leaders as prominent as Dr. Martin Luther King or as unrecognized as my next door neighbor model an ability to make a commitment beyond personal needs and maintain humility after success. I hope that I can follow.

For White People

In her book *Black and White Racial Identity Development: Theory, Research, and Practice,*(Westport, CT: Greenwood Press, 1991.) Janet Helms suggests that there are predictable steps in the development of racial consciousness for white people. As is the case with Cross' stages for people of color, Helms sees no particular age range attached to each stage and no guarantee that all individuals will move through all stages. In fact, exactly the opposite is often true. In our race conscious society, where white people receive benefits just for being white, many live out their lives without thinking about their own racial or ethnic identity at all. When a white identity develops, seven stages have been outlined.

- **Being white doesn't count. (Preconscious)** How many times in your life have you been asked to answer the question Who am I? In response, white people who spend their lives in predominantly white environments commonly come up with a list something like this: mother, wife, partner, sister, worker, friend, liberal, middle class, Presbyterian, animal lover, dreamer, runner, reader, and so on. Being white doesn't count. I tend not to note the qualities that make me part of the majority. In the preconscious stage of white identity development I see being white as the norm, a common ground that goes without notice because white is the baseline. I notice race only when people are not white. (Sadly, some people may live their whole lives without ever becoming conscious of having a white racial identity.)
- **Uh-oh. You mean we're the bad guys? (Contact)** This stage brings an awareness of white privilege—the invisible advantages white people—including me—in life, because our society was designed with our needs in mind. If white privilege is invisible, what makes me notice? This awareness begins when I have significant contact with a person of color and can't miss seeing how racism operates. I make a close friend or fall in love or watch Rodney King being beaten to a pulp on TV. "Uh-oh. Why are those white people doing that? They're prejudiced fools! Uh-oh. I'm white. What about me?" I feel uncomfortable, guilty, shamed and angry.

- **I am responsible for educating you (Disintegration)** At this stage, the blinders have been removed. I begin to see racism everywhere. I get it! I feel outraged and committed to helping other white people get it. I join the *Race Police*, finding most other white people guilty. "They" are the enemy, I think to myself. And it has become my job to point out why. My most important daily task, it seems, is to object to racist jokes, exclusions, injustices and institutional policies, objections I usually express in a shrill manner entirely lacking in charm. I lose many friends. People I have known all my life tend to run when they see me coming. They wish I would stop it already, and they sometimes do everything they can to let me know it, belittling my earnest calls for justice, refusing to debate or just leaving me out. The peer pressure mounts, asking me to collude, to shut up and not to notice racism. But it's too late and I can never go back.

- **I, too, am in the group (Reintegration)** Once you notice the elephant in the living room, it's hard to ignore it. When the mist clears, I come to realize that it's not enough to point out what others are doing wrong. I understand that people of color do not perceive me as exempt from my group. I am white; therefore I am under suspicion. Protest though I may, rugged individualism—the desire to go it alone—turns out to be just another white luxury. This is intense. Why don't they understand that I am not like the rest of "them?" Why aren't they recognizing me as the next great civil rights leader? I thought my realizations were unique and beyond everyone else I know. I am beginning to hear that people of color consider my new truths to be old hat, mundane, even obvious. My belief in my own accomplishments is threatened. I start to get angered by the frustration, falling back on blaming the victims: people of color.

- **Now what do I do (Pseudo Independence)** I can't get through the living room without bumping into the elephant, but I still don't know what to do about it. I understand white privilege and am shamed by it, but feel overwhelmed at the thought of being responsible for moving that elephant. How did I get to be so white? Why didn't I notice? How can I change all that I am? At this point, I may become a racial wannabe, trying to "pass" as a person of color by taking on some of what I perceive as their cultural characteristics. But that usually doesn't work, and I move cautiously toward a next step.

- **Finding white pride (Immersion/Emerging)** The next step is to recognize the need to find positive racial identity for myself, reflecting a developing desire to embrace my own racial and cultural heritage as a source of pride rather than an unconscious element in my life. I seek new ways to think about whiteness, ways that offer options other than either unconscious privilege or the bad-guy role. I begin to seek out white people who have come to a positive understanding of what it is to be white and racially conscious. I seek out support from other white role models, people who have fought injustice and actively worked against racism.

- **I am a work in progress (Autonomy)** Finally, I develop an ability to see people simultaneously as both individuals and as members of my group. The elephant begins to respond to the sounds of my voice. I feel good about bringing up race within my own circle of influence, because I can begin to see some ways in which I am changing and my changes are affecting lives. Feeling heard releases energy and creates increased zest, a sense of empowerment, greater knowledge, an increased sense of self-worth, and a desire for more connections. I define ways in which I can actively work to interrupt racism while I also understand that there is much more to learn. My goals are to continue to learn more and to identify my personal areas of influence. Whose lives do I affect and how? Whom do I talk to? In this stage I am afraid of making mistakes. I often apologize in advance just in case my words or actions may not be sufficiently sensitive to the experiences of people of color. But I genuinely hope to learn from my mistakes. As a result, people of color often view me as an ally. I understand that I am a work in progress that I will never be completed or perfected, but I also understand and that I must do what I can—knowing that, *unless I am challenging the system of racism, I am colluding with it.*

Facing the Issues

I (Beth) remember that in the airport, someone came up in disbelief to stare at Sofia and ask if she was ours. I quipped, "Yes she's only 12 hours old and we are all doing great." Ted and I laughed the whole way home about the stares and reactions the clever response had drawn. But the truth is, as the days went on my beautiful brown daughter with her full head of jet black hair provoked this response on a daily basis, and the more they asked the more I wasn't sure what to say.

Ted was quick and to the point. "She's our daughter. Do you have any other questions?" That usually shut them up and he kept reminding me that we didn't owe strangers on the street any explanations. For myself, I found the struggle more emotional. I imagined that somehow people could tell she wasn't really mine—see through the façade of motherhood I was trying to paint on but which still felt so fragile and uncertain. I questioned if I was somehow ashamed or embarrassed because she was Latina and we weren't, "If I really felt good about her heritage then why wouldn't I tell them?" Eventually I learned to differentiate between people who mattered and people who didn't. I sometimes told more and sometimes nothing at all. I grew more confident in myself and didn't worry so much about strangers.

I hadn't anticipated those feelings would surface again when we adopted James. I was surprised the first time someone asked, "Whose child is he?" when I was unprepared to answer. The resolution came quicker the second time around, but what I hadn't considered was Sofia being a witness to these new interactions.

We moved when James was just a year old to a new house in a new neighborhood. When our neighbor finally had the nerve to approach, both kids were collapsed in the double stroller after an energetic excursion to the park—Sofia was all ears. "So, I guess you do a lot of baby-sitting?" the neighbor asked. Jean was definitely in the category of someone who needed to understand so we stood for a while as she cooed over the children and told me about hers, already grown. She's actually been a good friend to our kids, inviting us to Chinese New Year celebrations with her family and always giving birthday and holiday gifts. After our chat that day I asked my three-year-old Sofia if she knew why Jean had asked about babysitting. "Oh Mommy, she can't figure out how we go together because we are all different colors. Some people just don't get it!"

Now the kids and I have three or four ways to respond, depending on our mood, when we get questioned. A few years ago, right before bed, James began to cry. I heard Sofia tell him, "People are mean. Because we are brown, some people don't like us. I know it's hard, but we can't let them win." I wanted to run in and scoop them up, tell them I could protect them and that it would be ok, but I know I can't do that. Watching your five-year-old learn to toughen up is hard, but better tough than unable to survive.

When you choose to become a family that is different from most, you must be prepared to confront your own racial biases in both overt and subtle ways. We all bring assumptions and unexamined ideas to new situations. The first step in the process is also the one that never ends. You can expect to find that you carry within yourself both negative and positive internalized attitudes about adoption and race. Our society is biased in many ways, and each member of society (whether we are personally touched by adoption or race ourselves) is a student of the lessons society teaches us. But attitudes can be changed.

Acknowledging your own racism and "adoptism" is painful, particularly since it means that you carry prejudices against your own child. Though you may feel yourself free from these biases, it is more likely that you just don't recognize them fully yet. Transracial adoptive parents are afforded continual opportunities to examine and develop new attitudes that expand far beyond the overly simplistic and often inherently negative values held by a society undereducated about adoption and race. If you haven't had much experience with these issues, your antennae are not yet well developed. If you think that racism is getting better, you probably aren't dealing with it much. If you think that most people feel adoption is a good thing, you probably haven't yet had the opportunity to experience people's "special" reactions to special families. The more you know, the more you will realize how much race and adoption matter. The more you realize how much they matter, the more you will know how much there is to learn. We must acknowledge where we are beginning from so we can become conscious enough to change. If growth and learning sound like fun, jump in, because it will last a lifetime and then some!

Institutionalized Racism

"If the young are to avoid the unnecessary burden of self hatred, they will have to develop a deep faculty for identifying, fractionating out and rejecting the absurdities of the conscious as well as the unconscious white racism in American society from what is worthwhile in it."
—Charles A. DeLeon in the *Journal of the American Medical Association*

What is institutionalized racism?

Institutionalized racism is subtle and covert discrimination backed by power and resources. A National Council of Churches Workgroup report (quoted in Itaberi Njeri, "Words to Live or Die by," *Los Angeles Times Magazine*, May 31, 1992.) stated, "Both consciously and unconsciously, racism is enforced and maintained by the legal, cultural, religious, educational, economic, political, environmental, and military institutions of society." Racism is more than just a personal attitude. It is the institutionalized form of that attitude.

Effects of facing daily racism

In the book *Living with Racism* (Boston: Beacon Press, 1994.) authors Joe R. Feagin and Melvin P. Sikes suggest the following

1. Modern racism must be understood as daily experiences. Overt discrimination is likely to increase in public places and includes avoidance, rejection, verbal and physical attacks.
2. Recurring encounters with racism have a cumulative impact that is

greater than the sum of these events might appear. These encounters affect members of the community in a domino effect. Most racist acts are not perceived by the victims as isolated events.

3. Repeated experiences of racism shape both one's way of living and one's understanding of life.
4. Daily experiences of discrimination restrict social, economic, and political mobility for peoples of color as groups.

Internalized Racism

When you live in a society that commonly accepts stereotypes of people of color, you internalize those stereotypes and begin to see them as truths rather than assumptions.

1. Do African Americans commit crimes or receive welfare more often than do white people? No. Does the media make us believe that they do? Yes.
2. Are Chinese people all musical and good at math? No. Does the media make us believe that they are? Yes.
3. Are most Latinos part of a gang? No. Does the media make us think that they are? Yes.

You get the idea.

We all—and we do mean all, people of color and white alike—internalize these images and these assumptions. Our schools do not teach enough about Asian, Latino, Native American or African American contributions to society for us to recognize that there are many. We don't hear many media stories about the growing black middle class or the Asian poor in this country—as a result it is easy to forget that they exist. This internalized racism can be seen in children as young as three who show preferences for white dolls as "pretty and clean" over dark skinned dolls as "dirty or ugly" (*Different and Wonderful*, Darlene Powell Hopson and Derek S. Hopson, New York, Simon & Schuster, 1990.) Internalized racism takes the form of fear when a white woman walks down the street and sees four African American men walking toward her. It takes the form of appeal when we find ourselves looking at Jennifer Lopez and Cameron Diaz with their newly blond hair and feeling they look more beautiful than they did as brunettes. It looks like factual truth when we don't know that Africa is minimized while Europe is overemphasized on the maps we see daily of the world. (Arno Peters *Projection Equal Area Representation Map*, New York, Friendship Press, 1991.)

We are all indoctrinated by societal realities. Some of us are more likely to notice and question the implied precepts of racism than are others. It all comes back to whether we move from the shared pre-encounter stage of racial development to the stages which follow. People of color are usually more likely to have encountered experiences which push them into the next stages, but no one can avoid the internal implications of the external "isms." All anyone can do is move through the stages toward integration and rejection of the isms as truth.

Can transracially adopted kids be exceptions to this experience of racism? No. Parents who want to help their kids must break through the lingering myopia they have about racism. Jim Mahoney, a therapist who works extensively with transracial families, reminds us that children of color face institutional racism ranging from where freeways are located to difficulty in securing loans. No matter that their parents are white, our children's appearance will cause them to experience racism in many ways:

- They will be scrutinized routinely upon entering a 7-11 convenience store.
- They will likely make less money than your white child will.
- They will be more likely to die a violent death than your white child will.
- They will likely experience more unemployment, layoffs, and vague depression than you did or your white children will.
- They will receive incompetent care from caring white teachers, therapists, physicians, nurses who will misdiagnose your child of color's behavior as depression or "the blues" and will say, "It's just a phase."

Other people won't know that your adopted child of color is struggling with a hidden dual role expectation: she must function as a member of your family when with you. Without you, in the dominant culture—at the mall, store, library, McDonald's—your child must be culturally competent and know how to participate in the larger culture, which offers him less than it offers you, his parents.

Organized Racism: Taking a Stand

Skin heads, Nazis, Ku Klux Klan, the white power movement… we know what these groups are all about. Racial hostility and discrimination are tools to protect white privilege and power. As humans we share a chilling history: people group together to express hostility through attack, genocide, exclusion and avoidance. Though in their current forms hate groups do not seem to be in the majority in the United States, is there any question that they abound?

Understanding the enemy is always important. Raphael Ezekiel (*The Racist Mind*, Princeton, NJ,: Harvard University Press, 1996.) has been working on a study of organized racism. He suggests that people join hate groups because they feel powerless, resentful, fearful, and isolated as individuals and are attracted to the notion of being part of a "force capable of ruthless action." Such movements reassure members again and again that "white power is your family" and that "we're going to get what we ought to have. We're going to make our own breaks." Ezekiel writes, "These are people who don't feel their lives are important and who need to find meaning in some kind of behavior."

Are organized hate groups a threat to our families?

Only rarely have we heard a report of a cross burning in the yard of a transracial adoptive family or of a reign of terror inflicted on a transracial family due to race. Though we don't want to minimize the horror such events cause, we believe that this kind of targeted racism is rare and thus the least of the problems transracial families face. More damage comes not from flagrant displays of hatred by people with shaved heads and swastikas but from mainstream people who incorporate racist thought and action as fundamental parts of our culture. A white clerk avoiding the hand of a Latino customer; police stopping blacks driving through "white" neighborhoods, the infrequency with which we recognize the contributions of people of color, or the shock and pain of our children when they are excluded from a white child's birthday party when all the white kids are invited....

Affirmative Action

We must step up to the plate, both to recognize and to stand up against the racism that exists in everyday life, no matter how subtle or pervasive. Standing back or taking time off is another form of white privilege, one our children and their people have not yet been given the right to indulge in.

"In affirmative action," writes Faye Crosby in the book *Understanding Affirmative Action* (Washington: American University Press, 1996.), "designated individuals monitor the operations of institutions and so can notice (and correct) injustices in the absence of any complaint. This monitoring role is crucial, because an accumulation of studies have shown that it is very difficult to detect discrimination on a case-by-case basis, even when the case involves the self." Not too many years ago in California there was a proposition on the ballot to stop affirmative action practices as they applied to the entrance of students to the statewide universities. As the onslaught of radio and TV ads reached its frenzy, eight-year-old Sofia offered this insight: "If they make it so they don't make sure to let in fair numbers of people of all different colors into the school then it seems like they will only invite their friends. Most people only know people like themselves. They don't live with people of different races or really *really* love them. If they don't I don't think they will notice so much that the numbers aren't fair and pretty soon there will only be one kind of people and that will be bad." Sofia's words were deeply prophetic and accurate regarding the impact of removing affirmative action from the entrance process of the UC system. Only a few short years later the schools are facing devastating drops in the numbers of African American and Latino students applying to attend and being admitted.

The reality is that institutionalized affirmative action exists for white people. Inheritance laws allowing us to pass our property on to our children have never been interrupted and so the wealth of our ancestors has remained within our families. We have legacies in elite schools and colleges where our sons and daughters are given first chance at admission because of our own history with the school. The list can go on and on. We must speak out about the reality of a "less than level playing field." We must take a position and that position must be with our children, for if we are not with them then we are most surely against them.

Racial Hierarchy

> "The darker the berry, the sweeter the juice."
> —African proverb

What are your boundaries?

In our race-conscious culture the lighter one's skin, the greater one's privileges. Popular culture and music croons that "white is right, Asians are the model minority (almost like white.) If you're brown, get down, and if you're black, step back."

Would it be a surprise to you to know that more white prospective adoptive families feel comfortable adopting transracially when the child's birth parents are light-skinned than when the birth parents are both dark-skinned? That more prefer a biracial child than one who has two African American parents? That more prefer to adopt Latino or Asian children to African American children? Probably not. Most of us acknowledge the racial hierarchy in our country: the darker one's skin, the greater one's challenges. And we do not suggest that parents reach beyond their racial comfort level in forming their family. Humans do not thrive in environments in which essential characteristics are not accepted. No child should grow up in a family unprepared to cherish him. But the truth is that if parents buy into the racial hierarchy that places lighter skin over dark or Asian over black there is danger for their child. In the end, if racial hierarchy is embraced, then your child falls below white and ultimately is "less than," and that means *less than you*.

White is Right (Not!)

> "He felt again a little of the panicky bewilderment of the child he
> had been ...and felt a kind of anger, even now, at the anxiety he had

suffered, which he thought had shaped more of his present nature than he dared acknowledge."

In his novel *The Conversations at Curlow Creek* (NY, Pantheon Books, 1997.) David Malouf's character Adair describes his amazement that he survived his parents' inability to help him see who he really was. He had not been aware at the time he suffered the anxiety how much it shaped who he turned out to be in the world. In a parallel manner, difficulties occur when adoptive parents undermine their child's heritage by thinking that their child can receive white benefits by virtue of being their child, even though their child is a person of color. If they make no real effort to connect the child to her birth culture, basically assuming that she will "pass" for white and will never have to deal with racial issues, chances are that she will eventually pay the price.

Our children are resilient and can survive in spite of our limitations, but don't make the mistake of believing that your light-skinned child of color can create a secure identity by trying to "pass" as white or simply not identifying racially at all. Parents must help their children embrace all aspects of their heritage. As white parents, we must challenge our own prejudices, rather than waiting for people of color to teach us. We are taught to stay separate from people who are different from us, but we must constantly challenge that idea and plunge into multicultural life by risking mistakes and taking responsibility for the mistakes we are sure to make.

If all transracial adoptive parents regarded being of color as an advantage for their child, if we truly believed that having a dual racial heritage was positive, we would stop at nothing to help our children reap the advantages of their birth cultures.

Prepare, Don't Protect
Who needs a map?

Having good tools makes most jobs much easier. Maps are tools developed after exploration of a territory in order to provide direction for the folks who come after. We expect pilots and drivers to be able to follow maps, not to forge a path en route. Children journeying through life will get lost if they have to find their way alone before they're able. Maps based on other people's experiences can help them steer away from danger and find the good stuff more easily, *but sometimes we are afraid to provide them with accurate maps.*

Some parents think that their job should be to create a world for their child where the sun always shines and she will be protected from all harm. This in turn leads to the belief that children should not be given maps because they already are in a trouble-free place where all of their needs are being taken care of. Some believe that a parent's job is to prolong their child's stay in the Eden of childhood. White middle-class society's romantic vision of an innocent child at play, unaware of even the smallest difficulties in life, can be used to build a parenting style with more payoffs for parents than for children.

When, under the pretext of concern for their welfare, we keep our children helpless and dependent, we allow ourselves to appear big, powerful, and protective—dominant—in our own eyes and, for a time, in our kids' eyes as well. Being the protector supports a parent's need to be needed. Being the protector does not serve the child's need to learn self-reliance and self-determination. We get the benefits—not our children. We must learn to ask ourselves, Who am I taking care of now—my child or myself?

White parents often hope to "keep their children innocent," enjoying a "race-free" childhood for as long as possible. In contrast, the life experience of parents of color often encourages them to prepare their children to cope with injustice and with demeaning social messages from a very early age. White parents of children of color need to learn to tell the truth about racism and to help prepare their kids to deal with it.

Read the story *Amazing Grace* by Mary Hoffman (1994, New York, Dial Press). Grace wanted to play the part of Peter Pan in the school play, but the other kids said she couldn't because Peter Pan could not be portrayed by a girl or by a black person. Rather than trying to fix the situation for her or diminish its importance, Grace's mother and grandmother helped boost her ambition and confidence by offering the inspiring achievements of a black ballerina and by supporting her efforts to prepare in advance so that she would truly be ready for the audition. As white parents we may not have had role models to prepare us to respond to our children in this way.

We can't protect our children from life

Even in the most protected of environments it is possible for bad stuff to happen. In a racist society, even the youngest among us will sooner or later have a negative experience relating to race. Imagining that as white parents we can somehow prevent this from happening is wishful thinking. We must support our child's sense of dignity and competence instead of our own need to rescue. Parents in same-race families can anticipate what is coming and are not likely to let their children out into the world without tools for taking care of themselves, just as no parent would let their child learn how to cross the street without clear tools for avoiding getting hit by oncoming traffic. Critics of transracial adoption remain concerned that parents who themselves have never been targeted by racism and do not understand it cannot provide a child with the map needed to survive the negative experiences that will occur. Children need to know how to anticipate and cope with social bias in order not to take it personally. There are many tools we can give them and they are best learned when supported and affirmed by those that a child trusts most, their parents.

We must learn how to take all events in our stride and go on

We as parents can create a map that helps our children find their way. We can identify bias when it comes up in books and on TV and talk about it, give it a name, make it easy to recognize and respond to when it comes up again. We can model as well as strategize in advance appropriate responses to racial incidents and realities. We can focus more on our child's efforts to move along her own path and less on outcomes, encouraging our child to value her own ability to deal with challenging situations. We can become actively involved in antiracist activities to model an assertive way of dealing with difficult events and practices. We can stimulate and encourage open communication with the family about racial and ethnic issues and about all the other hard issues that have strong, emotional impact for our children. But, ultimately our children must also learn from a trusted family friend who is of the same racial and ethnic origins as the child. This person will bring a kind of authenticity to the tools and strategies that white parents cannot have.

Talking with Your Child about Race and Racism

The key is talking with our children, not talking to them

Every parent soon learns to distinguish the meaning of their baby's cries, using nothing but its tone. We seem to put this talent away when our children get older. Many of us would rather talk than listen. In sensitive areas, we need to learn better listening skills. Young children may not talk at all about racial issues, but feelings may emerge in their play or in their preferences for crayon colors ("black is a yucky color"), ice-cream flavors, or skin colors of dolls. Parents can learn a lot about what young children are thinking by setting aside regular time to play with their children, allowing their children to direct the play and simply observing the core issues illustrated by the imaginary actions of the characters they create.

How, at this time, does your child understand being adopted transracially?

As children grow, their understanding of adoption and sensitivity to the role played by race in our society changes. The best way to understand what your child is thinking is to listen. Conversations about movies, TV, stories in books, news events, and the like offer opportunities to get his opinion on events that are not directly tied to his own daily life. Asking questions to understand what your child is thinking about and what his questions are is an important place to start.

> *When our (Gail's) Korean-born daughter was about ten she was fascinated by jigsaw puzzles, wanting to know how things fit together. Her questions about current events or movies usually were focused on, "Did that happen because the people were different from each other? Is that why they have wars?" And the book* Sarah, Plain and Tall *by Patricia MacLachlan, (NY, Harper and Row, 1986.), was so compelling to her that she read it at least ten times and carried it around with her, the way younger children carry their teddies. She said she liked Sarah, the main character in the book, because even though she was different from everybody around her she didn't just try to fit in.*

There was a pattern to our daughter's interests. She was exploring many different approaches to one theme: how do things that are different from each other interrelate? What does being different mean for me, since I am different from my family members and most of my friends? Paying attention to the patterns and themes your child is processing in everyday life provides additional information about how she views her own position in the world.

Ask specific, concrete questions that don't elicit one-word answers

What does your new teacher do best? What is different about this teacher from your last teacher? Who is your reading buddy? What did the kids say when your teacher read that story to the class about slavery? How do you want to show your birth family when you make your family tree? Ask what seems appropriate, but don't bombard your child with questions. Your goal is to talk less and listen more in order to understand what your child is dealing with.

How do you yourself respond to racial issues?

Parents may tell themselves that they feel comfortable raising a child across racial lines, but when faced with issues that threaten their child's well being, feelings of uncertainty, anger and perhaps shame can arise. Don't assume that your feelings are the same as your child's. Don't overload the situation with your input. If you bring race into every situation to the exclusion of everything else, your child may avoid talking about it with you at all costs. The best advice is listen more, talk less. You need to understand your child's experience, not direct the action.

Don't turn into a psychological dentist...

attempting to extract feelings as if they were bad teeth. We sometimes assume that superficial answers to our anxious questions mean the child is concealing painful emotions, but we may be looking for something that isn't there. Most children are not subtle. If a child is not labeling something as a racial incident, perhaps it isn't one. Encouraging your child to talk when she says, "I'm okay. Leave me alone," may be overload. It's possible that nothing is really wrong. On the other hand, don't assume that because there is no discussion there is no problem. Trust your intuition and everything you know about your child, but don't overreact or invade your child's right to be the star of his or her own personal drama by taking it over for yourself.

> *Allison, a Chinese child, age four, had been adopted by a white family as an infant. Allison's family was now in the process of adopting domestically. They were participating in an open adoption, and Marissa, the expectant mother, had come to stay with them for the last month of her pregnancy. Allison's parents had told her about the planned adoption but were concerned about how this process and the proximity of an expectant parent would affect Allison. One evening while they were reading books together before bedtime, Allison asked her Dad, "Where is the baby going to go after Marissa has her?" Dad managed to change the subject and put Allison to bed without falling apart. He and his wife spent the rest of the evening discussing their plans about how to respond to her question.*

What do you think was behind Allison's question? What suggestions would you come up with for handling the issue? Do some of the suggestions involve limiting Allison's exposure to Marissa? What kinds of feelings would be brought up for you as Allison's parents in thinking about these questions?

Here's how Allison's parents handled the situation...

> *The next day, Mom and Dad asked Allison what she meant when she said she wanted to know where the baby was going. Allison explained that she wasn't sure if the baby was going to sleep with Marissa or with her parents or in her own room. Allison wanted to be sure the crib was in the right room before the baby came.*

Allison's parents had responded to her questions on the basis of their own assumptions and fears. Needless to say, listening to what our children are really asking is the first step in giving them the information they want and need about adoption and race.

Explaining words that designate color

> "Uncle Jesse's hands are dirty cause they're brown on the outside and white on the inside," Seth (Gail's son) announced when he was about three.
>
> "No," I said "I bet your Uncle Jesse washes his hands in the morning when he wakes up and before lunch and dinner just like you do and they're just as clean. It's because he has more melanin in his skin than you. Melanin protects our skin from the sun but the palms of our hands don't need as much protection as the backs of our hands. We don't open our palms to the sun very much so the melanin makes just the backs get darker. Everybody has some melanin in their skin but Uncle Jesse has more than you do. So the backs of his hands look darker than yours but the palms are light like yours."
>
> "Why can't a cow have kittens? Why and why and why?"
>
> "Because cows have little calves and cats have kittens. Goodnight my child, good night." That was easy. It was a line from one of our favorite bedtime songs and we each knew both the question and the answer, but Seth wasn't done asking yet. His ability to link ideas was terrific for a three-year-old:
>
> "Why don't you you have yellow hair like me, Mom?" he sang. "Why and why and why?"
>
> "Because people don't have to match to be a family. Some families have people that match and some don't. Goodnight my child, good night."

Sometimes words don't mean what they say. Why are people with brown skin called "black" and people with pale skin called "white?" What are people of color? Are they green or blue? When do we use color designations and what do they mean?

Melanin causes skin color. This is a hard concept for very young children to understand. Explaining that *black* is a word used to describe African Americans, *brown* to describe Latinos as well as other people of various races and *white* is a term used to describe people whose ancestors came from Europe becomes even more complicated because the colors do not match the skin color of the people. Black people are not really the color black, but have skin that is one of the many possible shades of brown ranging from beige to deep ebony. The specific color of one's skin is caused by how much of the pigment melanin each person has. Black people have the most, so they get to have the darkest skins—sometimes, but of course someone who is black can be lighter skinned than someone who is white. People who are called Latinos may be of

European, African and/or Asian descent and embody every skin color imaginable.

Because the word *white* is used as an adjective to connote cleanliness, goodness or purity, there are also connotations of those qualities associated with the racial designation. White people are not really white, but usually one of many shades of beige ranging from pale peach to deep tan. We must be clear with children that when used to describe people, "white" is not better or worse, it is just a way of describing the people who have less melanin in their skin—people whose ancestors originally came from the European continent. The word *black*, on the other hand, is often associated with things that are dark and fearful. This is a powerful example of attitude manipulation reflected through the language of culture, even throughout the Bible. Black is a term of pride that has been used in slogans such as Black Pride, Black Power, Black is Beautiful, etc. The word *yellow* is associated with gold, butter, lemons, jaundice, old age, something cheaply sensational as in "yellow journalism" and a fungus (as in the yellowing of the leaves in plants). The word *brown* is associated with mud, sand, chocolate, coffee, "brown shirts" (members of the Nazi S.S. in Germany), tanned by the sun, excrement, and paper bags. The word *red* is associated with having red hair, American Indians, communists, excitement, anger and more. When children are old enough, it is important to talk to them about the connotations color designations imply for all. Paying attention to the meanings attached to words and helping our children scrutinize and assess their proper usage will give them the confidence to choose the right words to describe themselves and others.

Respecting Feelings

Seeking Solutions

If we acknowledge that we live in a racist society, our challenge, as adoptive parents of children of color, is to raise kids who feel good about themselves as individuals, as members of their families, and as members of their race. At the same time, we must provide then with the skills to function against racism. Our job is to help them feel safe and useful. We must protect them against attitudes that are dangerous and destructive to their growth, safeguarding at all costs their ability to have faith in their own dreams. The best way to begin is to explore our own racial attitudes and emotional responses. Children learn first about the world from our actions and attitudes as parents. Each experience of success builds self-respect.

Looking in the mirror

One of the most common questions we are asked is, "How can I effectively parent a child of color if I find racist attitudes in myself?" First and foremost, remember that whether our skin is white, black, brown, yellow, or tan, in a racist society we all assimilate racist values. What color are the people held as experts in most fields of interest by the media? What color are your personal family doctor, dentist, lawyer and other professional providers? What color are the people who are presented as appealing and upstanding in the advertising you encounter day in and day out? What color doll would your three-year-old pick as the prettiest, cleanest or nicest? Who are our national heroes and our political leaders? Despite their growing numbers, the African Americans, Asians, Native Americans and Latinos who are on top still stand out as exceptions to the European American norms of our culture. This, in itself, is racism, the kind of racism that acts as a barrier to self-respect for children of color.

When to start—now

We must take inventory of the racist stimulus around us and understand its impact on our children and on us. We must be prepared to answer honestly questions concerning how and why this has happened. We must acknowledge the truth: that all of us participate in the perpetuation of racism by "simple" actions: by watching TV shows in which African American men are portrayed solely as comic figures, rather than as romantic or heroic leads, or by subscribing to newspapers and magazines in which racial stereotypes are perpetuated or racial differences simply ignored. We must acknowledge and appreciate that differences exist and that they make a difference most of the time. Telling our children that all people are treated equally isn't true. It's more valuable to be straightforward, helping them to anticipate the stereotypes, to focus on positive differences among races. They need to understand and feel pride in who they are. Then, once the groundwork has been laid, they can anticipate racism and cope. Standing up to racism is difficult and not always possible, but worth the effort. What better way to build self-esteem?

There are no easy solutions. In spite of the fact that people of color have not yet been accepted as fully entitled members of this society, keep working to expand the solutions. Each moment of success builds more self-respect. Each solution enlarges the potential from which greater solutions will emerge.

Positive Racial Identity and Transracial Adoption

Children adopted transracially have special challenges in developing strong racial and personal identity. How we see ourselves—our self-image—and how we value ourselves—our self-esteem—are shaped both by the way we perceive our racial or ethnic heritage and how we perceive society's views about that heritage. A healthy racial identity means that we appreciate the strengths and unique beauty of the culture with which we are identified and accept our membership in the group. Positive racial identity depends on our ability to identify fully with our ethnic roots, yet remain confident that race or ethnicity does not limit our opportunities in life.

Racial self-esteem

A central task of childhood is to define and come to value one's "self." The process of gaining a positive racial identity stems from children's early care-taking experiences. As they are loved and cared for by their parents, children hear again and again how much we value the sunshine in their warm brown skins, their tight curly hair, their shining, almond-shaped eyes. Over time children come to believe that since these characteristics are cared for and appreciated, they must be of value although they differ from the characteristics of the parents. Racial esteem flourishes in those children who sense that their value comes not from what they do but who they are. They begin to feel valued for themselves and for their uniqueness.

Good care-taking and a respect for children's individuality form a first foundation and then, once children have learned that they are lovable, they need to learn that they have valuable skills. As they master each new task, they will feel more confident about themselves. Without a solid foundation, their accomplishments will never be enough. Without the skills, the foundation is inadequate in a race-conscious world in which they will be asked to prove whether they measure up or measure down, depending on which eye and which beholder is asking.

Although children's self-esteem is initially shaped by others' perceptions of them (and it will always be influenced by those external perceptions,) once their cognitive capacity to do so develops (at about age four or five) children begin to think for themselves about what it is that makes them okay. Eventually their internalized picture of self becomes more important than the views of others. If the inner picture of self is not clear and of value, children will develop the skill of "impression management," presenting what they believe others want to see. This preoccupation with external expectations and values tends to diminish their comfort with themselves. In the context of their racial identity, they attempt to avoid racism, rather than developing skills for coping with it.

Racial identity

When trying to understand why they were transracially adopted, children are vulnerable to developing low self-esteem. They may feel "abandoned" by both their birth parents and their racial or ethnic community. They ask, "Why didn't I get adopted by a family like me?" or even "Wasn't there just one family in my birth country who would adopt me?" This sense of rejection can leave children adopted transracially with a weak core at the center of their self-image.

Some children adopted at an older age may have learned in their early years to distrust people of a background different from their own. If, prior to their adoption, their caretakers were of their own race, coming to trust and connect to new parents of a different race is more challenging than it is for children adopted at birth. On the other hand, if they suffered abuse or neglect prior to their adoption by people of their own race and felt rescued by adults of a different race (white), they may be extremely vulnerable to thinking that people of their race hurt children. If this misconception is not challenged, they may either struggle with internalized self-hate or become the one who hurts as a fulfillment of the lesson of their experience.

When children feel positive about their birth parents, they are more likely to feel positive about their heritage and themselves. In a transracial adoption, the importance is intensified because the birth parents represent the child's race; if children do not feel positive about their birth families, they may have difficulty integrating their birth cultures.

On the other side, if a child's only contact with or image of people who share their race is through their birth parents, they are likely to grow up with some unfortunate assumptions. "Everyone from China places their girl babies for adoption" or "all black people are too poor to parent their children."

Whether or not there is direct contact between the child and birth parents, it is useful for adoptive parents to help children find a supportive view of their culture by examining the messages their child is receiving about their birth family.

How to help

Increasing racial self-esteem is an ongoing process with two parts:

1. Parents can help on an everyday basis by engaging in everyday efforts to create an affirming environment.

    - Being consistent in what we communicate and following through. When we send mixed messages about people of other races/ethnicities, kids are confused. It's great to have books with pictures reflecting characters who look like our child, but the child will perceive a mixed message if adults fail to own and read books for adults which are written by, for, and about members of the child's race or ethnic background. Similarly confusing attitudes are conveyed if we offer books that show characters only of the child's race or ethnicity while overlooking other groups.

- Providing specific praise or criticism that offers clear opportunities for improvement when needed. For instance, instead of saying, "You have beautiful brown skin, Kevin," we can say, "You look great, Kevin, and I particularly like the way you remembered to oil your skin." Instead of saying, "You look messy, Kim," one might say, "Your hair looks a little better, Kim, but I expect you to do more than just get the knots out of it."

- Allowing children choices. Making choices helps children to build confidence in their judgment. Expand your child's options to include as many peers and adults as possible of the child's racial heritage. Then be ready to support—without editorial comment—any choice that your child makes. In the end it needs to be your child who determines who is important in their life. This means that banking all your identity marbles on one family or event is dangerous in the extreme as the chances of your child's sensibility coinciding with a single opportunity or personality are slim.

- Encouraging each child's abilities. Help your child become expert at something—learn a traditional folk craft; study karate, judo, dance; develop a hobby; acquire some information—that will make them competent in an area that reflects their interests and goals. It will be a major bonus if that activity is also related to their racial or ethnic heritage. Once the child becomes more expert than anyone else in her circle of friends, parents can help find ways to share the specialty with others or to teach others about it.

- Providing a peer group. Everyone does better if they have an arena to share with others experiencing their issue—a place to talk about racial encounters and feelings of isolation—in the psychological safety of their own group.

2. Using the opportunities that can result when children suffer an acute blow to their racial self-image to address the identity crisis.

   - Trust your child's antenna. Don't try to make things better by explaining away your child's perceptions of a racial incident with comments like "Oh, I'm sure Mrs. Avery didn't mean it that way, sweetie." Racial blows are already damaging to the core of self. This is a time when positive and respectful validation is key.

   - Be an ally. Finding the balance between wanting to make it all better by slaying all the dragons for our children and wanting to make it all better by denying the dragons out of fear for our children is never simple. To make them strong we must allow them to practice and decide. Sometimes they will do a great job; sometimes they won't. We have to let them practice while the stakes are less than life or death in preparation for the moments when they may be.

- Model the struggle of handling difficult issues. Don't shield your children from your own struggles with how to respond. Let them see you feel hurt, discouraged, tired and weak so they can understand that survival and success are born out of getting back up and in the fight even when it seems to be more than you can stand. Talk to them about your own mistakes and show them how they allow you to grow.
- Expose your child to models who have have suffered the indignities of discrimination and become successful. From Mulan to Malcolm X to the immigrant family down the street or the Native Americans at your church, teach them to recognize the incredible strength and dignity of many many people of color facing everyday life challenges. Experiences of racial injustice are less likely to be internalized if your child is aware of positive counter-examples.

Fight your inner programming

Pain is something I (Beth) have been intimate with myself, of late. When my mother died, I joined a group of five other women who had recently lost their mothers. Our group went for eight weeks, three hours per week. Somehow it never seemed like enough. I found myself and my fellow "Motherless Daughters" wanting to talk and talk among this group of women who understood in a way that it seemed no one else on the planet could. My need to grieve found refuge and expression with people who would listen and who would accept my process —whatever shape it took—as one to which I was entitled. I lost my mother through death, but my grief has reminded me that my children have lost a mother through circumstance. As a motherless daughter to children who lost their first mothers through adoption, I found new insight that no matter the source, grief—takes its own time and warrants its own expression.

In our motherless daughters group, the cardinal rule was our agreement to listen and give attention without comment. We shared pictures, stories and legacies of our mothers, both positive and negative. In speaking about our mothers, in an uninterrupted and uninterpreted way, we were in fact honoring their significance in our lives. The very act of naming them to an audience who actually cared and paid real attention allowed each of us a profound opportunity to identify our grief and caring for them, which felt enormously healing. Within the group, we were able to unburden our feelings without anyone jumping in to try to fix them or explain them away. We all found ourselves relishing the opportunity to cry, ventilate or even get

*angry in a non-judgmental environment that validated our feelings
without pushing us to move on.*

*All of us felt as if the world's agenda for us was to "feel better" and
"move on" from the deaths of our mothers far more quickly than any of
us found possible or reasonable. We experienced fear that we might
lose our connection to who our mothers had been, and as a result
perhaps even who we were ourselves, if we moved forward without
great care and caution.*

*We talked of recreating our own selves, becoming new people.
Finding a way to do that in the context of the selves who already exist
presents many challenges. Sometimes it was hard to accept that
something which hurt so much, and which all of us would undo in a
second, could also result in positive changes or outcomes by which we
came to feel better. This ambivalence was difficult to admit within the
group. All of us felt it impossible to explain to outsiders. They too often
jumped in to interpret our feelings as meaning that somehow our
mothers' deaths were "for the best" or a "relief" in the face of sad
circumstances, a response we universally found appalling.*

*All of us found ourselves caught off guard by unexpected triggers
or experiences that brought up strong feelings about our mothers. We
each had felt angry or vulnerable when we didn't want to expose our
true feelings at the moment they arose. Sometimes only after we had
had a reaction did we realize that the emotion had anything to do with
the deaths of our mothers. This was unnerving and frightening. We
wondered if we would ever be able to operate normally again. The
consensus was no, but finding understanding and recognition helped
in creating our new "normal."*

Dr. Kenneth Watson writes; "Children face 'self-esteem crises' at times
when the magnitude of failure at some particular thing either eclipses their
past successes or reconfirms for them that they are 'total failures.' Parents, or
other caring adults, can turn such a self-esteem crisis into an opportunity to
enhance a child's self-esteem by following three steps—in order." They are:

1. Accept the child's feelings of worthlessness. This is the hardest step,
   but one that cannot be skipped. It means letting children "own" their
   feelings of pain and despair, even if things do not appear to us as the
   children see them. It means that when a child says, "I'll never amount to
   anything—I'm just no good!" the adult must resist saying, "Of course
   you will, look at all of the things you can do." It means that when a child
   says, "I'm hopeless, nobody can ever love me," they must resist saying,
   "Of course they can—and do. I love you." Children who are hurting
   must sense that those adults who wish to help them are not denying

them the pain they are experiencing. Of course adults do not have to agree that the children's premises are accurate, only that their pain is real. They can do this by the silent acceptance of the feelings of the children; by an empathetic sigh or hug; by a soft sad exclamation like, "Oh..." or, if they must use words, by acknowledging the child's suffering by a statement such as "What a terrible way to feel." And then they must wait and endure with the children the pain the children are feeling; perhaps, if they can, by finding a feeling of similar pain within themselves.

2. Provide an opportunity for the child to build competence through achievement. When children sense that their parents, or other caring adults, are tuned in to their pain, the adult's new goal is to add to the children's sense of achievement by arranging for them to participate in some activity that will result in success. Parents need to look for a specific "task" that is developmentally appropriate and falls within the range of the child's abilities or potential at that moment. They must be careful that the activity is not too trivial or too general. The point is to set the child up for honest success.

3. Reinforce achievement with honest praise. Once children have experienced success, they should be praised simply, honestly, and directly. For instance, you might say, "You did a good job fixing your hair today, Kenya." As a child's self-esteem grows, parents can begin to build the mechanism of self-praise. At such moments they might say instead, "I bet that you feel good about the fine job you did fixing your hair today, Kenya." For children with a yet stronger self-esteem, one might say, "How do you feel about the good job you did fixing your hair today, Kenya?" An even more "self-determining" level of praise would be, "How do your feel about the job you did fixing your hair today, Kenya?" Using children's names on all occasions of praise reinforces the children's sense that the achievement belongs to them.

According to Dr. Watson, it is tremendously challenging for parents to follow these three steps in sequence. When our children are injured, we are apt to bleed. Society and our hearts have programmed us to "kiss it and make it go away." If our child is sunk in despair over a particular failure or sense of total incompetence, we rush to fix it by re-framing what happened as "not so bad" or denying it altogether and trying to offer support with praise.

Try on the hat yourself. Don't you hate it when someone you need support from tries to minimize your feelings or explain your pain away? "You don't understand! You don't even care!" are often our angry conclusions, as we slam our emotional doors shut and leave that person behind. Children respond similarly. In fact, the only useful role we can play is to empathize and to let our children know that we understand that their pain is real. Only by communicating in a believable way that we understand what they are feeling and are willing help share it, will our children be able to receive our messages. If they do not sense empathy, they will assume that we are too unsympathetic to understand or too callous to realize the impact of their experience.

If our reassurance and their own subsequent achievements are going to have impact on our kids' self-images, we have no choice but to apply Dr. Watson's model for how to respond in the context of racially motivated challenges and crises—in order. The three steps are worth repeating:

1. Accept the child's feelings of worthlessness *when reacting to racial slurs and attacks.*
2. Provide an opportunity for achievement *to counterbalance the internalized harm the attack has forced.*
3. Reinforce achievement with honest praise *that acknowledges the child's racial identity.*

You Can't Make too Big a Deal about Race

How can you help your child cope with her feelings about race and racism?

Don't try to undercut her experience or imagine that you can "make it better." You're not in charge of her experience. She is. Your child is the expert. Allow her the right to all of her experiences. Don't try to fix them.

Appreciate what your child is letting you see and hear. What you can do is acknowledge that feelings are acceptable, it's okay to feel bad when difficult things happen, growth is possible, and nothing feels the same forever, even though in a bad moment we all think it will.

Acknowledge that racism is real without fearing that your validation will encourage your child to become a victim. We teach our kids about their right not to be touched in their private parts or in ways that make them feel uncomfortable. We teach our kids that strangers can be dangerous because we know that this information makes them survivors, not victims. For the same reasons, we know that acknowledging the truth of racism is essential if we want our children to be able to avoid being victimized by it. Perhaps the greatest legacy for children from groups that have suffered the indignities of injustice is to understand that surviving despair and pain causes one to come out stronger on the other side.

Remind yourself and your child that racism reflects poorly not on the target but on the one who holds the racist attitudes. Racists are responsible for racist beliefs.

Strategies: Seeking Diversity
What if You Were the Only One?

"A white mother said she would feel too uncomfortable in a situation where she might be the only white person. Her child is the only person of color all the time, but being a minority for a few hours was too much for her?"

—Beverly Daniel Tatum

Day-to-day living—what we do, who we see, where we go. This is how and where children learn the most important lessons of their lives. More than our words, and regardless of our intentions, children take our actions to heart. If there are many people of color important to your life, you will deliver the message that people of color are important and valued. If your child is the only one, how will you avoid the message that she is an exception to her race, or that there is something wrong with his ethnicity?

When white families adopt children of color, we unconsciously expect a great deal of the children. We expect them to integrate into our white families and become full members of our cultures. We expect them to learn our language, accept our values, and, often, to spend the majority of their waking lives with white people like us instead of with people who resemble them. One way to get an inkling of how enormous a stretch we are demanding of them is to seek out situations where we will be the only white person present—either in church, at a particular shopping center, in a class, at a restaurant, at the movies, in the mall, etc. When people of color are in the majority, it usually affects our sense of safety, confidence, and acceptance in ways we did not questions before.

Sometimes white parents say that they are afraid to be the only white person in a group. All of us understand that in the U.S. such fears are common and are fed on a daily basis by the media, the entertainment industry, institutional racism, and our own individual priorities. The question is how dare we demand more of our children than we would feel comfortable asking of ourselves? How may times have our children had the experience of being the only person of their race or ethnicity in a group? Sometimes having the most of something isn't so great. Seek out regular situations in which you will share your child's experience of being "the only one." You will learn great respect for her ability to cope.

Does Diversity Solve Everything?

"For every complex problem there is a simple answer… and it's wrong."

Having said that, H. L. Mencken would probably disagree with the simple and often repeated guidance parents receive: to cultivate diversity. Making connections with people living your adopted child's culture of origin is hardly a simple solution either, but, even so, on its own it is not enough.

Diversity doesn't guarantee connections

The residents of Berkeley, California, pride themselves on the diversity of their community. At its one public high school, a strong goal is to erase disparities in student achievement marked by race and class. With above-average SAT scores and multicultural courses from Swahili to Asian American history, Berkeley High has long been a symbol of successful, integrated urban education.

But Berkeley is also struggling to open the patterns of self-segregation among its students. Even though the population of the school is broadly diverse, reflecting a broad range of ethnic and racial groups, at lunch time the black kids sit together in the cafeteria, as do the Asian kids, as do the Latino kids, and so on. In such a setting, where do the multiracial kids sit? Where do the transracially adopted kids sit? Are they included members of their racial and ethnic groups, or do divided loyalties make it uncomfortable for them to take part in a segregated group?

> *When Carrie and Dennis moved across town they did so because they believed it would be better for their two Asian children to live in a neighborhood with real racial diversity and people who looked like them. As a white couple they had felt comfortable living in their all-white neighborhood but since adopting the girls all that had changed. After they settled in, Carrie began to visit preschools. She started with the Cantonese immersion school but found the local Montessori school more to her liking. The Cantonese school was very academically oriented and had even the three-year-olds sitting at desks. The Montessori school was far more child-centered, providing young children with opportunities to explore their feelings. The problem was most of the kids were white.*

We have seen numerous situations in which well-intended families moved into communities of color in order to build bridges to their child's culture. For example, when choosing a school, they often end up choosing one that reflects their values and not the racial diversity they moved there for. This demonstrates the incredible complexity of developing significant relationships beyond the limits of one's personal familiarity.

Some families live in racially diverse communities but still spend the majority of their everyday time primarily with white people—with friends, fellow workers, teachers, shopkeepers, service providers, mentors, and so on. This can be particularly dangerous since their children see many people of their race all around them, with none of them being invited into the intimate landscapes of family life. It is very likely that children will interpret this as a conscious choice on the part of their parents—a choice to keep those people out rather than a lack of ability or knowledge about how to invite them in.

A diverse environment makes connecting easier

Immersion is a key stage in the development of racial identity. Just as it's hard to learn to swim without a deep enough pool, without ready and regular access to a given culture it's pretty hard to immerse yourself in it. So, although diversity is not the whole solution for transracial families, it is certainly one of the most useful ingredients.

Imagine that over 99% of a beach's pebbles are an ordinary gray, but you're hoping to find a rare type of shiny brown pebble. If you fill a bag with just a small handful of pebbles, then it may hold none of the brown pebbles you seek. If you are a multiracial adoptive family living in a small town or rural area where the majority of people are white, you will need to stretch to your greatest possible capacity to find creative ways to compensate for your child's loss of access to people living the culture of his birth. Bring him to experiences with his cultural group as frequently and for as long in duration as possible. Please consider culture camp experiences and long vacations in communities where people of your child's heritage live, so that you and your child will have a chance to make friends. Contact the closest college about finding a student of your child's heritage who might like to become a mentor. Try everything. Stop at nothing. Because the majority of your child's life is spent isolated from others that look like him or her, so you need to use every opportunity you can to create access.

Our children need regular and comfortable connection to the cultures with which society will identify them. And as parents, we must work to become conscious of the impact of our choices on our children's cultural identity. Learning to develop and employ this consciousness, though challenging, is well worth every effort you can give it.

If You Are Living in a Mostly White Area

How does growing up in a white community affect children of color? Your choices determine your child's comfort. If your daughter were a grown-up now, looking back at where she grew up, what would she say?

- "I had a wonderful childhood. Our town was great for me. I always felt proud to live in a nice safe neighborhood where I was fully accepted and included."

- "It must have been my personality. I grew up feeling tolerated, but never popular. I wasn't really surprised when I didn't date as a teen. The white boys were not interested and there were no Asian boys in my school. Maybe if I hadn't been so shy, I would have had a better time."

- "I've often wondered why we didn't move to an area where I wasn't the only Latino kid around who wasn't a farm worker or somebody's maid. I don't know how it would have been if there had been other kids who looked like me around while I was growing up, but I think many things would have been easier. I never knew what it felt like not to be different, or to have friends who knew so much about me they weren't afraid to let me know when I was messing up until I went away to college and found other Latinos. My life is so different now, and I am much happier. If you really care so much about me, why didn't you move?"

Can't afford to move

Maybe you're thinking, "Yeah, yeah. You think it's so easy? What about my job, or the family business? You think you can just pick up a business that has built a local clientele and move it someplace else? We couldn't afford not to have an income. Did you expect us to start over? What about our house and the work we put into it? My grandmother's garden? There are trees in our garden that were planted by our great-grandparents. They are our roots. We couldn't leave them. We thought we were giving you the best we could—a nice place to live, the best schools. I guess we never really understood what you were missing."

Can't afford not to

Consider all of the options and the needs of each family member. Ask yourself whose needs are being served and whose needs are being given higher priority. Moving is one of the most stressful of human activities because it means leaving the familiar for the unknown. Give yourself credit for being able to consider it seriously at all!

Ask yourself if you live in a white community because you are white and would be uncomfortable not being in the majority? Are you asking something of your child that you can't take on for yourself?

If you are sure that moving is out of the question, what can you do to connect your child to more diverse communities?

1. Do everything within your power to make friends with at least one family who shares your child's racial heritage. Build up the strongest friendship you can with them and beg to be invited to spend time hanging out with them in their neighborhood, where your child will have a chance to make friends with other kids who share her racial experiences.

2. Join in recreational, religious, or educational groups or activities in the closest community you can find with members of your child's racial or ethnic group.

3. Make it a point to shop, go to restaurants, or see movies in the company of people of your child's heritage, no matter how far you have to drive, drive, drive.

4. Seek out special events such as museum exhibits, street fairs, theaters or musical productions that will attract an audience largely of your child's heritage and be sure to attend, no matter how far you have to drive, drive, drive.

5. Seek out beauty shops and barber shops located in a community that caters to people of your child's heritage and become a regular there.

6. Choose professionals of color: doctors, dentists, lawyers, teachers, etc. whenever possible, no matter how far you have to drive, drive, drive.

7. Think twice about private schools because often the few families of color in your area are not sending their children there.

We (Gail's family) moved from a proud-to-be-radical, diverse college community of less than 5000 people in Ohio to the San Francisco Bay Area when Liza was nine years old. Mel had grown up in Brooklyn and I am from Chicago. Because at gut level we'd somehow believed our kids were just like us, it had come as a shock to understand that they were phobic about cities and terrified of subways. I'm almost sure that the shock of Liza's losing her yellow baby blankie (that drag-everywhere can't-sleep-without-it rubbing-against-her cheek patch-of-comfort that had never left her side) when the family spent the weekend in the metropolis of Cincinnati, was what convinced us. We felt absolute that it was time to make a move and introduce the kids to a bigger world. Since we were both self-employed, moving was possible. Anywhere we could afford, had a diverse population and was open-minded enough to welcome our family could be considered. Even with so few limits, the stakes seemed so overwhelming it took us five years to do more than stick red pins in a map. Deciding to uproot four children who didn't want to move, ALWAYS struggled with transitions and loved the community we lived in required us to have enough knowledge about any new place to feel satisfied we would be making life better, not just creating another huge loss for each of them. As much as we thought they needed a more urban environment, we were like puppies, sniffing out the one perfect spot that smelled just right. Eventually, even the places that seemed most promising got ruled out for one reason or another. We would probably burst before we could decide.

San Francisco had been among our top five choices from the start.

At that time, I think anyone who had secretly longed to be a flower child or travel with Jack Kerouac but lived in a place like Yellow Springs, Ohio or Paw Paw, Michigan, dreamed of someday moving to San Francisco, a Mecca of natural wonders and cutting-edge people. We'd ruled it out because we couldn't afford it and didn't think we were cutting-edge enough to fit in. Then a friend called and offered a job and we started packing.

Moving the kids twice seemed out of the question, so when an enterprising realtor helped us find a great house in the single weekend we had to look, we bought it. The realtor's name was Connie, she was an awful person who lied to us and we believed everything she said. "The schools are fabulous," she said. "The community is sooo diverse." I'm confident she even hired a crew of people of color to act like they lived in the neighborhood because when we drove around without her, trying to get a feel for things, I counted twelve black people and four Asians on the streets, none of them ever to be seen again. In fact, nothing we saw raised any questions for us. Our fantasies about San Francisco had not prepared us for the fact that some parts of the Bay Area are racially mixed and some are not. That's how we came to move our black, biracial, Asian, and white children to a predominantly white community. So with the best laid plans, trying to be so cautious and so careful, we had done a terrible job choosing, it was only going to get worse, and our kids would never recover.

In her first week at her new school someone put a note in Liza's locker, calling her "Nigger." Oh God. We did everything we could think of to support her.

Twenty years later, each of my children agrees that the move was positive for them. Facing new challenges created new growth, not instantly but eventually. What we didn't deliver to them in a neat package, they were able to have access to by driving the extra mile. As Annie Lamott says,

"The truth is that progress is usually small and sneaky. The lie is that only big will do...Big is the magic we look for first, but grace is what makes things work out against all odds. If it were too big, it might sweep away all the bits of knowledge and insight we're granted as we go along. If it were too big, it couldn't get through the almost invisible cracks and holes in our walls, in our stone hearts; knowledge comes in tendrils."

How to Make Connections

A group of white families who had all adopted Chinese baby girls attended a community celebration for Chinese New Year at which a *meal was served. They had been planning this for months. They saw it as a real opportunity to connect their daughters to people of their own heritage. They sat together, all dressed up, the girls looking beautiful in their ceremonial costumes. at one table. They were devastated that no one from the Chinese community approached them or offered any sign of welcome. In fact some of them felt as if people were glaring. They wondered if they had made a terrible mistake bringing their daughters to this event*

The women of the First Chinese Baptist church society talked about it for months. Those white ghosts showing up as uninvited guests, to put on a show with their Chinese daughters. Didn't they understand that to celebrate when even within some of the church members' own families, children and parents had been separated, daughter from mother? How could they forget past wrongs done to them or keep from thinking bad thoughts? It was a bad omen to start the New Year with such bad face. They would not open the event to the public again. Not ever.

Relationships are made one at a time, in tiny links, experiences joined together end-to-end to make a chain. Trying to become part of something we don't know much about may at first feel like pushing against a heavy wooden door, but, after time, when you begin to connect to people one by one, the door becomes lighter and lighter, until eventually it is like pushing aside a soft chiffon curtain.

Before you go

There are many sub-groups within every racial/ethnic community. No group is monolithic or able to be characterized by a set list of traits and traditions. It is critical to look at the range of groups that are part of your child's culture in order to strategize appropriate approaches to particular communities within that "culture." Most groups have some members who are more approachable than others. It is discouraging to approach a group that does not welcome outsiders. It is important to identify those segments of a group which are most receptive.

Communities with experience across racial and cultural lines are likely to be more open to interracial friendships than communities that do not value or know how to make these connections. Most monocultural communities are resistant to further impregnation by the dominant culture since they are usually fighting already to keep the youth of their community within the bounds of their culture. So, approaching a Korean church that is the only Korean language church of its kind in the state may be more difficult that approaching a Korean community center which has a fully bilingual program. The church is probably working to maintain its primary culture, making it less open to outsiders who may tend to "dilute" the effort, than the community center which is obviously trying to bridge the issues for Korean Americans in living biculturally.

Despite the potential difficulties of making forays into new communities, it is essential that the transracially-adopted child have role models and cultural guides. Here are some tips to help you know where to begin.

- Do your homework. Know something about the culture prior to approaching a community. Surround your children with evidence that you value and respect their heritage. No matter where you live, you can get books, music, dolls, and artwork that celebrate your child's racial identity. This can be a positive experience for the whole family, even when it is difficult. Read books, join a group on the internet, seek a buddy family through a local organization or help line, seek a mentor through a local university, and/or find a cultural guide through a national organization.
- Follow protocol. Know and demonstrate respectful behavior based on the values of the cultural group. If possible, individually speak with people who are part of this cultural group in order to understand what these values are. Be observant and take time to study and discover. Make a conscious effort to follow the cues of the group instead of assuming that your normal behavior will be well received.
- Develop a relationship with someone trusted by the cultural group to function as your cultural guide.
- Gain appropriate entrée: obtain permission to enter the community (usually done through the cultural guide). Call before attending any public event and explain your interest. Find out if you can meet with anyone in advance who would be willing to sponsor you and your family at the event and help you to understand how best to fit in and behave respectfully.
- Develop a collaborative network. Build relationships with community organizations and natural supports.
- Acknowledge the reciprocal nature of relationships. In gathering information from the community, it is always important to remember to give something back. Schools and not-profit organizations are always looking for volunteers!
- Encouraging a respect and appreciation for other cultures will enhance your children's own cultural identity. Developing an affinity with other historically disenfranchised groups is one way to combat the sense of isolation that a transracially-adopted child might feel. Attending a Chinese New Year Celebration, A Cinco de Mayo festival, or a Gay Pride Parade not only encourages these cross-cultural bonds between natural allies, but also opens up a whole realm of possibilities for white parents looking to foster their children's minority identities.

Take the risk for your children's sake

"Our greatest fears are often of things that do not happen."
—Marcus Garvey

Good for you! You've done it! You're attending an event where many people of color are present and you see plenty of people in the room that you'd love to talk with. But how do you meet them? Everyone else looks completely comfortable and is chatting away in small groups and you're the one standing by yourself feeling like chopped liver. What's the first step?

Definitely blame your mother! It must be her fault that you just can't walk up and introduce yourself to somebody. Definitely. Didn't she tell you, "Never talk to strangers!"?

According to the *New York Times*, ninety percent of us learned fear of stranger lessons so well that we would rather deliver a public lecture (most people's second worst fear) than walk into a room where we don't know anybody else. So on this one, you're completely normal. And that's good because it gives you a lot in common with everyone else in the room.

There are ways for you to approach someone and manage to be comfortable. Just try. No one ever died from saying "hi" at a meeting where potential new connections have come for the same reasons you have. The worst thing that can happen is that someone won't like you. Big deal. Look how much effort it took for you to come here in the first place. Time is too precious to waste an hour or two not talking when you could be sharing a moment with a potential new contact. Take the risk. Here are three things you can do which will help you break through your fears and meet someone new:

1. Remember that you share common ground with these folks. You have common interests. That's why you're all at this event. They are not strangers. Yack about those interests.
2. You can plan and practice how to introduce yourself with something as simple as "Hi. I'm Deb Brown, and this is my first meeting. Can you tell me a little about this group?" Even we can manage that one, and you can too.
3. Shift the focus and concentrate on making someone else feel comfortable. Ask them questions about themselves and then introduce them to someone else. Each one leads to one.

Does your child need something separate from you?

Definitely, that is in fact the goal. Letting go is difficult. Our children grow up much faster than most of us anticipate. Despite the joy of each new stage most of us also experience the sorrow of leaving the last one behind. But our children need our permission and recognition that eventually they will want to be in groups or at events where they go with people of their same race only. They deserve the experience of not having to explain who we are or why we are tagging along. The benefits of these opportunities at monoracial experiences are important as a way of saying to them, "You are Latina and you deserve the pleasure of experiencing that without me serving as the guide or getting in the way."

> *I (Beth) worried about what they would teach her. Ted worried about whether she would know how to act. As we sat by the window, casually pretending not to notice that she was three minutes late returning from her first trip to the all Latino church and Sunday school of our friends, we really weren't fooling anyone including ourselves.*
>
> *I don't know exactly what we expected when she returned. Did we imagine she would reject the Lesbian parents of her best friends from school? Did we think she would decide she would like to move in with her Sunday School teacher rather than being in our own family? Did we envision her becoming somehow less our daughter by connecting to people that were different from us and more like her?*
>
> *When she flew in the door she was flush with the excitement of a new and happy experience. She goes every week now. She never invites us. What we had forgotten was how good we feel when we see our daughter find some piece of herself, knowing herself better… becoming. What we forgot in our worry was how much of loving is letting go.*

Of course joining a group independently doesn't begin until our children are old enough to go on their own or with other friends and families. Identify what your child needs from these experiences—is it social, emotional, educational? If you are dropping your child off in a group setting you haven't had the opportunity to know well yet, you need to be sure that you have asked the group leader or facilitator about his or her goals for the kids in the groups. What do they understand about adoption? About racial or ethnic issues? About children of your child's age? Who participates in the group? Our children have so many opportunities to feel different that it's refreshing and supporting when they are given the chance to be in the true majority.

Adoption Group Activities

Feeling different makes us feel isolated from others. This is why group activities—whether social, educational or therapeutic—are so useful for adopted and foster children. In the company of others who have felt the same things, children can see that they are not the only ones. They are not the only children in the world who sometimes feel the way they do.

If you are looking for family validation, a support group with other adoptive families is great. Through the fun of shared activities, children and families can discover through their own experiences that adoption is another way for families to form—a different kind of normal. Adopted children benefit from the chance to meet one another. For children who believe adoption has happened only to them, it is reassuring to meet others who share their experiences.

Typical activities offered through local support groups include potluck dinners, informal discussions, educational workshops, parties, holiday celebrations, picnics, mentoring programs, day camps, fairs, family camps and a wide variety of recreational activities. Support groups offer a safe and supportive place to raise questions, express uncertainty, vent frustration and brag about successes. They may be an informal gathering of a few parents or the local chapter of a national adoption association.

The best way to find an existing group in your area is to ask local agencies and national adoption support organizations for referrals to post-placement groups in your community. These groups are usually eager for new members and are likely to be extremely welcoming. Local private agencies will be listed in the yellow pages of your telephone directory under adoption.

If there isn't one in your community, start one!

The first thing we would suggest is that you broaden your outreach to include both families who have adopted transracially and same-race adoptive families of children of color. The purpose of the group should be two-fold: (1) support for parents and kids and (2) building significant relationships with other parents of color. Not only will you have a broader base of families in your area who may be interested, but you will form a stronger group if some of the adults are of the same heritage as the children.

Groups that have enjoyed the greatest longevity are those that have both recreational events (including the kids) and some adults-only meetings from time to time where parents can share information and experiences they have in common, learn from a visiting lecturer or view and discuss a video or book on racial or adoption issues.

Culture camps

Summer programs where they can be immersed in their birth heritage can be invigorating. Culture Camps are generally short-term summer camps, usually lasting a week or so, designed to help school-aged adopted children and their siblings immerse themselves in the adopted child's birth heritage Curriculum is generally focused on activities to introduce the children to the art, crafts, history, music, dance, folklore, food, and language of a particular culture. Some camps also include activities designed to help campers explore adoption issues through discussion groups or creative activities with adoption themes. The best camps make it a priority to recruit counselors who are natives of the culture being explored. Sometimes counselors have themselves been adopted. For many of the children who attend, the highlight of the camp experience is the opportunity to be "the same" as nearly all the other children in their groups, sharing similar physical features, the same birth heritage, the experience of having parents of another race and the experience of being adopted

Strategies: Concrete Tools for Operating in a Racist World

Mainstreaming—What Are the Rules?

Fitting in

We have all had the experience of not belonging. It is uncomfortable and unpleasant. Whatever the circumstances, most of us are familiar with the sense that if we don't behave the "right" way, then we cannot belong. For adopted children, and especially for transracially-adopted children, this sense about "fitting" (or not) is especially acute. There is no way to avoid it completely. But we can provide tools to address the desire to fit in and we can teach our children skills to help them make connections. Mainstreaming means identifying the common traits and styles shared by those who are growing up in your child's birth culture, and enabling your child to develop and use those traits. Knowing how to operate within the ethnic mainstream will facilitate his or her comfort with and acceptance by others of the ethnic group,

If the word "mainstream" troubles you, it may be because many of us who come to transracial adoptions are not part of the mainstream ourselves—in fact we often take great pride in being people who reject social conventions and norms. We think of ourselves as internally-motivated, unlikely to be influenced by others and without great need of external approval. As parents, we tend to be nontraditional rather than conventional, leaders rather than followers, drivers rather than passengers on life's roads.

Transracially-adopted children are likely to view the matter from another perspective. Because their lives have involved making a fundamental transition from one family to another and one culture to another, they tend to be sensitive to situations in which they feel different, often yearning to belong or fit in. This desire to be "one of the group" has great importance in children's relationships to their birth culture. Parents can help by understanding that, however much they themselves value individuality and reject conventionality, transracially-adopted children have more than enough experience in feeling different and may seek to conform. Our children may feel especially gratified and assured by sharing the hairstyles, manner of dress, and social codes common to others of their race.

These external markers can be visible vehicles of belonging. Since young African American girls do not generally wear their hair loose or in an Afro, if your daughter does wear such styles she will be marked—once again—as an outsider, exiled from the larger community. If you fail to accord them some of the most visible mainstream markers, then the community will be that much more likely to judge your family as incompetent, which does nothing to help your child's sense of identity.

> The other day James (Beth's son) called Ted at work to say, "Dad, I need a hair cut. Let's make a calendar so we can go to the barber every week instead of whenever." I knew Ted had to be remembering, as I was, the first time we had gone to that shop six or seven years ago. James had lasted only a few minutes in the chair before his complete melt-down made all hair activities impossible. Robert looked at us and him and thought, as he told us three or four years later, "They will never be back. Poor boy." But his kindness kept us coming the first year as James cried before, after and during and the second year when he sat with "the look" and the third when he puffed up as his barber shop friends greeted "little man" and his sister "pretty woman" at each visit and so we kept coming.
>
> "Dad, you need to understand, we like to take care of our hair. I know you don't care but it matters for us and you gotta get me there until I am old enough to do it myself." My husband couldn't wait to call me back after their conversation was over. "Did you hear what he said? He counted himself as black instead of white. At least maybe we did one thing right. Thank you, God."

Hair, clothes, ear-piercing: there is a long list of cues you should become familiar with so that the decisions you make, while not undermining your child's sense of family membership, also allow participation in his racial or ethnic group.

It's hard to be on the team unless you know the rules

Give your children the social skills to act appropriately in their birth culture as well as in yours. In order to teach this lesson, you must first explore and recognize the difference between the two. Some ways to do this are by consulting with people who are living in the culture, reading, taking a parenting class targeted to parents of your child's birth cultures, and getting information from friends and acquaintances willing to play the role of cultural guide, mentor, or buddy family. Then you need to clarify for your children the difference between acceptable behavior within the home and the safety of the family and acceptable behavior outside the front door in other social settings. Children of color (and perhaps particularly those raised with white parents) are always scrutinized carefully and can be subjected to harsh judgments from outsiders. If you and your children overlook this fact, then they will have a distinct disadvantage in their interactions with the world. Politeness and knowledge of appropriate social mores can go a long way to opening doors and relationships for our children. They need to learn the values regarding good manners, the social norms regarding greetings, and respectful naming. There are often vastly different than norms in European-North American culture.

As a young teenager Liza (Gail's daughter) called up her friend Tomika on the phone and heard her friend's mother call out, "It's that rude girl, calling for you again. You tell her not to call here anymore! That girl doesn't know how to act. I don't want you spending time with her, you hear?"

Tomika told Liza not to call her at home anymore. She would get in too much trouble.

But why? What had Liza said that was rude? She had been trying her best to be polite. Tomika was her best friend. Why didn't Tomika's mom like her? It wasn't fair.

Tomika finally explained that her mother couldn't stand it that Liza would call up and say "Is Tomika home?" instead of asking to speak to her in the proper and polite manner, "May I please speak to Tomika?"

Liza was hurt, but she and Tomika remain friends to this day so she didn't really lose her friend over it. What she couldn't get over was how we, her parents, had betrayed her by not teaching her appropriate telephone manners, in her mind, universal for every African American family. The truth is we didn't have a clue anyone would find her phone manners offensive. Both of us had been communicating exactly that way all our lives and had never gotten the idea that anyone considered us rude. We were totally oblivious in general and even less aware that there might be different ideas about phone etiquette in the black community than we were used to. Brilliant, huh? All we could do was apologize. Even explaining that we just hadn't known has never been good enough. We should have known, she thought, and I agree.

In my family (Beth), it was a sign of familiarity and fondness to call adults by their first name. When my best friend Tosca began to spend more and more time at our home, eating meals and sleeping over, my mother insisted she call her by her first name. One night Tosca and I were talking on the phone. Mom invited her to dinner. "Mommy," Tosca cried out, "Margaret invited me for dinner. Can I go?" I heard the muffled voices that I recognized as disagreement between her and her Mom and then her mother on the phone saying they would be right over. Mrs. Ng arrived and anyone could see that Tosca's tail was between her legs. We all laughed later when we understood that Mrs. Ng had assumed that Tosca must have mortally offended my mother by using her first name.
None of us know what we didn't know…

Values or information?

My mother (Beth's) had a strong sense that there are right and wrong ways to do things in the world. Her goal was to provide her daughters with the best skills, to allow them to be the best they could be. Let's take place-setting and bed-making, for examples. Learning to know which fork goes where was taught while she helped us set the table for imaginary—and very fancy—dinner parties. We would get out the silver chest and have fun deciding how many courses we could come up with, making the task as complex as possible. Later, when I was confronted with social situations which intimidated most of my friends, I felt comfortable and in control. I had a sense of belonging.
Similarly, when it came to bed-making, according to my mother there was only one right way. But when I journeyed out into the world of sleepovers and saw other ways of making beds, I began to question this dictum. It did not prove helpful in the way the place-setting games had because in truth there is not social more for bed-making that has ever come in useful as a point of connection. This "rightness" had been presented not as information but as a value.

Bed-making is one thing; racial identity is another. When the stakes are high, you've got to be careful to provide information, not just subjective evaluations. Decisions will need to be made regarding values and behaviors that are essential to membership in the family and those which are common to a child's birth culture.

Conflict of values

"What do you feed them to make them so shy?" a white friend who happened to be a child psychiatrist asked at the annual school barbecue (Gail). It was the kind of chitchat that counted as a complement to me as a young mom, especially coming from a professional. Our kids went to a lab school on a wooded college campus. Seth and a bunch of other little guys, none older than seven had just come running across the field stripped naked and laughing hysterically, rushing at the blankets filled with parents like baby bulls. "Wait for me, wait for me!" came a Tinkerbell voice from way behind them, a butterball brown figure running to catch up. Liza, at three, was fantastic. Her glistening baby body was also naked, the only girl, the only one so small. None of the parents could keep from laughing—not at her but with her, although her brother was rather annoyed she was getting all the attention yet again "Go, Liza!" someone shouted. "Come on baby, you can get 'em!" At the time, "streaking" was IT on campus, the coolest of the cool. Students running around naked in public was still disconcerting to me, but to my knowledge, our children were leading the first streaking at their school.

Actually, I was not all that surprised. Liza and Seth had always been more comfortable without their clothes than in them and nudity was not altogether unusual within the privacy of our home. I was a tiny bit worried that some people might not approve but I was rather proud of my gutsy kids. Especially Liza, who had done it on her own. She knew what she wanted, and by God she had gone for it.

"Go get her dressed right now!" hissed Mrs. Wilson, a black professor at the college, glaring at me from under her glasses. "WE expect our children to be well-behaved. WE do not allow them to run around naked in public." Her voice was low as if she wanted only me to hear but blaming and terribly unfriendly.

"Oops," I said sheepishly, immediately understanding that Mrs. Wilson was speaking for the black community and judging my kids on her own terms. As reprimanding as the message she was sending my way was, I knew she was trying to help my baby and that I'd better follow her directions, quickly. "I see what you mean," I said, picking Liza up and wrapping her in our blanket. "Seth, go get your clothes on now! Come on Liza. Show me where you left your clothes. We'll come back as soon as you're dressed."

It is likely that you, as a white parent, may experience some conflict in values with the child-rearing traditions of your child's birth culture. Much of white mainstream culture in North America emphasizes and esteems individualism, each person's "right" to lead life in his own way and to express himself as he chooses. But many cultures of color place higher priorities on taking care of the group, regarding the group before the individual. Given the likelihood that values and behaviors are not likely to be the same in the two or more cultures our children straddle, we must ask ourselves how we plan to give them the behavioral tools to succeed in both.

Along with the emphasis on individualism comes mainstream white America's belief in self-determination and meritocracy: that good talent rises to the top of its own accord and that excellence is always valued and rewarded fairly. The premise is that a level playing field exists; a world that is fair. Given the realities of racism, this notion cannot be accepted.

It's really not as difficult as it sounds. Behavioral dualism is an asset; if parents are not confused, it's not likely their children will be either. After all, we exhibit behavioral dualism in all kinds of common circumstances: in the cultural difference embodied in interfaith or interracial marriages; in the different homework and bedtime rules in the two homes a child might have after a divorce; in the different behavioral expectations in home versus school or in church versus the playground. Negotiating these differences is generally an ordinary daily task. Told just once (or twice), most kids figure out what is acceptable and what is not, adapting back and forth as circumstances require. In the case of different expectations between white culture and the child's birth culture, our kids can also find ways to fit into both, as long as they know the rules.

Our job as parents is to help our children understand the difference between what might be okay at home and what is okay in public settings. In a common example, we have found that many white parents allow their children a fairly wide range of choices in the private realm, allowing children to question authority and at times to say no to an adult. This is not a value shared by many communities of color. A child who refuses to obey her parent in the grocery store or other public setting is not a popular figure, and the judgments will be harsher and more damaging if the child is of color and the parent is white. A common conclusion made by rush-to-judgment onlookers is to conclude "Those folks don't know how to take care of that baby" or to wonder, "What is that child doing in that family?" On the other hand, if your child knows the difference between what she can do at home and what she can do in public and acts accordingly, the problem is solved and she has the tools to interact well with and be judged favorably by members of her racial and ethnic group, an important goal.

Providing cues

Community connections begin with claiming. Giving our children the language to claim their heritage is extremely important, but the language isn't all that it takes for our children to feel established within their racial community. Fitting into a culture also involves all of the physical senses.

Sight: What are the physical characteristics of the people in our children's racial groups? Certainly, a group will offer a wide range of visible characteristics, but there are also mainstream norms. These norms are often very different from white norms. If you are parenting a Native American child, you need first of all to educate yourself about the importance of clothing in Native American culture. "It's just clothes," you might say. But if your Native American child—especially your child with white parents—is to be accepted as part of that community, then you have to pay attention to clothing. Native Americans choose clothing in a wide variety of styles, ranging from conservative to trendy, ethnic to hip-hop. There are many options about clothing and jewelry, and you need to be educated enough to distinguish the mainstream from the uncommon.

Taste/food. It's important that your child be able to identify and enjoy foods central to their racial or ethnic heritage, such as knowing what meunudo or greens or kim chee is. Maybe you and your child could take a cooking class in which you will likely meet a person of your child's race or ethnicity. Giving your child the tools to understand how and what to eat will make them feel less awkward in situations where people will expect them to know.

Tasting your way through a culture is a delicious way to learn something about it, but in this case, tricky business. Too often transracial families limit their exposure to food and drink alone—making their importance outweigh their actual role in the culture. Food can help your child develop comfort with and connection to the culture of his or her birth, but the important thing is not to reduce your child's sense of heritage to mere food sampling or to confine these foods to holiday traditions. Americans have a reputation for being rather self-centered tourists, measuring experiences in other cultures against their sense of themselves as the center of the universe. It's important that your introduction to the tastes and foods of your child's culture be respectful. Here are some ways of showing respect through food

- Break bread with friends to whom the food of culture is every day fare.
- Relish their stories of childhood memories about delicious traditional foods
- Learn about food preferences within the culture and the broad range of foods that are typical
- Expose your family to traditional foods, not Americanized versions (e.g.

authentic Mexican cuisine vs. Taco Bell)
- Learn how people in the culture rate food products. What kind of bar-becue sauce is considered best? What brand of Mexican staples would Mexicans usually buy?
- Look for restaurants with native-culture clientele. Become regulars in order to open doors to connection.
- Learn about food-connected cultural manners. What are the traditions around
  - Offering food to guests?
  - Food taboos?
  - Use of utensils or fingers? Being served or helping yourself?
  - Making eating noises?
  - Cleaning your plate? Leftovers?
  - Food as medicine?
  - Hot vs. cold?
  - Sharing food? Drinking from the same cup?

Sound/music. If all they have ever heard is folk music, your children may feel hesitant to attend a school dance when the time comes. Having a buddy teenager of their race can give them a sense of ease with the mainstream music of their culture. The same holds true for spoken language. If we de-value what may sound to us like "street" talk or "improper" English, we may be removing what feels like an "in" linguistic style. This is not to say that our children's shouldn't learn "proper" English, but various racial groups have ver-nacular forms of social speech that our children are entitled to come to feel comfortable with as well. Use the same respectful approaches and caution in approaching music and language as were discussed regarding food.

Smell: If you visit a market catering largely to the Asian or Latino or African American communities, you will likely go on a vividly different olfactory adven-ture than you experience at the markets you have usually shopped before. It is important that your child have some familiarity with the scents common to his or her culture in order not to feel repulsed or confused by them. Include the fragrance of food, hair, and body products.

Be sure to create a healthy sense of respect and balance in bringing your child's culture of origin into your family. Learn it well enough to make it a part of who you are. When your child's primary experience with his birth culture is through visits to "exotic" ethnic restaurants, street fairs in "other" neighbor-hoods, or even a short visit to her country of birth, your efforts to instill racial or ethnic pride may result instead in a limited tourist passport, or even worse, something akin to a trip to the zoo—a chance to look-see but then go home to "normal, regular, plain old (white) everyday life." Though rich in meaning in their own ways, the symbols of a culture cannot be presented as the whole without trivializing what it means to live within that culture. After all, if immigrants to America were introduced to American life only by making occasional visits to McDonalds and Disney World, imagine the misconceptions they would have.

Skill Mastery
Low self-esteem

As we have mentioned before, transracially adopted children of color tend to struggle more than most with issues of self-esteem. Young children want to be like their parents, and when parents are of a different race or ethnicity, the child may feel at fault and of less worth because on a fundamental level they can never be like them. This has nothing to do with whether the parents are asking the child to be like them or valuing their racial identity, it is simply the truth. Powerful messages from society regarding racial hierarchy and connection will compete with the adoptive parent's heartfelt message to the child that she is loved, important, and deserves care, that others can be trusted, and that she is not alone. What helps? What makes children feel good about themselves?

Becoming competent

Early childhood educators agree that children feel good about themselves when they have experiences of accomplishment and attainment. Young children love to acquire new skills. While the mastery of any notable skill will help a child feel more confident about his or her place in the world, the mastery of skills related to the child's particular culture will help the child develop positive racial identity as well.

Parents can facilitate this development by keeping alert to their children's talents and interests and then patiently encouraging the child's skills. This suggestion may sound obvious, but consider what happens in many families when a child decides he wants to learn to tie his shoes. At first, parents patiently show the child how to do it and often sit with him, offering encouragement and ongoing support. But it isn't easy to learn to tie your shoes when your fingers are not fully coordinated and you have not yet integrated the steps, so most kids get frustrated and then act out. Parents may try diverting the child's attention to other activities, or may suggest that he just take a break—anything to diminish the frustration (both child's and parents'). Parents may find themselves hesitating to return to the task and its frustrations. So the child is left alone with the challenge, getting quite discouraged in the process.

In contrast, parents can help both their children and themselves by developing an understanding of how skills are mastered and an appreciation of the single-mindedness of new learners. Parents can easily become bored with the 27th rendition of a new song or the 3000th occasion a child shows us that she can write her name, but in truth our children need our praise even during the 267th rendition of "Twinkle, Twinkle." Their experience of success—and our acknowledgment of it—reaffirms their competence. It is often tempting to respond, "Well, you know now how to write your first name, so let's learn how to write your last name, too." This response must be considered carefully. We need to look at our children for their readiness to move to a next level. Dangling ever-increasing expectations can easily introduce a sense of shame and diminished competence, instilling a stronger sense of what the child can't do than what he can. Self-esteem is developed by experiences of accomplishment, not by being ever-reminded of future skills as yet unaccomplished. We must provide what our children need to move to the next level, what they are ready and capable of accepting.

But tailoring expectations to the child's current abilities does not suggest that you should diminish expectations for your child's effort and accomplishment. Parents can actively commit themselves to encourage not just the ordinary developmental achievements (like learning to tie one's shoes) but also the uncommon development of excellence which can become expressions of the child's interests and unique abilities in areas such as swimming, music or sports. As an example, the dedication to his son's skill mastery expressed by Tiger Woods' father represents an extreme of this strategy. Hold out high expectations for your children. Any child will be served by a parent's commitment to assisting a child's development of abilities or talents to their fullest possible degree. Because of society's lowered or negative expectations, children of color need to feel personally successful and accomplished. Communicate to your child your belief that she can excel at those things for which she has talent and strength and that she can do well in all things to which she sets her mind. Our children need to know that it takes hard work and great stamina to overcome difficult odds, that this struggle is their legacy and that they cannot allow others' reduced expectations to limit their determination to achieve.

Authentic success contributes to strong self-esteem. Be sure to provide your child with the tools and resources to develop real skills.

Personalizing Culture

What do Michael Chang, the first American to win the French Open in tennis; Connie Chung, a news anchorperson; Myung-Whun Chung, an opera conductor; the writer Maxine Hong Kingston; I.M. Pei, one of the world's leading architects; Dr. Samuel C.C. Ting, a winner of the Nobel prize in physics; and An Wang, owner of Wang Laboratories and one of the richest men in the United States have in common? Could your children answer this question? Each of these famous people is Chinese American. Perhaps you knew that, or could guess on the basis of their names or physical appearance. Most young children would need to have this information pointed out to them; they wouldn't have the experience to guess each person's culture without being told.

The problem is that as adults, we sometimes forget to mention to our children the ways in which they are connected to their birth cultures. We may try very hard to incorporate culturally appropriate music, art, literature, food, activities and people into the lives of our families, but then forget to let our children know about the link between themselves and their heritage.

> *One thing Mel and I look back on proudly when we think about connecting our kids to their cultures was that we loved world music and filled our house with it. Folk music and Sunday hootenannys were regular features in our lives. On Friday nights we all went to the college for outdoor folk dancing. Habitually our friends and their kids would gather in our living room with an assortment of guitars and drums and we would sing and share covered dish suppers. If you didn't like to sing, you could play the spoons. We felt really proud of ourselves about those gatherings, making music with a diverse group of people— teaching our kids to sing in other languages, to enjoy a wonderment of rhythms, to improvize, to carry a tune. What a shock when one of our pride and joys as an adult announced in public with clear disapproval, "It would have made such a big difference to me if I'd just heard some black music growing up. I wouldn't have felt so out of it with my friends."*
>
> *"Give me a break! We played Jazz and gospel day and night. What about Miriam Makeba, and Odetta ? What about... uh, uh...singing spirituals in the car with Poppy?"*
>
> *"Man, oh man," she said, slapping her forehead. "That was black music? How would I have known that was black music? That was old folks at home music—that was background music, that was our family muzak. It was in the air all the time but it wasn't black music to me. I wouldn't have guessed in a quadrillion years that it had anything to do with me."*
>
> *"Oh." I murmured. "I mean, "Uh, oh." I guess I just learned something. Giving things names and explaining why they're there makes a difference, you think?*

In adoptive families, where the child may be the only person of a particular culture in the family, it often happens that the parents believe that they are exposing their child to positive racial or ethnic reflections and experiences, only they don't help the child understand his special connections to those reflections and experiences. They simply become, from the child's point of view, "grown-up stuff—of little or no interest and certainly no particular relevance.

For example, you might say to your child, who was born in China, "Honey, come watch this guy. He's a great tennis player and his name is Michael Chang." But that's very different from saying, "Honey here is a man whose family comes from China, just like you, and he is a world champion tennis player. You can be proud that someone like you is one of the best tennis players in the world. Would you like to watch him play?"

For example, the whole family is going out for Sunday lunch and you decide to go for dim sum. Unless you say so, will your Chinese daughter realize that this food comes from the country of her heritage and not from the birth culture of your Latino son?

You have a set of Chinese story puppets that represent figures in a traditional opera. You like to stage the opera, using the puppets to act out the parts. But unless you make a point of it, how could your Chinese daughter understand that these puppets and this music are a part of her heritage and not of her African American sister's?

Pointing out the specifics is the only way to help your child discover ethnic connections between himself and the world around him.

Reading Matters

My (Beth's) son James rarely asks questions about having been adopted. When James was five or six, we read Two Birthdays for Beth.

"I wonder why Beth isn't sure she likes having two birthdays?" I asked.

"She wishes she just came out of her mommy's tummy. Blah, blah, blah," James said. "She doesn't always want to talk about it."

"Does she feel sad?" I asked.

"Yes, and sorta mad," said James.

"Sometimes she gets mad at herself but she tries not to, 'cause she didn't do anything wrong. Her other parents loved her. So do her real mom and dad." (To James, "real parents" meant us at that point.)

Though James had never actually spoken about his feelings on adoption before, he had heard us talk about it with Sofia and as a general family topic. I told him I could understand why Beth felt sort of mad and sad and that I thought that was OK. When we finished the book, James got up and spent ten minutes searching his room for his copy of Love You Forever. *James and I cuddled up in our favorite reading chair, finding particular pleasure in the comfort of the story's refrain: "I'll love you forever, I'll like you for always. As long as I'm living, My baby you'll be."*

Just as most of us are gratified to discover characters in books who resemble us, whether in appearance or attitude, background or circumstance, many adopted kids love books that include adoption and children of color love to encounter characters who resemble them in both obvious and subtle ways. Such books can be hard to find in ordinary bookstores. Sure, you might find a bookstore display celebrating Black History Month, or a table offering a dozen books reflecting Asian characters. In the Parenting section you'll find a few books about adoption mixed into the selections on breast-feeding and baby names. But to be relegated to limited sections and "special" occasions both marginalizes race and adoption and reflects only a token sampling of the wonderful array available for those who embrace these issues at the center of our lives.

Fiction can be a mirror, reflecting and validating people your child can identify with racially as well as a window, providing opportunities to step into someone else's shoes. Reading is also a safe way to explore issues without personalizing them. Being able to have some distance from a challenging topic may help your child think about the issues more clearly. For children whose lives don't fit the fantasized "Ozzie and Harriet" stereotype (and whose really does or who really wants to?) finding stories whose characters resemble themselves can be an exhilarating and transformative event. So it is, too, for parents and other adults touched directly by issues of adoption and race. To stumble upon a description and analysis of how young children are likely to handle grief and loss issues, for example, can be a "Eureka!" moment for a parent struggling to understand a newly adopted toddler. And not only can books parallel our experience, they can lead us to worlds otherwise unknown, offering us insight into unfamiliar ways, introducing us to new points of view. By exposing our children to the endless varieties of human relationships, we teach them not only about accepting others but about accepting themselves as well. So in seeking books for your family, please consider those stories that differ from your family's experiences of adoption, history, cultural and racial identity, family life, as well as ones that echo and reflect it.

Here is a simple, three-part method to help you use books to talk about challenging and core issues.

Select a story about a child dealing with one of life's deeper or more challenging issues. Anything from the loss of a pet, to trying to fit in at school, to feeling parents are not being fair. The book does not have to be about adoption or race to deal with core issues for your child. What you are looking for is something your child will be touched by or excited about, a story to jump start conversation.Create a cozy, quiet atmosphere where nothing short of an emergency on the level that the house is burning down around you, will disturb your special time to read together. Cuddle in and take all the time in the world to read the book you have chosen to your child. The setting should feel intimate and very, very safe.

Talk with your child exclusively about the characters in the story to understand his feelings about the plot and the personalities. "How did you like it when the boy did that?;" "What do you think he could have done differently?;" "Do you think his friend made a good choice?;" "I think the Dad was being really unfair when he did that, what do you think?;" After awhile, when the conversation comes to a natural end, think about whether you and your child have already gone deep enough just with the questions and discussion that has happened so far. If you want to take it further, lean back in your chair and say something like…

"Gee, this story reminds me of the time in my own life when…." Then slowly tell a story from your personal history and be sure to include a deep description of how you were feeling during the time the story happened. Your description of your emotions will likely have a lot of impact on your child. Answer all of his questions. Then, gently, ask if the story in the book reminds him of anything that ever happened in his life. If the mood has been set and he feels truly safe to share, you are likely to be amazed at what you hear next. Listen with every pore of your body. When he is finished, hold him close. If it seems appropriate, talk about his story, ask questions. You may find out how he really feels about things that you didn't even know he was thinking about. Read to your child every day, every single day.

Helping your child find her own voice

It is also important that children be encouraged to understand the importance of their own stories. From the first moment children can scribble, parents can facilitate this process of self-discovery and self-expression by encouraging children to write their own books. These books needn't be elaborate. Some families make a point of helping children write books about every new thing that comes up in their lives, creating a collection of family literature to be placed proudly on the bookshelf among works by other great writers. Perhaps you'll even decide to bind these efforts into a single volume, reflecting a child's thoughts over a year.

Even before children are old enough to write, parents can record in writing the stories that their children tell. However you preserve your child's storytelling, the important lesson is that your children come to think of themselves as the authors of meaningful stories of their lives, and come to understand as well that their voices will matter and be heard.

What your child needs to know

- That heroes come from every race, gender, and ethnicity. For a book to be positive, heroes need to behave authentically, hold positive values, and be represented without stereotypes.
- That the lives and lifestyles of "minority" families are not "odd" or unusual. White middle-class America is not the measure against which all other lifestyles must be compared.
- That things happen in life without regard to race and ethnicity and at the same time race and ethnicity are a part of every situation.

Dealing With Racism

Don't wait for an injury before you talk about racism. Discrimination hurts everyone, but white parents are especially susceptible to surprise, because we don't anticipate it. Racist things happen, and they hurt. Recognize that racism affects your child's life on a regular basis. Don't add to your child's stress by over-responding to every situation. Prioritize. Fight the battles that make a difference. Model obtainable goals. Children need direction and hope.

Strategies for Parents

Speak No Evil

Of utmost importance is that your kids know that racial slurs cannot be ignored. There are no excuses, In these days of demeaning music, racist jokes, and loose tongues, let's make one thing clear to our kids:

In this family there is a zero-tolerance policy toward racist remarks and behavior.

Here are some examples of effective responses to use when racial slurs come up.

Adult to adult: "I am not comfortable with what you just said and I'd appreciate it if you would never repeat it. Your remark is offensive, because it says some people are worth less than others are, which is neither true nor funny. The world has more than enough anger and pain, so how about putting a lid on contributions like that?"

Adult to child: "Talk like that hurts people's feelings. I won't let you talk that way here."

Train your child to know

- Race and gender come with birth; no one can choose or earn either
- You are always available to talk about things that concern her about race. Practice talking about race in many contexts so that you won't be nervous when you talk with your child.
- It's okay to be different. The goal is to recognize, accept, include, honor and celebrate the diversity of human beings. As people, we are more similar than different. Our differences benefit us all.
- You love him and he is not alone.
- She need not let anybody, of any color, limit or define her solely by race or undermine her acceptance of herself.
- He doesn't deserve bad treatment and is a good person just as he is.
- Whatever doesn't kill you strengthens you.
- There is always something he can do. He has all the tools he needs to be attractive, nice, clean, and smart. He will get up every morning and do what he has to do and get up every time he falls down. The answer lies inside him.
- People who act rudely don't know him and have no right to comment.
- Some people are toxic, always negative. If she is near them, realize that that's how they are. It has nothing to do with who she is.
- It's useful to talk about issues of oppression and to identify the racism directed at them.
- She is in charge of her own attitudes.
- He has one life, whether he spends it laughing or crying is entirely up to him.
- One person can make a difference.
- He is part of a group from whom he can gain strength and comfort.

Make your commitment to your child clear. This is especially crucial when rejection from others occurs. Involve your child in groups that foster appreciation of differences. Make sure your social life includes frequent activities with people of other races. Prepare your child to know that things happen and that they hurt. Don't set your child up to be an ambassador of multiculturalism. The more diverse her circle becomes, the less often she will be targeted unfairly because of race or ethnicity.

Children of color are often unfairly accused of being troublemakers. As white parents our antennae are not always accurate in approaching teachers or others in positions of authority over our children. We want our children to be respectful and responsible in such settings but we also must recognize and in turn allow them to recognize the negative stereotyping that exists in schools and other institutions. Talking about acceptable behavior, listening for cues about whether the standards are the same for all the children, no matter their race, is particularly important when parenting a child of color. Helping yourself to learn to spot unfairness is the first step in validating your child's experiences of being targeted.

On the flip side, prepare them and validate their feelings about so called "positive" stereotyping; which is painful and damaging because it too makes assumptions about people that have nothing to do with them personally. Asians who are labeled "the model minority" and expected to be good in math and at details are often victims of "positive stereotyping," as are blacks who are expected to have good rhythm and to excel at sports. Having options builds self-confidence.

When something bad happens

- Be a true ally. Make sure your child knows that you know that she is not at fault.
- Use the power of the family to brainstorm a list of things she can say or do when racist remarks or situations come up.
- Don't deny, explain away, or make excuses for what your child experiences as racism.
- Validate your child's hurt, offer comfort and share feelings.
- Don't imagine your child doesn't notice or hear something that was said in their presence.
- Not talking about it means you condone it.
- Make sure that your child is clear that being blamed may not be related to his or her actions.
- When your child is the target of a racial slur or is treated unfairly, offer him or her a dignified way to regain composure and withdraw from the situation. Saying something like, "I'm going to give the puppy a bath now. Would you like to help?," can provide some respite from the hurt until he is ready to talk some more.
- Model appropriate reactions to racism. Acknowledging that they have a right to be angry, validating the reasons they are angry and commiserating with them about injustices they observe and experience will go a long way toward helping your children work through their feelings and to strengthen the bond between you.
- Help your child to externalize racist remarks rather than internalize them. This is a critical coping skill for children of color if they are to handle the onslaught of negative messages they will likely encounter in their lives. This skill can be developed through the observations and modeled anger of their parents.
- No one can know the perfect way to respond to insensitive remarks all

the time. In fact, people commonly respond to racist insensitivity with shocked disbelief and stunned silence. It is only later that we gnash our teeth and think up clever ways to handle the situation. Giving yourself permission to handle racial insults imperfectly is to acknowledge your humanness. Don't be ashamed. It's not you or your children who need to be embarrassed. Use your reaction to process the event with your children. "Wow. Can you believe he said that? My jaw just dropped open; I didn't know what to say!" Make a game out of all the things you wish you had said. Sharing and processing experiences is an important way to externalize racism.

- Sometimes parents of children of color tell them that they have to try twice as hard and be twice as good to convince biased people that they are not bad A racist will not be changed by a child's "good" behavior. Your child may no longer trust your judgment if you give them advice that doesn't work.

- Don't feel guilty for your race. Especially when you and the person who hurt your child are both white, it is important for your child to hear you acknowledge that some white people really do abuse their power to hurt others.

Strategies for Children

Children must learn to assign more importance to what they think themselves and less to what others think. Teach them to pick from an arsenal of strategies for responding to in-their-face racism.

Ask a question

When someone makes a racist comment they can ask, "What do you mean by that?" or "Why do you ask?" These questions put responsibility back on the offender. Talking can clear up miscommunication.

Disagree

What others say is just their opinion. Your child could say, "What does that mean? I don't think it's true. I thought people were supposed to treat others the way they wanted to be treated themselves."

Confront

They don't have to grin and bear it. If someone hurts their feelings, they are entitled to say, "I don't like that," or "Stop it."

Make a joke

Help them find ways to make a joke about what was said. Share jokes with your kids that poke fun and make it clear that peoples questions are sometimes stupid:

- "You think my hair looks like Brillo? Thanks, man. It's really great when someone else discovers your best qualities without your help."
- When asked, "Why is your brother's skin so dark?" Respond with, "I guess Mom left him in the oven too long again.."
- "Do you have a green card?"
  "Yes…American Express"
- "Do you speak Chinese?"
  "Sure… Chinese."
- (In a restaurant, mistaking a Latino patron for a waiter) "Can I see a menu?" "Would you like to borrow my glasses?"
- "Do (pause) you (pause) speak (pause) Eng(pause)lish?"
  "60 words a minute."
- "Where did you learn to speak English so well?"
  "In utero."
- (At college) "What affirmative action program are you here on?"
  "Mom and Pop."

Whisper responses to a bully

The bully will have to get quiet in order to hear your child if they lower their voice to a whisper. This places them in the position of power, turning the tables on the taunter.

Withdraw

In many ways this may be the most important lesson our children can learn. At times, it can save their life. We have to caution against overuse because the world can get smaller and smaller, but conserving energy and picking winnable battles is the strategy of all great armies. Teaching our children that the fight against injustice is the holiest of all wars is nothing less than inspirational. As in all wars, knowing when to fight is truly a life and death matter.

Talk with a friend

We have to help our children understand their need for allies. Talking and connecting can help rebalance their minds and release the pain.

Use the power of the family

Brainstorm together about things to say in difficult situations. One example is to practice staring, as a family. Staring in unison at those in public who stare at you can feel great and helps mitigate against feelings of rejection and pain.

Teaching kids to spot "isms"

The truth is that unless you are actively working to change the system of racism, you are colluding with it. When we teach kids to recognize bias, we are also teaching them how to create change.

Learning from bad examples

Mom knew something was bothering Tasha the minute her daughter got into the car that day after school. The little girl's eyes were downcast and she was quiet and sad. But it wasn't until they had dropped off all the other kids in the carpool that Tasha would say what was wrong. It seems that at story time Miss Green, the kindergarten teacher Tasha loved with all her heart and soul, had read a new book to the class. The book Zilla Sasparilla and the Mud Baby *had left a deep impression.*

"They all said I was the mud baby, Mom. Everybody teased me," said Tasha, her eyes averted, her voice very small.

"Oh," said Mom, "It sounds like a mud baby is not a good thing to be."

"I'm not a mud baby," Tasha cried. He's stupid and dirty. They washed him all clean with milk. Johnny said that tomorrow he was going to pour his milk on my head at lunchtime and see if I got clean. I'm not going to school! Why did Miss Green have to read that stupid book!"

"Let's go borrow that book from your school right now," said Mom. "Maybe we can figure something out."

Safe at home again, Tasha settled into Mom's lap in the rocker, a cookie in her hand. Before Mom started reading, she explained to Tasha that sometimes people believed that something was a certain way because they had never learned about or seen anything different. She asked Tasha to try to remember when she herself had been very, very little, before she had gone to school, when she stayed home all day with Mom and their dog Timmy and their cat Cleo.

"Can you remember the first time we went to the zoo? How surprised you were that there were so many kinds of animals. You were so little that you thought dogs and cats were the only animals in the world, even though you had seen pictures of other animals in your books. You didn't believe that they were real until you saw them for yourself."

"In the same way," Mom explained, "some white people who don't know anyone who isn't white sometimes think that most people in the world are white. People who don't know better sometimes think that

something is wrong with people who are not white, describing them as dirty or bad. Keeping this attitude is not okay, and we use the word 'racism' to talk about this so that we can make it stop. When I read this book to you, let's see if we can find out if there is racism in this story. If there is, let's think what we can do to make it stop."

Tasha was pleased, listening hard to see if there was any stupid stuff in the book. She found quite a few things. The story was about a woman who pulled a baby out of the river and wanted to raise him as her son. The river was described as "wicked," and the baby was seen as not human before he was washed in milk and named. Once he had been washed clean and named, he was a "real" baby and was never to be called mud baby after that.

After talking more with Mom about it, Tasha wasn't ashamed anymore. She thought the lady who made the book ought to feel ashamed.

"What do you want to do about this?" Mom asked Tasha.

"I want to tell Miss Green and all the kids about racism."

"Do you want my help?"

"No! I want to do it myself."

"Anything else?"

"I want to tell the lady who made the book why kids like me won't like it and that she should never make a book like this again."

"That's a great idea. Do you want my help?"

"Yes. Can we write a letter to her now?"

"Okay," said Mom.

Give your kids the words to call it like it is

We can help children learn to recognize racism, adoptism (the belief that families genetically linked are best) and all other "isms" if we make an effort to point them out when they come up in reading, on TV, in music, or at the movies. Make a family game of trying to spot "isms" of whatever kind. We may not all react to the same things in the same way, but in making a priority of examining the messages embedded in materials, we can all become clearer thinkers. Children can learn to ask questions like, What is wrong with this story? Whose feelings this would hurt? To whom is this not fair? Who is doing what in the story? Why are they doing what they are doing? Who is solving the problem" Who is left out of the story? Who is being described incorrectly? And (most important of all)…What can we do about it?

Code Words and Cover Stories
What do you do with all those "supermarket strangers?"

Code words and cover stories are intervention tools a family can create together to help children feel in control when they are experiencing invasive questions or racial/ethnic bias.

When an interested stranger launches into a series of questions about where your child was born, whether or not you are a family, etc., it is important to take care of your child before worrying about the stranger. The best strategy is to turn to your child and let her decide how she feels like responding. A series of code words and cover stories, maybe developed around the kitchen table. Allowing members of the family a way to communicate privately in public settings can be a quick device to halt the escalation of unpleasant situations without exposing your child to embarrassment in front of peers or other adults. A child armed with a repertoire of code words known by his parents and brothers and sisters is a child who feels in control and part of a unified family team.

Code words can strengthen a family's sense of "us"

"Are you having a spike?" The word "spike" is used in one family when anyone wants the others to know he is experiencing intense feelings and wants to end a conversation. Sometimes the parents use the word when they suspect that one of the children is having a difficult moment. One day, on a shipping trip to the local mall, this family ran into Mrs. Cipari, a woman they hadn't seen for a while who seemed to have nothing more important to do than to ask each of the children what they wanted to be when they grew up. She asked the oldest daughter, who is Asian, if she was planning to be an accountant, the youngest brother, a sturdy boy of black and Asian heritage if he wanted to become a golfer like Tiger Woods, and the third child, a Latina girl, if she would like to grow up and become a gardener. "Oh dear," Dad interrupted, apologizing grandly, "I seem to be having a spike. Sorry but I just can't stay and chat. I've got to finish my shopping and then get out of here. Come on kids. Please hurry, honey. I've got to go. Say goodbye to Mrs. Cipari and we're out of here."

Another family uses the word "bubbles" when anyone feels ready to burst with frustration. One hot summer day while they were waiting in a long line for tickets to the matinee, a blonde girl with long, straight hair who looked to be about seven years old started throwing spit balls into their black daughter's many braids. "Where are the bubbles?" the mom asked in a loud voice, startling away the nasty child. "I knew we'd need the bubbles if we had to wait in line too long." Nobody else in line could seem to understand why everyone in her family was laughing so hard. They seemed to be having a great time.

The purpose of these signals is not necessarily to give the most diplomatic, funny or terrific answers to curious strangers, but to help the family support one another in public situations. Code words and cover stories can be wonderfully useful. If you would like to read more about them or have access to other examples of how to use them, read *Real Parents, Real Children* by Holly Van Gulden (New York: Crossroad Publishing, 1997.)

S-T-R-E-T-C-H

The healthiest adoption adjustments have been made among children whose families have managed to redefine the very meaning of family. According to Dr. David Brodzinsky, this strength is seen when the "differences among family members are celebrated and the culture from which the child originates brought into the family in meaningful ways." Too often the child is required to make 100% of the changes. As one young woman adopted from Korea put it, "When I came to my family, I had to stretch to learn a new language and new ways of doing everything from using the toilet to how to pray. I wish my parents and brothers and sisters could have stretched a little bit too, and incorporated some of my traditions into the family instead of me making all the changes. Even now it still seems like a big deal for them that I keep kim chee in the fridge, because the smells sometimes get into the milk."

Here are a few suggestions for ways the family can s-t-r-e-t-c-h.

- Learn to speak your child's language of origin.
- When going to the mall, movies or a restaurant, drive those extra miles if it means being somewhere frequented by families of your child's race or ethnicity.
- When taking vacations or sending your children summer camps and other recreational activities, choose places and experiences where they can interact with people of their race where you might be in the minority.
- Include the folk tales, legends, and lullabies of your child's culture into your normal every-night bedtime rituals.
- Think of family as being both sides of the coin—include your child's birth family in your prayers and theirs.
- Become proficient in preparing and enjoying some of the foods of your child's culture and include them in equal prominence as you plan your family meals.
- Learn about and incorporate into your family traditions the holiday traditions of your child's culture. To the extent that they can be blended into your religious observances, include them with as much time and space you devote to the traditions with which you were raised.
- Think of the family as a sunflower in the way Marshall Singer of the University of Pittsburgh suggests. The "face" of the sunflower is the

core family, the place where all the petals attach. Each of the petals represents a view of the family as perceived by members of the other groups to which the family belongs. The truly multicultural family can never really think of itself as belonging to only one group. All of the family members need to develop a sense of connection and kinship with groups that reflect each individual's culture of origin.

Talking Straight about Holidays

"…and the truth shall set us free."

It's great to be American—but our history is a mixed heritage, filled with pride but also shame. Your child of color deserves to be introduced to both sides of every story, particularly the stories surrounding national holidays like Thanksgiving, Christmas, and Independence Day, which are celebrated throughout the country from a European American perspective. If they are to become informed and critical thinkers, children must learn from both sides, preparing them to stand up for what is right and to resist repeating or continuing the injustices of the past or present. Help them understand that though the truth is not always pretty, we are strong because we know it and can talk about it.

What your child needs to know.

- It's limited to see only one side of important events.
- Humans survive hard times because they take care of one another.
- We are all more alike than different.

Here are some tips to help you know where to begin.

Thanksgiving

Tell the story of Thanksgiving from the perspective of Native Americans as well as European immigrants. In *Anti-Bias Curriculum* (Washington, DC: N.A.E.Y.C., 1989.) Louise Derman-Sparks suggests this version, "Suppose you live in a house you love. Every day, your parents tell you that the trees, streams, mountains, and animals around you are your brothers. They teach you never to harm any living thing. One day, some strange people who look nothing like you come from far away on big ships. They have long sticks called guns that kill your brothers and the animals. You are afraid but your parents invite them in because all living things are brothers. Mom and Dad teach the strange people how to grow food and how to live in your house until one day the strange people make your family leave your house, taking it from you and keeping it for themselves. Every year after your family has left; the strange people have a big party in your house. They call it Thanksgiving and it celebrates taking your home away from you. How does this make you feel?"

Christmas

Let your children know that although Christmas is celebrated as a national holiday, it really reflects a Christian religious belief system. (We will discuss religious diversity and cultural issues more thoroughly in Section 3.) Kwanzaa (a 20th-century constituted African American holiday which is cultural rather than religious,) Hanukkah (a Jewish religious holiday) and the tradition of Winter Solstice also fall within the month of December. Discussing common themes and traditions, such as the use of firelight (candles and bonfires,) and the involvement of special music and food are ways to help them understand more than their own experience and perspective. All are holidays that celebrate community, sharing, and caring for one another. Another reminder that we are more similar than we are different.

Fourth of July

Let your children know that one out of every five Americans was a slave in 1776, and that America's declaration of independence from British rule did not change slaves' lives. Educate yourself about other holidays of independence like Juneteenth and Cinqo de Mayo.

Start Now, Do Something

> *Transformable racism involves false beliefs and assumptions that can be changed by pointing out the facts.*
> —Blanche Radford Curry

You can begin to transform yourself , your family, your community, your world by taking some simple steps …

- Reach out. Invite a family of a different background to spend a day with you.
- Use your influence to push toward expansion of the curriculum at schools in your community to include cultural diversity, starting with preschools.
- See to it that any group you are part of is racially inclusive.
- Ask yourself if any group you are considering joining is antiracist in principle.
- Don't smile and let things pass. Express your opinion if racist or ethnic jokes are told, even if you are the only person in your group to do so.
- Listen to people of color talk about their experiences with racism.
- Talk with people of color about racism. Many white people have never had even one conversation about the issue with anyone who is not white.
- Talk with white people about racism. You may feel more open about expressing fears and doubts in a homogeneous situation.
- Question meritocracy. Is trying hard or believing all anyone needs to succeed? Does excellence guarantee success or rewards?

- Make it family policy to encourage open discussion about racism
- Ask more questions. If more white American boys were ending up in prison than in college, would people be talking about building more prisons?
- Take risks by openly taking a stand against racism in unfriendly situations.
- Take risks by openly taking a stand against quieter, unintentional comments about people of color that are racist in nature, even if delivered in friendly situations.
- Don't try to make things easy. Work to make them real.
- Support antiracist causes.
- Write letters to the media in response to racial events.
- Get actively involved in groups fighting against racism.
- Name racism whenever you see it.
- Connect to other parents raising children of color with whom you have urgent interests in common.

Useful Books

Birdseye, Debbie Holsclaw; *Under Our Skin: Kids Talk About Race* **(NY: Holiday House, 1997.)**
    Six teenagers of different ethnic backgrounds candidly discuss cultural heritages affect their daily lives, their views on race, and their experiences with prejudice.

Gibbs, Jewell Taylor; *Children of Color* **(San Francisco, CA: Jossey-Bass, 1989.)**
    Traditional and innovative intervention strategies and techniques for helping children cope with the effects of discrimination. Deals with a broad range of Asian, Latino, African, and other heritages.

Jacobs,Bruce; *Race Manners* **(NY: Arcade Publishing, 1999.)**
    A startling wake-up call to black and white interaction, sure to change your thinking. Jacobs, an African American, explains that he wanted to write a book "that people could use, a book that would help each of us pick our way through the minefield of racial booby traps many of us encounter each and every day; [that would] lay bare everyday racial behavior and help make sense of it." Using concrete examples, he points out and then challenges our every-day assumptions about race and racial difference. His arguments are reason-

able, understandable, and penetrating. This book really does provide an important contribution to our times.

Lazarre. Jane; *Beyond the Whiteness of Whiteness* **(Durham, NC: Duke University Press, 1996.)**

A mother's recognition of white economic, social and moral complicity in the power structure of racism. "I am Black," Jane Lazarre's son tells her. "I have a Jewish mother but I am not 'biracial.' The term is meaningless to me." She understands, she says–but he tells her gently, that he doesn't think so, that she can't understand because she is white. This book is her memoir of learning to look into the nature of whiteness in a way that passionately informs the connections between herself and her family. This book is an important contribution to understanding white privilege and unconscious racism. It is clear-eyed, thoughtful and clearly written, essential reading for white parents of children of color.

Olmos,Edward; *Americanos* **(NY: Little Brown, 1999.)**

"The book captures the beauty of the culture that is never seen, not even by ourselves," Olmos writes, asserting, "The face of America should include us." This spirited bilingual book depicts a broad range of Latino life in the United States. "Latinos come in all colors, races, and creeds. This book is about understanding that we're all different—that's what makes us all the same. We're like thumbprints." Photographs compiled from the amazing work of 32 Latino photographers and 18 writers captures the beauty and grace of Latinos in the United States, making Americanos as colorful as the culture itself.

Reed, Ishmjael; *Multi-American* **(NY: Penguin, 1998.)**

Speaking out on a broad variety of issue—including assimilation, racial conflicts between minorities, the gay rights movement, and stereotyping—this collection of essays by non-Anglo writers takes readers far beyond the issues of Black vs. white, introducing the authentic voices of Rainbow America in all their diverse, angry, proud, celebratory glory.

Shipler, David; *A Country of Strangers: Blacks and Whites in America* **(NY: Knopf, 1997.)**

An intelligent, penetrating and intriguing look at how Black and white Americans perceive each other. Shipler's book "is an effort to make black and white people less foreign to one another. I'd recommend picking up a copy of this book as a kind of cultural guide to the all-time most frequent pitfalls in listening, speaking and acting across the racial divide," wrote Patricia Williams in her *New York Times* review; "Unlike other examples of this genre, such as Studs Terkel's excellent *Race: The American Obsession*, which assembled interviews from people of all races, Shipler's book maintains a more studied gaze from one side of the fence to the other... even as it notes how full of holes the fence is—"

Tatum,Beverley; *Why Are All the Black Kids Sitting Together in the Cafeteria?* (NY:Basic Books, 1997.)

In high schools and colleges daily, young people can be observed segregating themselves by race. Integrating racial identity is a different process for people of color and white people in this society. Beverly Daniel Tatum explains this tendency as a way of affirming racial identity and outlines the process of developing racial pride through a series of predictable stages. A fascinating and clearly presented map of steps toward integration of racial identity, this book affirms the need to understand and talk about the processt. Includes chapters on understanding Black, white, Latino, American Indian and Asian Pacific identity. Highly recommended

West, Cornell; *Race Matters* (Boston, MA: Beacon Press, 1993.)

"As moving as any of the sermons of the Rev. Martin Luther King, as profound as W.E.B. DuBois's *The Souls of Black Folk*, as exhilarating in their offering of liberation as James Baldwin's early essays," writes the *Washington Post Book World*. And Marian Wright Edelman says, "Cornel West is one of the most authentic, brilliant, prophetic and healing voices in America today. We ignore his truth in *Race Matters* at our personal and national peril."

Wildman, Stephanie; *Privilege Revealed* (NY: NY University Press, 1996.)

Filled with penetrating images about the challenges that come with an understanding that race matters alongside the goal that it should not, *Privilege Revealed* reveals the complexity of race in all our lives. Of particular interest to adoptive parents is chapter five, "The implications of making comparisons between racism and other isms," which starts with a story about Tony Grillo, an Afro-Cuban woman who comes down with cancer. "Cancer became the first filter through which I see the world. It used to be race, but now it is cancer," she says. A terrific blend of clear theory and compelling stories, this is a read-it-from-cover-to cover book that belongs in every home library.

Section Three
❧ ❧ ❧
Family Matters

Together. No Matter What.

By Beth Hall

My mother was diagnosed with certain death almost a full year before she died. When she called to tell me, I cannot remember anything that we said, but I do remember the searing pain in my body. In that year we had many decisions to make. All of the hows, plans for the future—time spent together now—how should it be? My children were only four and six, my mother worried about them seeing her sick, wanting them to remember her as she had been rather than as she was becoming. At each juncture, we found ourselves unwilling to turn the precious little time she had left over to strangers. We and she found the need to be cared for by us to be ever growing.

We spent the last night of my mother's life with her, in her home. My sister and myself, our children (her adult daughter and my son and daughter, aged five and seven) and my mother's life long friends, whom we had called because her time had come, spending a few minutes to say their good-byes, making their peace in their own ways. After the visitors had gone, the kids expressed concern that we would forget how we had taken care of her. With my children on either side, my mother frail in their arms, we took their pictures, a jarring reminder of how ill she had become lying next to their youthful health.

We spent the entire night in her room. We played her favorite music; we ate while she only gulped for air. We were with her when she died. As the priest prayed, we held hands and wept for her passing. Wept for our loss. Wept for her suffering. We watched as her body was wrapped and carried away. I had never seen my little boy cry with such whole body grief as I saw that day. His pain overtook him. He sobbed and sobbed. We did not leave her house for three days. Together—we ate, we cried, we laughed, we planned, we remembered—together.

I had found support in many areas for the experience of caring for her on a daily basis as the things she was able to do for herself diminished. And I found a new friend in Esperanza, a long time friend whose importance to me had never held the significance that would develop during this time. Esperanza grew up in Africa where her family was traditional.

Esperanza told us how it was in her country. How everyone who died, did so at home just like Grandma. How when the elders became sick the whole family took care of them and slept with them in their bed in case something awoke them from their dying sleep and they needed to be comforted. She told us how everyone from the eldest to the very youngest took part in making the elder comfortable, in telling them stories of their ongoing lives and giving them courage and comfort in the face of death. She told my son and daughter how she had moved to the US and told her friends lying in bed with her Tia (Auntie) while she had died. They had made fun of her and called her weird and strange. She had felt ashamed because she had been glad to be with her at the end and they made her wonder if she had been wrong. It took her years, she explained, to understand that taking care of family was part of her culture, "part of yours too," she told my two beautiful babies, James and Sofia.

James began to cry. His little body shrinking against Esperanza's large comfort on the couch. Sofia spoke first. "My Mom feels bad because her mother died. Sometimes James and I miss our birth mothers. We wanted to be with our Mom because we know what it feels like to miss your Mom. It doesn't mean you don't love your other family but you just feel sad. I am going to tell my friends that I don't care what they say. In our family the most important job is to take care of our family." And James added, "And we, uh,uh,uh, are going to know how to act, sob, sob, when we grow up, sob, uh, uh, because we already learned how to act African when we miss our Grandma…" And we all collapsed in tears.

Secretly I thanked God that somehow we had followed our hearts and kept the kids near, because we had in fact given them a pathway to connection with their birth cultures. How could I have forgotten that targeted or stressed people and cultures always hold onto the core of what can never be taken away by those in power or controlled by external forces like wealth or society? They hold on to family, to relationships—the relationships which only they have and only they know. Somehow we had given that to our children in the face losing my mother. Esperanza put words to what is often true in their birth cultures and which they had lived in the midst of our own family.

It was in Esperanza, rather than most of my other friends, that I found support for the involvement of my children and family in my mother's journey toward death. Most of my friends and even members of our extended family and certain teachers and advisors were concerned about the level of involvement our children were having with my mother. In the last months, she could not manage any of her bodily needs without help and most of her comfort came in physical responses and soothing for her pain. They were worried that we were frightening our children. That we would leave them with nightmares or horrible memories of their Grandma, with whom they had spent so much time and had such a positive relationship. And secretly we were wondering ourselves—ten fold. But somehow at each new juncture of care, each new moment of incorporation, watching my mother give over to yet some new bodily indignity, we could not leave them out of what they had been so intimately involved with up until then. So they were present in every sense. They saw it all. They watched her die in every sense, in every way.

Six months after my mother died, we decided to rearrange our home so that the kids could have their own rooms for the first time. They each delighted in choosing their paint colors and using their imagination to create a space that was theirs alone.

They had been in their new rooms only three months when my sister was diagnosed with a cancer that would require radical surgery and a long stint of radiation therapy. It was too soon since my mother's death and we were all stunned. Sofia spoke up first. "Auntie Barbara, you will move in with us. I will sleep with James because we are used to sharing a room and you can have my room because you will need to rest. You have to be with us. We belong together. We are a family."

The Experts Speak Out

"I come from a family in which diversity is the norm. My only cousins are biracial: White/Japanese. There are Christians and Jews, Mormons and Buddhists, not to mention a few agnostics and atheists in my immediate family. I was raised eating borscht, with cornbread and tofu on the side. As a child growing up, I was surrounded by, and imbued with, the idea that differences are something to be celebrated and treasured. I love this about myself, my family, and who I am. I have come to see this 'difference' as a great advantage I have in life. There is a certain freedom in not having to worry about being the same or fitting in."

—Chedgszey Smith-McKeever

"Adoption has shaped my life through the losses experienced by my birth mother and by my adoptive parents. It shaped my life as I tried, all alone, to figure it out. No one would talk. No one would explain. My questions were unanswered. My adolescence was so difficult— wanting to please my parents but having to please myself...needing to know myself."

—Joyce Maguire Pavao

"Generally, adults are very good at using the term 'unconditional love,' but I don't think they practice it very well. As a child I often felt, and I think a lot of children feel this way: 'Sure, you love me—as long as I'm doing right'; 'Sure, you love me—as long as I'm fitting whatever image you've set for me.' I think that if you show your children that you show your love for them only when they're good, even if you say you love them all the time, the child often feels that your love is conditional. We do this in ways we don't even realize. As long as I am doing what I am supposed to or what you want me to or living up to whatever expectations you have, then I can count on this love. But if I can't get the love when I'm not perfect, if I'm just me; if I can't make mistakes and feel comfortable making those mistakes and being loved through those mistakes, then there is conflict. So I would say to those parenting of challenging children: Learn to be patient with them. Try to understand the depth of the pain that they are experiencing. No matter how loving the people around them, knowing that their parents didn't want them, whatever the reason, hurts. To grow up parentless or to grow up without your birth relatives around you, without people, sometimes, who look like you."

—Shane Salter

"*My father talked and talked and talked; I stopped listening. I required no lengthy explanation of what it meant to be adopted. It meant I was not my father's child. It meant I was a secret, even from myself. In the three years since that day in my father's study, I have realized of course that I am not my mother's child, ether. I am not allowed to talk about my adoption outside my family ('It would only hurt your mother,' my father says. 'Do you want to hurt your mother?'). My stomach hurts when I even think about telling anyone, but it hurts, too, when I think about having another mother and father someone. I try to talk to my parents about it, but my mother's face changes even before I can get the first question out, and my father always follows her out of the room. 'You're our child,' he says when he returns. 'We love you and you're ours.' I let him hug me, but I am thinking that I have never heard my father tell a lie before. I decide that all the secrecy is for my father's benefit, that he is ashamed to tell the world that I am not his child because he is ashamed of me. I think about the Ford my father bought in Dallas three years ago; it has never run right, but he will not take it back.*"

—Lynna Williams

"*My parents wanted a son to carry out the family name and to be the heir of the family. They wanted a son so badly that it never oc- curred to them that they might have a daughter. I was named Ho Leung Wong before I was born. Ho Leung is a combination of my father's and mother's names. Ho means courageous and Leung means as bright as the moon. Together the names mean very smart. But girls were not allowed to go to school in ancient China, so any name meaning smart is a boy's name. I was my parents' biggest disappoint- ment and my name will remind me of that for the rest of my life. Even so, I did not want my adoptive parents to change my name. It is mine and I am me.*"

—transracially adopted teen

Family Matters

*"At our best level of existence, we are part of a family, and at our
highest level of achievement, we work to keep the family alive."*
—Maya Angelou

Strengthening Family Identity

Jigsaw Puzzle

Parents of transracially adopted kids often ask, "Why is my child acting like
that? Is it because of development? adoption? race? something else?" In a society which values whiteness above all other shades, parents must help their
children deal with the reality of racism but not become victims of it. They must
acknowledge their child's need to deal with loss and anxiety caused by adoption, while at the same time fighting for the legitimacy and enduring status of
the family. Given these demands, parents often wonder where to focus when
confronting the usual challenges of life with children. Taking inventory of where
an issue comes from may shed new light on how to handle it.

Johnny will start preschool soon and needs to be potty-trained. Playing in
the backyard, he suddenly pulls down his pants and sprays urine on the fence,
shouting to make sure everyone sees. Potty training... Now this is a developmental milestone every child passes through; it transcends adoption and race—
or does it?

After all, differing cultural expectations make a difference in the expectations for the preschooler and in the way others of his race view his behavior.
And what about the genetic role regarding one's physical ability to control
oneself? And what about the tendency for adoptive parents to worry about the
opinions of other adults and to seek approval for being better than good parents? How about gender? Johnny's display is "boy behavior;" girls can't do
this. No single factor is alone in its impact on a child's behavior, nor on a
parents' response.

Letisha comes home from fourth grade in tears, carrying her family tree
assignment. When you suggest that you could speak to the teacher, she falls
apart. "But, Mom, everyone has to do it. And it has to be *this way.*"

Letisha wants to be just like everyone else. With her dual family background, it may seem impossible to try to make both her families fit the rigid structure of a family tree. Perhaps she feels shame. If her parents focus on adoption only, she will end up feeling frustrated by their failure to understand and they will feel frustrated for exactly the same reason.

Maria was dropped off at 11:30 by a noisy car full of kids. Her curfew was 10:00 p.m. Confronted, she got furious. Her parting shot, "I can't believe you don't trust me."

Maria is working on independence, but because she is Latina, it is more dangerous for her to be driving around with other rowdy teenagers—especially if they are also of color. If the police should stop them, they are much more likely to get into serious trouble. Will Maria and her friends know how to act so as not to threaten the officer? And if they do "behave," can the person in authority be relied upon to give them a fair chance? And how much does Maria's need to act out reflect her need to make up for the loss, grief, and anger she feels over her adoption? And what about her parents' response to her stinging comment? Are they more susceptible to her negative judgments for fear that they are not legitimately her parents, or out of the anxiety that she may abandon them for birth parents where she feels a better "fit?"

There are many layers to every family issue, each one an essential part of the whole. Nothing can be either overlooked or overemphasized except at the loss of the integrity of the whole. The danger is that we will either minimize our differences or emphasize only a few. Neither approach will reflect reality, and oversimplification will unintentionally abandon the children to work through the issues without our help. The benefit of embracing the larger picture is the creation of families and children who are learning to handle a world growing ever more complex. The very fact of living within a strong family can empower children to view life from a position of strength and comfort rather than from fear and retreat.

Developmental Stages in Transracial Families

Influenced by the work of H. David Kirk (the Shared Fate theory of acknowledgment and denial of difference,) William Cross (stages of racial identity discussed earlier,) Peggy MacIntosh (author of July/August 1989 seminal article on the concept of white privilege—"White Privilege: Unpacking the Invisible Knapsack," published in *Peace and Freedom*,) Jerome Smith (entitlement in families) and ourselves (the term *adoptism*,) infertility educator Patricia Irwin Johnston suggests that, for people touched directly by adoption (birth parents, adoptive parents, adopted people) there are predictable stages to the process of assimilating adoption issues to one's life. The process of coming to understand that there is a "genetic privilege" in society at large and that it has given rise to a negative corollary—"adoptism," drives this development.

What is Adoptism?

Andrea, a birth mother, has moved on from her experience of placing her child for adoption, becoming a successful doctor and mother of two (more). She is a survivor who faced the worst choice she could imagine, and not only made the best choice she could but lived through and with it. "People try to be there for me, they try to understand but it's hard to hear the words that they offer because what's behind them, unsaid, is the way they really feel: Knowing I wasn't ready to be a parent.... Disappointing my family and friends, who *thought* they knew me.... Wanting my child to be with me but knowing I'm not the best choice.... Perhaps the hardest of all is to hear someone say, 'I think what you did was wonderful but I could never do it myself.' To be set apart is one of the hardest parts of being a birth mother—not only did I lose my child, but I am judged as wrong, out of sync with the deepest laws of nature for making a choice that no 'real' parent, who truly loves her children, could make herself." Andrea gives words to a reality and pain that isn't often perceived, *even by those who may love us best. Parents who choose adoption for their children are considered not as good or as valid as parents who parent their children.*

Ben is an adult who was adopted at birth. He is now married, and he and his wife have a two-year-old who was born to them. They are hoping to adopt a second child. He told us this story: "I remember when I told my best friend that Lynn and I were planning to adopt. I couldn't believe his response. 'Why would you even think of that?' he said. 'You guys make great kids. Why would you want to take in someone else's cast-off without knowing what you're getting?' All I could think was, 'Wow! You know I'm adopted and that's what you say to me? What do you say about me when I'm out of the room?" Ben gives words to an incredulity many adopted adults have expressed; that others hold a hidden bias about adoption and that they never know when it will pop out and cause pain. *Even those who love them best may say something unexpected, summoning up the stereotype that adopted means reject, cast-off, bad seed, etc. People who are placed for adoption are not considered to have been as valued by their birth parents as children who are raised within their original families.*

We met Sarah in the intimacy of a grief support meeting. Each person present had lost a child when a birth parent reclaimed custody. Three years before, Sarah and her husband had lost their son Greg (adopted at birth) when he was four months old. They had since adopted a little girl. Sarah spoke as a survivor, someone who had faced the worst she could have imagined and lived through it. "When Christine came and took away Greggie," she said, "people tried to be there for us. Everyone tried, but something always seemed off when they tried to comfort me. I just couldn't shake the feeling that underneath, even our closest friends secretly felt that her reclaiming him was somehow more right than his staying with us—right, according to some higher order of things. Feeling sorry for us was something separate. I know our friends and family did feel sorry for us but something else was at risk, something no one ever talks about. I've come to think that most people deep down believe that birth mothers and children belong together—no matter what. Nobody ever said that to us straight out, but it was there. I think even the people who love us the best had those feelings, but nobody would ever come right out and say anything. Feeling set apart from everyone was one of the hardest parts of losing Greggie for me. Not only did I lose my baby, I was judged wrong—out of sync with the deepest laws of nature for wanting him when she had first rights." More than one pair of eyes welled up with tears. Sarah had given words to a hurt that isn't often spoken: *that even those who love us best may not regard our families formed by adoption as valid compared to families formed by birth—even those who love us best.* There was a long pause in the conversation after she spoke, as the hard truth sank in.

Racism:

A belief that race is the primary determinant of human traits and capacities.

A belief that racial differences produce an inherent superiority of a particular race.

Prejudice or discrimination against someone on the basis of race.

Sexism:

Prejudice or discrimination against someone on the basis of gender.

Adoptism:

A belief that forming a family by birth is superior to forming a family by adoption.

A belief that keeping a child with his/her biological parents is inherently better than placing a child for adoption.

A belief that for those growing up as adopted people the primary determinant of human traits and capacities is genetics.

A belief that differences in family-building structures or methods produces an inherent superiority in families of a particular structure or method.

Prejudice or discrimination against members of the adoption triad.

These are examples of adoptism at its core. Adoptism is a cultural belief that families formed by adoption are less truly connected than are birth families; that birth families should be preserved at all costs and under all circumstances except the most severely harmful; that people who were adopted were first rejected, maybe for a reason. No matter what place you hold in the adoption triad, such judgments and discriminations feel the same. As a society, we tend to understand the dangers of bias based on race, gender or class. *Adoptism is no different. Adoptism is just as damaging.*

And we absorb the biases of our society as we grow up. As with racism and all the other "isms," it's through recognizing our deepest attitudes that we can change those that must be changed. Perhaps society's belief that parents must stay with their children is linked to the dark fears of childhood: "What will happen to me without Mommy and Daddy? Who will take care of me?" Maybe some of the bias against adoption is an extension of the voice of that child who can imagine no means of survival but for parents to take care of children born to them.

Whatever adoptism's sources, the important thing is that we can change ourselves and our attitudes. Recognition allows forgiveness. We can forgive others because we share their fears. We can feel part of, instead of separate from, victims or survivors. Understanding the bias takes away its power.

Predictable Steps in the Development of Adoption Awareness

Becoming a family is a process, not an event. Parts of the process must be repeated many times over. Competence and self-esteem grow by repeating successful acts, including the discovery or rediscovery of belonging to the family. Predictable stages in the development of the identity of a white adoptive parent of a child of color parallels those changes undergone during growth in the understanding of white racial identity

We have decided not to delineate age ranges for the stages of awareness that adopted children experience because, as David Kirk has pointed out, it is emotional triggers that tend to promote growth to a new stage. Each triad member moves through these stages *according to their own experience and the realities of the societal biases they encounter*. For the transracially adopted child these stages are intermingled, and often impossible to distinguish from, those of racial identity awareness and formation. Some of us stop at a particular stage never to be triggered to the next, some of us get stuck overlong in the emotions of another. Whether the adoption is inracial or transracial, adopted children and their birth and adoptive parents can be significantly "out of tune" with one another when it comes to thinking about these issues. Most of us pass through most of the stages, but there is no graduation because there is no end. This is a development process that continues to evolve throughout the lifetime of each individual. The stages look like this...

In Adopted People
Love is enough: Preconscious
All Adoptions

"I'm adopted and I'm special. My mommy and daddy were so happy when I came home. Everyone is adopted, just like me." Adopted people who have never known a family constructed in any way other than by adoption have no reason to wonder about there being a difference.

Older Child Adoptions

The preconscious stage is different for children who have cognitive memory of their first family, foster care or an orphanage. They are eager to see the new family as the solution to their loneliness or pain, but relief remains to be proven. "Once I am adopted I won't feel like this anymore. No one will be able to hurt me again. I will never feel alone or confused. I will know that I am lovable."

Transracial Adoptions

"I am beautiful. Everyone loves me with my beautiful brown skin and dark eyes. Some people talk about my color and race more than others. I don't know why."

Maybe adoption isn't so great: Contact.
All Adoptions

"When the kids at school started teasing me and asking 'Is that your real mommy?' I realized they think our family is strange and maybe not as good a family as theirs. I don't like it and it makes me feel uncomfortable, ashamed, mad and nervous that somebody might say I'm different and something's wrong with me." This often occurs at ages six to eight, when peer-reaction to their proud announcements that they were adopted have created children's own awareness that adoption isn't universally admired and accepted.

Transracial Adoptions

"I heard someone call me 'chink' and Mom and Dad and my teachers had to have a lot of meetings about it. I don't even know what it means but it must be bad because everyone is so upset. Most of my friends who are white don't have to go through this. I feel embarrassed and ashamed and secretly kind of mad about it. I don't know if I should tell my parents how I feel. They seem so upset about it, I don't know if they can handle it. But actually lots of the kids have called me chink before."

I am not the only one: Disintegration.
All Adoptions

"At this stage I really like having friends who were adopted like me. I like to be around other kids who understand my experiences and who don't ask me dumb questions. In new situations it always helps to meet other kids who also are adopted and sometimes they turn out to be my best friend. I am glad my parents want to go to adoption support group meetings."

Transracial Adoptions

"I am glad to have my brother and sister who are brown like me and also my friend who was adopted from Guatemala. He told me he thought he was the only one before he met me cuz his sisters are both white like his parents."

Not better, not worse...just different: Internalization.
All Adoptions:

"I just want to be a normal regular kid and be treated the same as everyone else. I wish my parents would give up on trying to fix everything for me and just let me be. I hate my parents for wanting to talk about it all the time. They think they are being so subtle but I know they are worried about it. That's probably what I hate the most because secretly I know it would be better to be like everyone else. One time when we went to see a movie about a kid whose family loses him as a baby I almost started crying. How embarrassing!"

Transracial Adoptions

"I hate it when the new teacher always asks me about my parents and especially when my Mom wants to come and give an adoption presentation about Korea at school. It's bad enough that I'm not white I don't see why she has to point it out."

I am who I am: Immersion/Emerging.
All Adoptions

"Being adopted has a new meaning in my life. I seek out peers and role models who have been adopted in my real life and from books, films, workshops and experts who will help me build a positive identity. I am beginning to see ways in which I am strong—different from my non-adopted friends. I value my ability to fit into most situations, I notice that I am more open and tolerant than most people I know. I tend to be clearer about what matters than some, I have already faced losses most of my friends haven't. I don't take much for granted and I am seeing this as an advantage."

Transracial Adoptions

"Now I realize that the only way to feel good about myself is to be like the other kids of color. It is at this stage that I want to embrace my own racial heritage as a source of pride separate from the heritage of my adoptive family. I want to know about the accomplishment of others who have come before me. If the only contact I have with people of my racial and ethnic heritage has different values than my family, so what. I really don't have a choice, because my parents are different than most white people. They love just me but they don't see that not everyone else does. They lump me with the kids of color who are adopted like me so I have to hang out with them. It does help when my parents talk about racism. I used to think all that stuff they wanted me to learn and think about just made me feel bad, now I realize they understand. Thank God."

Adoptive Parents
Love is enough: Preconscious
All Adoptions

"I was born into my family and most people I know grew up with their real parents. I have not really noticed any bias against adoption and I'm not sure I really believe it is very significant in the people I know. Being part of the majority, I never notice families with shared blood lines, only the ones who don't have them. Forming a family by adoption is something I really feel excited about. In fact there is a part of me that feels noble, like this was a right thing to do. I find myself constantly talking with people about adoption—there is a part of me that is down right proud. My mom used to say that Tommy, who lived next door was a 'brat,' and it was because he was adopted. But Tommy was just weird. I don't think people think of our child like that. As an adoptive parent, I just want to be like any other parent and have my child treated like any other child. Love is all we need to make our family strong."

Transracial Adoptions

Race doesn't matter to me. I love my child and will shower him with my love. That's all a child needs. That's what we got from our parents, that what all our friends give to their children, and that will work for my child as well. I'm just a normal American. I don't focus on my heritage so why should it matter? My wife and I are raising all of our children to understand that race shouldn't matter. None of our friends care, so we don't have any problems. When kids are encouraged to "notice" color or racism, they start to have a negative attitude and end up feeling alienated from white culture. We don't want them to take on the negative characteristics some of the people of their race do by blaming white society for their problems. Kids who are taught to see racism become angry. I want my children to have the same kind of life I have. They are our children. They deserve it."

Adoption as a lesser choice: Contact.
All Adoptions

"An unexpected event happens that catches me off-guard and forces me to acknowledge adoptism. Perhaps it is a personal event such as a stranger asking inappropriate questions in the grocery store ('Where did your child come from? How much did she cost?') or a story in the media which just happens to mention that the perpetrator of some vile crime was adopted or a movie called *Problem Child* about an adopted little boy. For the first time I come face to face with the reality that others see adoption as 'second best,' maybe even dangerous, for everyone involved. I'm shocked to discover that others 'feel sorry' for our family because we are not genetically connected . I am amazed at the intensity of their curiosity and judgement about our child's birth family. I am so shocked by how casually people—even strangers—violate family privacy boundaries that I sometimes feel that if I don't answer the inappropriate personal questions, I may be giving my child the idea that being adopted is something to be ashamed of. I start to feel anxious and angry about how people are responding to us."

Transracial Adoptions

"The first incident of overt discrimination against our child produces recognition that others are not color-blind and that the child we love is not being viewed as white, nor is he considered as good as white."

The contact phase has two steps: recognizing adoptism and then being turned around by it.

I can't wait to change the world: Disintegration.
All Adoptions

"Now that I've been awakened, I seem to see adoptism everywhere. I'm outraged and on my high horse, determined to bring about a sweeping change in our society or at least my own extended family and friends, finding most everybody guilty of unconscious bias. Bringing example after example to their attention, almost with every breath, I demand that adoptive families be seen as 'just like' families built by birth. I am busy lobbying tirelessly for the use of respectful adoption language and campaigning to ban all adopt-a projects. And in my spare time I am also a vigilant media critic. Just let them dare create negative portrayals of adopted people, adoptive parents and birth parents on TV and in the movies; they will not escape my scathing criticism. I am often put down by the people around me as a stridently irritating, overboard crusader. Although my influence is questionable, I can't let that stop me. I must do what it takes to protect my child. If I am able to stop campaigning long enough to pay attention to my children, I begin to notice as they get older and move through stages of individuation that they bring characteristics and temperament to our family that do not just come from us. Whether through the sum of many small experiences or a single hit over the head with a base-ball bat realization, I come to terms with the nature vs nurture battle where neither side wins."

Transracial Adoptions

"I don't know when I got to be so 'white.' I had no idea that life could be so unfair. Everywhere I turn I see people treating other people unfairly. I can't stand the idea that this is happening to my child. She and I can both go to the same store at the mall, but if they think she's alone the security people will follow her around—never me. How can that be right? I wish I knew what to do about it. Sometimes I feel paralyzed, unable to figure out an appropriate move. Once in awhile I secretly wonder if we made a huge mistake. Is our daughter going to hate us? Have we completely screwed up the life of our son? I had no idea how big racial issues were going to be when we first adopted. Now we do all that we can but I'm not sure we are enough or that it is possible to ever know enough. I'm also seeing how impossible our friends and family are. I can't be-lieve that we never even noticed the kinds of things they were saying before. They are so out of it, they don't even get it no matter how much we point it out. I know they hate to hear us telling them they are racist, but how can we afford not to get them to change if they are going to be around our kids?"

Not better, not worse...just different: Internalization.
All Adoptions

"I begin to understand the role of both gain and loss that adoption brings to the lives of adopted people, birth parents, and adoptive parents. I have developed a new understanding that life is not fair and that we are not judged fairly. Discouraged that my personal war against adoptism has not seemed to make a substantial difference, I am troubled, sometimes to the point of tem-porary emotional paralysis, to comprehend fully that my child's experience of the world differs significantly, and painfully, from my own. I am no longer interested in changing the world but am stunned by the new realities that my child's individual identity throws up into may face each day. This can be a challenging stage, a crossroads where I either perish or out of which I will thrive. Coming to embrace the very 'importance of genetics' that I had grown to fear can either push me to new strength or despair."

Transracial Adoptions

"I wanted my daughter to look so good for the party at her friend's Marissa's house that I took her to get her hair done at a salon. The problem was I didn't have anyone to ask for a referral and had to pick a place just be driving by. The place I chose was terrible. They did an awful job and I know they charged me double because I was too stupid to know what was right and too embarrassed to ask. I should have let Marissa's mother do her hair at her home like she suggested but I felt so humiliated. She didn't even invite me to come. My daughter has never even been to their house before and I was just supposed to let her do my daughter's hair? It feels really hard for me to let go and let an unfamiliar culture influence my child when I can't be a full participant myself. I feel like I'm caught up in a conflict of values: I want to preserve my child's beautiful innocence and I know she needs to develop survival skills that I can't give her. When one gets in the way of the other, I have a hard time. I know I should have sent her, let her do her hair, *but it hurts*."

I am who I am: Immersion/Emerging.

All Adoptions

"I am beginning to see that adoptive families have unique strengths that are different from families that are linked genetically. I can feel the dignity of being a parent in a strong family where individual differences are highly valued. I am beginning to forgive myself for not being able to give my child what only her birth parents are able to give. I am grateful for my own role. I no longer feel the need to compete with shadow birth parents to help my child figure out how his birth heritage shapes him. I have learned through experience to anticipate events concerning the bias of adoptism. I am aware that adoptism exists, understand that my family may be hurt. I have learned the valuable art of protective hesitation (not jumping in prematurely, but waiting to be sure what the situation requires and what the best strategies will be.) I no longer take everything so personally. Joining other adoptive families for mutual support and direction is helpful to me."

Transracial Adoptions

"Here we go. Now, seeing with new eyes the importance of racial identity to our child, I am willing to do what it takes to offer skills and support. I develop a new ability to anticipate events concerning bias and injustice. I learn the art of protective hesitation (not jumping in prematurely, but waiting to be sure what the situation requires and what the best strategies will be,) and I try to learn the parenting traditions of my child's birth culture, even if I am the only white parent in the class. I seek out books and films and experts who will help me learn about being a member of our child's birth culture and I join with other transracial parents for mutual support and direction."

For Birth Parents

Love is enough: Preconscious.

All Adoptions

"I don't know anybody who grew up with adoptive parents, but I'm pretty sure it's the best choice for my child even though it breaks my heart not to keep him with me. It's better for him and it's just not possible for me to take care of him the way I want him to be taken care of right now. This is the hardest thing I've ever tried to do in my life. It's sort of like a Cinderella story, he will be able to have the stuff I can't give him and I'm really hoping he has a great life. I know his adoptive parents will love him to pieces, they want a baby so bad. I hope he will know how much I love him too."

Transracial Adoptions

"I want the best possible family for my baby. I want them to love him like he is their own. Thank God these people believe that they can love any child, they know race shouldn't matter. My baby will grow up believing that too. Maybe he won't make all the mistakes I have."

Adoption as a lesser choice: Contact.

All Adoptions

"I didn't understand that many people think something's wrong with me for not being able to raise my child. Then I saw *Losing Isiah,* one of the few movies that has a birth mother as a character and what is she doing? Throwing her child away in a trashcan. I realize that most people probably think I was on drugs or crazy to place my child for adoption. It's a terrible feeling."

Transracial Adoptions

"On TV the talk shows always act like there are millions of people who want to adopt more than anything. They never say that they only want to adopt white babies. I can't believe I have to beg to have someone love my baby, like she's not as good as anyone else's."

I can't change the world: Disintegration.

All Adoptions

"I don't know how to change how I'm feeling, only that I want to do something. I begin to seek out other birth parents, read books written by birth parents and join support organizations. I want to learn how other people who share my experiences live with it. I may also join the adoption reform movement, doing what I can to change the public image of birth families. I have a new understanding that not all adoptive parents are perfect, and that my child may not be a perfect fit in her family. It can be deeply disturbing to me to imagine that my child is having such a different experience in life than my own and that part of it is about so many people looking down on adopted people, as if they were the 'bad seed.' I don't have any idea what to do about it."

Transracial Adoptions

"I saw a white family with a black child today. What have I done? This child's hair was horrible. Not even combed. Her skin was ashy. What if my baby looks like that? What if they really do use babies in America for body parts. I wanted her to have a better life. What will I do if I found out I ruined her life?"

Not better, not worse…just different: Internalization.

All Adoptions

"I am beginning to understand that a lot of adopted children have problems simply with growing up adopted and am concerned about if my child is really doing okay. I have accepted that she will be a part of her adoptive family forever. I understand that despite the challenges she is also likely to develop strengths because of her dual family status. I struggle with my sense of responsibility for the repercussions of my choice that seemed so much simpler then than it does now. I am working towards a confidence that I made the best choice I could under the circumstances—some days I even believe it!"

Transracial Adoption

"I went to visit my son's family again. It wasn't so bad this time. I know they are doing things differently than we do but he is a great kid and I must admit that he is growing up believing in himself. He asked me a lot of questions this time about being African American. The move has really helped him, one of his best friends is black! I know my friend Mei Lin really struggles because she doesn't know anything about her daughter whom she had to leave before she left China. Both of us have felt a lot better since we started reading some books about adopted people. I couldn't believe it when we found out Louise Derman Sparks was a transracial adoptive parent. We have been studying her Anti-bias Curriculum in graduate teaching school. Maybe Mei Lin's daughter has parents who are so changed by the experience of their that they let their kids find their full heritage too."

I am who I am: Immersion/Emerging.
All Adoptions

"I can see that for my child, her birth and adoptive heritages are intertwined to make her who she is. I will always be connected to her. There's no need for me to compete with her adoptive parents. Joining other birth parents for mutual support and direction is helpful to me. I understand and take responsibility for working on myself to be as healthy and comfortable as I can with my choices and life experiences. I prepare information for my child so I will be able to provide him with as many answers to his questions as I can."

Transracial Adoptions

"I wish that the adoption system had given me better choices. I wish that I had known to ask more about how they planned to raise my child since she wasn't like them. I wish I hadn't felt so bad about myself that I didn't see all the ways I could have helped them. I think about my daughter a lot. I plan to be ready if she ever looks for me. I want her to feel good about her heritage. I am working on myself, getting involved in helping my community because that's what I want my daughter to find. I want her to know she not only has me but this whole community to loves and which she is a member of. I wonder if she feels good about being an American Indian.

For all triad members—Our family is a work in process: Autonomy.

For each of the triad members the process is completed through the stage of autonomy, which is basically the same for adopted people, adoptive parents and birth parents.

All Adoptions

"We each come to realize that our family is a work in progress that will never be perfected. Because of our special circumstances, we will serve as a model for how people manage intimate relationships across genetic lines and of how to challenge a society that favors 'genetic privilege.' Families are forever. We know that members of a family can feel connected by love, law, genetic connection, common heritage and/or mutual commitment Not all of these is required for us to consider ourselves a 'family.' Strong families are built step by step. Members of strong families work at their family connection and help each other because if one of them has a problem, they all have a problem. Members of strong families don't let each other fail. Families are fluid. Relationships between us evolve and grow and change as each individual member evolves and grows and changes. Over time we get lots of chances to revisit the same issues, hopefully learning from previous mistakes but there is no final graduation. We understand that we have no choice but to challenge systems of adoptism and we are beginning to find ways to make our voices heard successfully. The work goes on."

Transracial Adoptions

"Adoption is the work of a lifetime. At this point, we have come to recognize that we get lots of chances to revisit the same issues. We recognize that our children have power all their own that will help them to stand tall in this race-sensitive culture. We recognize that we will never graduate from the school of understanding race, but that we will continually be given opportunities to grow. Our children recognize that they have the opportunity to be members of more than one family and more than one community. We are assured that our antennae become ever more sensitive, and that every day is another chance to be a good multiracial family member. Together we can make a difference."

Maintaining a Balance

Too much of what is written about adoption seems like bumper-sticker wisdom:

"Love is all we need."

"Love is not enough."

"Every child needs to know his history."

"Open adoption solves all the problems of loss and grief in adoption."

"Living in a diverse community solves all the issues of becoming bi-cultural."

"Making sure your child has same-race role models solves all their challenges of feeling connected and knowing who they are."

"Adopting children of the same race solves all the problems of children growing up feeling good about one's race and ethnicity."

"Winning the lottery [would] solve *all* problems."

Most of these are ideas that warrant consideration, but they are not complete answers. Adoptive parents who are hoping for simple answers to help their child integrate the past and positively embrace the future are going to be frustrated. There is no such thing as a quick fix. Sorry to say, but parents can't kiss away the boo-boo and make it all better.

Joan McNamara, an adoption therapist says, "Issues such as early trauma, learning difficulties, attachment issues, prenatal exposure to alcohol or drugs, medical problems, siblings in the family and siblings in other families, racial and cultural heritage, lack of information on early history, abandonment, separation and loss are interconnected." Everything about us—the sum of our parts—shapes the way others react to us and we react to ourselves. The more ingredients that are poured into the mix, the more complex the recipe for the individuals involved. But relinquishing hope for easy answers makes more room for the lifelong work of finding real tools to meet the challenges that come with the territory of living and being a productive human being.

Using teachable moments

Since part of a parent's job is to normalize the feelings of sadness, confusion, and self-importance that come with adoption and race awareness, it behooves us to make deliberate ongoing efforts to gauge our children's level of awareness and help them to move from stage to stage as they become ready. Everyday life can offer natural opportunities to address the subjects of adoption and race. Put these issues out on the table as part of every day reality. Initiating conversation demonstrates your comfort with these topics. If you think that the opportunities just don't arise, pay closer attention!

> *Our son Jeremy was three and a half when he was adopted (Gail). At our first meeting, the agency encouraged us to take him out for a burger and when he called us Mama and Daddy in the restaurant, we were his. But after we brought him home, he hung back from using those treasured names. We developed a routine to help him get more comfortable.*
>
> *"Go tell your daddy I need his help," I'd tell my new son, while his dad was waiting in the next room.*
>
> *"Come on," Jeremy would say, pulling on Mel's arm, "Her wants you!"*
>
> *"Who wants me?"*
>
> *"Um…Mama."*
>
> *"Good boy, Jeremy. Good job. Now go tell your mama I'll be there in a minute, as soon as I finish what I'm doing.*
>
> *"Him's coming," Jeremy would say, running back into the kitchen.*
>
> *"Who's coming, little man?"*
>
> *"Him's coming"*
>
> *"Who do you mean?"*
>
> *"Daddy?"*
>
> *"Good boy! Good job. Go tell your daddy to hurry up."*

Expect your child to ask questions in the car and in the grocery store more often than in a comfortable corner at a designated special moment. Impromptu important conversations happen that way, and you need to feel comfortable responding whenever your child asks. Conversations initiated by your child offer golden moments. It's a blessing when questions are asked.

Here are some examples of "conversational moments." Use them to jump-start your own thinking:

- A child is adopted into a friend's family.

  Initiating conversations as the result of events that happen in other people's lives can be a very safe and helpful way to talk with your children and hear what they are actually thinking about the subject themselves.

  "Did you hear Katerina's family is adopting a baby girl from China?" "How do you think Katerina feels about that?" "Did you notice that the baby looks different from the rest of the family? What do you think about that?…"

- Baby kittens are born and then given away to other homes which already have puppies.

  "Do you think the family should keep all the kittens?" "Since they are giving the kittens away, do you think they care about the kittens?" "Why would someone who already has puppies want to have kittens?"…

- Friends get a divorce and share custody of their children.

  Discussion about how different family share custody of their children can lead to consideration about the many ways families are made and behave. Children can see other children feeling bad and talk about whether those feelings mean that their parents do or do not care about them; whether the adults' motivations make the children feel better, etc.

- You wonder aloud how your child's birth mother is celebrating Chinese New Year.

  "Whenever we celebrate Chinese New Year I wonder what your birth mother is doing." This can lead to research on how it is celebrated in the region in which she was born or more conjecture on your part that she is probably thinking of new beginnings and that would mean she is probably wondering about her daughter too…

- Mention to your child that you've noticed how much she is starting to look like her birth parents or like a girl photographed in *Latina* magazine.

  "Now that your are ten, I think you look so much like Maria, your sister in Guatemala." "Can you see how similar your skin and hair are to the model in this magazine. She is beautiful." "Look at how much you look like this woman in the picture. She was given the award for the best teacher in New York City. There must be thousands of teachers. You should be proud that the best one is Latina like you."

The Value of Family Rituals

Everyday life will tell our children over and over that their family is "different." For them, it will become a common experience to be confronted with challenges, direct or indirect, explicit or implied, to the authenticity of our families. Ours don't look like other families; we have uncommon variety in our skin colors, hair types, facial characteristics, etc.

Our children don't share a certain family nose; they don't have the experience (so often annoying to those born into a family) of being met at family reunions with exclamations from distant relatives who joyously declare, "Oh my, you look just like your mother did when she was your age!" And so our children's experience largely lacks many of the ordinary affirmations of belonging.

At the same time, their lives are filled with lots of occasions when family difference evokes the strongest notice. When you pick your child up from school, there's the familiar surprised remark, "Is that your mom? But she's white!" At the park, while you sit tucked next to your toddler, digging in the sand, a friendly stranger asks, "Which child is yours?"

But we are family, nonetheless. Just as we want to help our children develop tools to enable their acceptance by their racial group, we also should remember to provide the tools that help demonstrate and strengthen our acknowledgement within the family of one another as family. We must act like family, with our own unique and exclusive family ways of doing things. If we pay a little attention, we can discover, identify, create or develop unique acts that reveal and affirm our belonging to one another. These family rituals are the bridges by which children can connect to the family in a way no outsider can.

Don't be thrown off balance by the word *ritual*. For some people, ritual has to do with religious practice. That's not what we mean (though participation in religious activities can certainly be one of your family rituals.) We're talking about the stuff you do that is, or can be, woven into the fabric of your everyday lives. The type of activity doesn't matter—whether it's that you all roll your eyes together when Dad goes on his "silly" kick or that every child participates in making a shared present at holidays (despite their groaning,) or that you have your own special ways of waving goodbye—just make sure that you are doing things that suit you, that are unique to your family, that allow for significant interaction among family members, and that your children come to understand that they are unique to your family, shared by none other.

Why build a family ritual?
- Just for fun!
- To reinforce family ties

- To celebrate family history
- To strengthen family identity
- To create memories
- Why not?

In my family (Beth's), we have made up songs about ourselves, in which the kids are named in the context of a silly activity or something they've done. I would be too humiliated ever to sing these songs in front of anyone except my family. But whenever I do sing them (which is often,) neither child will tolerate getting short shrift, each wants equal time and verses. In fact, they remember verses that I have forgotten. These silly songs have become a circle around the children, a circle that marks "us" from "everybody else," that includes them in and defines for them their membership in this family.

In our family (Gail), all six of us ate dinner together every night except if something really important got in the way like you accidentally got run over by a truck and could present a notarized excuse from the doctor. My husband and I didn't start our married life with eating togetherness as our sacred vow; it's something that started when Shira was adopted and decided to keep it going as the family grew. What we actually did was this. On the refrigerator door was THE CHART. Every night you found your name listed next to a job: cook, set, clear, wash, garbage, or smiley face. Smiley face meant haha, lucky day—you just got to eat. You had a job everyday even if you were two years old. Peanut butter and jelly or oatmeal for dinner were as common as tacos or stir-fry. Before the meal, we would all hold hands and sing. Each night someone else got to pick the song, but mostly it was "Peace unto you, joy unto you,…love unto you,…peace unto you" which often was rendered peas unto you though everyone was allowed to stay alive. Then everyone had to say something, anything they wanted. Not mean stuff, no bad words, just private stuff that you didn't want to say in front of people unless you knew for sure that no one could dump on you. We all felt it was okay to take chances. Even if you said dumb things or acted stupid, nobody gets to make fun of you. One time one of Seth's friends asked why we did all that stuff and he answered for all of us when he said, "I don't know. It's just what it our family does and we can't stop."

Be alert to those things which already are or which could become family rituals. Maybe you'll create pet names for each family member; maybe you'll designate Wednesday night as "the whole family, and family only" night; maybe some silly situation will generate a code that you use when out in the world.

Family Pet Names

(Gail) "Only my family can call me that and live," Seth once told a friend who had somehow overheard his family name and dared to use it. I guess that pretty much sums up how it works in our family. Why is it that the pet names that stuck were not the sweeties Mel and I lovingly promoted but the nasty ones the kids came up with all by themselves? I used to try to guide them by suggesting and modeling endearing titles they could use for each other but it was hopeless. They were way too quick for me. If I outlawed one less than attractive name, out would pop another. If their dad just hadn't told them what his school nickname had been, they might have felt less licensed.... But you know what, the part that has mattered to all of us over time has not been the teasing. Even if the names were poopy, having special in-family names only we could call each other accentuated our feelings of belonging. My son Seth is the only person in the world who calls me "Mammilla." I was thinking about it just this morning and finally realized that his pet name for me is probably the reason why even today, at the age of 33, all he has to do to get whatever he wants from me is to ask. It's because I can't hear him say "Mammilla" without everything else in the world abruptly disappearing. Tears come unbidden and I receive the message it is so hard for me to receive— the one I spend my whole life hoping to hear...that someone really, truly loves me.

Just for Fun Rituals

Paint, water, brushes and a role of white paper are gathered. Everyone paints at once, while upbeat music plays. The resulting masterpiece is hung on the wall or used as gift-wrap.

Birthday Rituals

Have each family member draw a picture to be included in a birthday album for the birthday boy or girl to mark this year.

Who You Are Makes a Difference Ritual

One night, a dad came home and said to his 14-year-old son, "The most incredible thing happened to me today. I was in my office and one of the executives came in and told me she admired me and gave me a blue ribbon for being a creative genius. Imagine. She thinks I'm a creative genius. Then she gave me an extra ribbon and asked me to find somebody else to honor.

"As I was driving home, I started thinking about whom I would honor with this ribbon and I thought about you. I want to honor you. My days are really hectic, and when I come home I don't pay a lot of attention to you.

Sometimes I scream at you for not getting good enough grades in school and because your bedroom is a mess. But somehow, tonight, I wanted to sit here and, well, just let you know that you do make a difference to me. Besides your mother, you are the most important person in my life. You're a great kid and I love you!"

The startled boy started to sob and sob and he couldn't stop crying. His whole body shook. He looked up at his father and said through his tears, "I was planning on running away tomorrow, Dad, because I didn't think you loved me. Now I don't want to."

Present your child with a blue ribbon imprinted with gold letters reading, "Who I Am Makes a Difference." Invite him to spread this acknowledgment ceremony to other members of your family by giving him an extra ribbon so that he can pass the experience on by honoring somebody else.

Bedtime Rituals

The "for this five minutes" game. For this five minutes, every night before bed the child tells about good thing that happened today and then the parent does the same.

Memory-Making Rituals

Some day, memories will be all your child has of family life. Find an activity the whole family can enjoy—taking a walk together, learning a sport or a dance step together, singing together, or just playing together. Build this into your schedule of regular events everyone can anticipate and count on.

Ourselves Together Ritual

Stand in a circle and pass a ball of ribbon as each person makes a wish, allowing the ball to unroll as each family members continues to hold a portion. In the end, the ribbon, a symbol of the strong and bright connections among the family, will connect the circle. This can be used on adoption days, birthdays, family days, etc.

The Clean-Up Ritual

All family members gather in the same room for ten minutes and work as a team to clean up everything in reach. Each moves at his or her fastest speed, creating a multi-handed human "vacuum" sucking up anything that isn't nailed down and creating order in record time.

Gratitude Journal Ritual

Oprah spread the good idea of Sarah Ban Breathnach of keeping a "gratitude journal" in which, every day, you write down three things for which you are grateful. Repetition and accumulation build positive attitudes. Those too young to write can draw pictures in their journal instead. Entries can be read and shared. If writing and journaling aren't your thing, then share with each other daily or weekly things for which you are grateful.

Holiday Rituals

Christmas, Halloween, Passover, Thanksgiving, Graduation and the like can be affirmed and confirmed with deep joy and festivity according to individual family traditions. Anything goes in making up rituals—read a special story, bake special treats, make and use unique decorations, set a unique schedule, go to the same restaurant, give gifts, write silly poems. Whatever it is, make sure these events and holidays have a component that is for family only and that the same acts are repeated year after year.

Entrustment Rituals and Adoption Day Ritual

Commemorate with your child's birth family their entrustment of their precious child to you. Shape an event to commemorate your unique partnership. Acknowledging such an important partnership helps everyone process their feelings about it. Activities can include structuring a ceremony in which each person can speak his or her feelings; capturing through words, film or recorded sounds every detail of "what happened on the day I came home;" creating a composite of everyone's hand prints with paint or plaster of Paris; writing a song; reading a poem aloud; lighting a candle; holding hands in a circle… For those who don't have birth family members present, consider using art writing and other means of creating a ceremony acknowledging the child's birth family. Some communities have religious services with an opportunity to remember and pray for absent members of the triad. Create a ritual to celebrate the day your child's adoption was finalized with a family gathering each year. Here are some suggestions of things to do:

- Plant a tree in the child's name each year to mark his or her adoption day.
- Remember something wonderful from your child's first family.
- Remember something wonderful about the day you and your child first met.
- Create an art, music, theater, sports or dance event or attend one to celebrate a new heritage added to the family.
- Prepare a feast of foods of your child's heritage or go to a great restaurant.
- Have a party for extended family and birth family together.

Naturalization Day Rituals

Your child will always have a connection to his or her birth culture. Create a special way to celebrate the day that your internationally adopted child becomes a citizen. Create a family tradition to be repeated each year that honors both his or her birth country and his or her entry into American citizenship. Sing music of both cultures, eat foods of both cultures, recite poetry of both cultures, eat foods of both cultures, recite poetry of both cultures, do folk dances of both cultures. Being a member of more than one culture is something wonderful.

Mother's Day and Father's Day Rituals

Your child has another mother and father. Mark these holidays by making and sending home made cards or gifts to thank your child's birth mother and/or birthfather. Sometimes those of us who have been infertile or who have walked an otherwise painful path to adoptive parenthood have some pain at the notion of sharing this special day with another. If this is true for you, look at whether or not you are still struggling with feeling fully entitled to be your child's parent. From an outside point of view you are parenting every day, making all the decisions, being there for each new stage and moment. Sometimes inside we still struggle with being "real." The important part is to recognize that that struggle is internal and our own, not our child's. Loving another does not make loving one person less. In fact many of us find ourselves able to receive more when we give more. Try to be generous on Mother's Day and Father's Day and take care of yourself by finding support and understanding from other adults, support groups or therapy. If you do not have contact with your child's birth parents, create the cards and letters anyway, holding them in a safe place or special box for a time in the future when circumstances have changed and you can send them or your child can see them again, noticing how he felt at different ages and what messages he wanted to send to his birth family. Though making these materials will reveal feelings of sadness and many questions from your child, they will give your child the opportunity to explore those feelings and learn to manage them in the safety of and with the permission of their family. They will also provide you with a deeper understanding of his feelings about his birth family, greatly important and useful information!

Parenting in Adoption

Perspective on Attachment
Bonding vs. Attachment: What's the difference?

Bonding is a one-way process that begins in the birth mother during pregnancy and continues through the first few days of the child's life. It is her instinctive desire to protect her baby. Attachment is a two-way reciprocal process between parents and their children. Society tends to talk about bonding as if it is the most important connection but professionals hold out attachment as the important measure of children's long-term health and well being.

Adoption is only one among many causes, such as premature birth, child or parent ill health during the birth, a c-section birth, etc., for bonding between birth mother and child to be interrupted. Attachment, by definition, begins with relationship and can begin at any point. We need to be competent with language and talk about attachment. In any family, attachment must be achieved in order for the child to flourish. Time and interaction are needed. It starts with a promise—a promise from parents to child that says, "You count, and you can always rely on me." From this promise will come the baby's sense that the parents matter more than anyone else, leading to the baby's reliance on them. Parents then begin enjoying their ability to nurture with competence. Richly rewarding feelings grow back and forth as each comes to believe "we belong together."

After birth, an infant must reach a new physiological balance as a result of being outside rather than inside the body he shared for nine months. In adoption, he must also make an instant change to a new set of parents. Birth in itself is exhausting. Learning how to adapt to the world without the comfort of familiarity takes longer. No matter how warm the reception by new parents, extra stress on baby must be anticipated. Although baby doesn't understand these changes, he senses changes in sounds, smells, stress, and rhythms. His world is upset. He experiences a loss and reacts. Responses may include crying, difficulty sucking, bowel or bladder disturbances, or withdrawal. Usually such changes are temporary and reverse as he adjusts. Humans have an enormous capacity to recover.

Children handle stress in different ways. Some thrive no matter what; others are vulnerable. Resiliency studies on primates (Stephen Suomi, Laboratory of Comparative Ethnology at the National Institute of Child Health and Human Development) show that attentive care from foster mothers results in bold and outgoing offspring, adept at picking up coping styles. This makes them stronger. They become leaders. Surely adopted children can do the same.

How does adoption affect adoptive parents? Is it harder to form attachments?

Adoptive parents yearn to build a family while feeling terrified that something will go wrong. They may need to work through extra emotional issues before feeling able to form attachments. Researchers in neonatal studies have defined six stages in attachment for parents of infants born prematurely (M.H. Klaus and J.H. Kennel, *Maternal Infant Bonding*, 1976, St. Louis, Missouri.) Adoptive parents should understand them. They are powerfully related to our own issues.

1. Working through a grief reaction. Feeling guilty for any anxiety about fully accepting. Not trusting themselves and worrying they might harm baby.
2. Basing responses solely on information about physical characteristics.
3. Observing and taking courage from baby's reflex behavior: he can move; he is normal.
4. Beginning to see baby as a person. Observing and taking courage from baby's responses: turning to a voice or grasping a finger.
5. Daring to try to produce responses: when the parents touch her, she moves toward them or away. Seeing themselves as responsible for her responses. Beginning to see themselves as parents of this baby.
6. Readiness to let baby rely fully on them. Daring to hold, rock, feed him. Loss of primary fear that he will break, or being unable to comfort him.

Attachment does not necessarily occur instantly. For parents to feel deeply connected to a newly-adopted child, they must feel confident that they understand her cues—what a baby's cries mean and what will comfort him, what an older child thinks and what she really feels.

Post-placement depression occurs when adoptive parents feel that they have not connected quickly enough to their child. For children to feel deeply connected to new parents, they must feel confident that they will be taken care of and that their needs will be met. For older children to feel comfortable they must feel able to understand the cues of their new parents—what words mean, what is expected of them, what the feelings behind the words and actions are.

Attachment when children are placed at older ages

Imagine that you are taking a long-awaited vacation with your best beloved. You are midway to your destination on a luxury jet; the dinner, which was surprisingly good, is finished, and the movie is beginning. You nod off to sleep, relaxing into your partner's shoulder. Suddenly, there is a terrible crash. The plane goes down. When you regain consciousness you are in a strange place where everything is different. Your partner is gone. You can see no one else who was on the place. You are hurt; probably you've broken some bones in the fall... Where is my loved one, you wonder, "Where is everyone?"

People come to you, but they wear odd clothing and speak a language you can't understand. You don't know if they want to help you or to hurt you. When they try to move you into one of their shelters, you resist. You don't want to leave the crash site; all you want is to find your loved one. You have no interest in any of the new people. They smell terrible. The things they are trying to put into your mouth make you gag. You are bereft without your loved one. You are in pain and you feel so helpless and lost.

Time passes. Gradually you come to know one of the new people. She is kind to you and brings you water and food and warmth. You begin to look forward to her visits. As your body recovers, slowly so do your spirits. Eventually, you come to understand that no matter what you do, you cannot go back to the time before the crash. The grief is clear, but you make peace with the people in this new place. Over time, you assimilate, making a new life in this place. You become as fully at home as if you had been living there forever. But every time a plane goes by, no matter what you are doing, you notice it. Never again can you fly or be around airplanes without strong feelings flooding back, reminding you of all that might have been....

Did your child ask to land in a new culture, to learn a new language and accept different smells, tastes, sounds, colors, and way of life? Does he have to make a transitions of monumental significance to assimilate?

Much has been written about attachment in older children. What we know is that the process is made easier for children who have had previous experiences of attachment. We understand that children who are placed as toddlers or older need to go through the same process of connection with their new parents as infants. This is made harder by their previous experiences of loss and distrust but can eventually be overcome through the same cycles of recognition and needs being met.

What is often not acknowledged is that attachment between older children and parents is made more complex by differences in race, culture and ethnicity. It requires a greater degree of trust to connect to those who seem that much more different from us. Transracial adoption also invites challenges from outsiders. These challenges can accentuate adoptive parents feeling that they are not yet their child's legitimate parents and interfere with the process of creating opportunities to build intimacy between parents and children.

Sometimes children are being moved from one monoracial environment to another. An African American child, for example, who has grown up in an inner city neighborhood with her birth family and later with her foster family has probably assimilated a strong sense of distrust of white people. She may know them only as social workers and police who come into her neighborhood to take people away and make everybody upset. If that child is now moved to a mostly white environment, placed in a white family and asked to love white adults and call them Mom and Dad; we must understand how incredibly large is the leap that we are asking this child to make.

This is not to say that these placements are doomed. Adoptive families have the desire and capacity to connect. But without compassion and understanding of the pressure being placed on the child to negotiate issues of both race and adoption the process is far more likely to fail. Addressing issues of race along with adoption as a family deepens attachments. Reevaluating our assumptions about what makes a family belong together can help adoptive families find strength in who they are. With patient and continuous contact, attachment will deepen.

Patterns of Parenting

Influenced by Dr. Louise Hart's work on parenting styles in her book, *The Winning Family* (Berkeley, Celestial Arts, 1993) and our own experience with the many multiracial adoptive families who consult Pact, we have a sense that there are three broad categories of parenting styles common to families formed by transracial adoption: child-centered, parent-centered, and democratic. Parents evolve these styles because of their own philosophies of child development, their experiences with their own families of origin, and their own personalities. Each of these parenting styles has strong cultural components and assumptions about the world based on the privilege of being white.

We have come to believe that the best parenting strategy for transracial parents takes the best of each with an understanding that the goals and priorities are different depending on the situation and context of the parenting "moment" to which it is applied. Which of the following styles best describes your general approach to parenting? How conscious are you of your style and how consistent are you during everyday situations? Different uses of power and control—from letting the child be in charge to a home environment where the child is not allowed any choices and the parents hold power—create different results.

The first step consists of recognizing the traits—both strengths and weaknesses of each style. The second step is thinking about when and where the tactics of a particular style will be most helpful.

The child-centered parenting style

- Non-intrusive. Parents feel that they have no right to intrude in the child's natural growth. Using this style, they would let the child figure out his own adoption story and definition of race. Guidance is perceived as interference.

- Parents believe that the child will find her own way in her own time and that it is better not to direct her journey.
- Parent communicates that the child can search for or have contact with her birth family and the parent will support the process.
- Parents believe that the child will be better able to connect with others of his race if the parent stays out of the picture.
- Parents believe that it is best to send the child to camps, schools, etc. of the child's choice, but are cautious about getting overly involved themselves.

Many parents who choose transracial adoption think of themselves as self-directed individuals who are able to make choices that are inner directed and not overly influenced by others. They may have been raised by extremely autocratic parents themselves and, having hated it, vowed that they would be different with their own kids. Holding as a high value a desire for their child to feel confident and able to think for herself often leads to a permissive style of parenting with the idea that the less intrusion the child has, the more self reliant she will become. Unfortunately, raising a child by relinquishing all the power to the child provides too much freedom with the child missing out on the stability of limits, rules and structure. In permissive families, kids may not learn boundaries, may have trouble with limits, may lack self-discipline, may think they have the right to do exactly what they want when they want to, may have little awareness of social responsibility, and may strike out at their parents if they are not getting what they want when they want it. Children from these families often behave totally differently in public from their African American peers who have usually grown up with a kind of survival training stressing the need to be obedient and to follow directions instantly without question or resistance. If an adopted child is unable to cope with rules or act in a cooperative way, other children are likely to label her as different or spoiled; hardly a good idea for a child who needs contact with others of her own racial background. Parents who value self direction still must guide their children to be respectful of others and to be responsible for their actions. This requires involvement, discussion, and continuous interactions.

The parent-centered parenting style

1. Intrusiveness. Parents feel they must protect the child by indoctrinating her to their views, whether the child has an interest or not.
2. Dogmatism. Parents feel that their view is the only acceptable view.
3. Rigidity. Parents believe in particular solutions to most issues and are inflexible in their embrace of a certain philosophy (e.g., their "kind" of adoption—open or confidential—is the solution to their child's potential issues or problems.)

4. Idealism. Parents' stance to the child on adoption might be "You are just like everyone else; your birth was normal; your birth family is wonderful." There is an overemphasis on the great gifts the child has received from her birth parents.

5. Parents often believe that they can transmit the child's racial or ethnic heritage in a direct way, though they are not members of the child's race.

6. Parents study the child's racial/ethnic heritage and take on for themselves many customs, traditions and distinctive aspects of the culture rather than seeking connections for their child to people who are living in the culture and are of the same race as the child.

If parents have grown up in an autocratic family, this may be the only parenting style they know. They may believe, "It was good enough for me," and repeat it by default. Others who practice this parenting style are responding to what they believed was an uncaring family life which didn't give them a chance to experience what it means to be loved. Parents who take an autocratic approach impose their will through a rigid structure that allows the child minimal flexibility or freedom. Demanding respect, they believe they are helping their children if they teach them to obey without question. If a child exerts any will of his own, it's their job to break it, sort of like training a wild stallion by overpowering and punishing him. Children raised by autocratic parents work hard at keeping their parents happy in order to avoid getting punished. They are used to being told exactly what to do and often lack imagination or capacity for self-assertion. Because they have grown up having their feelings ignored in deference to their parent's feelings, they may distrust their own feelings and think of themselves as wrong. The autocratic style may work with young children but is not effective with teens.

For transracially adopted children, this style is useful with children of color who must learn to work around the limitations and stereotypes the world is forever placing on them. Children who learn to find positive ways of coping with unfairness, to make lemonade out of lemons, have a great advantage in handling the struggles of coping with racism. Understanding and recognizing the rules means that they can avoid danger and conflicts that can result for children who don't understand how they are viewed in public. On the other hand, an additional burden that may come from having autocratic white parents is that the parents are transmitting a system of values and a sense of history that distances the child from his culture of origin. A white parent who is rigid or dogmatic, always having to have the last word on racial and adoption issues, will, because of his own lack of insider status as a member of his child's culture, almost certainly be reinventing the very customs and traditions he is trying to transmit. A child cannot test her assumptions on others who have direct knowledge. What he passes to his child will be his interpretation and representation of reality, a view that will probably not prepare the child to deal with the real world. Parents who value obedience, respect rules, and boundaries still must guide their children to be able to connect with others to think for themselves and to be responsible for their actions. This requires providing enough freedom, flexibility and respect for the child for these qualities to be allowed to develop.

The democratic parenting style

1. Parents help the child learn the boundaries: Where is the safe place? Where is the dangerous place?
2. Parent is teacher, offering guidance, allowing exploration and self-determination.
3. Parents seek out valuable role models for their adopted children of color.
4. Parents listen to understand the child's experience of being adopted, communicating a desire to provide unconditional and permanent love, being open to discussion about birth family and circumstances of placement. They emphasize that the reasons for placement were due to circumstances, not the child; she was lovable and unflawed at birth.
5. Parents want to connect their child to adult role models of his race/ethnicity.
6. Parents seek to relate respectfully to people of their child's race/ethnicity.

Parents who share power with one another and with their children start from an attitude of cooperation with their kids. Everyone's needs and ideas are respected and children have choices. This style of parenting takes the best of the other two and tries to marry them in ways that give children the benefits of each while minimizing the deficits of each. As they grow, children raised in this way increase their skills at making good choices. Those who grow up in democratic families learn to make good decisions and take responsibility for their own lives. As these parents empower their children to think for themselves, they gain more facility for building satisfying futures. Transracially adopted children must learn to hold their own in white society because they are immersed in it on a daily basis. In addition, they must learn to respectfully take part in the culture of their heritage by learning the cues and then choosing what pieces are appropriate for them to assimilate into their own multicultural lives. Being raised in a family which they have real choices can make a difference, and have the ability to influence others and bring about change will raise any child's sense of self and be a lifelong model for building healthy relationships. For children who face the extra challenges of adoptism and racism, learning healthy ways to get along with others is a survival skill best learned from learning to recognize the rules and watching how their parents act. If your style of parenting is not democratic, we invite you to revisit some of your choices with the goal of helping your child to feel comfortable getting what he needs and giving to others. A family is fluid. The way we parent need not be static.

Preparing for Transitions

Many adopted kids respond strongly to change all their lives. This makes sense, since changing families at least once is a huge experience! Does your adopted child have trouble with transitions, with changes from one place, action, mood, topic or thing to another? A transition can be a "little" deal that comes up every day—such as stopping one game and starting another, coming to dinner, getting in and out of the shower, or moving from one class to another at school. It can also be as high-stress as moving from one family to another, moving from one country to another, adding a new member to the family, moving to a new house, or coping with divorce after adoption.

It is logical to imagine that children who have had to make a major life change—a change that affects most things they do—are likely to be more sensitive to change than are other children. When at conferences we ask, "Does your child have trouble with transitions?" the strong show of hands convinces us that transracially adopted children tend to have difficulties with change. Often their parents have all the while been thinking that they have probably caused the problem through less than perfect parenting.

Since it is impossible to predict in advance which children will have particular sensitivity with transitions, choosing to use a parenting approach which assumes a need for attention to transitions can help to head off problems. Here are some elements of such a parenting approach...

Helping slow-to-adapt kids make smoother transitions

Surprises are not welcome for kids who have difficulty with changes. Routines provide a sense of security and control. Think about your child's normal routine, and try to be clear with yourself about the ways in which your child depends on it. As much as you can, limit the number of transitions that will be required in a day. If a routine is going to change, what will be different? Where, when, why and under what circumstances will the beginnings and endings of events and activities take place? What will be the signals to cue the child about the transitions? Talk in advance with your child about changes that will come up. Create a regular time together to talk about upcoming plans. Let your child hear your sympathy and support for the challenge transitions offer. Send the message, "We respect that you like to know what to expect and to feel prepared. We want you to have advance notice so that you can have time to get used to the idea of what is going to happen, what you will be doing, and can feel ready."

Helping rushing-to-adapt kids make smoother transitions

> *We (Beth and her husband) told James that he was going to be switching schools early in his third grade year. We all recognized that his current school was not meeting all of his needs and he exhibited real relief in our acknowledgment of the pressure he faced in trying to compensate for the ways the expectations were not consistent with his strengths. We thought this meant that he would also be relieved to know that we were planning a move to a new school better matched with his strengths. What we forgot is that he is a child who worries about change before it happens. He is often able to manage transitions in the moment, but too much preparation results in lost sleep and over-worry. At his request, we had planned to use one of the normal classroom circle times to tell the other kids. As the day approached, James began to exhibit behaviors ranging from fights with other children to complete breakdowns. He became overly sensitive to offenses that were usually no big deal. When we finally recognized the signals and told him we didn't have to tell the other kids, he relaxed. We even added that although we (the adults) were still considering what to do about schools for next year we had decided that we should decide and he didn't need to worry about it anymore. James calmed visibly. Taking back the responsibility for the decision and the moment of transition helped. With time he even talked about the probability of the move, but he had clearly been able to leave the responsibility for managing it at the door of the adults—a distinction that allowed him to prepare for the change with less fear and more trust.*

Preparing for a transition can provoke anxiety in some children who find the expectation of change to be stressful. Anticipation can be all-consuming for the child who is fearful about the future and his ability to handle what it holds. Children like this still need to be prepared, but doing so with information about upcoming change is not the most useful tactic. Offering comfort by taking adult responsibility for aspects of the change and their outcome can help these children manage their fears and prepare without falling apart. Often these children need to act immediately on the change because prolonging the transition feels excruciating. Helping kids understand this need on their part will eventually lead to their own understanding of the difference between impulse control and anxiety management. Parents must model ways of distancing the provoking fear such that it can be slain or at least tamed.

Preparing kids for change

Children challenged by change can certainly be helped to feel more in control over their situations if they know when changes will come. As the saying goes, forewarned is forearmed. Here are some common-sense suggestions for things you can say and do to prepare your child for change.

- Provide accurate information.

  "This is a picture of what your sleep-away camp will look like."

  "The lake at our vacation spot is very safe. Jaws will not pop out of the water. Look at this internet site which says that sharks don't live in lakes in this area."

- Provide fair warning.

  "When you hear us singing 'We Are Family,' it means that it's time to come to dinner."

  "Tomorrow when I pick you up we won't be going home; we are going to Grandma's house. Do you want to put your favorite bear in the car so that you'll have it with you?"

  "I'll give your swing three more pushes. Then it will be Jaime's turn."

  "You have five minutes to go. Find a good stopping place."

- Provide transitional objects. A transitional object is a comforting item like a blankie or a teddy that provides extra security during times of change. It can also be an article of clothing or something less "obvious" for older children.

  "You can wear your special Barbie shoes when you go to the gym."

  "Of course you can bring your teddy with you when we go."

  "Let's make a paper chain with loops to tear off each day while we wait for your birthday to come."

  "Here's a picture calendar to help you count the days until your sister comes home from camp."

- Use your child's imagination.

  "Let's pretend to be horses and gallop all the way to the car."

  "When the timer goes off, let's go to a pretend party."

  "What if when we get to the party the ice cream has turned to Jell-O?"

- Offer support for the struggle.

  "I really noticed how much you wanted to stay longer at Gary's house to play. It's hard to do things that have to be done when you would rather play with your friend. I see you really working hard to try to make it smoother when your play dates have to end." Sometimes it's hard for a transition-sensitive child to reach closure, especially when she is doing something that matters to her. Let her know that you are waiting and that you will be glad to help, but that her choice is to finish up on her own in the amount of time available or to expect that you will have to take over and she will still have to move on to the next event.

- Help your child anticipate potential transitions before they happen.
  "I was thinking about how it is going to be for you to go to this new camp without a friend you already know. I wonder what kinds of things would help make it better when you feel alone or uncertain about being there. Do you think getting a letter every day would help? What about bringing a special book that you will read only when you need to feel better?…"

- Disappointments of any kind may be especially hard.
  When your childs experiences disappointment, she has to make a transition from what she had hoped for to what is possible. This accommodation to reality and disappointment may be very challenging. Provide a way for her to release her feelings.

- Offer praise for success.
  Every time your child makes a transition well, appreciate her and offer her affirmation. This is difficult work that takes place daily. Thank her for trying.

Birth Family

Messages about birth families

Who will your child go to with questions about birth parents? Do everything you can to ensure that you are safe, inviting and open to their deepest concerns about these incredibly important people in their lives. They are going to ask, wonder and explore. The only question is whether it will be with or without you.

Birth family issues may be even more important to transracial families

In transracial families, acceptance of birth families can be even more important than in same-race adoptive families, because rejection by the birth family can look like the rejection by the race of the child. Transracially adopted children may suppose that they were placed because of their race. They may think that people of their race or ethnicity rejected them because people of another race adopted them. If they don't have friends who demonstrate otherwise, they may think that all people of their heritage abandon their children. This may lead to an unconscious repetition of the pattern they have misperceived when they enter their own adult years. Openness can be of real value here, because it allows for connection to their racial heritage as well as to their birth family. Of course, not all transracial families have the opportunity to open their adoptions.

Don't minimize birth family significance

Whether you know your child's birth family and have ongoing contact or not, your children will have to resolve their dual family membership to become healthy functioning adults. To minimize the role of the birth family makes the child's connection to the adoptive family appear to depend on a lack of connection to the birth family. Encouraging a child to see his or her identity as either/or, expecting a rejection of birth ties as a prerequisite to claiming membership in the adoptive family is a recipe for disaster.

"Your real mom didn't want you!"

It's easy to acknowledge in theory that your child has birth parents. But what messages are you really sending?" Do you speak of them—even if you don't know them—as a fact of your child's life? Do you open the door to your child's questions, musing aloud, for example, "Gee, you're so clever with math; I wonder if you get that from your birth parents?"

Maybe you're thinking, "Yeah, fine, fine, of course, but we're too busy being a family to have time or need to worry about them. It's not that we wouldn't think about them; it just doesn't seem that important." But your behavior helps your child to see what really matters to you. If birth parents are not discussed openly, then children will assume that they shouldn't be spoken of. What will they do, then, with the questions that certainly will arise? Your child will explore them apart from you and the family unless you find a way to allow the process to unfold within the safety of the family.

Coping with fantasy parents

For adopted children, idealized fantasy parents have the power to solve all problems like Cinderella's fairy godmother. Fantasy parents of color can help children deal with the stress of having parents who are not themselves targets of racism, which arouses anger and guilt in the child. Fantasy parents can be conjured up at times of need and then fade away until they are needed again. It is normal and positive for children adopted transracially to integrate the differences between themselves and their parents by developing a clear sense of themselves as people with dual heritage—having adoptive parents *and* birth parents. From there it is a very small leap to idealizing birth parents and blaming adoptive parents, or, in open adoptions where birth parents are known, to invent a third set of parents who are made of pure fantasy. Having Will Smith, Maya Angelou, Margaret Cho or Ricky Martin as your imagined birth parent can counter some of the negative birth parent images that society in general assumes. For a child who has limited contact with any adults of color these fantasies also help them imagine a relationship with people of their racial or ethnic group.

When your child brings up his or her fantasy parents or places his birth parents in an idealized role, do you feel wounded? challenged? angry? alarmed? Remember, when your child is stressed, you are likely to feel stressed, too, whether fantasy parents come to the rescue or not. If your child brings them up, be careful not to overreact. Your child has been affected by something that he or she needs to work through. This can become a wonderful opportunity for you to get some new insight into how he or she is experiencing a stressful incident. Talk about imaginary parents opens a window, which can allow him to share his hurt and hopes with you. Listen and let your child be in charge of saying what his imaginary parents are doing. Your assurance that everything will be fine and that you will take good care of your child will be communicated by your acceptance of his fantasy. This coping device is no different from an adult's holding in mind an image of a perfect spouse who would meet every need and fulfill life in a perfect way.

Open transracial adoptions

When children have positive feelings about their birth parents, they are more likely to feel positive about their heritage and themselves. In a transracial adoption, the importance is intensified because the birth parents represent the child's race; if children do not feel positive about their birth families, they may have difficulty integrating their birth cultures.

On the other hand, if a child's only contact with or image of people who share their race is through their birth parents, they are likely to grow up with some unfortunate assumptions such as everyone from China places their girl babies for adoption or all black people are too poor to parent their children.

Whether or not there is direct contact between the child and birth parents, it is useful for adoptive parents to help children find a supportive view of their culture. This effort can be encouraged by gathering and sharing background information or, if possible, by developing relationships with the child's birth family.

Why do birth parents of color choose white families?

Our current adoption system is as institutionally racist as every other system in this country. The notion that MEPA and IEPA and the new openness to transracial placement will solve the problem of the large numbers of children of color currently waiting in the foster care system seems naive and unrealistic. In fact, although black families adopt at twice the rate (4% vs. 2%) that white families do, there are far more children of color in foster care and out-of-home, non-permanent placements than there are families coming forward to adopt them.

One of the common reasons expectant parents of children of color choose to entrust their children to white parents in adoption is a desire for openness after placement. White parents often have greater access to education on issues of ongoing contact between children and birth parents after adoption. There is often a larger pool of waiting white families who hold this value than there is among prospective parents of color. This is partly a function of the fact that the private adoption system is dominated by white practitioners and white pre-adoptive parents. Since open adoption is most common in the private sector of adoption, birth parents looking for openness are too often forced to choose white parents because same-race families are not offered as options. Many white transracial adoptive parents struggle with the fact that they would not have been their child's birth parents first choice had there been similarly minded families of color available. In our experience a transracial family is not often a birth parent's first choice but one that can be considered, based on the opportunities at hand. Second choice does not mean second best

Is ongoing connection with birth relatives positive?

When such a placement occurs, it may be of particular value to the child to have ongoing contact with birth relatives in order to help dispel any notion of rejection by her racial or ethnic group. Understanding why an adoption plan was made can help the child resist the misperception that the adoption was based on personal rejection. Openness and contact can also help dispute society's stereotypes of birth parents of color as either drug users, "welfare queens" hoping to get financial support, or sexually irresponsible people.

Having a connection to her birth family will increase your child's sense of entitlement to her cultural heritage while at the same time offering a terrific way to learn cultural cues and to develop a sense of ethnic belonging. It is important to remember, however, that birth parents should not be made to feel obligated to be the child's only racial role model.

Although this is not a treatise on the advantages of open adoption we want to at least to list some of the considerations we believe are important in considering ongoing contact with birth parents of transracially adopted children.

1. Your child's birth parents are stakeholders in their child's success in your family. Without a successful adoption they will have to contend with an added aspect of their own guilt and shame for placing their child. As a stakeholder of the same race as your child, you are not likely to find a more committed partner in promoting strong self-esteem in your child.

2. Often open adoption relationships are uneven because there is a significant difference in power and sense of "standing" between the adoptive parents and the birth parents. Openness in the transracial context offers

real opportunities for birth parents to bring yet another "expertise" to the table—that of being a person of color in the world.

3. You have known your child's birth parents in an incredibly vulnerable moment of their life, a time where crisis of whatever form drove them to decide they needed or had to place their child for adoption. Giving them the opportunity to see you in a vulnerable way, struggling to understand or manage connection to your child's birth culture, can create a reciprocal intimacy that can really help your child to see that you love them (since you love members of their birth family.)

What are the challenges of ongoing connections?

1. Neither the birth parents nor adoptive parents may have previously developed relationships across racial lines. The high-stakes situation of adoption adds extra sensitivities to the stresses of learning how to interact positively with someone who may be living in a very different cultural and/or economic group.

2. Cultural values may differ, but their differences may not be explicitly recognized, which can create conflicts. In some white families, for example, agreeing to do something at a particular time generally means what it says. If the arrangement is to meet at 1:00 p.m., white people usually apologize profusely if they are fifteen minutes late. In some black or Latino families, on the other hand, an agreement to meet at 1:00 p.m. may mean that anytime between 1:00 and 3:00 is fine. Because neither family understands their different cultural values in this regard, the door is open for conflict.

3. Though the birth parents share with the adoptive parents the responsibility for connecting the child to his heritage, all too often the task falls to the birth parents, since they have long experience in interpreting cultural messages about race or ethnicity and in developing ways of coping with racism. The adoptive parents may not have developed multiple ties to the racial community beyond the birth parents. This situation often feels to the birth parent like a betrayal of a contract the adoptive parents were thought to have made. Relying solely on birth parents for this work can then become a source of resentment between families. The birth parent role is sufficiently challenging on its own without the exclusive responsibility for the child's racial growth. Under any circumstances, whether or not contact with birth parents is fully open, the adoptive parents are best advised to pursue as many significant relationships as possible with willing adults who share the child's race and who are willing to serve as cultural guides for the child.

Extended Family

Most of us do not choose transracial adoption without thought and preparation. We spend many agonizing hours, months and sometimes years deciding whether we will be good enough parents to our child, whether we really can love someone intimately across racial lines. Will we be competent as an adoptive parent? Will we really feel like a parent to a child of color? We would not dream of suggesting that anyone should just become a transracial or international adoptive parent without this scrutiny and self-reflection. Yet most of us ask our extended family to do just that!

I (Beth) called my mother to inform her of our second adoption only two hours before we went to pick James up at the hospital. Truth be told, we needed her to watch our eighteen-month-old daughter while we went to pick him up. I remember she was pleased we had named him James, after my father who had died in same hospital in which the baby was born. She was pleased to have her first grandson. But I was deliberately unwilling to tell her what race James was. For me it was all about demanding her absolute allegiance to my family based on my choices. One wrong move or comment and she would be in very dangerous waters. She had expressed concerns about our ability to incorporate an African American child into the family, believing that the hierarchy of racism made it easier for our Latina daughter than it would be for an African American son. The truth was, Ted and I had spent countless hours discussing the same issues. But from her I barely tolerated the question when she asked his race. "He's black," I retorted defiantly, "Is that a problem?" "No," she said. "I just want to know who my grandson is. I can't wait to meet him."

Five years later, I was at church with my mother and the children. After the service she was talking to some of her white friends when I overheard her say, "You have no idea what it's like to be black. I bring my grandson to the hair salon and I am the only white person there. They are so nice to me. They welcome me into their world. I have to wonder if we would welcome them that way. I think it's easy to judge when we don't know."

It took me five years to think for one minute that anyone in our family other than myself, my husband and my children were on this journey of building a transracial family. I was so sure it was my job to advocate and to educate and to "know it all." It never dawned on me to expect that my children could find advocates in our extended family. I was so busy seeing the danger and treacherous things that they didn't understand that I never bothered to see the support and growth. When I told my sister about what our mother had said to her friends at church and my own inability to give her any credit in understanding my children, she shared her own story of adoption.

"Remember how close I was to Grandma? Did you think I didn't know she was the one who opposed my adoption? She told me about it when I was a teenager and going through a really bad time. She told me she had been sure that she couldn't feel the same about me as you because you were born to the family and were connected differently. She said that she was right. She didn't feel the same. That it had taken her more than eighty years—until I came along—to know that she could love someone so much without that connection, without any obligation. Whenever I feel different or alone in our family, I always remember that Grandma loved me not because she said she would; she didn't sign on for the adoption the way Mom and Dad did. She loved me for me. Period."

Extended family members can forge relationships with our children that can be among the most supportive and important they have. Family have an intimate view of their lives and if they are willing to grow and understand can offer incredible insight and understanding to our children without being in the charged role of "parent." Giving our family members time and opportunity to know and understand our children and their experiences is a gift to both of them.

When family members don't act right.

My grandmother (Gail's) was neither a sweet nor a kindly woman, particularly in her later years. Underneath her good-natured façade, Bubbie was proud, fiercely protective, and deeply suspicious of anything new. As a Polish Jew, losing family to the pogroms and later the camps, emigrating to a new world where she had a difficult time, both her fears and her defenses made sense. Neither made her easy to live with, however, nor was she an ideal candidate for the role of great-grandmother to transracially-adopted kids. Through no choice of her own, we dealt her in. She loved my children, though she never understood adoption. She never understood how the atrocious racial slurs she made in a seemingly innocent way affected us. Her bewilderment when we complained felt genuine. Let's face it—she never saw the world from anything beyond her original prejudiced view.

Kate and John are an interracial couple, white and black. They adopted Jasmine, the biracial daughter of Barbara, who can trace her ancestry to the Mayflower, and a black man. Barbara's parents are

authentic bigots. On the night she finally got up the nerve to tell them
that she was pregnant, and that the father of her baby was black, they
kicked her out. "The shame," her mama said. "A mongrel! You'll not
bring a pickaninny to this house and call it our grandchild. Get rid of
it like you got it—on your own." Barb's father sat like a stone in front
of the fireplace, polishing his pistol, never looking up. She pleaded,
but they would not budge, and she was just sixteen. When Jasmine was
five, Barb's mother passed on. Barb's Dad said he'd like to see his
grandbaby but Barb wants to keep him away from Jasmine forever.
Kate and John would like Jasmine to have the opportunity to meet her
birth grandfather. They don't want to go against Barb's wishes, though,
nor do they want to chance that he would hurt their daughter like he
hurt her mother.

An African American boy invited Carol's white niece to the prom
and Carol's sister wouldn't let her go. Carol was deeply distraught. Her
daughter, Anna, who attended the same high school, is African
American. What a painful shock to have prejudice come up out of the
blue from an extended family member Carol and Anna both love and
had assumed shared core beliefs about family, race and acceptance.

These problems offer double binds, difficult to approach. As parents, our priority must be our children, not our extended family members. Only the parent can take care of the child. Every child deserves to be safe from racism in the haven of the family. The relative is prejudiced, and yet the relative is a member of the family. Is this an opportunity for the demonstration of unconditional love, teaching our kids that we don't like this person's ways or ideas, but that we can still love her? Or do we have to separate from this person because ongoing contact may be toxic? These are Catch-22s, not readily solved, with lasting messages, no matter what the resolution.

But there's one approach that will not work for sure. If contact with extended family involves prejudice and adoptism, children are confronted with attitudes we cannot ignore. Too many stories of children who are confronted with racism within their extended families show the parents absent from their child's experience. This can only seem to the child to be tacit acceptance of the racist views being touted. Don't leave your child alone in the family, the place where they deserve to feel safest. TALK ABOUT IT. DEAL WITH IT. CONFRONT IT.

Crime or disease?

The model we normally use to deal with racism is "crime and punishment." Let's say my grandmother commits the crime of racism; now how shall

I punish her? Cut her off? Refuse to see her? Reprimand her angrily? Responding with righteous indignation and anger just does not work. Who opens their heart or changes in response to being chastised? I feel guilty at being connected to someone who is bringing pain to my children, a pain that I know as a parent, but not as a victim of the racism itself. That fact brings me even more pain.

An alternative model is to understand racism as an illness. Depending on the degree of racism, it can be moderate or severe, and in some cases, terminal. This model allows the victim of racism to have power. We feel sorry for sick people, but scared of criminals. Helplessness and fear caused by victimhood imposes another victimization on the sufferer. Those who understand that racism is a disease and that those who have this disease deserve pity are in a better mental and spiritual state to respond to the racism.

Feeling compassion for the person with the illness doesn't mean that you let the disease spread, of course. We can feel compassion for someone with TB and do our best to help him recover from it, but we also take steps to contain the TB, to avoid spreading it further.

We should not let racist behaviors and policies continue unopposed any more than we should let those suffering from, say, Ebola virus to spread the virus further. Racism needs to be quarantined. We can't let the sick people go on spreading the illness. But we can take action in a spirit of loving kindness and understanding. Perhaps your spiritual beliefs can provide you with some concrete actions you can take to this end. In the midst of the emotional shock brought on by racism amongst family members, opening our hearts and listening to the source of our spiritual strength can help us find the right path to deal with the situation.

Often the last thing our children need to experience is further loss of caring adults from within the family circle. We also have to recognize the truth that we can't change our relatives. We can't limit our life choices, or our children's, based on others' limitations. What we can do is change the ways we respond to people in the family who behave inappropriately in regard to race and/or adoption. Someone who is toxic must be removed or severely limited but before we commit to such radical surgery we must explore other options in fighting the disease.

What to do

Here are some particularly useful suggestions adapted from *Raising the Rainbow Generation* by Drs. Darlene Powell Hopson and Derek S. Hopson for dealing with racism:

- When possible, prepare your children in advance. Let them know what attitudes you think the relative holds and where you think they came from. Explaining why and how they were formed teaches your child an understanding of other points of view, even those with which we don't agree. By extension, this teaches tolerance. State clearly that you do not agree. Give your child permission to challenge the remarks in an appropriate manner.

- Challenge offensive remarks immediately, not by starting a family feud, but by gently asking simple questions. "What do you mean by that?" "Why did you say that?" "Why do you feel that way?" This approach gives your relative a chance to describe how her views were formed. You can then point out that those views are not acceptable to you or say that you want to find out the facts and invite your child to explore the facts with you. Emphasis is not on challenging the relative as a person, but on the fact that your attitudes are different and you would like to discuss the issue again when you've gathered more information. This approach makes clear to your child that you disagree with the family member's attitudes and that you take the issue seriously enough to want to prove your point with them.
- Don't let the offender say it. Interrupt her midstream and say, "I won't let things like that be said in my home." She may be speaking out of conversational habit, because no one ever made clear that such remarks were unacceptable.
- Talk about differing racial attitudes the first moment you are alone after the remarks are made. Clearly state your objections. Stress that you still love your relative, but that you believe her attitudes about race are all wrong. Encourage your child to talk to you any time if she hears similar remarks elsewhere.

Being ambushed by previously unsuspected racism in your family may call for a different tactic. You might want to begin by asking your child what she wants to do so long as it does not put her on the spot in a way that makes her feel you are abandoning her to deal with situation alone. Giving her power in this situation can offer a good way for her to feel that she can be in control, not just a victim. She may want some time to think. She may be able to come up with an answer for how to respond to the crisis that works for all of you. Teenagers respond positively to genuine adult respect for their views and willingness to take them seriously. Your child may decide that she doesn't want to take action at all. If so, it is important that you support that option as well or prepare the child ahead of time that you do not consider that an option.

Kate, John, Barb and Jasmine's situation described above may call for the involvement of an objective outsider—a therapist who can serve as mediator, who can explore the hurts and the losses, and who can help this family do what is ultimately best for Jasmine. Perhaps they can find room for working out loyalty issues between Barb and the adoptive family while leaving room for what may be a positive relationship to grandpa for Jasmine.

Interracial dating can provoke a reality check in families where silence has been assumed to mean support but instead meant acceptance of what relatives could not change. Carol's daughter Anna obviously will need support, as will the African American boy who invited Anna's cousin to the prom. Carol must help her sister to understand how her ban on interracial dating for her white child feels not only to her black niece, but to the entire family as well as to her personally. Carol's extreme hurt and anger need to be voiced. Hopefully new conversation can result. Hopefully, new ways of relating will result. If Carol cannot change her sister, finding a way to understand her limits and allowing Anna and the rest of the family to help decide how to cope with them is paramount.

Disengaging from family altogether, even for extreme acts, can set dangerous fears afire for adopted people who wonder about whether they too could be sanctioned if they don't act "good enough." All we can control is our own reaction to what others do. You can't control your sister's or your mother's or your father-in-law's behavior. Sometimes an incident or pattern within the extended family will allow you and your immediate family to acquire a deeper understanding and mastery over the issue of racism. When used as an opportunity to find out what works to overcome and what does not, this can at least allow one to feel as if some good has come out of a negative. Such knowledge is going to be necessary for our kids, who have a lifetime ahead of them in which to come to terms with this disease.

This issue is worth the friction it may create. The healthy growth of your child is at stake. Differences can exist between you and your loved ones. The bottom line is that in not saying or doing anything, you condone what was said or done. Silence cannot be an option in your home. Parents must stand with their children. Otherwise you stand against them.

Siblings in Adoptive Families

If your spouse said to you, "I love you so much, honey, and you're so incredibly fabulous that I've decided to get another husband (or wife) just like you. Don't worry. I will have time for all of you," how would you feel? And how would you feel if, after your expletives and after you said, "Forget it! Get rid of them!" your partner answered, "What's wrong with you?" "You're crazy to feel that way," or "Whoa! Cool it! I'm not here to listen to you whine," or "Face reality. I can't send him back. We're a family now," or "Don't be so negative. Can't you see how cute he is and how much he loves you?" or "I did it for you honey. I thought you'd love a buddy!"

If sibling rivalry is fueled by a desire to find security by having the exclusive love of one's parents, it seems logical to imagine that any child who has been moved from one family to another might be especially sensitive to the issue of security and would be more prone to view siblings as rivals. Family culture and closeness, gender, age, position in the family, size of the family, similarity or disparity of interests and talents, personality, experiences in birth or foster families, as well as each person's sense of psychological fit within the family are issues that shape sibling relationships.

Since the children and parents in adoptive families have differing genetic backgrounds, they cannot expect to be as prone to be "alike" physically, intellectually, or emotionally as are people who have a birth connection. So they may be more "at risk" for poor matches. On the other hand, their attachment may be strengthened because of the consciousness of all of the family's members that matching is not key to family connectedness. Adopted siblings, like any siblings, are the only people in the world who share a set of parents. This singularity may be beneficially intensified for children more sensitive to the need to be "like" someone else.

Why having siblings helps

Children in transracial families can benefit greatly from having siblings who grow up, like them, sharing parents of a different race or ethnicity. Relationships with our brothers and sisters are often the longest relationships of our lives. For children who moved from one family to another and have a greater sensitivity to family ties and issues of intimacy, growing up with siblings who share both the warm, positive feelings of the family unit and the challenging experience of having a family that looks different can really help. And it may be of benefit even to have siblings to fight with as one struggles to define one's own place in the family circle. Here's a look at how this played out in one particular family—Gail's

> *Our household includes two cats and two dogs. They sometimes fight with an energy and dedication that makes me comprehend world wars—and my children. Most of the time our pets live peacefully within our family, sharing space and food and taking turns curling up with the humans. My four children are now grown. Because they all live within driving distance from one another, we get together frequently. We tend to linger around the dining room table, where the conversation inevitably turns to retelling one funny story after another: who did what to whom, and why... Sometimes, the conversation rekindles the same old feelings they had when they were little, reviving the same old torments. It's something like a structured game of "gotcha last." Except now that they are adults, they keep things in bounds*

(most of the time) and seem genuinely to enjoy remembering one after another childhood experience, the majority of which their dad and I didn't know happened in the first place. Many of their experiences turn on racial incidents that they had protected us from. As I listen to their stories, I am also surprised and warmed to see in such clear detail the level of support they bring to one another, just by being siblings— and even when they are fighting like cats and dogs. I know that their differing interests and temperaments, which have led them in different directions since childhood, have grown more pronounced as they have moved into adulthood. But I can also see the many sturdy bridges they have built, which allow them to connect to one another and their shared membership in our family. These bridges appear to be highly traveled pathways that the children keep in good repair and frequently polish and paint. I think of our family as typical of the majority of transracial families. If the lives my children have chosen as grownups offer any message, it is that being close to one's siblings is a shared and important value among them. If it is possible for parents to provide transracially adopted children of color with siblings of color, we'd greatly encourage you to do so.

Should siblings match?

Society tends to view multiracial families as marginal. In fact, multiracial families live out a unique leadership role.

Pros and cons

Families formed by transracial adoption do not and cannot genetically match. Sometimes families struggle with the question of whether they should adopt the same race child a second time so the children will "share" their experience in the family, both being African American or Chinese or whatever. As two parents whose children are all of different race, we have seen the evidence that it is valuable to children to share the experience of difference and bias because they can offer one another support from a knowing place. We have also seen that our children of all different races find more in common with one another than different. Sometimes children can interpret parents adopting a "matched set" of children as an unspoken belief that biology is more important than commitment to family, that adoptive families are second best and their parents were trying to make up for the loss of genetic connection by matching the kids by race. This can be dangerous if the children interpret their family to be second best with the ideal being the family formed by birth.

Celebrating strengths

Strength can only come from accepting our family as different and celebrating the strength of those differences. The challenge of connecting children to their birth cultures is larger when more than one culture is involved. If children share the same birth culture, parents are not stretched as far as when they must built bridges to two or more distinct racial groups.

Building on the diversity inherent within the family by adopting siblings of different birth cultures can validate the foundation of our family structure. A family that believes it belongs together even though no one matches is demonstrated by not making a deliberate effort to adopt children based on their specific race alone. Siblings in such families attach to one another and have opportunities to practice living empathetically and compassionately with one another because of their shared experiences within the family. This becomes a family model in which each person holds his own unique space and makes his own important contributions to the family circle with a minimum of competition. Multiracial families, by their very ability to live harmoniously under one roof facing the day-to-day challenges of family life, demonstrate the skills society needs to heal racial and ethnic strife in our society. In this sense, we are pioneers who have tremendous leadership skills to contribute to the growth of our civilization.

White siblings in transracial families

"Look, here's the reality," Seth said recently. He grew up as the only white child in our (Gail's) family with three siblings of color. "Overall, it was a positive. We had great times and what I've realized about growing up in our family is that because we were all so different from each other, I was constantly encouraged to go with my strengths. I just got my education earlier than other kids do. I learned how to be more sensitive to and less threatened by differences than most people I know. I can be non-judgmental and that means I can get along with more people. My whole world is better because of that. When you're a kid, you want to be part of everything and I always felt different. I thought everyone expected me to be the 'All American' boy. On the outside you're white and all of a sudden, you're not. What you look like doesn't match what's inside. I worried if the white kids would still like me when they found out I was different but I also knew my friends had to be open to difference. Anyone who thinks one race is worth more than another one could never be my friend. It was easier to trust my black friends. I felt like I had more in common with them. What I think parents should do is just talk about it. Let your white kids know

*that people don't expect you to be a certain thing. Who you are is okay.
Help them build a strategy to know how to introduce themselves
instead of winging it all the time. Let them know they don't have to
carry a flag for the home team or screen people based on their approval
of the family model. What kids like me need is to know the family
understands how it is for them. Anyway, it's a different deal now. It's
getting a lot easier to be different than it was 25 years ago. It's not so
rare anymore."*

Many parents who already have white children (either by birth or adoption) wonder if it is fair to bring children of color into the family. Will it create too great a burden? Seth's story points out the incredible gift having siblings of color can be for children who might not otherwise have experience with the struggles against bias that can make them strong and proud.

White siblings of children of color face unique challenges that are not often addressed. Few white people in the world understand the challenges of racism more directly than children who see their brothers and sisters being targeted and who face bias themselves but not when they're on their own, nor when people they meet don't know about their family. As siblings, they need support for their unique experiences. Imagine that you are a white child with a sister who is Latina and a brother who is black. How do you think you might feel in each of the following situations?

1. Your brother is well coordinated and has always been good at sports, while you have always been clumsy and less agile. When it comes to picking teams he's always a first choice and you're often the last

2. You are sitting at a table in the school cafeteria with a group of white kids when someone makes a racist joke.

3. You are thrilled when you are invited to the big party of the year at your school. When you get home you find out your brother and sister are not When the family talks about it around the dinner table you all acknowledge that it is probably because they are of color and you are white.

4. Your sister, who is not as good a student as you are and who has a lower grade point average than you do, is admitted to the college you were hoping for; her acceptance is in part because of their commitment to diversity in the student body.

5. You are not as good a student as your sister. Your grade point average is lower than hers. A local community group gives you a scholarship but not your sister, even though you both applied.

When there is conflict between a person's hopes for himself and the world's responses to his siblings, white siblings of children of color are likely to come face to face with loyalty struggles. Are they required to spend their lives up on a soapbox, protecting and supporting their siblings? If they don't speak up every single time a racial issue arises, are they being disloyal to their family? If they consciously use the white privilege that society grants them, are they betraying their brothers and sisters?

Finding the pieces to the loyalty puzzle is a challenging activity throughout life, one which is never 100% complete. Children do not choose their family structure, nor do they necessarily understand or hold their parents' philosophical attitudes. They may feel a myriad of emotions when challenged by racism, ranging from confusion, surprise, rage or depression to a developing desire to act as an agent of change.

How can you help?

1. Help your white child understand that it is very natural to feel a mixture of emotions toward siblings, both to like them a lot and to resent them a lot. Help them to understand that because our families involve extra issues relating to race, it is likely that the normal mix of feelings about siblings will reflect the issues of race and ethnicity.

2. Clarify the distinction between feelings and actions. It's useful for your white children to be able to name their feelings and to voice politically incorrect wishes like, "Why don't you get rid of them?" but it's not okay for them to hurt their siblings by participating in racist activities. Our task as parents is to help them voice their anger and to help them see that these restrictions are as the same as those their siblings face regularly because of our society's racism.

3. Let your child know that you understand she may be having negative feelings. Use direct and sympathetic phrases to keep the conversational door open. "I can see how rough this situation is for you," or "It must be very hard for you, having to deal with this issue when your other white friends don't have to," or "Please let me know how you feel, because I care about your feelings."

4. Give your child the opportunity to become an ally of people of color in the fight against racism and bias. This can be a powerful and proud place for them to explore their ability to stand up for what they believe in and who they see themselves to be as members of a multiracial family.

How parents can help siblings connect

"Demanding good feelings between sibs leads to bad feelings; acknowledging bad feelings between sibs leads to good feelings."
—Adele Faber and Elaine Mazlich

- Be realistic in your expectations about sibling relationships. Did you always get along with your brother? Did you willingly share friends with your close-in-age sister? It is not uncommon for siblings to be close as very young children, become more distant from or unpleasantly competitive with one another as they grow, and then rediscover one another as adults.

- Treat each child as the individual he or she is. Don't base parenting decisions on making all things equal. Just as no two adoptions are alike, and no two sets of birth parents and their circumstances are alike, no two children are alike and so can't be expected to feel the same way about adoptions issues in their lives. Some kids wonder, some don't. Some kids enjoy extended family relationships with open adoptions and some don't. Some adopted people search and some don't. What children need more than "fairness" is to know that, as their parent, you are "on their side," ready to help them meet their needs—whatever those may be.

- Never compare your kids in either positive or negative ways. This advice is more challenging than it sounds.

- Do all that you can to nurture a sense of shared family culture. Carefully cultivating and highlighting religious and holiday traditions, the family's shared mealtime and bedtime rituals, favorite foods and family recipes, books and songs and games and repeated visits to favorite places all contribute to each child's sense of "us" as a family unit.

- Instead of trying to love them equally, show kids how they are loved as unique individuals. Instead of giving them equal time, allocate time with them according to the needs of the situation and the child. Giving children individual time with Mommy or Daddy minimizes rivalry because the needs of each child are getting met.

- Watch for and support ways in which children, separated by age or of opposite genders, discover things they enjoy in common. When you discover things shared by your children that are not things you yourself enjoy, use them to contribute to their sense of conspiratorial generation vs. generation intimacy.

- Avoid artificial twinning. Two genetically-dissimilar kids who will nearly always be parented as a pair are set up to be compared by peers and teachers and coaches. This sets those siblings up for competition and greater struggles in finding their own sense of self

- Acknowledge your child's negative feelings with words that name the feelings, but help them express their wishes. Offer suggestions for creative activities to help them act out their feelings. Don't allow siblings to hurt each other or themselves physically. Teach children ways to get rid of angry feelings by expressing them with words.

"You are sooooooo special." One-Child Families (and some-times others!)

I better understand now why I sometimes take myself too seriously, why I don't always laugh when the joke's on me, why it's important for me to be recognized as special, why I attach myself so strongly to a few people and how losing them plays into my only-child fears of abandonment.

—Darrell Sifford

Single child transracial adoptive families are more common than ever before. Many parents are concerned that they may be cheating their child of a "real" family experience or they feel guilty when their circumstances do not allow them to consider adopting a sibling. Facing the challenges of society's concept that the "ideal" family is a multi-child, monoracial, two-parent, two-gender, genetically-linked group is big stuff. Many of the issues that commonly confront only children are similar to issues that are common in adoptive families in general; the combination of factors may create a cumulative double-whammy effect.

Will my child be spoiled rotten?

Being able to devote your undivided attention and all of your resources to your child is a positive condition that parents of multi-child families sometimes envy. When there is only one irresistible child to be doted on, the child's" every task may seem remarkable. The absence of competition for time, consideration, or intimacy can free kids to enjoy the world with less worry about finding a place in it. The little prince or princess possesses a secure place front and center, releasing them to progress to interesting things beyond the self. For the child of color who is not always given first place in the world at large, this attention can counteract the potentially internalized "less-than" messages they receive from the outside.

On the other hand, receiving too much attention can create a demanding little one who is over-dependent on parents. Only children can be less flexible and uncertain about how to negotiate relationships with peers because they haven't had to practice at home. If a child of color with white parents acts like she is better than others and deserves exceptions from rules, then potential problems are increased with people in her birth community may feel that she is acting "uppity" or "too white."

He thinks he's grown up

In only-child families, parents sometimes become social peers at home. This can place pressure on the child to conform and please the parents in order to fit in and garner approval. Young children unconsciously copy their parents and unknowingly develop similar beliefs and behaviors. They want to emulate and please. This common desire is greatly amplified in families with one child, creating a circular pattern in which the child's emulation pleases the parent, which in turn encourages the child to devote more attention to emulation, which pleases the parent, which encourages the child... This pattern of reinforcing similarity is in conflict with the transracially adopted child's need to develop a racial identity that is different from his parents.

Single parents must be especially careful not to encourage their child to think of himself as a grownup and assume responsibility for taking care of his parent in inappropriate ways. He may also grow possessive of his relationship with the parent, objecting to the parent's relationships with other adults.

"Super Kid" pressure

Growing up under the microscope with parent(s) who feel they have just one chance to create a state-of-the-art child may place unattainable expectations on the child. Parental concern and involvement must be balanced with space for the child to make mistakes and to individuate from her parent. Children of color with white parents may feel additional pressure to excel so as to be a credit to the family as well as to others of their race and ethnic background.

What can you do?

A transracially adopted child who must negotiate intensified feelings about similarities and differences needs parents who can be extremely realistic about their child, without continually viewing him as too "special." Though nurture affects development, your child is entitled to feel good about following a pattern of growth influenced by nature. A child who feels terminally special may be shocked to discover, over there in the "real" world, that she is not as special or as smart as you said that she was. And if being special is what made her important in the family, this can feel like an overwhelming loss.

- Encourage your child to see that differences between you are a source of richness.
- Avoid criticizing your child for being different from you and don't over praise similarities.
- Maintain an active social circle so that your child knows that he is not your major companion or confidante.

- Take every opportunity to say, "Good for you; you did it your way. I don't know how you thought of that."
- Encourage cooperation with others and playing by the group's rules. Don't try to create exceptions or special treatment for your child or make excuses if your child has difficulty following the rules.
- After an only child has misbehaved, it's good to allow for a cooling-off period. Provide a place where the child can process the interaction without being banished from the adult. You might say, "Sit down next to me and think about how you will handle this situation differently next time."
- Only children are often sensitive about being alone. Punishments utilizing a time-out or exclusion are often best avoided.

Families that Grow through Birth plus Adoption

"There is no such thing as 'natural.' A natural dancer has to practice hard. A natural brother has to be there all the time, and a natural fool has to work at it."

—Joe Lewis

Sisters

My parents (Beth's) loved to tell the story. They described to my sister and me the two ways children could come into the family: through birth and through adoption. In the end, it was me, not Barbara, who burst into tears...the adoption scenario had sounded so good! It wasn't long before we all realized that it wasn't so simple.

I think I was about eight years old the first time someone told me that there must be something wrong with my sister because she was adopted. I remember being upset. I remember getting angry. I would never be that kid's friend again! ... I also remember secretly wondering whether or not that kid was right.

Barbara had gotten into my stuff again. She made me sooooo mad. I was so unfair sometimes, having a seven-year-old sister. There she was with my broken doll; she said it was a stupid doll anyway. I had never been so angry with her. I blurted, "You're not my real sister anyway. You don't even belong in this family!" I still feel guilty when I remember that I said that, an eleven-year-old's design for vengeance. The most painful part of that memory is that I was tearing at the fabric of my *family, which ultimately left me terribly insecure. I spent a lot of my life feeling the need to defend my sister against the questions and judgments of the uneducated. Adoption was a normal and comfortable part of our family vocabulary. Two out of our three cousins were also adopted. The problem was that I never allowed myself to ask or voice the secret questions and doubts that I couldn't help but learn from society.*

Society has strong expectations for family matching. I have always looked like a carbon copy of my father. My parents loved to play games. As I grew up, I found that I shared that trait, too; I could remember the cards that had already been played, that sort of thing. Just like our parents. Barbara doesn't play games anymore; it was much harder for her to fit into that particular family pattern. On the other hand, she can hear a tune once and sit right down to play it. I struggled for years with piano lessons. Though I still try I am barely able to bang out simple children's songs. Genetics!

When I hear parents say that it makes no difference to have one child adopted and another not, I cringe. We adoptive families are in a minority. There is strength in that fact, but only if we can stand up and be honest about that which makes us different. Blended families can work, but like any family that works, it takes honesty about who we are and who we are not. This I know: when our parents tried to mold us into sameness that might have worked in other families, we felt uncertain and insecure about our ability to fit. It was when our parents acknowledged the truth of our differences and singularities that Barbara and I were able to bask in the confidence that comes from having a family that supported each of us, both of us, one hundred percent.

It was only much later in life that I was able to face my fears and come away with the answer: we were different and unconnected in ways that other siblings were not. We can be the best of friends and the worst of enemies. We have been there for each other and we have let each other down. We are similar in certain ways and could not be more different in others. My sister and I are still just what we have always been—sisters.

Strategies

It is even more important in families where children come to the family through birth and adoption to acknowledge that these paths are different in important ways. Loving our children is not about treating them equally or the same, it is about loving them for who they are and supporting them according to their unique needs.

When children born to and adopted into the family are different races, the same issues become visible to them and the outside world—the negative messages come earlier and faster. The same strategies that apply to any siblings apply to these siblings but the truth and differences we must acknowledge are often scarier for the parents who don't want to communicate stronger or clearer love for the children they gave birth to.

The facts are the facts. Giving birth to a child, being genetically connected, is powerful. Teach your children to speak about genetics, to value nature along with nurture or risk the outcome of their own burden in trying to figure it out on their own. Telling adopted children that we wish we had been able to carry them in our wombs so we could experience that kind of intimacy with them reminds them of how much we love them not how little. Wishing we had a better understanding of them because we were more like them allows them to experience us as parents who put their needs over our comfort, a powerful message of support and love.

Spend time with each "kind" of child, acknowledging the guilt and fears of the children you have birthed, acknowledging the frustration and sense of loss of the children you have not. Those who are parenting from both perspectives may be most able to help their children believe how uniquely they are loved and supported. You can remind your children that you do know better, they are not the only "kind" of child you have, and yet they are still loved, still 100% members of the family. The possibilities for unequivocal, unconditional love are profound and all the parenting experts agree—that's good for kids!

International Adoptive Families

All of us who are adopted come to our families with histories behind us. That isn't good or bad; it just is. For the most part, adopted people know that they are loved and cherished by their families. They feel that they are exactly where they belong. And yet, many unanswered questions remain deep inside, and need to be resolved.

—Susan Soon Keum Cox

I'm a regular American kid

Each child is an individual who, due to her age, temperament, past experiences, and current circumstances, will negotiate in her own way the challenges inherent in the disruption of one life and integration of another. But despite these variables, acclimatization to this new personal universe is likely to echo a common pattern; first, a submissive honeymoon period, then a time of testing and rage, and eventually, integration. It is still rare for internationally born children to be brought home within the first weeks of their birth. This means that the children, no matter how well cared for— in an orphanage, in their birth family or by a foster family—are making a transition that relates not only to their attachment to care givers but is also cultural in nature.

This look at common stages of adjustment for internationally-adopted children has been adapted from the work of Jean Nelson-Erichsen and Heino R. Erichsen from their book *How to Adopt Internationally* (Fort Worth, Texas, Mesa House Publishing, 1997.)

1. **Don't make waves**: This child is subdued, compliant and contented or responsible but noticeably well-behaved. Parents may notice a "far away look" or behavior that seems "shell-shocked," depressed, withdrawn or grieving. The culture shock is intense.

2. **Good morning, America**: The child is curious, perhaps fascinated. She is "waking up" to the new world and begins to make connections. Everything is different. "What is the place?" she's trying to ask herself. "Who are these people? What is this food? Is there enough for me? Will I be safe here? Can I trust them? Is this too good to be true?"

3. **When will you give me away**? The child begins to recognize that the world's expectations of her are in conflict with her old culture. She is frightened, defensive, and defiant. Her behavior seems determined to cause rejection. This period is marked by the child's attempt to deal with a critical concern: "Nobody is ever going to keep me. I may as well be as bad as I can so that these new parents just give me away and get it over with." In older children, breaking rules, stealing food or money, bullying other children, testing and acting out are common indicators of emotional upheaval. Parents sometimes describe this stage in its extreme forms as a "trial by fire."

4. **It's not so bad; Guess I'll stay**. The child begins to acquire the skills necessary for coping with the new environment. With the acquisitions of these skills comes an increasing sense of being comfortable. The learning curve has progressed to the degree that he can understand the cues for what things mean and how people are likely to respond. Attachment to new parents has become safe.

5. **All-American me**. Kids in this stage don't want to talk about their pasts; they say that they are regular American kids. The child has taken on all the surface qualities of a "normal" American kid born in the U.S. He is likely to be unwilling to talk about his first culture during this stage, or may verbally reject it. Resentment and anger may be focused on birth

parents and/or birth country as a means to attach and fit into the new environment.

6. **I am all I am**. The child has found a way to balance who they were and who they are. Susan Soon Keum Cox, herself adopted from Korea, says, "Those of use who believe in the merits of adoption—who care about the future for the thousands of children who, were it not for an adoptive family, would never know family at all—must pledge our solidarity to making adoption more encompassing, more 'real.' By recognizing the additional challenges and opportunities of helping internationally-adopted people retain both their personal memories and their cultural familiarity, we can help them cherish the fullness of their identity and place in the world."

Strategies for connection
Bilingual advantages

Paul Robeson spoke twenty-five languages as a way to absorb the many cultures to which he was determined to belong. He consumed a language for the cultural essence it contained and became loyal to all the groups whose song he sang.

Adoptive parents often wonder whether it is important for their children to become fluent in the language of their culture of origin if they speak English as their first language.

There are many benefits to being able to communicate directly in the language of one's birth culture. The real question for adoptive parents is one of priority. Though many agree that bilingual facility "would be great," oftentimes we find that the development of a second language is viewed as an elective, like piano lessons, requiring special effort and practice, demanding strong commitment from parents, who must arrange for instruction and not only create but insist upon opportunities to practice.

In transracial or transethnic adoption, bilingualism should not be an afterthought. Comfort in the language of one's birth heritage is an extremely powerful tool that should not be easily dismissed or skipped over because of "higher" priorities. Although it is possible to feel truly at home in the Latino or Chinese communities, for example, without the ability read and speak Spanish, Mandarin or Cantonese, being fluent in the language is a definite plus that is valued as a "mark" of membership. For children who are already less confident about their membership in the group, it can create a much greater sense of belonging. The acceptance by other members of the culture will increase in direct proportion to your child's fluency. Furthering the ability to read and speak another language can deeply contribute to an adopted child's understanding of his roots.

For Latinos in particular, language ability holds even greater importance because more than for any other immigrant group, the tendency of Latinos has been to retain the Spanish language. All of us have our greatest potential for learning language while we are youngest and are already learning one language between the ages of 0 and 5. Exposure to a second or third enhances our ability to hear and learn the subtle differences and nuances throughout the rest of our lives. Imagining that we will eventually get to it is naïve. The time is now. Do it.

Being bilingual enhances thinking skills

In addition to deepening their cultural ties, there are other benefits in mastering two languages. Sandra Ben-Zeev, an Israeli researcher, has studied the effects of bilingualism in children. Using both Spanish-speaking and Hebrew-speaking children as her subjects, she suggests that children fluent in two languages have greater cognitive flexibility than children who are monolingual. They also tend to understand language as systems enabling different perspectives. She suggests that bilingual children:

- Analyze language more intensely than do monolinguals.
- Are capable at an earlier age of separating the meaning of a word from its sound.
- Are better able to play with words
- Excel at substituting symbols, revealing an increased ability to grasp broad concepts without being dependent on individual words to convey all meaning.
- Understand better that the structure of a language is different from the meaning of individual words.
- Are better able to classify objects and then to re-sort them using different criteria.
- Have a greater tendency to elaborate without being asked.
- Tend to approach some tasks with a stronger analytic strategy.
- Are better able to use verbal hints as cues to successful task completion.
- Exhibit unusual attention to details in restructuring exercises.
- Demonstrate greater ability to note details that allow a better integration of a narrative or picture sequence.
- Demonstrate greater social sensitivity.

> *I (Beth) came upon Sofia one afternoon crying in her room. She had been browsing through her baby book, looking at pictures of herself, her four siblings in Guatemala, her birth mother. When she was able to speak she showed me the letter she had written. "I love you all. I had planned to tell you myself but I realize now that I can't. I am sorry I can't speak Spanish."*

For children who are able to be in contact with their birth culture or birth families being able to speak the language will add greatly to their sense of confidence and ability to communicate. Developing the ability to make sense of what one sees while enabling a child to express himself and create connections, bilingualism should be seen as a great gift for our children in particular

Visit to a birth country

What makes you feel most in touch with being an American? Is it reciting the Pledge of Allegiance? Voting? Enjoying the entitlements of the American way of life? Fighting for our country in times of war? Traveling to another country and noticing your difference from its people, while noting as well what is familiar?

Webster's Dictionary defines nationalism as "a devotion to one's nation; patriotism; the doctrine that national interests are more important than international considerations." After a child moves from his homeland to the United States and a new life as a full member of his adoptive family, she often becomes naturalized as an American citizen. We hope your children will develop the ability to feel allegiance and pride in being American. But we must also remember that it is important that the child adopted internationally continue to feel pride and membership in his birth culture. Can a person feel patriotic toward two countries at once? We can look to children of parents from two countries and say yes—but not without work on the part of their parents in providing access to both.

Tourist identity or kinship?

It would be a massive oversimplification if we were to reduce the issues of dual heritage to a question of the differences between patriotic feelings and feeling oneself to be a true member of a culture. There is a difference between feeling like a tourist and knowing that you really fit in. Tourists experience other cultures from the vantage point of the outsider; they are readily able to compare the land and people they are visiting with their home culture. In contrast, people who feel themselves to be part of another culture can imagine living within it forever; there is no need for comparative analysis— what is, just is—naturally. What is, is sufficient—naturally. What is can be fulfilling. Internationally adopted children who come to the United States as infants or very young children are unlikely to ever feel fully a part of their country of origin. Their Western or American upbringing will not be erased by return trips or education. What they can feel is a strong sense of heritage and connection through the legacy of their birthright, if given the opportunity to explore their membership.

Imagine your little girl was born in Guatemala. You believe that it is important for her to feel connected to her homeland, so you have gone to great effort to add books, music, and art of Guatemala to the family collections. Your daughter even has a Guatemalan flag in her room and a doll in authentic dress with a matching costume for herself. One night a week, you try your best to prepare a Guatemalan supper; you count yourselves as truly lucky to have the opportunity to regularly attend an international adoption support group especially for families who have adopted Guatemalan children. which allows her to have friends who also were born in her home country. You are planning a family vacation to Guatemala and the whole family is getting ready by studying Spanish and reading aloud from a wonderful assortment of travel books. Your daughter is excited but also anxious about the upcoming trip. She wonders aloud how it will feel to be in a place where everyone looks like her. What if she doesn't fit in?

For your child to feel like an insider on your trip to Guatemala she would need to feel confident that she could understand the meanings of people's actions and language and be able to behave according to the rules of the culture. This "inside knowledge" could be possible if she knew enough about the language, behavior, manners, attitude and history of the culture. Being an insider really doesn't demand that she feel loyalty to the country or not. It does not matter that she is just visiting and will anticipate and welcome her return to the United States. What matters is that she feels a sense of nonjudgmental kinship with the people living in the culture, just like the kinship that relatives do feel for one another.

Planning for your trip.

If you are fortunate enough to be able to consider a trip to your child's country of birth with them or as a family—prepare to prepare. There are going to be a range of intense feelings, some extremely positive and some tremendously complex and challenging, triggered by the trip. Feelings of all kinds help children to learn and grow. Anticipating what is coming is the best offense. Here are some common responses from various members of adoptive families. Everyone will benefit if every member of the family can understand in advance the wide range of feelings that are a normal part of this important experience

The adopted child's view

- "If I go, do I have to stay?"

- "Everyone looks like me! I'm not from Mars! I look really good. I love it; I love it; I love it!"

- "Can't we help my birth family and give them some money? They don't have anything. They don't even have a TV and we have three at home. How come we have so much and they have so little?"

- "I look the same as people here, but I am so different. I don't want to stay here. I don't like it because people expect me to know things I don't know."

- "I thought the kids in orphanages got adopted. It makes me feel bad to know that some kids never do."

- "Hey, I don't want to go sightseeing anymore. I want to go to the game room in the hotel."

- "It makes me mad that people expect me to speak the language here. Why can't they tell that I'm an American?"

- "I'm so glad that I got to visit my birth country. It's so perfect here and now I know where I come from and why I am the way I am."

- "If I had grown up here, I would have been me but different. I think it would have been hard in certain ways because nothing what I'm used to. It's kind of weird, but I'm glad I am who I am."

The view of Siblings who were not born in the country

- "If we go, will my brother have to say there?"
- "Hey this place is a neat place. Where's the McDonalds?"
- "How come she gets all the attention? I should have stayed home. Nobody here like me."
- "Why does it smell so funny here? Why is the bathroom so weird?"
- "My sister is really lucky, to come from such a beautiful place."
- "My brother is really lucky to be adopted and get to be an American."
- "I wish I had a birth country besides America.

Adoptive parents' viewpoint

- "How will it change our family if we go?"
- "Will we be viewed as our child's parents or will our family be challenged?"
- "Is it better to go with a group of other families, or should we go by ourselves?"
- "Is it better to go with our child or send her with a group of other adopted children on a homeland tour?"
- "When should we do this? What age would be best for our child?"
- "Can we afford to go?"
- "I'm really glad we made this trip. It seems so important to my child."

- "I'm scared. What if she wants to stay here forever?"

- "Her birth parents are so sweet. I wish we could communicate with them better."

- "I wish we had done a better job of learning about this culture. If it's the last thing I do, I'm going to learn more."

- "The food is really good. I hope we can recreate it at home."

- "Thank goodness we worked so hard to prepare. It feels really comfortable to be here and to see our son so thrilled."

If your child's only education about her birth culture is through guide books and history texts, she will probably be unable to create connections with the people of that culture because they will be too unfamiliar, too different from her experience. She is also likely to fear their rejection because she doesn't know how to fit in. She needs the chance to learn about the living culture from someone who is already part of it.

Countering negative cultural images

Internationally adopted children will encounter other Americans' negative images of their birth country. Children adopted from a county which has waged a war with American troops, such as Vietnam or Korea, may be confronted with hostility felt by those who have suffered trauma during their military experience or those who have lost loved ones in the war. Children coming from Eastern European countries such as Romania and Russia will be challenged to explain the negative TV and newspaper stories which have depicted dramatic accounts of birth parents who were said to have sold their children in exchange for TV sets or fat wads of cash. Children with origins in Latin America may fear they were kidnapped from their unsophisticated birth parents by wily baby snatchers seeking to make fortunes from American adoptive parents who paid big bucks for babies. In light of these challenges, adoptive parents must counter the negative pictures others will repeatedly paint.

As with all transcultural adoption issues, our best advice is to develop significant relationships with high-functioning people who are proud to be part of your child's culture of origin. All the secondary resources in the world cannot counter negative stereotypes as effectively as can one flesh-and-blood friend who is proud to be Vietnamese or Korean or Romanian or Russian or Mexican or Guatemalan.

How important are ethnic vs. racial and cultural connections?

> *As we (Beth and her husband) sat in the classes in preparation for adopting our first child, we were clear that we would adopt from some country in Latin America. Imagine our dismay when we heard the advice that we would need to connect to the community of our child's birth culture. Surely they didn't mean that our child would not feel especially connected to our closest friend, Jesús, a Chicano, or our neighbors from Cuba. We had envisioned these people as primary mentors for us and our child in the journey of connection and cultural exploration. Had we gotten it all wrong?*

With all the best intentions, professionals sometimes seem to communicate that internationally adopted children need to find connection and heritage in an exclusively country-specific (and sometimes even region-specific) way. While it is true that many members of the Cantonese community do not fully identify with those who speak Mandarin, there is also a larger understanding of being Chinese as well as the even broader experience of being Asian. White parents in particular must be extraordinarily careful not to limit the connections their child can pursue because of decisions about which group or what community they want their child to connect to.

Sometimes there is no real Guatemalan community in a particular area but the Latino community (primarily made up of Mexicans for example) may be strong and proud. If parents talk with their children in ways that specify their heritage in an exclusive way, the child often feels more alone than necessary. We also have to be really honest—and this is a hard issue—by asking ourselves whether it could be that we are more comfortable with the seemingly exotic or distant idea of our child's country than we are with a local community we don't understand or may have negative biases about. Is your desire to connect your child to their birth country motivated in part by fear of the need to connect with local people? You may have prejudiced thoughts about people you fear may judge or reject you. It is always important to acknowledge how challenging some of this feels and figure out what part of the roadblock we ourselves bring to the table.

Being exposed to those who hold reverence for a people's rich history and respect for its future is the key to creating positive identification. S-T-R-E-T-C-H to develop authentic connections with real people in whatever ways you can.

Single-Parent Transracial Families

If you decided to adopt a child as a single person, you bravely took on the full responsibility for raising your child on your own. You also chose to take on the extra issues of transracial adoption. The single parent transracial family is different from the two-parent family in that there's only one of you calling the shots. Single parents we have worked with have taught us that there are advantages to not having to reach consensus with a partner when facing complex situations. This autonomy can free one to act more quickly and perhaps more decisively. The down side is not having someone who is equally invested in becoming educated about and responsible for your child's issues with whom to share the awesome task of doing your best. But single parent or not, you've got to build a sense of family identity, unity and strength in the face of challenges, express or implied, from those who doubt you're "really" a family.

The most effective way to come to feel like family is to act like family: a parent takes care of and provides for child; a child responds to and is attached to a parent. When you act like a family, others will begin to see you as family.

Why can't I have a daddy (or mommy) like everyone else?

Children of single parents are going to be frustrated some times because they don't have two parents like some of their friends. Even in a time when many kids don't, transracially adopted children are more likely to notice who they are different from than who they are similar to. Difference is in such overabundance in their experience that the frustrations can get mixed up. The girl who is screaming about wanting a Dad may really be frustrated about being the only Chinese member of the family. Parents have to be willing to listen, ask questions and not personalize their child's response as a criticism of themselves to help them sort out their feelings and learn to live with what is.

Single parents sometimes report less scrutiny than do two parent transracial families because the adoption is less obvious. Like same-race adopters, single parents are confronted with the assumption that their child is born to them (and the father or mother was the "other" race the child visibly resembles.) Parents have to walk the balance between showing their child that they are not ashamed or embarrassed about their adoption and acting like it is the only important piece of information about the child or family by always mentioning it publicly.

Feeling guilty for choosing to become a single parent

None of us is ever going to be Super Parent, no matter how hard we try. And one parent alone cannot provide exactly the same environment as the dual efforts a couple can put forth. But we know of no significant research that indicates that it is better or worse to grow up in a single-parent family.

What is clear is that this experience is different. It is possible to build delightfully intimate and enriched relationships between parent and child, while it is also important that roles stay clear, allowing the child to remain a child without slipping into the role of companion to his parent. It seems a waste of time and valuable energy to lament being only a single parent. Instead, that time can be used to create positive activities to strengthen your family. Increased challenges simply create more opportunity to grow. Sometimes having more can be a special gift.

Becoming a single parent when it wasn't the original plan

Sometimes things happen that we didn't plan and can't control. Adopted children are particularly sensitive to loss. If one parent dies or a divorce happens, both the remaining parent and particularly the child can be expected to have a strong reaction to the loss.

In the case of a death

When an adoptive parent dies it is reasonable to expect a child to have a more intense reaction to their loss than would be the case for a child born to the family. Why? Because this loss will tap into the loss of the birth family with which the child is already contending. The left-behind parent is already coping with personal extreme grief, so coping with a child who is in grief overdrive can be really challenging. Your own experience can help you to be more empathetic to your child. You and your child can share your mutual sense of the unfairness of a world that has handed each of you losses that you didn't deserve or expect.

Most parents in this situation find themselves struggling with the guilt and anger that are a part of the normal stages of grief. You may experience guilt because your child is going through yet another loss; anger at God, your partner, or the world for forcing single parenting on you. Single parenting is often a choice you would never have made up front. Finding support for yourself must be a priority or you will not be able to help your child process their feelings, which often look like "naughty behavior" or being the "rock of Gibraltar," way beyond his years.

In the case of a divorce

Divorce is very tricky, because society blames adult parents for their failure and for the ensuing pain that is inflicted on the children. Parents who are willing to give up on one family member (their spouse) must answer to their adopted children, who will need to know why they should believe that their parents will never "divorce" them. The parents are often so angry with one another that it's hard for them to focus on the needs of their children.

Get help and support. Recognize that your child is going to have a strong reaction. Society may suggest that there is no need for the children to stay connected to both parents since they are not their "real" children anyway. Nothing could be further from the truth.

Providing gender and racial role models

While single parents can create wonderful families, it is particularly important in single-parent families that children have significant relationships with other adults who offer them support and involvement. For children of single parents, opposite-gender role models are essential. For children of color with white parents, cultural role models are essential. The challenge for single parents is to develop relationships with adults who can become family friends, available to the child in truly intimate ways. This task often means expanding one's outreach into the community, even when the obligations of work, childcare and family life seem to leave no time for anything beyond the daily necessities. The truth is that, once accomplished, these connections can create more time and space in your life for you and your children to be apart when your needs aren't in sync with each other. Reminding yourself of this may help when the task feels daunting.

The ways and means are as individual as the personalities involved. What matters most is first to make the commitment to the process of making new friends or deepening relationships with old ones; then, staying committed to making time, both family time and adult time, to spend with these important people. Between your child's birth and her eighteenth birthday you only have 6,570 days (and you have already spent some portion of them)! There is not a day to waste. Your child needs these role models as much as he needs air and water—and so do you!

Gay and Lesbian Families

In the general world of adoption, it is not unusual for agencies, facilitators, or attorneys who accept gay and lesbian prospective parents to suggest transracial or special needs adoption as their best opportunities to become parents. This practice of pairing "hard to match" parents with "hard to place" children has both pluses and minuses. On the positive side, adults who live with cultural homophobia are likely to possess increased sensitivities, coping skills and strategies that will help them understand and support children of color in facing racism. On the negative side, transracial adoption and raising children with same-sex parents are each complex issues and challenging by themselves. Not everyone should take on both

Adoptions by gay or lesbian parents involve many issues—both legal and emotional—that otherwise do not come up in the adoption process. Many people do not approve of gay or lesbian parents. Adoptive parents—and their children—are likely to experience some form of prejudice or bias because of their non-traditional relationship. These will be added to the experiences of racial bias that will confront your child as a person of color. Often, people who have experienced prejudice of one kind are better prepared to handle it in another form.

Children who have grown up with gay and lesbian parents have told us that they felt their parents were more accepting and unbiased about racial issues, having already faced so much prejudice themselves. Transracially adopted children are often able to understand the connections between all kinds of differences which can feel like a support for their own experience in the world. When California voted on its version of the so-called "defense of marriage" law, one ten-year-old transracially adopted child of heterosexual parents wrote the following.

> *Life would be boring if everyone was the same. For instance, if the only thing in the world that we could eat was pizza we would get sick of it in about a week. Everybody in the world is special and if you are Gay or Lesbian you are even more special because you are different than the majority of people. Being different is special. If you are adopted and look different than your parents you are different and that is special like being Gay or Lesbian. So if you voted yes on Prop 22[sic], take a moment to think it over again and maybe next election you can vote NO!*

Multiple Issues

Adopted children of color with single-sex white parents have as many opportunities to feel different as anyone could wish for. The special challenges facing white parents to provide significant gender and heterosexual role models as well as racial role models are of course present in gay and lesbian families. The need to prepare children to deal with homophobia as well as racism adds an extra layer of complexity to everyday family life.

Adoptive parents who want to keep their homosexuality confidential cannot fairly ask their kids to keep secrets. Secrets have been show historically to be lethal in adoption. Children equate secret information with "bad" and if the information is about their family status or their adoption they will internalize it as bad. If adoptive parents are comfortable acknowledging their lives publicly, their children will almost certainly feel themselves to be in the spotlight at times when they would prefer to be just like all other kids. Having gay or lesbian parents is going to create one more reason kids will not always want to acknowledge or bring their parents along because for them it is one more way of being different that will be felt at times as embarrassing or a liability.

As with all complicated parenting situations, it is important to pay attention to the children's needs and priorities, most especially at the times when those needs are different from their parents' needs. Your child's frustration with you does not mean that they do not love you or derive the benefits of having you for their parent. It means that they are frustrated with the struggles and skills they are trying to master to feel good about themselves and find their own comfortable identity.

Religious Choices and Beliefs

The Role of the Church and Other Religious Communities for People of Color
Allies and instigators of society's racial struggles

Organized religion has played a significant and often dominant role in the cultural survival of many communities of color. The Catholic church has been very politically and culturally important in both Latino and many Asian cultures, both in the US and abroad. The African American churches have been major leaders in the US civil rights movement as well as sacrosanct gathering and replenishment resources for black Americans facing the struggles of life in our land. The Black Muslim movement has been significant in addressing the needs of African Americans through the Million-Man March and its focus on afrocentric thinking. The Jewish community played a significant role as allies to the civil rights leaders and movement throughout the last century.

Whether you as a family subscribe to the beliefs of any of these religious groups or fundamentally oppose them will certainly dictate whether and where you and your children participate in a spiritual community. But whatever those beliefs dictate, it is important for all transracial parents to recognize the importance of the spiritual and religious community in the lives of people of color and to teach their children to understand that it represents a significant cultural support that they need to understand to get a full feel for their cultural legacy and heritage.

Teaching tolerance: Conflicts involving religious groups

We cannot ignore the reality that along with a supportive and cooperative role, religious groups also have developed certain conflicts with other religious communities. Louis Farrakhan has made anti-Semitic statements. The Baptist church has asked its members to boycott Disney because of their policy on hiring gay and lesbian people. The list goes on. These conflicts set up inherent uncertainties for children who have been transracially adopted. How can they feel safe in their religious community when they are members of both the "insider" group and the targeted "outsider" community?

Our families are not going to change the way of the world, at least not overnight. What parents must do is talk with children about these internal conflicts and inconsistencies. Standing up against intolerance within your own religious community is essential if you want your child to have any sense of connection or investment in your family's religious beliefs. Expressing your own sense of sorrow and discontent with the views of intolerance will allow your child to feel freer to express theirs as well. Acknowledging their struggle within the community in which you feel totally at home is painful, but acknowledging the truth and the difference of your child's experience is the most important piece of support you can offer them.

Choosing where to worship

Because Christianity has pervaded many of the world's cultures and finds expression among many ethnic groups in America, children adopted from Asian, Latino, and African American heritages are likely to find opportunities to practice Christianity within a church setting in which they are not in the racial or ethnic minority if the family's religious connections are flexible enough to allow them to change congregations or even denominations. This is not always the case for families who are already deeply invested in a religious community or a religious belief. The luxury of choosing a religious congregation based on the racial or ethnic make-up of the congregation is usually only available to those who are part of a mainstream denomination or who are already members of churches which have congregations that serve populations of color.

If your religious beliefs make participation in only one particular denomination or congregation a must, then you will probably feel the need to include your child in that choice since it is one of the aspects of full membership in your family. If your beliefs are more flexible or unexplored, considering a church with great diversity or one where your child will be in the majority is a wonderful option.

Jewish Families

When you meet a stranger, does your private radar tell you if he or she is Jewish? Do you imagine others will identify someone who doesn't "look Jewish" as a Jew? Many Jews struggle with the tension between being targeted and receiving privilege. Some fear that assuming Jewish identity will appear as a denial of white privilege. This issue is more complex for Jewish parents of children of color, who face multiple identity issues.

Can an adopted child of color develop a Jewish identity?

> *"When I examine my own Jewish identity, the historical and social 'facts' are preeminent. Every time the UJA or the Holocaust Museum sends me a mailer (always reminding me to 'never forget'); every time I read Hadassah magazine; every time I read Sholem Aleichem or I.B. Singer; every time I think about my grandparents, I'm reminded of what it has meant—the sorrows of history, historical triumphs, ethics, values, music, Israel-Arab relations—to 'be' Jewish in a non-Jewish world. At the same time, when I look at my son I'm reminded that he isn't biologically linked to any of this particular history. It's not that I regret 'getting him into all this.' Rather, I wonder what kind of a 'Jewish identity' is possible for an adopted person born to non-Jewish birth parents, and especially for an adopted person of another ethnic group."*
>
> —Val Lipow

Jews make up two percent of the total population in the United States. Though in fact there are groups of Asian, Latino and black Jews through the world, it is undeniable that in the United States, people of color who are Jews are in a decided minority. Because of this social reality, it has been our experience that Jewish families, more than Christian families, have reason to express deep concern about religious practice and identity for their children of color.

One Jewish family's experience

> *Our (Gail's) children face challenges to their connection to Judaism that we ourselves do not experience. We are a Jewish family. From the beginning, we believed that to deny a Jewish experience to our kids would be a barrier to their sense of full membership in our family. For their sake, we embraced religious activity perhaps even*

*more that we had done before we became parents. We see our children
as irresistible —'to know them is to love them.'*

*But when my children repeated comments made to them by members
of our congregation, it woke me up to all that I can take for granted and
all that my children cannot. 'Your real mother wasn't Jewish,' or 'You must
be glad you weren't aborted.' Other Jews have always questioned if my
children really belong, no matter how my children behave or what they
believe. And others often respond with amazement because my children's
skin colors don't 'match' their Jewish names.*

*Though they could read Torah and adored matzo balls, their
acceptance depended on having Jewish parents. Without us with them,
they felt like outsiders. Now that they are grown, they point out sadly
what we never noticed when they were small: that none of their
teachers looked like them; nor did any of the rabbis; nor did any
religious stories or songs or pictures reflect children like them. They
never got main parts in the Purim plays or Chanukah pageants. In
their minds, the congregation's members could be divided into three
groups: those that were too saccharine to be for real; those who didn't
want them there because they were goyim; and one or two who were
friends. Only now do we recognize the great difference between their
experience and ours; only now do we understand the importance of
acknowledging those differences*

*It I had it to do over, I would never again defend, deny or try to
explain away comments my child perceived as biased even though
people important to me uttered them. Now I would have more realistic
criteria for choosing a synagogue and I would be more conscious of the
conflicts my children felt when they both did and did not feel Jewish.
In case you are thinking, 'Well, thank goodness none of that could
happen to my child because we live in a diverse area and know lots of
other Jewish adopted children of color, my kids grew up with other
adopted Jewish kids, too. We knew lots of adoptive families, and my
children had lots of Jewish adopted peers. Knowing those other kids
helped, but it did not connect them to the larger Jewish community.*

We can't change other people. Jews' history of persecution has made it
predictable that Jews would be at least as suspicious of outsiders and self-
protective as anyone else. And the world inside the synagogue doesn't' much
differ from the world beyond it. Don't assume that the Jewish community will
unconditionally embrace your children just because you do.

That does not mean that they can't feel Jewish. It just means the focus
may be in a different place than in the synagogue. Maybe for adopted children, being Jewish is neither a cultural nor a religious identity so much as it is

a part of family identity. Perhaps for your children, too, it will be within the warmth of the family circle, where they can surrender to the hora and beg for more bagels, sing prayers and never have to endure anyone questioning their belonging, where your sons and daughter will enjoy the pleasure of counting themselves fully as Jews. Our approach is to enjoy what works, acknowledge what doesn't, and don't try to fix what we can't.

Providing for Your Child's Future

All parents need to consider what will happen to their children in the event of their death or incapacity. Single parents (and older parents) have to be even more certain that they fulfill their parental responsibility to make safe and appropriate arrangements for their child because their life expectancy is shorter or they have partner for back up.

Considering these questions in the context of transracial adoption means acknowledging that choosing who would care for our children if we were unable must include considerations about their ability to connect with and understand our child's adoption status and racial community. Many parents ask brothers or sisters or even sometimes their own parents to parent in the event of death, but are they prepared to maintain connections with your child's birth family if you have an open adoption? to support your child's option to search for their birth parents if and when they are ready? to educate themselves about adoption issues that your child is likely to face? to think of themselves as a family of color, invested in creating significant and intimate connections for your child?

Each family's answers will be their own. But don't presume that these decisions can be made as they would have been made had you given birth to all of your children or adopted members of your own race.

When Family Members Have Special Needs and Issues

Adoptive Parents Are Not to Blame

Some children are born with brains that function in unusual ways because of a disorder of brain chemistry. They may develop ADHD, learning disabilities, schizophrenia, etc. No one can control the particular arrangement of genes inherited by each human being. A child's genetic makeup is determined by chance, the combination of genetic messages from birth mothers and birthfather. Tests done at the time of birth cannot yet determine most brain disorders that will show up over time. While nature may be stronger than nurture, remember that good nurturing and a positive environment can make all the difference in the world to a child's development.

The good news is that parents can do a lot to treat problems caused by defective genes in our children. The bad news is that too many parents of children with attention deficit disorder, anxiety or eating disorder, learning disabilities or school phobia or other psychological, emotional or educational disorders feel, inappropriately, that they are at fault—that if only they were better parents their children would be well.

Though most people don't blame parents for a child's physical disease—asthma, cerebral palsy, or diabetes, for example—they often are eager to blame the parents (both birth and adoptive) for other kinds of difficulties: "Well you know, her Mother works;" or "Her parents have always been too permissive;" or "His Dad works all the time and is much too distant." When kids are troubled, teachers, relatives, friends and strangers are happy to give unsolicited advice, whether or not they know what they are talking about.

Because of society's biases about adoption, adoptive parents may be especially vulnerable to the things people say. Their self-evaluation of success as parents may depend on raising healthy children. If their children are troubled, adoptive parents are susceptible to feelings of tremendous guilt, imagining that it's all their fault. Adoptive parents have a tremendous investment in living up to the image of Super Parent—proving the theory of nurture over nature can seem to be the only means of legitimizing our value. But self-blame does not help your child. You can help your child and yourself by accepting a brain disorder as a true illness. Seeking help to address this illness will make a positive difference.

Reframing

Reframing means changing perspectives so as to look at the glass as half-full instead of half-empty. It means examining the same information with a different or positive point of view. It means understanding the challenges that one is facing as a condition or disease rather than something a child or parent has caused. For example, though children and adults with ADD are often easily distracted, rigid and hyperactive, they are also tenacious, riveted on details that interest them, full of energy, and inventive. Thomas Alva Edison, who contributed so much to our way of life, likely had ADD. On the one hand, he got thrown out of school, but on the other, he had the patience to repeat an experiment thousands of times. Because of this tenacity, the light bulb was invented.

Children need to be familiar with the achievements of people with learning difficulties who have used their talents to advantage. Nelson Rockefeller, Anne Bancroft, Woodrow Wilson, Albert Einstein, Bruce Jenner, and Greg Louganis are all examples of people with learning difficulties who did not give up. Your child should know their stories. Equally important, in order to counter the cultural myth that race and ethnicity "cause" or increase learning difficulties, children of color need to be surrounded by examples of the many people of color without learning challenges who have made important and significant contributions to mankind.

Similar examples can be found for mental illness, early childhood experiences of abuse and trauma, and almost any condition or experience our children may be facing. Make it your mission to seek positive role models of people with challenges similar to your child's as well as making sure they see examples of people who look like them who do not face the same challenges so that they will not presume the challenge to be affiliated with their race or ethnicity.

Reframing provides a model for thinking about interaction between coping strategies and people with challenges. For example, children with diabetes can learn to take insulin and modify their nutrition and activity patters to help them prevent risk and lead full lives. Adults provide education to the diabetic about "anticipatory coping" skills and strategies. The diabetic learns to anticipate and prepare for the daily conditions of life with diabetes. Some conditions, such as asthma, change in their manifestations, requiring different degrees of intervention, throughout the life of the individual affected. People with asthma often modify their environment and activities according to their asthmatic reaction.

Strength can be found in how we look at things. Children can be helped to develop a can-do attitude, resisting those who blame racial issues for their challenges.

Getting Kids Tested—What If They Are Labeled for Life?

"Without an understanding of the challenges the adopted child, birth family, and adoptive family can face, schools and other community institutions often, unwittingly, work against the best interests of adoptees and adoptive families.... All of the children who are adopted, or who are foster children, or who are in other complex family situations and working hard to make sense of these complexities, have emotional obstacles to dealing with these challenges and divided loyalties. This extra emotional work—what I would call a normative crisis under challenging circumstances—influences the learning styles of these children."

— Joyce Maguire Pavao (*The Family of Adoption,* Beacon Press, Boston, MA, 1998)

Recognizing that children who are experiencing challenges at school may or *may not* have learning challenges or mental disabilities is critical. Remaining knowledgeable about what is happening for your child at the time questions come up is important. You may find out that a segment on family history and heritage has been the major curriculum during the week a teacher says that he or she is noticing learning issues. You will want to question whether they are simply experiencing a reaction to challenging questions and feelings as a result of the assignment.

On the other hand, being overly cautious about what is really happening for your child is no favor. There are many benefits available to children who qualify for Special Educational Resources. Just understanding their strengths and weaknesses in learning is a benefit to any student. Many of the best private schools are moving in the direction of testing all children as the knowledge base grows about learning styles and the importance of how a child is taught in response to how they learn.

Transracially adopted children particularly benefit when their struggles are demystified. Already vulnerable to challenges of self-esteem and identity, the more they know about who they are the better they will be equipped to develop coping skills and strategies. Transracially adopted children may blame their race for their difficulties, particularly if their learning disability is the characteristic most unlike their adoptive parents and in part because they have internalized the false idea that people of color are less intelligent than whites. Parents need to learn how to reframe the issues so they do not fall into this pothole.

LD (Learning Disabilities)

Children with learning disabilities want to learn and to belong, but their neurological wiring often frustrates their efforts Learning disabilities affect all kinds of people—highly intelligent and not very smart; white, black, brown and tan; people with pre-natal exposure to chemicals and those with ideal pre-natal histories; children and adults; poor people and rich people; families who are educated and families with no education; children with stay-at-home parents and children in households with a high degree of stress; families with a history of LD and people with no genetic predisposition. There is no formula or checklist to discover who is susceptible and who is not.

When adopted children (and especially visibly adopted children) are diagnosed or suspected of having LD, many parents think that there must be a reason. It just isn't so. Researching genetic history may be useful in the context of getting clues for narrowing the field of issues and beginning to develop coping strategies, but often it is just a blame game—leaving birth parents shackled with more guilt and everybody still in the dark as to what exactly the issues are. The most important thing you can do for your child is to watch, listen and observe. Where are the disconnects? How do the struggles get triggered? What helps and what doesn't? You are always the expert on your own child. But in the case of your transracially adopted child, it is critical to hold onto this truth, and not let the world of experts tell you they *know* what is going on. Learning disabilities take almost as many forms as there are people affected by them. Parents must take the role of leading advocate, making sure their children are not the victims of adoptism and racism that always go along with the system's view of their child. You will have to become educated in a whole new way, to a whole new world of terms (IEP, ADHD…) and approaches.

What kids with LD worry about

> "We were always stared at. Whenever we went outside the neighborhood that knew us, we were inspected like specimens under glass. My mother prepared us. As she marched us down our front stairs, she would say what our smiles were waiting for, 'Come on children, let's go out and drive the white folks crazy.' She said it without rancor, and she said it in that outrageous way to make us laugh. She was easing our entry into a world that outranked us and outnumbered us. If she could not help us see ourselves with humor, however wry, that gives the heart its grace, she would never have forgiven herself for letting our spirits be crushed before we had learned to sheath them with pride."
> —Dorothy West, 1995

According to the *Survival Guide for Kids with LD (Learning Differences)* (New York: Free Spirit Publishing, 1990) by Gary Fisher and Rhoda Cummings, there are six major issues for kids with learning difficulties:

1. No one explains what LD is, so we spend a lot of time worrying about what is wrong with us.
2. We feel confused in school about what we are supposed to do.
3. Our parents, teachers and the other kids are not patient with us most of the time.
4. We do not have many friends.
5. Kids often tease us and we get into trouble.
6. We do not like being called retarded or dumb.

It's easy to see how all of these issues can be compounded for kids who are transracially adopted, particularly if they think their difficulties are a function of their race or ethnicity. To highlight their relations, reread each of the six points, adding the phrase "because we are different" to each sentence. Thus it is especially important that parents talk with their children about these issues, separating race and ethnic bias from the challenges of coping with learning differences.

ADD (Attention Deficit Disorder) and ADHD (Attention Deficit Hyperactivity Disorder)

"Dear. Docter bronson

At firs I was afrade to go and See you. I was scard you would giv me shots or do a brain operation on me. I was afrade youd tell my parince that I was a sereyes mentel case or a totle severe domy. Instead you told us about my atintion defenet Now that I know abote it I can do something about it I am working on it my atinthoun is a problem but it's not as bad as I thought and I'm not as bad as I thought I do bad things sometimes but Im not a bad kid and now ^know it's not wrong to have mind trips as long as your mind doesn't travel to fair away at the rong times I think my ititioun will get stroner and strger and I will get to be even more ever ready and super steady eddie.

Thanks your pall

Ever read eddie"

> —Dr Mel Levine *All Kinds of Minds, A Young Student's Book About Learning Abilities and learning Disorders,* (Educating Publishers Service, Inc, Cambridge, MA, 1993)

Twenty-eight percent of adopted children are currently being diagnosed with attention deficit disorder. Perhaps this is an accurate reflection of the truth. Perhaps the world has an easier time diagnosing children they see as "problems," like adopted children, like children of color, with this syndrome. We are hearing stories of doctors prescribing Ritalin and other medication over the telephone, never having met the child but only having heard the description of the symptoms. Parents have to be extremely cautious and be sure that they aren't buying into the "quick fix" of an easy answer to deeper issues being displayed through their child's behaviors. Parents also have to listen to Ever Ready, Super Steady Eddie. It helps to understand who you are and what the obstacles and issues that you face are all about. They become old friends that no longer need be fears, tigers that can be turned to pussycats with understanding and work. The support of parents who accept and understand makes all the difference

Transracial Adoption and Pre-Natal Substance Abuse

Sandy and Mira were veterans of adoption. Having adopted twice they felt well prepared for the emotional roller coaster of meeting expectant parents. Going to the hospital was exciting, but they were cautious in not wanting to count this new baby girl as a member of their family until her birth parents had taken the time they needed to be sure they were making the best decision for their daughter. Already parenting two African American children, Sandy and Mira had changed significantly as a family, experiencing the joys of multiracial living as well as the pain of their growing awareness of the racism surrounding them. They were totally blindsided when the social worker approached them.

"As you know, this little girl is at extremely high risk for FAS (Fetal Alcohol Syndrome.) Are you really prepared to parent her and provide all of the special care and services she will need? Surely she would be better off in the system, where she could be adopted by a family who will receive AAP (state funds for special needs children placed through the foster care system.)"

What was stunning was that they hadn't known any of this. They had met her birth parents. They had been told there been no use of any drugs or alcohol... but it was true she hadn't had any prenatal care... and they hadn't had much time to get to know each other because the baby had been born three weeks early... Their growing sense of panic was exacerbated by the 2:00 AM hour. They couldn't call anyone, so they got on the Internet. They spent the night praying and investigating; the outcomes and expectation were daunting. But when they called us in the morning they had come to the place of believing that if the birth parents still wanted to proceed they would find a way to love and parent this little girl with all of her issues.

Sandy and Mira have never forgotten the lesson they learned that day. The social worker had given them this information as if it were fact. When the pediatricians, neurologists and other specialists were asked for opinions, it became clear that the social worker had made it all up on her own. She believed herself to be able to tell by looking at the baby that the child had FAS. She knew the incidence of alcohol and drug use for young African American women with no prenatal care. She thought that she was doing them a favor by telling them before they made a huge mistake. That was her side. Six years later, Leilani shows no evidence of FAS. Her birth mother had always said she was alcohol- and drug-free throughout her pregnancy. The social worker saw what the system had taught her to see and Sandy and Mira had almost taken her word over their own truth and knowledge, never suspecting the racist and adoptist viewpoint confronting them.

We receive calls daily from families and professionals telling us about children of color adopted transracially who have clearly been exposed to drugs or alcohol in utero. Sometimes there is physical evidence to the contrary yet still the presumption persists. Children of color, and particularly those placed for adoption, are far more likely to be "diagnosed" with such history whether the evidence supports it or not. Parents must be extremely cautious and not assume what they do not know without a great deal of evidence and investigation.

When your child has been exposed

Children affected by prenatal substance abuse face certain predictable challenges. When these are combined with the challenges of transracial adoption, parents have many levels on which they must help their children learn success in a world not designed for their success. Acknowledging challenges is the first step toward coping with them while avoiding the trap of blaming oneself. To refute the myth of terminal uniqueness—"I am the only person in the universe who has to face these issues"—it is useful to be aware of some typical problems encountered by transracially adopted children bruised before birth by their birth mothers' alcohol or drug experiences. The following is a list—and they are not dead-ends.

- Difficulties participating in the reciprocal circle of attachment, so important in adoption. A child's internal circuitry can make it hard for the child to be able to communicate his needs and hard for adults to be able to satisfy these needs. Without secure attachment to one's family, it is difficult to connect to anything, including one's birth culture.

- Difficulties establishing or maintaining strong connections. Handling the complexities of connection to two cultures is difficult even for children without brain chemistry challenges. For children with greater sensitivity to transition and variable experience, it may be particularly difficult to build positive racial (as well as personal) identity while struggling to absorb and synthesize the extra information necessary to understand and operate within two different cultures.

- Difficulties with learning and thinking patterns can add to the overwhelm of trying to exist as a member of both one's adoptive family and one's racial group.

- Difficulties with thinking things through to logical consequences are common in prenatally-exposed children. They can be easily frustrated. This quality of impatience can be a barrier to establishing the coping skills needed to deal with racism in our culture.

- Difficulties with establishing a positive self-image. The child may continue making the same mistakes despite repeatedly working to correct them. He may persistently believe that his race is the reason for his difficulties, even thought there is no valid connection.

- Difficulties loving herself. This can lead to an assumption that being "bad" depends on her skin color.

- Difficulties telling the truth. Covering up a lack of understanding or knowledge by lying can hinder the child's ability to deal with the complexities of racism and situations that, in this society, even the most capable person finds it difficult to discuss.

- Difficulties being perceived as lazy or oppositional because the child repeats the same mistakes. Because of their racial bias (conscious or unconscious,) adults who interact with the child may interpret these difficulties according to a racist expectation that child of color are lazy, undisciplined or unmotivated.

- Difficulties with erratic memory. A task learned one day may be forgotten the next but remembered later. Learning and remembering are tools which help one feel identified with racial or ethnic heritage. Not remembering songs, appropriate behavior, or history can create additional challenges.

Benefits of knowing the truth

For your child, knowing that his birth mother used drugs or alcohol during her pregnancy can be a relief. If your child is having difficulty learning and/or processing information, it can be liberating to know that the challenges he is facing are not his own fault.

When chemicals such as drugs and alcohol exist in a mother's body when the baby's brain is forming, these chemicals can have an effect on the brain's development. It is brain chemistry—not the child's efforts—that are responsible for learning difficulties. Prenatal exposure to drugs, nicotine or alcohol may explain why she finds it difficult to avoid repeating the same mistakes over and over again, even when she is trying hard to do better. His depression or over-anxious behavior is almost certainly traceable to the actions of others, not to his actions or yours.

Many adoptive parents who have children affected by in utero drug or alcohol abuse go through a period of intense anger directed at the birth parent/abuser. This is a reasonable and natural reaction to understanding that your child's pain was caused by another's actions. As with most painful realities, one needs to move through the anger and grief in order to slowly forge out a place of acceptance. Processing the emotions involved makes the condition easier to live with and to develop coping strategies. In fact, alcohol-and -drug-exposed children can greatly benefit from the articulation of these feelings. Expressing anger at the perpetrator of the "crime," is one way of relieving guilt and frustration with their situation. Adoptive parents need to be careful to tell the whole story in the responses they share with their child. so that the child does not misconstrue that since their birth parents used drugs or alcohol they had no positive qualities. But if you don't tell your child about their birth mother's use, then they can't possible reap the benefit of having healthy and healing reactions.

For some children and parents there is also great benefit to understanding or knowing others (even if not their own birth parents) who have struggled with or still are struggling with addictions. Knowing that these are diseases and that the use of drugs and alcohol is often not a choice but a compulsion can be helpful. Certainly honesty about the genetic predilection to be susceptible to the same addictions is essential.

Sometimes children who understand why they are facing emotional or learning challenges have an easier time finding strategies to cope with them than do children who don't have answers or explanations. Coping tools can help counterbalance problem areas. They can help her focus her attention on positive compensatory activities rather than incorporating the blame and shame too often internalized by these children.

PTSD (Post-Traumatic Stress Disorder) and Previous Abuse or Trauma

What causes PTSD and how is it related to adoption

Post-Traumatic Stress Disorder occurs in both adults and children. In children it may occur when a child experiences a traumatic event in which he feels overwhelming fear or complete helplessness. Betrayal by someone on whom one depends for survival (as is true with a child's dependence on a parent) can produce PTSD symptoms. To a child, being separated from one's parents can seem to be a betrayal. This sense of loss can affect their ongoing world-view.

Unlike adults, young children have limited ability to make sense of such experiences. Traumatic experiences may shake their beliefs about safety and shatter their assumptions of trust. When a difficult experience may so exceed the child's normal expectations it may provoke reactions that seem "crazy" but which are in fact, normal responses to abnormal events.

The three main symptoms of PTSD are

- Intrusions, such as flashbacks or persistent nightmares in which the traumatic event is re-experienced.
- Avoidance, when the child tries to reduce exposure to people or things that might bring on memories of the trauma.
- Hyperarousal, a physiologic state of increased arousal, such as hypervigilance or an increased startle response.

Not everyone who experiences a traumatic event will develop PTSD. In disasters, in which many people are exposed to the same event, different individuals experience differing reactions. Differences in susceptibility to PTSD may stem from prior history. There is also evidence that early traumatic experiences may increase the risk of developing PTSD after another traumatic experience in adulthood.

Adopted children, particularly those who have been moved multiple times or moved at older ages, but also those who are sensitive or susceptible, seem obvious candidates for PTSD. The trauma they have experienced would upset and cause reaction in any human being. Looking for the symptoms and understanding what helps has direct applicability for the adoptive family. The adoption community talks about many diagnoses and issues that children sometimes face, it has been our experience that this one has been ignored more than its potential usefulness would dictate.

Proactive parenting

Adoptive parents who children exhibit symptoms that fit into the cluster of predictable response to PTSD need to take initiative in considering whether any of the available treatments for PTSD might be appropriate for their child. It is essential that parents be proactive when their children are experiencing such difficulties, because children who exhibit PTSD symptoms frequently also meet diagnostic criteria for ADHD, anxiety disorder, depressive disorders, conduct disorders, attachment disorders and other diagnoses.

Professionals untrained in the dynamics of adoption may easily misdiagnose the child's problems, creating treatment plans that could have a negative outcome. Mental-health professionals may be able to provide superior treatment when they are alert to the possibility that a child has experienced trauma prior to adoption. Treatment must be individually tailored and should be based on a thorough evaluation by someone familiar with adoption and with PTSD treatments.

Parenting tips

Behavior of a child suffering from PTSD may be provocative, out of control, rejecting, or embarrassing. Here are some things that parents can do:

1. **Explain what's up**. Be predictable. Unpredictability will make a child more anxious and, as a natural consequence, more symptomatic. For children hypersensitive to control issues, it is alarming and distressing to sense that their parents are disorganized or anxious. If you are feeling overwhelmed or out of sorts, help your child understand why, explaining that your reactions are normal and temporary.

2. **Listen more**. Reassure your child that there are realistic ways to make what happened to her turn out okay, that she can survive, and that you are there to help. Don't avoid or overreact. Simply listen.

3. **Provide choices**. Structure interactions as choices: "You have a choice— you can choose to do this or you can choose that." This opportunity to choose provides a sense of control and can help defuse anxiety.

4. **Spank not**. Even if your touch is appropriate, a child who has been physically abused is very susceptible to tactile triggers related to early memories. Never use negative physical discipline.

5. **Perfect your Garbo**. Use a calm, low voice when your child is out of control. On bad days, when your angel is screaming and refusing to listen and you are fried and furious, it may seem impossible to keep your voice calm, but what if your child was verbally abused in the past? Don't try to reason with a child who is out of control or when you are out of control yourself. Call a time out.

6. **Play it again, Sam—with a smile!** Due to difficulty concentrating, many children need frequent reminders about the rewards and consequences of unacceptable behaviors. Parents should not assume that a child will remember or learn from one situation to the next.

Useful Books

Bowlby, John; *Attachment,* **(NY: Basic Books, 1983.)**
John Bowlby's classic psychological study of attachment. John Bowlby was one of the first to study attachment issues; his theories have had strong impact on the current generation of clinicians trying to help children with attachment issues. No one hoping to understand the body of work contributing to current theories can afford to miss this classic text.

Faber, Adelle; *Siblings Without Rivalry* **(NY: Avon Books, 1988.)**
"My sister's first words were 'I'm telling mommy!' Our rivalry finally ended when I left home at 18." This helpful book expertly handles such topics as teaching parents to stop treating their children equally instead of uniquely; helping children express their angry feelings acceptably; motivating children to solve their own problems; and handling fighting. This best-selling book puts the reader right into the middle of a fictional workshop, sitting with other frustrated parents, asking questions and working out solutions. Uses action-oriented stories to show parents how to teach children to get along.

Johnston, Patricia Irwin; *Launching A Baby's Adoption,* **(Indianapolis: Perspectives Press, 1997.)**
A clear and insightful look at the issues of infant adoption including the parent's history and past experiences with loss and expectations for the future, the child's genetic and prenatal heritage, naming, bonding, attachment, and birth parent contact. As always, reading Pat's writing feels as effortless as listening to a warm but very intelligent voice flow in your ear, chatting easily about the things that matter most. Important information for prospective and new parents launching into a new life experience.

Krementz, Jill; *How It Feels To Be Adopted,* **(NY: Knopf, 1988.)**
This classic is still the best book we've found on a child's view of how it feels to be adopted. 19 kids from diverse backgrounds confide their feelings. Required reading for Pact parents.

Lifton, Betty Jean; *Journey of the Adopted Self, A Quest for Wholeness,* **(NY: Basic Books, 1995.)**
Asking why adopted adopted people feel alienated, unreal, invisible, unborn, this book offers psychological grounding for the deepest issues in adoption from the perspective of the adopted person. Lifton believes that only by restoring connection to the past can one move ahead with dignity and hope. The New York Times Review says, "'Inside every adopted person is an abandoned baby,' Lifton writes—not a rescued baby but an abandoned one. Shocked first by separation from the birth mother and later by learning 'that he both is

and is not the child of his parents,' the child splits his psyche into 'the Forbidden Self and the Artificial Self.'"

Mathis, Sharon Bell, ed.; *I Wish For You A Beautiful Life* (St. Paul, Minnesota: Yeong & Yeong, 1998.)

Letters written to their children by Korean birth mothers of the Ae Ran Won agency At the Ae Ran Won agency in Korea, each birth mother is encouraged to write a letter to her child at the time of placement. *I Wish For You A Beautiful Life* is a collection of letters from voices not often heard, providing a window into the birth mothers' innermost emotions at a very difficult time in their lives. What thoughts are typical? Hope that the children will have a positive life, sadness over personal losses, love for the children, and a level of guilt that sheds new light on what it is like to be a birth mother in Korea. This book is not intended for children.

Melina, Lois; *Raising Adopted Children* (NY: Harper Collins, 1986.)

This book explains the need to recognize that the job of being an adoptive parent brings with it some challenges different from those faced by "just parents," while it offers the essential basics of parenting an adopted child. Offers information on bonding and attachment; talking with children about adoption, sexuality and the adoptive family, adolescence, transracial adoptions; behavior problems and more. Well-organized, clear, and accessible.

Pavao, Joyce Maguire; *The Family of Adoption* (Boston: Beacon Press, 1998.)

An expert by training as well as an adopted person acutely sensitive to the core issues of adoption, Joyce Maguire Pavao offers one of the clearest voices in the world of adoption, alert to the deeper truths that may otherwise go unnoticed. Reading her book is like listening to a wise friend; she links her personal experience with the knowledge gleaned from many disciplines, creating that elusive "ah ha" experience.

Watkins, Mary & Fisher, Susan; *Talking With Young Children About Adoption* (New Haven, CT: Yale University Press, 1993)

This book is the best currently available to offer clear direction on how to listen rather than tell. Written entirely from the perspective of adoptive parents, some of the stories cited reflect an approach to birth parents which we find distressing. Though the author's point is to understand what children are thinking rather than to hand them a politically correct doctrine of adoption thinking, we still find it troubling that no discussion of these stories is included in the text. Despite this flaw, the book is extremely valuable in helping adoptive parents reshape their view of the purposes of talking with their children about their children's experiences of adoption. A Pact bestseller.

Watson,Kenneth W. & Reitz, Miriam; *Adoption and the Family System* **(NY: Guilford Press:1992.)**

Uses family systems theory to consider practical strategies for families connected through adoption. Employing a clean, clear-thinking writing style, Reitz and Watson look at adoption issues as interactions of family systems (birth families and adoptive families) over generations. Each individual is seen as a member of a larger system, influenced by and influencing the others over time. This book is a clear distillation of strategies for understanding the larger picture. Intended to provide an overview to professionals, this is a great book for anyone who wants to understand the broader and deeper issues of adoption. It is an exceptionally comprehensive, sensitively written, all-around superior guide, certainly one of the best on the market.

Section Four
🔹🔹🔹🔹
Through Development's Lens

All in A Name

By Beth Hall

Stage One:

When Ted and I decided to get married and have children, his father was furious that I wasn't changing my name. "Is there something wrong with Gallagher?" he asked repeatedly. I was so thrilled when Ted would say, "I am marrying Beth Hall and I want her to keep her own name because I want everyone to know that I love her, not an extension of myself."

Stage Two:

On her first birth certificate was written *Baby Girl Arroyo* and on her second *Sophia Anne Gallagher*. *Anne* because it was my middle name and her birth mother's first—somehow completing the circle of two mothers that were both hers. *Gallagher* because we couldn't saddle our child with a name that would harness her to hyphenation hell when fifteen letters might as well be infinity.

Ana said she wanted us to choose the name because this baby was going to "be ours." I knew it was a lie but I was so enticed with ownership of this child that I could not resist her argument. Somehow Ted knew that our first daughter would be Sophia. It was so brilliant. A name that could be beautiful in either Spanish or English.

I held her for the first time when she was three hours old. As I bathed her little face with my tears, I wanted never to let her go. The social worker said her birth mother was having a hard time and it might be best to just leave without letting her see the baby again. I questioned briefly and then agreed, needing to make this baby mine. When we got home I found myself weeping inconsolably. I knew I had somehow stolen Ana's baby and I hated myself for being the "lucky" one. Before the signing of papers, I flew back and brought our mutual daughter for her to see. I cannot recall one person who thought this was a good idea, but I felt I turned a corner that day. I knew that I had to tell the truth. I knew that adoption could never be *my* experience first. I knew my daughter would need Ana to *choose* to place her with us. I wanted Ana to know this would be a relationship of trust in two directions, not just one.

Stage Three:

He had already been born by the time we first heard about our son. We felt sophisticated and eager to involve his birth parents in the naming process. On his first birth certificate was written *Jason Terrelonge* (for his mother's maiden name) *Arterberry* (for his father's family name). On his second *James Jason Gallagher*, for my father who had died in the hospital where James was born—somehow significant of the circle of greater hands that moved our spirits together and made us family. We felt incredibly generous as we agreed to retain Jason as his middle name in honor of their gift. We found ourselves to be such grand people that we could grant all their wishes. I honestly didn't understand why they (his birth parents) didn't appreciate more our willingness to retain his given name. It seemed so progressive, so affirming of our child's mutual identity. Somehow I had expected more.

Stage Four:

I don't know when I finally had the wits or courage to ask our Latino friends why they always misspelled *Sophia*. I already knew that we had chosen a name with bicultural significance and that we had put our Anglicized mark on it by spelling it according to our own limited knowledge at the time. It was embarrassing. As Sophia grew older she relished in recounting our misguided planning and we all laughed as she explained our lack of foresight. Sometimes I see our choice of that spelling in direct opposition to our words when we said we wanted her to identify as a Latina rather than as an an Anglo like ourselves. By age six she felt entitled to spell it both ways and loved to correct adults by changing it at frequent opportunities.

In James' first year at "big school" he asked, "Why does Mommy have a different name?" I recognized his need to be identified with me. All my feminist pride and very important reasons for self-identification ended there. I realized how stupid I had been not to change my name and insisted that I would change to Beth Gallagher, the same as my children. And again, a man in my life (this time aged five), insisted on my identity as important. He could not bear that I should not be me but wanted to know why he couldn't have both our names as his.

In that moment was born our plan to change our children's names. It took, of course, months of deciding what everyone wanted. Ted and I wanted to hyphenate all of our names; the kids, on the other hand, wanted us to keep our names while they changed theirs to match with us both. In the end we found their argument and desire to be in control compelling.

Sofia realized that this was a chance to correct the spelling error that had muddled her beautiful Latin name, so we knew that that would change as well. One night, before we went to court, Sofia said: "We talked about names in school today. I don't think my birth mother really loved me. She didn't give me a name. I wanted her to give me a name."

"I can't imagine how hard it must have been for you to realize that right in the midst of your class," I said. Her seven-year-old body was wracked with tears for an eternal eight minutes. I found myself trying not to fix, not to interpret—the grief of the baby, the seven-year-old and the teacher all commingled in the one small body on my lap.

We asked the kids if they wouldn't also like to take back their birth family names. Sofia was thrilled to add Arroyo to her original—especially in the face of having no other from Ana. James was totally focused on needing to have both my name and his father's. "Not now," he said. "We can always do that later." I hadn't thought of that!

Stage Five and still counting:

Oh well, James is right. We do know how to do it now. And I find myself wondering at my own need to change their names so completely and to collude with this dual identity that society demands of the adopted. I am amazed by my children's willingness to live with something that I have not even asked of myself. It's all in a name.

The Experts Speak Out

"I have no boyfriends and no boy is interested in me. A lot of my girlfriends are pretty average looking, and they all have boyfriends. They say, 'You are so beautiful. You're so pretty.' And I think to myself, then why don't any of the boys like me? I know the answer is race. But we never talk about it. It is never acknowledged. At the end of the 9th grade I started hanging out in the Mexican section of town even though my parents went ballistic. I tried to learn what Chicano people do. I didn't really know how to dance and I don't speak Spanish. Some of them thought I was stuck up because of that and cause I'm shy."
—Sophia Greenberg

"As an adopted person, I need desperately to believe it is all right for children to be taken care of by adults outside of their families, and that they will not only be all right but will thrive. For if this were not true, then how could I possibly have the hope of being whole myself? As an adopted person, I need to know that it is true. As they say, the proof is in the pudding. I look at my daughters. They are vibrant, affectionate, bright and curious. They love new experiences and meeting new people. There is no doubt in my mind that being adopted affects parenting in a profound way. But how it manifests itself is as idiosyncratic as each parent, as unique as each child."
— Susan Ito

"While at college, I had to choose whether to 'be black' or not."
—Jennifer Robbins

I see all my students of color go through a stage where they try to reject their own racial identity. It's what society teaches them. It doesn't do the child any good to make him feel bad about it. Because from the child's perspective, the perception that it's better to be white is logically correct. When the kids look out on the school yard and all the teachers are white and all the janitors are not, they don't need to be told which is better to be."
—3rd grade teacher

"I was the only black kid in my grade school. Getting invited to more birthday parties than anybody else was cool even though later I found out it was because the kid's mothers made them so nobody would think they were prejudiced, but not having long flowey hair like my girlfriends cost me. We dreamed of becoming cheerleaders. it hurt me

to figure I wouldn't get picked because \ cheerleaders were all blonde and skinny, not black and big like me. It wasn't till I went to an all black high school that I found out that black guys liked super sized girlfriends, I could cheer if I wanted and I was Fine just being me."

—Angela, age 16

"In school I had more trouble with the racial barrier than I did with being adopted. I first became aware of the racial difference when I looked at a picture of my family and noticed that I was a little bit darker than everyone else. The most difficult thing was having people not believe that Leni was my mother. People would ask, 'Is that your mother?' So it always came up that I was adopted."

—Casi Wildflower

Through Development's Lens

*"Most advice on child-rearing is sought in the hope that it will
confirm our prior convictions."*
—Bruno Bettelheim, *A Good Enough Parent*

Infant, childhood and adolescent development has been exhaustively
documented by a host of experts. This section is designed to help you understand what new growth challenges your child is likely to face and when they
are likely to occur so that you can feel prepared. It's more like a set of guidelines than a timetable. How long it takes to get where you are going depends
on your speed, how often you stop and whether or not you make any detours
along the way. Your child will move through these stages in her own good
time. Some of what we describe will take place for her but some of it won't.
All we can be really sure of is that your child will start out a baby and before
you're ready, transform into an adult. Then again, not everyone does...

Adopted kids face the same developmental challenges as do other kids
but their responses may seem magnified because of the extra layer of challenges of separation and loss that are part of their emotional playing field.
Deep down you know that no child-rearing advice can be tailored to fit your
family exactly. You alone are the best expert on your child. Only you have
earned intimacy through ten trillion interactions and observations and only
you really know the prehistory of each new stage your child reaches. On the
theory that you also love your child more than the experts who offer advice,
(at least when she's not spilling her grape juice on your white shirt) we imagine that you also have more at stake in wanting to help her become ever more
satisfied with herself.

One of the stimulating opportunities all transracial adoptive parents receive at no extra charge is the chance to relate the wealth of general knowledge that exists about physical, emotional, and intellectual growth to the unusual and stimulating circumstances of our own kids. Conscious parenting

calls for an understanding of children's development as well as of racial identity and of family development. This is not an opportunity for worrying about developmental comparisons. Each child has innumerable individual qualities that make her unique, so she will move through developmental stages in her own time and in her own way. It will be helpful for you to recognize the stages and what is known about them and to understand that others have traveled your child's path before.

Along with physical, intellectual and emotional growth come the ability to understand adoption and race differently at different stages and levels of emotional and cognitive sophistication. Helping your child build a positive racial identity and stretching your own racial awareness is a lifelong process, informed by experiences with the outside world. Our needs and dreams change as we grow. The challenges we face from the outside world influence our connection to one another and create an endless stream of opportunities for strengthening attachments and intimacy among family members. Finding satisfying responses to challenges enhances the core of self esteem and confidence of each individual within the family, each of whom must find his or her own answer to the questions of "Who am I" and "Why does our family belong together?"

Sorting Out the Issues

> *"The parent must not give in to his desire to try to create the child he would like to have, but rather help the child to develop—in his own good time—to the fullest, into what he wishes to be and can be, in line with his natural endowment and as the consequence of his unique life history."*
>
> — Bruno Bettelhiem

Parents often ask us how they can figure whether a particular issue their child is working through is an adoption issue, a development issue, or a racial issue. Think about it. Does it really make any difference how we label the issue? We don't believe sorting in that way sheds any light on the situation. What matters is that it's an issue your child is having, period. Your job as parent is to help, offer guidance, offer support, and hold his hand as he struggles, all the while taking all components of your child's individuality into consideration. And then, before you've analyzed what he's up to to your own satisfaction, he will have moved forward to the next stage and you will get to try your part again. In the end, spending time labeling issues or trying the "figure out" where they come from probably takes energy away from focusing on what kind of support and help your child needs in the particular circumstance she is struggling with. Exploring all aspects of your child's personality and circumstance makes more sense than limiting yourself to only one layer of the onion.

Taking a look at both the external and internal forces acting on all of us helps us to understand predictable passages of the journey which in turn helps us to move forward. This is a journey with no finite ending. As in all aspects of life, there is something new to consider every day.

Infants

Perspective on Infants

"At a gestational age of six months this baby had already been attending to rhythms of movement, sound and chemistry, getting to know her mother and the few visitors who drew near to her world. By eight months she was listening in on conversations, playing with the cord, jumping at loud noises or fretting at hormone surges, and complaining about the food.

"In the weeks and months after her birth, we see that this baby— and every baby—is some kind of complicated combination of what she came as, what she has seen and experienced, what she is being 'taught' about herself and the world and about confidence and safety and trust and love. Her attachment to her new family is growing. Her cognitive awareness of her birth mother is dim because her cognitive capacities are limited, as is her language—which means merely that she has no words to describe her observations and experiences. But she has not forgotten. She has other capacities for storing her awareness.

So all the while never let us forget that a person is watching, witnessing, storing impressions. It might change our behavior—it would certainly change our attitude—if we understood that. And it might improve the adoptive launch."

—Michael Trout ("The Optimal Adoptive
Launch," *Pact Press*, Winter 1994.)

Moving from the care of birth parents to adoptive parents has an impact, even on newborns. There are some common behaviors that represent normal responses of adopted infants to the changes they experience. Some adopted babies will not evidence any of these patterns. Others will be poster kids for them all. Our goal in highlighting some functions that may be influenced by either heritage or adoption issues is to add to your sense of what may be normal for your child.

Physical development

Being born is exhausting. But in addition, adopted infants must often make an immediate transition to new parents. No matter how warm the reception by new parents, extra stress on Baby must be anticipated when Baby experiences changes in sounds, smells, stresses and rhythms that are inherent to the fact of moving from birth family to adoptive family.

Lesson One: If your baby communicates stress, it isn't your fault.

First time adoptive parents often expect (or at least desperately hope) that Baby will instantly find contentment in their arms because they are so thrilled to have a child. If Baby expresses discomfort of any sort, new parents may blame their own lack of experience and think it is their fault. It can be a profound relief to understand that uncomfortable physical responses are normal for humans of any age when adjusting to a completely new environment.

Think of how adults respond to change… moving, job changes, new marriages, divorce, adding or losing family members, even vacations are known to cause stress. We take for granted that instructions for travel in foreign countries advise travelers about health precautions and medications for normal (and predictable) complaints. Yet think about how often the story of someone's vacation includes grumbles about traveler's revenge, tourista or other bladder, bowel, eating or sleeping problems despite their good preparation and proper precautions. Babies respond to the disappearance of all that was familiar and secure, not to your parenting skills.

Since behavior is the language of babies, normal responses to a complete change of environment may include incessant crying, colic, bladder or bowel disturbances, difficulty accepting an agreeable formula, difficulty sucking and/ or sleeping problems. The key word here is NORMAL.

Making a move from one environment to another can create a high-needs child. Considering the predictable stresses of change, isn't it a blessing if your little one is able to urgently demand the attention that she needs rather than shut down or withdraw? Your baby has not had the standard arrival to your family, so standard baby advice won't do. Having high needs means that your little one may simply need more: more sensitivity to his or her needs, and more understanding that his or her needs are not being met according to original expectations.

Studies available through the Office of Minority Health Resource Center (http://www.os.dhhs.gov/prog) show that the level of stimulation created by the sounds of voices, television, and radio is often greater in families of color than in white families. This sort of cultural difference is of particular interest to families parenting transracially who otherwise might not have thought to explore duplication of stimuli from their child's before-birth environment.

Lesson Two: Don't compare your child's physical growth to any other child's.

Growth is the process of becoming larger and more mature. Most pediatricians compare your baby's weight and height with growth charts compiled by the National Center for Health Statistics to determine ideal weight and height. These growth charts have been based on large–scale surveys that were conducted in the 1970s of white children from middle and upper income families. Clearly, different growth charts should be developed to reflect differences that exist in different population groups (racial/ethnic, socio-economic etc.) (University of Michigan, School of Public Health, 1975) Until they are developed, however, it's important for you to understand that because this is so, the "ideal" or the "standard" may not appropriately reflect growth expectations for your child. For example, did you know that researchers have found that in early infancy African American babies tend to be smaller than are white babies? But by their second birthdays, the black children in these studies tended to be heavier and taller than the white children they were compared to.

Differences in developmental milestones are very relevant for children who have been in orphanages and other group settings during their early months or years. Standard developmental milestones are really markers for interaction and process *in response to the world around the baby*. For the orphanage resident, where the "successful" child is the one who is cooperative (translate non-demanding), quiet (translate passive) and easy-going (translate low-need,) her timeline for such milestones will be different than for the child who has been in a setting rich with stimuli and interaction. Each baby develops in his or her own way, anyway. But add to that the previous low-stimulus experience of your child and it seems downright silly to place the same expectations on children who come from orphanages than those who have been with a single, caring provider from birth. This does not mean, however that if your child seems different from other babies of the same age you should not pay close attention to his or her development process and consider consulting experts; just remember that these differences are not automatically indicative of a problem.

Of course your baby is different—remember where he has been! He will be different from you, from his adopted or born-to-the-family siblings and certainly from your neighbor's child, your pediatrician's chart or some busy body at the store who is remembering from a vantage point thirty years old. This is the first of many times you will be reminded that you are the expert on your own children. Each has different genes and different experiences. Each is fascinating to watch and enjoy once you let go of the anxiety and stress of looking for some graph called "normal" by which to measure their progress.

Heredity and nutrition also help to determine how quickly and how much your child grows. What you can expect is that motor skills will develop in an orderly sequence following the maturation of the spinal cord. First will come lifting of the head, then rolling over, sitting up, crawling, standing, and walking. Every child reaches these milestones at his or her own speed. Learning to talk starts with cooing, then babbling, to imitating speech, to saying first words, to using words together. You can look forward to many changes during your baby's first couple of years. No matter your child's growth rate, once she had attained these significant milestones, her growth begins to slow down and becomes more gradual. For most children, by age two you are looking at a toddler.

Understanding the realities of development will give parents a great advantage in choosing a pediatrician. Interview potential pediatricians about their knowledge of different growth curves and norms for babies and children of different races. Ask them if they have any experience with children adopted from orphanages. If they don't and if your child has been institutionalized, there are specialists across the country who can send them information and be called in for consultations. If they do not appear excited or interested in such information, they are probably not ideal pediatricians for this child, even if they were great for other kids.

The most reliable characteristics of normal development are your baby's alertness and curiosity and growing confidence and ability to interact in the world, defining your baby's growth from a perspective of his or her exciting changes rather than comparison to anyone else gets you and your child off to the right start.

Lesson Three: Once you recognize your baby's behavior as positive—his way of telling you what he needs—it becomes easier to seek ways to nurture him.

There's no such thing as a spoiled baby. Old-fashioned thinking said that too much holding or coddling could spoil children. As if it is important to teach babies from their earliest moments on earth that life can be harsh and they must make adjustments to survive. First, our children were taught that lesson at the core of their experience. Second, every attachment expert in the world agrees that success in the cycle of expressed needs being met—baby expresses a need, caregiver reliably meets baby's need, baby grows in confidence that by expressing need, his needs will be met, over and over again—is essential to healthy development. Third, pain can be healed by successful and repeated experiences of the cycle of attachment—*at any age*. In this cycle the child is excited by a need (hunger, fear, desire—whatever) and expresses that need. The parent fulfills the need and the child feels satisfied, relaxed and at ease. In the process he learns that his needs will be met and that he can trust his parents to be responsive.

If she cries loudly when you put her down but is happy to be held, hold her. If he acts hungry, feed him on demand. If she doesn't sleep through the night, be there to comfort her. If he isn't happy being held by your friends, don't pass him around. Focus on your baby's responses. When in doubt, respond to his cries. He is trying to tell you what he needs. It is likely you will discover exactly what it is through your own instinctive and natural process of trial and error. Babies, children, all human beings, have a strong survival instinct. They are very good at teaching us what they need. Babies don't manipulate, they communicate. In the rare event that you are not able to help your infant find a way to feel comfortable or the right formula, visits to your pediatrician will uncover any problems early and offer solutions.

Reward your child for the incredible trust and openness he shows each time he communicates a need to you by trying to meet that need. Reward yourself with the pleasure and intimacy born of the attachment you are creating and nurturing in the process.

Experienced adoptive parents know that although many adopted children are likely to have sensitivities to the huge tasks involved in making successful transition to a new family, every child is also unique and will go about the process in his own way.

Intellectual development

Lesson One: Children start learning from the minute they are born

For the first four months, most babies spend all their time learning about their bodies. They gather information through their whole bodies and use all of their senses in each investigation. Most things get mouthed, anything they can fit between their lips. They seem to be asking the question, how does this feel? How does it fit in my mouth? Adopted children are simultaneously deepening their attachments to their new parents during this transition period.

As a result of their transition, adopted infants may be either over-responsive to stimuli or hard to engage. At this stage, the best way parents can teach is by bringing the world to their child in understandable form and giving words to his or her feelings so that eventually he knows what he wants and learns to signal with intent. A parent's ability to be intricately in tune with baby's wants enables the child to feel confident and provides a foundation of experiences that will help the child associate pleasure with his own identity.

Psychologist Daniel Stern, a researcher who has studied infant-mother interactions at Cornell University Medical Center in New York, has shown that infants and mothers continually engage in lengthy reciprocal exchanges, with the mother matching the infant's intensity and tempo, adding variations to elaborate the communication. Mothers who intrude on the baby because they are more in tune with their own needs than his cause the child to be more attuned to her needs, too, and thus more likely to develop a false, compliant self. "What is at stake here," Stern wrote, "is nothing less than the shape of and extent of the shareable inner universe."

Parents can become involved in their child's learning process and incorporate positive images and experiences of racial identity and connection right from the start. This means finding ways to communicate before your child understands your words.

Lesson Two: Focus on your child.

Listen, watch, reflect her feelings back to her without deference to yourself. Convey information by letting your baby see, touch, and hear ways to express her own feelings coupled with a sense of being appreciated, validated and approved. For example, when Baby gets very excited about her foot and puts it in her mouth, she may let out a happy yip and look at Mom. Mom can look back and pump her arms in the air, like a cheerleader. The pumping motion lasts only as long as the baby's sound but is equally excited, joyful, and intense. Through such creative echoes parents not only reinforce Baby's behavior, but communicate with her which builds their relationship and shows Baby that her experience can be understood and shared with another.

After a period of high arousal brought on by a physical or psychological need having been satisfied, most babies relax and are most open to interaction. This is a good time to pick your baby up and cuddle close. Pick your baby up from the front and hold her face-to-face with you to support the process of attachment.

Using the same toe-sucking opportunity as an example, parents can make up a silly song just for Baby and touch each body part they are singing about. You can't get much sillier than this one. "Hi ho, hi ho…"I love your golden toes. Your perfect toenails smell like butter. What sweet feet you have. Soon you'll be running on the ceiling." Don't expect her to understand the words, but know that she will feel how happy you are with her because of your smiles and laughter as you sing just to her. You can make up new songs with words, which will be different, every day or (if you can stand it and your baby doesn't run away from home) you can sing the same song over and over. Baby will thrive on these frequent interactions and learn self appreciation, including appreciation for her racial heritage, a sense of humor, and most important, that you and she are intensely connected.

Some of the things you are likely to do naturally that will help your baby advance include talking, reading, and singing. Read at least one book to him every day. Make a point of selecting books that positively reflect his cultural heritage. Sing at least one song, either silly or splendid, that will pass on new information about culture, rhythm and tone. To teach new words talk about your day or what is growing in your garden or how to make cous-cous. While having fun, your baby will learn to love learning. The more we talk, read and sing, the more we activate brain activity that affects intelligence.

Emotional development

Physical development, intellectual growth and emotional development; in infants these are so intimately connected that perhaps they are really the same thing. In *First Feelings* (NY: Penguin, 1985) Stanley Greenspan, M.D. and Nancy Thorndike Greenspan explore three milestones in the emotional development of infants. We offer this brief introduction to their work as a useful foundation for parents hoping to understand the challenges their infants face. Understanding the normal progression of emotional development can help parents to see their child's progress from stage to stage and to relate these stages of emotional growth to experiences common to transracially adopted children. As the Greenspans state, "a child's feelings can't be separated from her experiences with herself and others and emotions help to define and organize all experiences."

Self-Regulation

The first emotional milestone usually occurs between birth and three months. The baby has made an adjustment from the dark and relatively quiet atmosphere of the womb and has become able to both feel calm (self-regulate) when experiencing the sensations of sight, sound, movement, touch, taste and smell and is even actively reaching out for them.

What might make this more challenging for an adopted baby? Expectant mothers who anticipate separating from their children after birth are understandably experiencing great stress during their pregnancies, particularly during the latter stages when what was once an intellectual plan may be creating panic as the reality of the separation approaches. It's a good guess that the baby awaiting birth under these circumstances is not living in a "relatively quiet atmosphere" at all, but feels more like a rowboat adrift in a raging sea. When this child is bombarded after birth with the sensations of the world, he may be too distracted to self-regulate, or he might not have developed any ability to experience calm. This in turn can make it harder for him to use his senses to become attentive to the world. Parents can help orient a baby who has reason to be cautious about experience toward an ability to embrace life by helping him to regulate his senses and by providing opportunities to experience a wide range of feelings.

It is normal for adopted infants to be either over or under sensitive to sensory experience, a reasonable response to their circumstance. Helping takes conscious effort on a parent's part but is of great value. Observe your child's responses to see which senses create greater response or sensitivity. Encourage regulation by paying attention to what movements your child finds calming as you rock and play with her, noticing how she responds to sounds, visual games, touch, smell, taste and movement. Use what calms her to teach her to calm herself while at the same time slowly working on engaging the senses your baby finds difficult. Your help in comforting her shows her how to be soothed and relaxed, something she can't yet do for herself. Treasure your baby's growing ability to be calm and alert. Each moment of mastery is a foundation for the next step, learning how to love.

Falling In Love

Forming a relationship between parent and child generally occurs between two and seven months. Baby has learned to take great interest in her parents, expressed by smiles and excitement as she explores your faces, feels your movements and hears your voices. Her ability to be responsive is growing as she becomes socially alert. If an adopted child has already had multiple caregivers by this age he will likely have increased anxiety about making loving contact. This can be expressed by becoming either overexcited or withdrawn. Parents can help their child form a relationship with them by

- making special efforts to be warm and interesting;
- paying attention to positioning themselves so Baby can see them and feel secure;
- anticipating Baby's attention span for intimacy in order to switch to another activity before she gets fussy, then later returning to wooing;
- being alert and responsive to a withdrawn baby's fleeting gestures;
- for a hyper-excitable baby, wooing her with calming gestures.

As in stage one, parents can help by being sensitive to Baby's individual differences rather than to their own emotional responses. Sometimes the parent's own sensitivity to rejection fostered by the circumstances that have led to adoption need to be acknowledged. Some negative reaction to Baby is common for all parents, suggest the Greenspans, "and need to be considered a problem only if it interferes with your being intimate and relaxed with her."

Responding With Trust

Between three and ten months, Baby has usually developed intentional communication. He responds and has learned that his responses lead to reactions on the part of others. He is learning that he can cause things to happen, a foundation for trust. Again, children who have had multiple caregivers may face challenges based on their less-predictable experiences. His smiles may have not brought reactions in a previous setting. If he has had repeated experiences of not being responded to, he might have learned gradually to stop showing feelings. Parents can help their baby learn reciprocal interaction by learning to read his signals accurately and responding to him reciprocally with empathy. Begin by determining a behavior that is easy for Baby to do and use that as the basis for interacting, making special efforts to gain his attention. If Baby is a low-sender, respond to *any* signal Baby sends. If Baby is excitable, first relax him, and then focus on making interaction relaxing and fun. It is important to help your baby practice interaction in all emotional areas: pleasure, rage, assertiveness, dependency, love and security, and the capacity to calm down.

Children who have not had the opportunity to experience these stages in the "normal" age range can still learn to become attached and connected. They still need to go through the three-step process of self-regulation, falling in love and responding with trust.

Special Issues in Infancy
Becoming Attached

> *"Children have never been very good at listening to their elders,*
> *but they have never failed to imitate them."*
> —James Baldwin

Adoptive parents often feel terrified that something will go wrong with attachment in their families. Researchers in neonatal studies have defined six stages of attachment between parents and children that may help you to understand normal steps in the process. Don't worry about doing everything right. Your security about being a good-enough parent will eventually help your baby feel secure. There's no rush. Take time to watch, touch, laugh, play and have fun. You and your baby have a lifetime to continue deepening attachments.

Here are some practical suggestions for enhancing attachment:

Feeding: follow a schedule based on Baby's cues. Put her needs—before she is even fully aware of them—before your own. Feeding on your schedule or removing bottles before Baby finishes nursing teaches her not to depend on you. Fit feedings to times when Baby is open. Don't feed your baby at cross-purposes to the cues Baby gives you. It is a more important priority to help Baby feel that you are responsive to her needs as she feels them than that she eat on a schedule determined by you or your doctor. Hold your baby closely when feeding her, looking at her and making this time as intimate as possible.

Eye contact: Looking into Baby's eyes leads to touching his check or picking him up. When you put him down, likely he will follow you with his eyes. You will feel good. An exchange of smiles may follow. If eye-to-eye contact is threatening, Baby may turn pale or withdraw. If you notice this reaction, let him look at you at a distance rather than face-to-face, allowing him more time to develop comfort with closeness.

Holding: Holding, touching, cuddling, stroking, and kissing send positive messages back and forth. Show affection through touch even if your baby stiffens, but don't force yourself on your baby Always pick her up from the front and hold her face-to-face with you. Do pick her up when she cries. Behavioral theory says that this reinforces crying, and that if you do it enough you'll have a crybaby, but attachment research has disproved this. Respond to her cues! If this is an area of challenge for your child, take a baby massage or exercise class. These are often opportunities to learn your baby's signals and for your baby to learn to take pleasure in your touch.

Sound: sing, recite poems or nursery rhymes. Encourage him to respond to your rhythms. Sensitive babies may need the volume in the household lowered. Experiment until you find his comfort zone. Other babies have been in more noise-full environments and will appreciate dancing to music or being taken to the park.

Playing: As Baby reacts positively to you, you are getting feedback on successful nurturing techniques. When something doesn't work, try new ways. Give yourself permission to take time to learn preferences. You will feel more competent as a parent. Notice the first time you are able to tell a stranger which way your baby likes to be held or how he best burps. These are testaments to your effectiveness as a parent—opportunities for you to feel connected and attached.

Enjoying Baby's beauty: Take time looking. By brilliant design, infants have big wobbly heads, enormous wide-spaced eyes, and tiny soft-skinned bodies. Adults may be programmed with instinctive nurturing responses triggered by the immature features of babies. Gaze at your beautiful child. It softens and opens your heart.

Timing: Your baby is most open to attachment after a period of high arousal brought on by physical or psychological need. Satisfying a need creates relaxation. Baby is most open just then. Though you may feel like being alone and resting, cuddle up.

Hypersensitivity: Understand that he may be following a normal course of slowed adjustment after stress. Be especially gentle. Try wrapping Baby in a blanket so that his or her arms and legs are contained, but if she stiffens and resists restraint, forget it and try other comforting techniques, such as rocking, walking, driving or wearing your baby close to your body in a sling carrier. Keep experimenting with comforting tools and you will hit on one that will work, at least in that moment. If your baby has high needs and a persistent personality, you will both have to do some adjusting in order to shape each other's behavior.

Parent in public: Participate in "Baby and Me" activities, which encourage you to touch Baby in the company of others; consider infant classes and support groups, etc. You must learn to wear the mantle of parenthood and believe in yourself in the role in order for your child to recognize that indeed you are his parent.

> *James (Beth's son) was one of those kids who struggled during his early time in the world. Comfort was a hard place to find and nothing seemed to agree. He spent his first three days in the hospital nursery while everyone was deciding what to do, and I always wanted to blame that time on his difficulty in accepting touch, food and sleep. But the truth is he was held a lot during that time and he just was who he was. We changed his formula six different times. He contracted thrush, scabies and had a cold before he was a month old. He liked to be held but only for short periods of time and he never slept for longer than two hours until he was many months old. With Sofia, we had held onto the easy assumption that her calm and comfort were really about our being great parents with incredible intuitive skills and compassion. Now we knew differently, and I for one regretted every gratuitous piece of advice I had given to those new parents I had deigned to enlighten with my presumed wisdom. James and I took infant-parent massage classes three times a week, and although he needed to change positions a lot, he didn't leave our bed until he was eight months old. Even then it was more because of our sheer exhaustion from his frequent awakenings than any plan or foresight by us. He was more than a year old when a friend pointed out how much pleasure James seemed to receive from touching me. I began to notice the way he followed me around and never left my nearness if he had a choice. Truth be told, he is my cuddliest kid, though please don't let any of his friends read this. Somehow even though we had focussed on what must be "wrong" as he struggled to find comfort in our world and family we managed to create attachment in the very midst of his greater-than-average need. Born out his need were countless millions of opportunities to live the cycle of attachment which accidentally, through no knowledge of ours, was exactly what he needed to feel close and find security. Phew! Sometimes I am so grateful for the "difficulties" life offers.*

What matters is your commitment to attaching no matter how long it takes. Build on signs of progress. If it takes time for the baby to act as if you matter more than anyone else does, enjoy interacting as connections grow. The best signals for knowing whether or not you're on track will come from the baby. Gather strength from simple pleasures; smiles and developmental milestones are proud signs of growth. Baby may take more or less time to attach than you do. Your partner may take more or less time. It may take days, weeks, months, or a year. Don't feel like a failure if attachment takes longer than you imagined. Most important is building a family together, for the long haul.

What's in a name?

> *"It is through our names that we first place ourselves in the world."*
> —Ralph Ellison

Names have great significance. In most cultures it is a sign of respect to greet a person by name. Names are given, often with a blessing, as if they were magic charms to provide the good and shield from the bad. Names are a way of claiming our children. Family traditions, culture or the dictates of our hearts may guide our choices of names.

Infant Placement—whose name matters?

When there is a placement plan for an infant adoption, adoptive and birth parents each may have the opportunity to name the child. Sometimes they each choose a name and the child grows up having two distinct names. Since adopted children normally have two birth certificates, in such a case the original, filled out by the birth family, will show the name given to the child by the birth parents along with the birth mother's name. Though this record is still sealed in most states, current efforts of the open records movement are finding success, and it appears likely that in time adopted people in all states will be able to have access to this original birth record upon request. The second birth certificate, currently created at the time of the finalization of the adoption, reflects the name the adoptive parents have given to the child and shows the adoptive mother and/or father as if they were the "birth parent" of the child. Normally it is the name the adoptive parents have chosen that the child is known by in everyday life. The name given by the birth parents, though not in everyday use, is often perceived as a private and precious gift to the child, an intimate statement of caring and bestowing the spirit of the birth family's tradition to the child. When a child has two names, it is important that each set of parents respects both names and treats them as the sacred gifts that in fact they are.

Sometimes, as adoptions become more open and communicative, birth and adoptive parents agree upon a name that both will use and this same name is reflected on both birth certificates. This choice is often made when one of the parties has strong feelings about what the child should be named and the other does not and is happy to accept the name the other suggests. A variation of this choice which also results in the child having only one name occurs when birth and adoptive parents collaborate on a name that combines names each likes into one. Children named in this way all have a first name and a middle name and some of them have many middle names. In this model it is often the name the adoptive parents' choose that becomes the child's first name and the birth parents choice that is one or more of the middle names. The benefit of arriving at a single name together is that it sends the message to the child that all of his parents have been able to work together to make this important decision. It also eliminates any potential confusion or loyalty issues about going through life with two names.

Racially & Ethnically Consistent Names

If given the chance, we like to suggest that adoptive families consider names that will fit easily into their child's birth culture. Most people would not expect a person with the name Shoshanna Greenberg, for example, to have brown skin. If the name Shoshanna Greenberg were on a list most of us would be surprised if the person who stood up when it was called was an American Indian. Adopted children of color have so many ways of being different from their peers, it might be useful for parents to consider whether the name they are considering will set the child apart once again. Claim your child by offering a name that is valuable within your family and culture, but consider doing so with a name that also fits into his birth culture and promotes his membership in both.

> *What possessed us (Gail) to change our first child's name when she arrived from Korea at close to age four? Our rationalization was that since she would need to learn English and the names for everything else in the world would be new to her, it would seem logical if her own name changed as well. And we thought having a Korean name might be a barrier to her fitting into her new life in America. And we wanted to. So in our wisdom we replaced her beautiful Korean name, Ae Lan Kim, and gave her a Hebrew name, Shira, meaning "song." No kidding. Yes, she was named after her great-great-grandmother, according to the ancient custom of our religion. Yes, that did support her membership in our family. Yes, we had given her a name that felt rich with hope and meaning in our imagination, an offering of the spirit. Yes, we gave it bursting with love for her. And yes, it was a drastic mistake… we were so naïve then that it didn't occur to us what it would feel like to lose one's name, one's birth family, one's country,*

one's language…shazam! Her name was all that our daughter had left, but we took it from her thinking we were making it easier for her to fit into our world. We had no thought that our world had a responsibility to accommodate itself to her. When the truth dawned on us, we felt criminal for adding losses to her losses. In the meantime, in spite of everything, Shira, born resilient, a survivor at her core, managed to grow up and become a mensch.

Adoptive parents need to claim their children and the desire to do so through naming is hard to resist. We think that it feels easier to rationalize the decision to exchange a name in a foreign language, which may be harder for English language speakers to embrace, for an "American-sounding" name. Often parents cite examples of Asian Americans who name their children predominantly Anglicized names rather using the names of their heritage or language. There are no absolutes to the question, but proceed with caution and take both the losses and the gains into account. Question whose comfort the choice of names is really addressin—yours or your child's.

Re-naming (older) children

In his *Narrative of William W. Brown, A Fugitive Slave, 1847*, William Wells Brown said, "*A new master might often change a slave's name and this indicated that the slave had absolutely no rights which a white person were bound to respect.*"

When a child who is old enough to recognize his own name joins a family through adoption, we think the child is better served when adoptive parents keep the child's first name as the name by which he continues to be called. The research of State University of New York at Buffalo psychologist Peter Jusczyk and his colleagues suggests this name recognition occurs in most babies by age four and a half months. Asking a child whose whole world is changing to also change her name may be experienced as being asked to be someone other than herself. Sometimes families tell us that they don't like their child's first name, but would you reject a spouse or new friend for such a reason or ask them to change their name? It is important that your child feel valued and accepted into your family for who she is; *not for whom she might think you want her to be.*

More than one adoptive parent has changed a new child's name for reasons that made absolute sense to them, perhaps because their child's name seemed too hard to pronounce, or because it didn't fit their cultural norms, or because it would break family tradition if they didn't name their first daughter after her maternal grandmother, or because they'd agreed before they married they would name their first daughter Heather, or just because. All we ask is that you think about the naming issue from your child's point of view.

Talking about adoption

Your baby may not be able to understand what you say but she will get that you find her beautiful and good each time you tell her the story of her life and how she came to belong to you. There are many important reasons why you should start this story on the first day she joins the family and tell it again and again for the rest of her life, but perhaps the most important one is that children who are highly valued learn to value themselves. Children who hear over and over that they are wonderful and special begin to know it is true. Children who hear their adoption story as the most fabulous story there could be have a heads-up on feeling good about adoption. And the more you practice, the better your storytelling will get. Start when they are babies and your joy and interaction is enough. All you have to do is tell the truth. By the time they are old enough to actually understand the words behind your message, you will have successfully fallen in love.

> *Once our family (Gail's) got to spend a week on the Danish island of Aeros̨çoben. We stayed on a farm with a totally crazy family who rented out the top floor of their house to us. They spoke Danish only and we and our four young children were limited to English. The first night they surprised us and came upstairs for a visit wearing funny masks and little outfits someone must have left for them that had big pink lips saying "Welcome to the USA" all over them, and carrying candy. For hours we sat together, not understanding a word each other said but doing circus clown routines we inspired each other to invent and laughing until we burst. All of us all fell in love with them and they with us. What we couldn't understand didn't matter. What we came away with was that Aeroçoben was good and beautiful and so were we all.*

Mongolian Spots

> *The first time I (Beth) gave Sofia a bath, she was only beginning her second day. We still laugh when we look at her picture. She was having none of it and never has there been a child with a wider mouth or redder skin than our darling who was with every shred of her body screaming to make us stop. And we did—not fast enough for her—but for the next month we did not dare to immerse her again, struggling to keep her clean with quick swishes of a wash cloth and lotion before wrapping her back tight in the swaddle that was her safe haven from the world of water and soap. Imagine our horror when she was already 9 days old before we noticed the terrible bruise on her bottom. I was devastated and insisted that Ted return from his first day back at work*

immediately because I was sure we had done something terrible to hurt her. We stressed for a day, called my mother and sister, both experienced enough to know, endured their indictment that we must have set her down too hard; how could this have happened? She was twelve days old when we slinked to the doctor fearful that we would loose her for our gross acts of incompetence. She laughed the simple laugh of someone who has seen it all and began the education of parents who knew less than nothing about their daughter.

Mongolian Blue Spots are flat birthmarks with wavy borders and irregular shapes. They are common among people of Asian, East Indian, African and Latino heritage. They are seen in only 10% of European Americans but over 90% of people of color. Bluish gray to deep brown or black markings, they often appear on the base of the spine, on the buttocks and back, and even sometimes on the ankles or wrists. Mongolian spots may cover a large area of the back. The pigmented area has large concentrations of melanocytes (skin cells filled with melanin) and exhibits normal skin texture. They commonly appear at birth or shortly after birth and can look like bruises.

Benign skin markings, Mongolian spots are not associated with any illnesses, complications or risk factors. There is no known prevention and they generally fade in a few years and disappear by puberty, though they occasionally persist into adulthood. There is no need for treatment.

Well-meaning white people who have no experience with these markings on people of color have been triggered to make accusations of child abuse against adoptive parents. For this reason, it is important to be sure that both your child's pediatrician and the caseworker that completes your post-adoption work record information on the presence on Mongolian spots. You can assist in the documentation of this information by taking snapshots of the spots and providing prints which can be included in your child's file.

Racial Issues for the Families of Infants

Obvious racial or ethnic differences between parent and child can be a stumbling block to one's own sense of attachment or to outsiders' ability to perceive of the parent and child belonging together. Feedback from others or feedback that is self-generated can generate uncertainty in the parent, which can create awkwardness in the dance of attachment. It will be the richly rewarding feelings that grow from physical interactions between your infant and yourself, back and forth, that will allow each of you to come to believe that you belong together. Within time your own experiences with your child will override any questions based on political or social assumptions or bias.

How will you respond to strangers' comments?

When your family becomes multiracial through adoption, you become public property in a way that you probably heard about in advance but that may still *feel* new when it's actually happening. Most people are curious by nature, noticing, wondering and making assumptions about what appears to be unusual. Guess what? Now, that's you. So now that you can't put the baby in the cart at Target without becoming the target yourselves, life is going to feel different. It's not important what other people say or do; none of us can transform all the people we will encounter in life into folks as lovely as we believe you to be, so there will always be some jerkheads out there pointing their fingers and stuttering their gibberish. We can't waste our time worrying about them or imagining that we will change them before our children start to notice. What matters here is how you feel when these things happen. The best advice: Keep on keepin' on.

We are all apt to be most self conscious at the beginning of new experiences. It is normal that this public scrutiny will cause some stress when you first experience it. The good news is that you and your children will get used to it, even come to see some humor in figuring out family responses to it, and learn to use it as a tool to strengthen your family. The words in our family language we whisper to comfort when our kids face something hard are "s'epass, s'epass—this too shall pass." It's a long life. As we grow the responses of the undereducated become so easy to dismiss. S'epass, s'epass to you.

Sometimes parents describe the shock they felt the first time someone assumed that their adopted child was born to them and a partner of color. They often feel a sense of shame or guilt because of their realization that although they love their child of color, they had not translated that to loving an adult of color in the most intimate peer relationship imaginable. We would submit that the relationship between parent and child is one of the most intimate in the world although not of a sexual nature.

This jarring moment of truth is really a great initiation into the realities of parenting across racial and cultural lines. Your beautiful baby will grow more quickly than you could possibly imagine to be a man or woman of color looking to find his or her own life. How will you feel if she is barred from marrying someone who is white because of her race? How will you feel if he marrries another person of color and your family becomes even more "mixed?" Initial feelings of surprise, shame, and uncertainty are normal. Don't hate yourself—frankly, none of us has time for that. Role up your sleeves and begin the work of falling in love not only with your child but with others of your child's culture and race. You will grow to understand that it would be a privilege to be intimately involved with a person of color in every kind of relationship.

Providing positive reflections

From the very beginning, celebrate the world's diversity with your infant. Think about the opportunities within your own home and community. You are embarking on the most exciting journey of your life. Don't hold back. Enjoy the richness that is flowing in your family's direction, as you become a member of the wider community of the world

Feeding schedules, style of holding, bathing, dressing, lullabies, stories, ideas about feeding… all cultures have particular styles that flavor their approach to these issues. Wouldn't it be great for you to know what they are and for your child to have comfort with these practices as well as your own? When the time comes that you decide to have anyone besides yourself take care of the baby, make a high priority of searching out a person of your child's ethnic or racial culture. If you are not using childcare, consider hiring a parent's helper who will be there with you and your child. When you select the cassettes and CDs you will play for your child, make a high priority of including music that reflects his or her culture. When you select colors to paint your baby's room, all of his or her "stuff," the images your little one will see from the crib or bassinet, make a high priority of including colors and images that reflect his or her culture. It's never too soon to start. You will be glad you did. The advantages are many. From the very beginning, your child will develop a familiarity with cultural mannerisms and you will benefit by having a trusted resource close at hand to teach you the common ways people of your child's culture address infant care.

Preschoolers

Perspective on Early Childhood

Between the ages of approximately one and three, children begin develop an extraordinary range of new skills, expanded curiosity about *everything*, and a capacity for stubbornness, saying "NO!" and power struggles. Day-to-day dramas tend to increase as she changes and parents often have trouble assimilating those changes, still treating her as a baby. She is on a new emotional teeter-totter with an increased ability to conceptualize the world, explore, and take action, but she is still dependent on you for security and warmth. Finding the right balance will be a milestone for you as you learn to respond to the new challenges her growth brings and for him as he negotiates this new stage in his life. Please enjoy every minute. It's a time frame providing much to celebrate as your baby becomes a toddler and the challenges for you in what are sometimes called the "terrible twos" only last a millisecond in the long range of life.

Physical development

Toddlers are extremely busy. By age two or so, they usually have learned to crawl, to stand up, to walk, to run and then to walk backwards. They must learn to talk and then to ask questions. They do not have a realistic idea of their own abilities and often try to be more or less independent than their parents think is appropriate. During the toddler years, your child may be struggling so hard and taking so many risks—like learning to throw a ball underhand, to manipulate smaller objects, to climb on the furniture, to climb up stairs, to explore everything she can get to—that she will often get frustrated, have mood swings and act just like the stereotype of the "terrible two" even if she isn't actually two. Likely her world has expanded beyond the family circle as well and she has play dates with friends her own age from day care or her playgroup. If she's getting sick more often it's because her exposure to common childhood illnesses has increased and her immune system is immature making her less able to fight off infections.

It is logical to imagine that children adopted at birth face fewer challenges as toddlers then children who are adopted as toddlers. It is also important to remember that levels of sensitivity and reactivity are always individual. Children who are adopted as toddlers must attach to and adapt to a foreign culture—the culture of their new family. They may have to learn a new language as well. Their immature immune systems have to fend off infections that may be entirely foreign to them. Delays in development are likely to occur while the child becomes acclimated to his or her changed environment. The remarkable resiliency of the many children who change families during this time period is spell-binding. Considering what these children accomplish, often during the briefest adjustment periods, it's hard not to believe that anything is possible.

With all children, the parent's job is not to prevent frustrations in their toddler's life but to help him learn to cope with them. This happens after the necessary stages of attachment usually associated with infancy have occurred. The same set of steps will occur in children adopted as toddlers. They still will need to start "over" and accomplish the dance of attachment prior to learning to manage the larger world of relationships and interactions.

Intellectual development

Have you ever watched a one-year-old suddenly understand how something works? Pulling the string makes the light go on, the lid fits on top of the pan, shaking the bell makes a ringing sound….As if he's asking, "really?" He repeats his action about eight million times in a row in order to make sure he's got it, overjoyed with each repeated success. His important job is to try everything, touch it and put it in his mouth. As he practices winding the handle to make the monkey jump out of the jack-in-the-box, he is also discovering object permanence, that things don't disappear forever when they go out of sight. See, there's that funny monkey again. Mom will come back when she goes to work. When he is hungry, instead of crying in his crib, he can now take Dad to the fridge. He shows that he understands the function of objects by brushing his hair with the brush or holding the phone to his ear even though he doesn't yet speak. At one he may know only a word or two and by two he will often have a large vocabulary.

Toddlers engage in classification to make sense of their expanding world. Two-year-olds love to sort and categorize objects into groups, learn their colors, separate dogs from cats or cars from trucks. Awareness of visible racial and ethnic differences starts here. Toddlers also begin to think before they act, and begin to know right from wrong. At this age most children can understand more than they can express even though they have a rapidly expanding vocabulary and may get frustrated if they can't make themselves understood. Sometimes as early as the age of two, toddlers begin to wonder where they came from and how they got into their families. For adopted children it is key that they come to know that they were both born *and* adopted, and that it is all right to be curious. Attachment and separation phases alternate, leading to their first perceptions of individuation, the idea that "I am me."

Again, all of these tasks may take longer to accomplish for a child adopted as a toddler and it is reasonable to imagine some developmental delay; he has so much more to do than children who've settled into their families from birth.

Emotional development

Much of a toddler's development seems to be both cognitive and emotional at the same time. At one, most kids are focused on interactions just with their parents and figuring out how to get their attention. They often become anxious about separations if parents must leave but otherwise are fearless and will try just about anything. Children engage in parallel play with other children but easily fight over toys because they don't know how to share. Conflicts with a capital C will dominate most interactions with toddlers, because parents will need to control their child's explorations with safety measures and Toddler will hate the words "NO NO!" By eighteen months, most kids will show more interest in playing with other toddlers but see them as objects to push and pull rather than as peers. Preschoolers may be startled by how other children respond to their demands. It is natural for them to be extremely "I" focused and unable to consider others' feelings.

Imitating adult tasks will be fun for kids at this stage, but this is also the time when separation anxiety has become a really big deal. Many kids benefit from having a transitional object like a blankie or teddy they can't be without and from which they seek comfort when Mom or Dad is away. It is normal for adopted two to five-year-olds to be particularly fearful of separation. They often have anxiety about being abandoned, getting lost, or no longer being loved by their parents. All children must work out their awareness of their smallness compared to their parents' size, as well as resolve internal conflicts about their urges toward autonomy. Bedtime, animals, almost anything can feel scary for kids of this age. Toddlers want to be big, but they also want the benefits of infancy. For a child who must move to a new family during this sensitive period, it is likely to take some time before he feels safe. For adopted kids who tend to be more sensitive to loss: other stresses such as illness, divorce, death, separation, moves or financial upsets can provoke a lot of "acting up." Children this age act out their emotions through their behavior, so parents must be careful to understand their children's reactions and distinguish between "bad behavior" and behavior that indicates the child is feeling bad. Emphasize that no matter what, you are there for your child. Toddlers feel that they cause everything that happens and are very reactive to criticism. Because of their increased emotional and cognitive skills, this important time to begin connecting toddlers to their birth heritage.

Many experts view early childhood as a series of alternating attachment and separation phases that establish the child as an independent person who can relate happily to family members and friends, and be capable of having intimate relationships with others. Toddlers are faced with an internal conflict between wishing for autonomy and feeling anxiety about separating from the primary caregiver. During this stage, when you must guide and protect your child, you become the embodiment of "no." Not surprisingly, your child becomes frustrated, demonstrating this frustration in behavior ranging from crying to throwing, hitting, biting, pinching and temper tantrums. For adoptive parents, who sometimes worry that this frustrated behavior has something to do with the child having been adopted, it helps to know that this kind of behavior is typical of toddlers. Children who are adopted sometime after infancy usually follow the same attachment and separation paths as other children, but possibly in a different time sequence. Parents should encourage both attachment and separation behaviors at the same time. The key is in the balance.

Special Issues in Early Childhood

"Our children give us the opportunity to become the parents we always wished we'd had."

—Louise Hart

Did I grow in your tummy, Mommy?

(Gail) That day when the car pool dropped her off after playgroup, she could hardly contain herself, she was so excited. She could hardly walk because she was trying to carry her teddy under her shirt, his belly held into the elastic of her waistband with one furry teddy-bear foot peeking out through the hole in the side pocket of her pants.

"What's that?" I asked and she stared at me like "Don't you know anything?" But she said, "Kimmy's mama's got a baby in her tummy. We got to feel it kicking! Mama, was I kicking in your tummy?"

I smiled the kind of smile that betrays me at funerals, feeling weird and far away and not having any idea what to say even though I'd been rehearsing my lines for this moment for centuries, "Oooh," I lied cowardly, "Hurry! I need to go to the bathroom! And then we need to take Lulu to the vet for her checkup. I'll tell you all about that at bedtime."

Between ages three and six, children begin to wonder where they came from and how they got here. When kids start to question where babies come from, their comprehension of what adoption means begins. One idea leads directly to the other. You can't talk about birth without your child wanting to know about her own birth. You can't talk about her birth without talking about adoption and how she got to you. Even if you've been telling her the story of her life since the day she first came to you, even if you have celebrated her adoption day as a National Holiday second to none, even if you have an open adoption and she knows her birth mother, don't be surprised if she asks the same question at irregular intervals but many times over, "Remember when I was in your tummy?" It's up to you to find a way to talk in your own natural way about adoption. In the beginning, simply letting her hear your positive tones is as good as it gets.

At this stage, children are working very hard to understand all relationships, and their family relationships are the first to be scrutinized and explored. As greater comprehension dawns, little ones need to understand they were both born AND adopted, not one or the other. It takes years of periodic returns to the subject of adoption before children will fully grasp its meaning. She was born same way every other kid on the planet was born. She was in her mother's tummy. You became her mother after that. Adoption is in addition to birth, not a replacement for it. Children who learn early that it is all right to ask questions and be curious usually carry this behavior over and feel confident continuing to ask questions and express curiosity as they grow.

Language skills allow children to explore the world in a new way. Parents need to view their children's questions as an opportunity to talk about feelings and experience, not to worry about having "right" answers. Children in this stage engage in fantasy and "magical" thinking. They are trying to develop a reliable sense of what is happening in their world. During these years, their world is expanding enormously; and so in turn must their repertoire of responses. There can be a great deal in the expanded world which threatens their sense of security. Two- to five-year-olds often have anxiety and fears, especially about being abandoned, getting lost, or being no longer being loved by their parents. Children must work out their awareness of their smallness compared to their parents and their urges toward autonomy and independence. They want to be big, but also want the benefits of infancy. Sometimes, competitive feelings towards a parent become a way of expressing individuation.

Many of us have strong feelings about sexuality and adoption. To offer our children the best possible understanding of adoption, we must first examine our own feelings and be clear about our goals for our children. Very young children will intuit the feelings associated with any subject long before they can clearly understand the details of a conversation about it. Children will pick up on mixed messages, so parents will do well to try to resolve their own conflicts. Therefore, while talking to your child it is important to distinguish clearly between discussing feelings and discussing facts.

Early discussions can be excellent practice ground. The first goal is to create an atmosphere of trust and openness. It is not necessary to convey every bit of detailed information. Children will understand and misunderstand information, but the feelings leave a lasting impression. It is also okay to acknowledge any difficulty you may have in talking about certain things, as long as you let your child know you are glad he asked and that you are trying your best to answer. Remember to label your own feelings rather than let your child infer them. If nothing else, you are giving your children a great model of how to cope with their own ambivalent feelings.

Research by Dr. David Brodzinsky has shown that adoptive parents, mothers in particular, are likely to overestimate their children's knowledge and understanding of adoption. He cautions parents not to stop discussion prematurely simply in the mistaken belief that a child who can "talk adoption" can *understand* adoption. There is some question about whether a child under six can understand the meaning of adoption at all. Children draw vastly different conclusions from information than do adults, and even children of the same age or developmental stage think differently. We cannot predict what meaning our children will attribute to the information we give them. When it comes to thinking about adoption, preschoolers use words without having a clear idea about what they mean. As development progresses, children have some ideas about adoption but tend to talk about birth and adoption as almost interchangeable ideas. Because their perspective is egocentric, they often come to the conclusion that their own experience is universal.

The best way to understand what your child is thinking is to play with him. You child's stories, "let's pretend" roles and the games she makes up are cues to what's going on inside her. How can you play the games your child creates? Stanley J. Greenspan, M.D. (*Playground Politics: Understanding the Emotional Life of Your School Age Child*, NY: Perseus Press, 1994) suggests "floor time" as a tool to help you tune in. Set aside twenty minutes (no phone calls allowed!); get down on the floor and play, just you and your child. Within this structure, allow yourself a spontaneous and unstructured role, following your child's lead. The goal, according to Dr. Greenspan, is to "march to your child's drummer" and to tune in to the child at his level. Floor time goes beyond 'quality time' because your child determines the direction of the play or conversation. Your child gets to be the total boss. Your job is to follow her lead; that's all.

> Jeremy (Gail's son) made up a game when he was three and a half and first joined our family. We played it thirty billion times until he was about seven. He was Dumbo, a baby elephant whose mom couldn't take care of him. His dad, Timothy Mouse, and I, Starlightstarbright, got to be mice parents who had wanted all their lives to have a "best beloved elephant" as their child.
>
> "You are walking down the road and you find me and you are so happy. You drive me home and put me in your nice mouse house and take real good care of me," he said in his Tazmanian devil voice. Holding up his arms he looked so vulnerable, so solemn with his old man face and legs that never bent—giving us permission to find him... to take delight in him! His second long hug and surrender into our arms was the first sign. His feeling of belonging to our family was growing, but he still held back, our little man stiff and hyper-vigilant against his sense of the continually approaching dangers of the world.
>
> Each time we played "his game" Jeremy expanded the plot to introduce new complications. What would happen when Dumbo grew too big to fit into Timothy and Starlightstarbright's mouse house? What would happen when he needed very big elephant food that wouldn't fit in the mousie-sized refrigerator? Or when people laughed at an elephant child following teensy mouse parents? Each time we played,

new concerns unfolded which threatened our elephant-mouse family,
but Jeremy was always able to imagine a way to solve even the most
difficult predicaments so we could remain together.

Our job was to say "oooh" uncommonly gently when things were
really sad and to pat his trunk and say "eek-eek-eek!" when they were
scary; Jeremy came up with all the answers, because he was in charge.
Together, we thought up stuff that Dumbo and Timothy Mouse and
Starlightstarbright could do to the bad guys who didn't think we were a
family—things that I don't have Jeremy's permission to share with you.
We became really superb at being SO happy when it turned out that
our family would always get to stay together. We learned more about
how our son was feeling about adoption and racial differences when he
was Dumbo, than perhaps ever again. When a concern became clear
enough to him for him to include it in his game, we took it as our cue
that he was trying to deal with it. And when the moment finally came
that he melted himself against us...when we heard his single small
sigh, and he closed his serious eyes...as James Thurber said, "Love is
what you've been through with somebody."

Being your boss for twenty minutes does wonderful things for your child:
it lets him know that you are interested in his ideas and that you care enough
to focus some time just on him. In the safety of your presence, he may be able
to play out some unclear feelings and feel understood, feelings that "big boys"
like him may not always be encouraged to demonstrate such as neediness,
anger, sadness, whatever. Use props like dolls, toys, craft materials, costumes—
whatever your child picks. This is his show. Learn to be an actor in the drama
your child directs. "What do you want me to do next?" is the question that will
lead your child forward. You don't need to work hard at analyzing the unconscious elements of your child's play or try to interpret his feelings about it.
However, as you have more experience, you will be able to notice recurring
emotional themes (such as questions about belonging, who is alike and who
is different or lost pets/children/animals). Your goal will be to assist your child
to communicate in a deeper way about whatever interests him or her.

For adoptive parents whose relationship to loss is different from their
child's, it can be painful to play the role of the lost pet or child without trying
to push the game toward a happy ending. Many parents can't resist slipping
into control mode. Greenspan suggests that if you have clear and accurate
expectations of what your child will do or say next, you are probably being too
directive. Your sessions should be full of surprises as your child pursues new
directions, fresh solutions to problems, different resolutions to old stories. As
you play, sit back and listen more.

It isn't easy to let your child be the boss, but it's the best way to find out what she's thinking. It isn't easy not to correct her when her perceptions are "wrong," but it is the only way to understand her perceptions. Hope to be surprised about what happens. If you can consistently guess correctly what your child will do or say next, you probably are still the one in charge. Enjoy being the actor, letting him be the director. Follow his lead. It's big-time fun. Here are some suggestions to make it easier:

- Let your child end her story her own way; don't push for a happy ending.
- Wait for his cues. Don't try to fill in silences by asking questions.
- Be patient. Don't ask too many questions.
- Answer all of her questions.
- Be happy to do anything your child suggests during floor time, as long as it is safe.
- Enjoy being surprised. Don't guess what will happen next.

Have fun. Don't analyze your child's play or try to interpret what it means.

Coping with loss

What makes adoptive parents hesitate to address their children's questions? Usually it is their fear of pain, anger, blame and their own loss. All children reject their parents some of the time. All children have troubled responses some of the time. As adoptive parents we often have special sensitivities about such times. Our own fears and pain are as much at play (if not more) as are our children's. Sorting out our baggage is never easy but we must begin early because the questions will come and they deserve unfettered answers.

Sooner or later your child will get the idea that if you are so happy that she is with you, then her birth mother must be just as sad she is gone. Like an infant struggling to lift her head for the first time, your child will face the challenges of her first baby glimpses of loss. Dealing with loss is a fact of life. All of us experience multiple losses throughout out lives. Unfortunately, most families avoid teaching about loss and in fact many seem to go to great lengths to avoid addressing head-on the losses experienced in their lives. Your child has already experienced the loss of their birth parents made more difficult by the absence of closure. Even in an open adoption where there is ongoing contact between the child and the birth parents, loss is present because the child has lost the opportunity to be parented by his birth parents and vice versa. Having wonderful adoptive parents does not erase this loss. For transracially adopted children, this loss is made visible by racial differences which may make their awareness of its impact more profound.

Helping children to acknowledge and understand loss in general so that they can deal with their specific losses productively can begin in early childhood. Having a pet goldfish (with its short life span) is a great opportunity to learn to deal with loss. "What will you miss most about Goldy? Should we flush or bury? What kind of funeral should she have? Who should be there? Do you want to get another gold fish?"

When will these issues come up?

Kids with a greater sensitivity to loss have a harder time shaking off the feeling of being sad inside. These feelings can be provoked when events (death, divorce, injury, illness) threaten security leading to transitions or new situations. In an effort to gain a sense of control, they are trying to find a cause for important events. Young children often have three basic questions: "Did I cause this to happen?"; "Will it happen to me again?" and "Will my parents be able to take care of me?" Small children may think, "I know I made it happen. My skin was too brown. That's why I got adopted."

To help your child cope with her feelings begin by validating your child's feelings. You can't fix it. You can try to understand. Talk with your child about the real causes of events. Be straightforward. Use correct terms. Children love facts, presented in simple terms: "People have different amounts of melanin in their skin that determines their skin color." "People have a different color of skin depending on where their ancestors came from." "Many people all over the world have brown skin, and they think brown skin is the most beautiful of all."

Talk about your own feelings and encourage your child to talk about hers, The preschool child tends to tell her story to everyone. She may be seeking support and may be checking the reactions of others to discover how she should feel. Remember that "I-made-it-happen" thoughts can be hidden for years. Keep listening to what your child says, for it may provide secrets. Be responsive to cues.

Help your child feel safe. When a triggering event happens it's normal for preschool kids to regress, and to show intensified fears (of the dark, of going to sleep, of going to a new place, of a parent leaving, or of the child being taken away) or to show sadness, anger, outbursts and boredom. The child is working through grief responses that may be bigger than the triggering event.

Don't insist on difference. Some parents think that the way to build a child's positive self-image is to make adoption or racial differences into a beautiful fairy tale. Differences can be celebrated without overstating them.

Don't insist on happiness or on overprotecting the child emotionally. Some parents cannot stand for their child to be unhappy. A child who is extra sensitive to loss will receive a lot of cues from the world for sadness. Pain is unavoidable. Adoptive parents as a class are faulted for being overindulgent. Prepare, don't protect.

Choosing child care and schools

Choosing childcare or a playgroup or a preschool that makes you feel comfortable and makes your children feel at home requires care. Proximity and affordability are not the most important issues. Here are some things to consider...

The environment you choose should be safe, caring, responsible, competent, racially and ethnically diverse, able to support your child's racial identity and able to nourish your child's spirit. Looking for this perfect environment is often the beginning of finding that we must make compromises on behalf of our children—a realization that can bring up feelings of real angst. Most of us are determined to be the "best of all possible parents" which makes it essential that we get our child into the best of all possible schools. Often no such school is available. After you have gotten over your frustration at what does not exist begin to look at what does and question your priorities relative to your child's. When looking at priorities like educational approach, personal style, diversity and affordability, if diversity is at the bottom of your list, ask yourself why.

Ask questions like, How many children of color are in the group? How many teachers of color are in the school? What holidays do you celebrate with the children? What would you do in case of a fire?" What kinds of rules must the children follow? Look for a situation where Michael Jackson, Michael Jordan, and Eddie Murphy could have been students at the same time without the teacher spending all of his time trying to get Michael #1 to speak up, Michael #2 to sit down, and Eddie to shut up.

Ask yourself, Am I comfortable with this environment? Do the teachers share my values about children? Is my child comfortable when we visit? Does the teacher make me uncomfortable in any way? The teacher or care provider should love children and should be experienced with children this age. Ask questions like How long have you been teaching? What kind of training have you had? Talk to other parents whose children of color have attended the school. Ask questions like, How did the teacher handle your child? How were the children disciplined? Did you notice any differences between treatment of white and non-white children? What kinds of games and activities took place? Did the children have fun?

When looking at how your child will be treated in this new environment remember, it's the feelings behind the words that matter most to young children. Many individuals censor children of color more rapidly, frequently and forcefully than they do white children. The person applying different standards may not be aware of the discrimination, but the toddler feels it and incorporates it into his sense of self worth. While white children may be effortlessly praised, cuddled, hugged, kissed, and admired, children of color are often offered a less appetizing menu of interactions with adults.

Many white adults are unaccustomed to being around children of color. It may be difficult for them to touch and cuddle. It is common for small black boys to be told by white adults that he dresses "sharp." How often is this adjective applied to a white child? In fact, African American boys are frequently complimented in different ways than are well-dressed white children, just as black men in our society are often viewed as hip or cool, labels less frequently applied to men of other races. Stereotypes may or may not apply. Even so-called positive stereotypes calling attention to admirable qualities are harmful, for the speaker has failed to see the child as an individual.

If you have any concerns, keep searching for a school or group where you feel assured that your child will be safe, happy and well treated. Remind yourself that this is a stretching process for you and your child. Believing in the philosophy and values of the school is critical. Being comfortable may not be an advantage. This time, while your child is young and still dependent on your presence in their learning and social environments is a great time to seek situations with room for growth for both of you.

Racial Issues in Early Childhood

"If you want to teach a child to be good, don't tell him how bad he is. Tell him how good he can be."

—Kwasi Geiggar

Toddlers and racism

What does the toddler of color learn from parents and caregivers about the value of her race? Do you and the other adults who regularly care for your child view him as a future CEO, astronaut, brain surgeon, orchestra leader, or janitor? Do you view assertive behavior as the seed of a lawyer or of a gang leader? If there are differences between the sense of future for white children and for children of color, this information is probably communicated in a hundred subtle ways, even to toddlers. Stereotypes about females may be radically different from stereotypes about males. Children are vulnerable to prejudices. The upper limit that adults imagine for a child affect their interpretations of the child's behavior.

When my kids' (Beth's) preschool decided to have a series of workshops for parents and faculty to discuss and learn about racial issues, we were thrilled. The kids were only two and three, but already we were spending lots of time in the bathtub and at the painting easel noticing the differences in our skin tones. "James is chocolate candy, Sofia is ginger snap cookie dough, Mommy is oatmeal and Daddy is coffee ice cream." We even had a song about it! During one evening's parent discussion, an African American dad and a white one (in an interracial marriage) expressed vastly different views on how to talk with their children about race. In the white father's home they were using color designations similar to our own. "It's great. We talk about milk and chocolate being mixed together to make milk chocolate, just the color of our son. I don't want to introduce the elements of race too early, our kids are going to be asked to fit into somebody else's check boxes soon enough. I want my kids to be free of all that stuff for as long as possible."

I knew I wasn't totally comfortable about the way our actions aligned with the sentiments of this dad, but I was still trying to figure out why when the African American father spoke. "As a boy, I remember going somewhere with my parents and being stopped by a white policeman. My father was pulled out of the car and made to grovel with his face literally in the dirt while my sisters and I looked on. I was only four, but I have never forgotten what he said when he got back into the car. 'Nobody can take away your dignity as long as you know who you are. Never forget to call yourself 'Negro—Mr. Negro to you,' in your head when the white man tries to bully you. I didn't say anything to that policeman. I let him do that to me to keep you all safe. But inside I said, 'Mr. Negro to you!' so he couldn't hurt me anymore.

We had to ask ourselves how much of our use of colors had been our own hope to keep that hurt away from our own hearts rather than the kids'. The next day we started using the real words— Latina, African American, people of color— and telling the kids why they had so much to be proud of.

Choose carefully those adults who will have repeated exposure to your child. It is essential that you feel confident that you understand their views on race and that their views about your child be free of stereotypes. Try to understand their style of discipline, their style of expressing affection and praise, and the amount of personal experience they have had with children of your child's race. Even though many people consciously believe in equal treatment for all kids regardless of race, there are subtle (or not so subtle) differences in how they behave with children, differences based on racial attitudes. Observation and conversation with others who have direct experiences with the person involved are the best ways to research this information, because the caregiver may not be in a position to assess qualities of which he is unaware.

What is your child thinking about race?

"If you understood everything I say, you'd be me."
—Miles Davis

Children often make assumptions based on limited information. In early childhood some children think:

- All brown people are adopted.
- All Chinese females are adopted.
- All Koreans are adopted.
- All Koreans are Jewish.
- All Latinos are Catholic.
- All interracial families are adoptive families.
- White kids are never adopted.
- If you are the same color as your parent, you weren't adopted.
- If you have brown skin, you're not an American.
- If your mom is white and you are not, you will have to be adopted.
- All Asian parents place their children with other families.
- All African American parents place their children with other families.
- All Latino parents place their children with other families
- All Native American parents place their children with other families.

Make it your business to know what your child thinks about these and similar statements. During the toddler and preschool years, your child will likely begin to have more significant contact with people beyond the immediate family. Pay attention to the images your child sees. Make sure they have many opportunities to see reflections of themselves in a positive light. Direct experiences with real people will diminish the impact of stereotypes. Looking at the world concretely, in the way a toddler or preschooler will, can be extremely helpful to parents who are trying to assess the diversity in their life and that of their child. Look for the message your child is receiving and then take steps to expand those messages in positive ways.

Ongoing connection with the child's birth family, where possible, will be a continuing source of positive racial reflections for your child. Your preschooler will be able to notice the samenesses between herself and her birth parents while also being able to notice and celebrate the ways the adoptive family is alike.

But not all children will have the same-race connections that open adoption brings. Baby sitters, child-care helpers, or nannies of your child's race will now be able to provide experiences within your child's cultural traditions—games, nursery rhymes, language, stories—that will enrich your child's connection to her birth heritage as well as familiarizing you with traditional or mainstream child-care methods practiced by your child's culture. If you do not yet have professional service providers such as pediatricians, teachers, etc. who are of your child's racial/ethnic group, review anew the field you have to choose from. It's important to provide your child with opportunities to build familiarity with successful people of color while conveying the message that people of color play important roles in our lives and in society.

In order to develop resources to help parents approach their child's culture with respect and to build bridges to it for the child, this is also the time to build on your relationships with cultural guides, putting new energy into friendships with adults of your child's heritage who will be lifelong role models for the family. Now that your child is old enough for play groups and play dates, provide peer support with other children of your child's race/ethnicity. Don't allow your little one to always be in the minority in his or her own life.

Preschool kids are ready to start exploring how to play instruments and how to sing with others in a group. Introduce instruments that come from their cultural heritage as possibilities. Find simple examples of instruments that are suitable for early learners. Percussion instruments are common to most cultures and are often an easy beginning place for young children. Most cultures have their own unique forms of drums and simple reed instruments such as recorders and flutes. Play music of your child's birth culture. Make a point of teaching your child simple songs and dances that children of his heritage might be taught. Continue to make sure that your child hears his language of origin and begin to teach first words: how to count in that language, what his name would be in that language, etc. Your child is old enough to enjoy cultural festivals, street fairs, etc. where he or she will be stimulated by the rich sounds and images.

Stories about history can begin to be introduced. Biographical information about people of the child's race or ethnicity who have contributed to society can begin to have a presence in the form of posters, videos, art, books, and toys. Household artifacts, clothes and the like should continue to be chosen with an eye to celebrating diversity and reflecting images of a variety of cultures. Your child's birth culture should remain dominant in the mix.

It is not enough simply to bring these things into the environment. Find ways to point out the connections between the objects and the child. Name the connections and personalize them. For example, "This is a picture of George Washington Carver, a very important man who did many good things for people in our country. He was of African American heritage, just like you. You can feel proud to know that someone just like you invented peanut butter. Many kids love peanut butter and jelly sandwiches better than anything, just like you!"

I Want to Be White Like You

Often young children adopted transracially express a wish to be the same color as their parents, leading parents to fear that the child may be rejecting his or her racial identity. It is also common for kids in this age range to assume that they will "turn white" when they grow up to be "like Mommy or Daddy!"

Did you know that many same-race families of color report that their children, beginning at around three or four, say that they wish they were white or lighter-skinned, expressing dislike of those who are too dark, too brown, or too black? Even young children begin to think of white as the norm or better and other-than-white as different or not-as-good-as. Not until they are six or seven years old do children master the idea that one's racial group is fixed and cannot change.

Preschoolers begin to notice the value the world places on skin color, eye shape, broad nose, thick lips, etc. From early childhood, all children internalize messages from the media and other social institutions that say light or white is best. Naturally, every child wants to be what appears to her to be the best. When a child in a transracial family expresses this wish, parents must first determine whether the child is expressing concern about racial issues or whether this is about belonging to the family (which the child may interpret to mean matching.) Every child is almost certainly going to experience and explore both concerns.

Don't assume that you know why your child is asking the questions he asks. If it is an issue about belonging, then it is the perfect time to talk about the reality that your family's connections are not based on racial sameness but the deep level of your caring about one another. If it's a racial issue, then it's time to talk about wonderful, accomplished people who are "dark" or "too brown," people known personally to your family as well as famous people. This is a reality check for a transracial family. Does your child have enough same-race personal connections to counterbalance the institutional messages of racism he is getting, as would be the case for children of color in same-race families. We must all become well versed in black history, Latino history, Asian history, Native American history, and so on, buying books not just for our children, but also for ourselves, so that we can talk about real people when doubts and concerns come up. We need to be comfortable talking honestly with our children about bias and the sadness and the pain it causes.

Children often wish to be white because all the people they see engaged on television in the activities they admire—a firefighter, a doctor—are white. Sometimes the color-sensitive words of songs express white as an ideal, such as a wish to be washed white as snow. Children of three or four are not too young to begin to deal with the truth in simple terms with parental support. If it is both an issue of race and belonging at once (and it usually is,) don't be hesitant to follow your child's lead and cover all of the issues.

School-Agers

Perspective on Middle Childhood

Between the ages of approximately six and twelve, your little guy will transform into a big kid. Physical growth slows down a bit but intellectual capacity explodes. Kids begin to understand what it means to think. Emotionally, your child's inner life will develop along with his capacity to identify and understand his own deeper feelings about adoption and racial differences. Once you become aware of how your child's capacities are changing, you will learn to work out effective strategies for dealing with his new needs and challenges. This can be a period where naked and not-so-naked questions emerge, providing an opportunity for sweetness to increase.

Physical Development

Yesterday your preschooler was a wired, high speed, just-try-it racer and in general stayed warmed up day and night, flying through his very busy little-guy jobs with so much joy that he could hardly contain himself. Today he's seven and has given you notice that he will be on vacation from red-hot growth until he's eleven. It is likely to go something like this: he'll probably have a smaller appetite but still gain about five pounds a year and grow two or three inches. He'll just get thinner, transforming his body shape from that huggy little toddler to a true big kid with real muscles. Now, when you watch him running down the trail in front of you, his posture and balance are so manly that you want to weep for your baby who has disappeared. But when you yell, "Hey, honey, wait up!" and he turns around to look at you, he's so terribly pleased with himself, you catch your breath. Watching your baby transform so suddenly is exhilarating and mind-boggling at the same time.

He can bounce a ball and run, but probably not both at the same time. Small muscle skills like printing with a pencil are happening but catching a fly ball comes easier. The large muscles in his arms and legs are more developed than his small muscles. Gender difference starts to play into children's way of thinking about themselves and relating to one another. Newly aware of his size and physical skills compared to his peers, he's got friends that matter to him for the first time. She's a social gal now, and they're a motley crew. Some kids are two heads taller and brawnier than the others, some coordinated, some clumsy. They play together like puppies that know their places in the pack. Size and abilities affect the way they get along with each other, how they feel about themselves, and what they do. Your kid's physical size and maturation rate is related to that of his birth parents and unless you can ask them about it now, you probably don't know anything about what their growth was like in middle childhood and what your child can expect. This is a common challenge for adopted children. If your child is a girl and you don't know her genetic history, you'd better get ready to prepare her for menstruation now since it could start as early as eight or nine. You don't want her to be shocked and scared and think she's bleeding to death. Many kids start to mature sexually during their preteens. It will not be unusual if your son begins to get erections or has his first wet dreams during this period. A discovery of masturbation may put that look of danger and glee on your son or daughter's face during this time. Kids today are maturing at much earlier ages.

Intellectual Development

Physical growth may be moving slowly during this period, but you're about to be absolutely blown away by a big change in your child's cognition. During middle childhood she will first become aware of how her mind works and will be able to think about how to think. How beautiful is that? And how good does it feel? Without exaggeration, this creeps up on you by surprise, like watching the sunrise, night turning to day without your being able to tell exactly when it happened, even though you were watching for it the whole time.

Suddenly your child has become able to control her attention and focus on what is most important. For the first time she can understand what to try to remember and how to remember it through encoding strategies, storage strategies and retrieval strategies. She is able to relate new information to what she already knows. Knowledge about a topic makes new information more meaningful and familiar so it is easier to store and retrieve. She is getting better at planning before acting. Elegant and useful new skills for problem solving begin to emerge. She can find a number in the phone book without looking on every page. With increased ability to think and reason, she's excited about games with rules, and collecting things. Reflective and analytical use of language enables her to handle riddles, puns, and jokes well. She is becoming able to appreciate subtleties and understand that what people say may not be what they actually mean, but she gets the point. She is learning about twenty new words each day as her vocabulary develops.

Piaget described this period of middle childhood as the "Concrete Operational Stage," a period when kids first begin to grasp the underlying principles of logical thought. For the first time they can classify and sub-classify objects along many dimensions, can order objects along measurable dimensions like length and combine distance with other physical concepts such as time and speed (spatial reasoning) in order to process information. As the ability to do this becomes automatic, children remember the commonalties between things and can apply concepts from one topic to another.

This is a time when many children are faced with either fitting well into the learning environment of their school or not. For those who do fit, this time can be one of great expansion and growth of self-confidence as new accomplishments and skills are developed daily. For those who do not, there can be serious challenges to self-esteem and knowledge. Is this kind of intellectual development affected by adoption? Studies have found that in IQ children resemble their biological parents more than their adoptive parents. But studies of disadvantaged kids adopted into advantaged families showed a considerably greater IQ than the average IQ of disadvantaged kids, so environment greatly increased IQ. Clearly heredity and environment interact in the production of intelligence.

If your child's learning style is different from yours or if he has very different interests, it may contribute to a sense of mismatch between you or make him feel misunderstood. Howard Gardner's theory of multiple intelligences says that there are seven independent intelligences based on distinct sets of processing operations. Understanding these different types of intelligence and recognizing that only a couple of which are really successful in typical school environments can help parents appreciate their children's strengths and fight for educational systems that suit their needs and challenges. All children benefit from this kind of approach to education but children with learning differences or other challenges cannot succeed without it. Helping children understand what kind of intelligence they possess can be very empowering at this age.

- **Verbal/Linguistic Intelligence** The capacity to use words effectively, either orally or in writing. Highly developed in: storytellers, orators, politicians, poets, playwrights, editors, and journalists. Students with a high degree (of verbal linguistic intelligence): Think in words; Learn by listening, reading, and verbalizing; Enjoy writing; Like books, records, and tapes; Have a good memory for verse, lyrics, or trivia
- **Visual/Spatial Intelligence** The ability to perceive the world accurately and to perform transformations upon one's perceptions. Highly developed in: guides, interior designers, architects, artists, and inventors, Students with a high degree (of spatial intelligence):; Think in images and pictures; Like mazes and jigsaw puzzles; Like to draw and design things; Like films, slides, videos, diagrams, maps, charts
- **Musical Intelligence** The capacity to perceive, discriminate, transform, and express musical forms. Highly developed in: musical performers, aficionados, and critics. Students with a high degree (of musical intelligence): Learn through rhythm and melody; Play a musical instrument; May need music to study; Notice nonverbal sounds in the environment; Learn things more easily if sung, tapped out, or whistled

- **Logical/Mathematical Intelligence** The capacity to use numbers effectively and to reason well. Highly developed in: mathematicians, tax accountants, statisticians, scientists, computer programmers, and logicians. Students with a high degree (of logical/mathematical intelligence): Reason things out logically and clearly; Look for abstract patterns and relationships; Like brain teasers, logical puzzles, and strategy games; Like to use computers; Like to classify and categorize

- **Bodily-Kinesthetic Intelligence** Expertise in using one's whole body to express ideas and feelings, and facility in using ones hands to produce or transform things. Highly developed in: actors, mimes, athletes, dancers, sculptors, mechanics, and surgeons. Students with a high degree (of bodily-kinesthetic intelligence):; Process knowledge through bodily sensations; Move, twitch, tap, or fidget while sitting in a chair; Learn by touching, manipulating, and moving; Like role playing, creative movement

- **Interpersonal Intelligence** The ability to perceive and make distinctions in the moods, intentions, motivations, and feelings of other people. Intelligence can include: sensitivity to facial expressions, voice, and gestures, as well as the ability to respond effectively to such cues. Students with a high degree (of interpersonal intelligence): Understand and care about people; Like to socialize; Learn more easily by relating and cooperating; Are good at teaching other students

- **Intrapersonal Intelligence** Self-knowledge and the ability to act adaptively on the basis of that knowledge. Intelligence can include: having an accurate picture of one's strengths and limitations, awareness of one's moods and motivations, and the capacity for self-discipline. Students with a high degree (of interpersonal intelligence): Seem to be self-motivating; Need their own quiet space; March to the beat of a different drummer; Learn more easily with independent study, self-paced instruction, and individualized projects and games.

Emotional Development

"It is with the heart that one sees rightly: what is essential is invisible to the eye."

—Antoine De Saint-Exupéry, *The Little Prince*

Now that he's a big guy, your darling can do all sorts of brilliant things besides find his teddy when it gets lost and saying "I love you" to you in his special way that melts your bones. Emotions, feelings, physical development and thoughts are interwoven, and when there is growth in one area it affects abilities in the others.

The chief task of elementary-school-aged children is to master the facts, ideas, and skills that will equip them to progress toward adolescence and independent life. During this time, children are supposed to consolidate their identification with parents and cement their sense of belonging to their family. Children have a strong inner life during this stage, as indicated by their dreams and fantasies; they are more attuned to the world inside their heads. Loss is one of the issues with which adopted children will continue to grapple throughout their lives. The full emotional impact of loss comes to children during this stage. Knowing that birth parents made an adoption plan for them often makes adopted children feel devalued and affects their self-esteem. They may feel their status in society is ambiguous. Your willingness to "connect" with your children about their adoption, instead of denying the differences between entering a family through adoption rather than through birth, can help them grieve this important loss. If facts and feelings about adoption are not discussed at all, children's fantasies about their backgrounds may be acted out unconsciously, expressing an unconscious self-identification as an unworthy person.

It's important to remember that all adopted children have feelings about their adoption, and that throughout their development they will struggle in various ways to understand why their birth parents made an adoption plan for them. You can help your children in this task by letting them know that they are not alone in these feelings and that you think it is good for them to express them and try to get explanations for what puzzles or troubles them. The more open family discussions have been from the beginning of verbal communication, the more likely it is that communication will continue, no matter how intense or complex the subject becomes.

Changes in self-concept and self-esteem

He has learned some words to describe what's going on inside him, and a new awareness of emotions enables him to be more sympathetic and capable of cooperation with others. His interaction with the outside world is increasing (focused on school) and he is able to attribute emotional experiences to internal states rather than blaming everything on somebody or something else. He is also learning how to handle mixed emotions like feeling glad you got him that super fast bike for his birthday and being scared about learning how to ride it. He is just starting to understand how to protect his own feelings by putting on a false front, hiding all the threatening emotions (he doesn't want to act like a baby!) and acting thrilled about his new bike! He is also getting better at reading the messages he receives from others and he has words to compare his appearance, abilities and behavior with other people. Though he may need help to express his feelings in appropriate ways when he is upset or worried, he has developed new skills so he can see a situation from someone else's point of view. Over time, she becomes more conscious of the fact that people can interpret the same event in different ways although she still has trouble understanding the feelings and needs of other people. Seven through twelve-year-olds are coming to know the difference between reacting to situations and initiating actions

Erik H. Erikson, a leading psychoanalyst in the field of human development and author of *Identity, Youth and Crisis*, defined this stage as "Industry versus Inferiority." By age seven to eight, most children form three separate areas of self-esteem—academic, physical and social—that become more refined with age. Industry has two components: developing new skills such as being able to accomplish one's tasks (self-directed goal-oriented behavior) and redefining oneself as a person who can do things. Often during these years, parents and teachers have higher expectations of them. Teachers insist upon the completion their work, so children get a message that what they have done naturally is no longer good enough. Self-esteem can often drop in middle childhood as kids see what others can do compared to themselves They need more love, attention, and approval from parents than criticism. For most, self-esteem rises toward the end of this stage. Pride takes on greater importance because children begin to understand that what they accomplish is the result of their own effort and they are better able to appreciate their own accomplishments. Developing a new mastery-oriented way of thinking helps kids to credit their successes to their own abilities and failure to a lack of effort. This approach leads to higher self-esteem and willingness to approach challenging tasks.

Moral development

With your kid was a little guy, you probably didn't dare give one kid two cookies and the rest only one cookie! Every cookie had to be the same size and none broken—preschoolers tend to be firm believers in equality. But by the time they get to middle childhood and have some experience with the demands of school, team sports, and friendships, kids often come to believe that the person who does the most work has earned the greatest reward—a view of fairness based on merit.

Before long, however—especially if they get a taste of what it is to be inferior to others in some areas of accomplishment or they experience some racial, gender or other form of bias—they begin to appreciate the value of benevolence. These children can become generous, wanting to give more to the person who is incapable of accomplishing as much as others. "That's not fair!" pops out of kids' lips more often during middle childhood than during any other period. It may be fueled by a growing sense that adoption is not fair because the kids don't get to help decide what will completely reshape their lives. Often, they do not accept rules that they did not help make which opens the door to the beginnings of the rebellion you thought you weren't going to have to deal with until he became a teen. Go ahead, suggest something to your child you think he'll fall all over himself to do. If he says something like, "That's lame," or, "No way," there's a good chance that at your house you're crossing the bridge to adolescence early. It's okay, honey, just take a deep breath. As H. L. Mencken so aptly said, "We are here and it is now. Further than that, all human knowledge is moonshine."

Peer relations

Friendships are redefined during middle childhood from being based on shared toys and fun to mutual understanding, trust and agreement to help each other in times of stress. Kids tend to make friends with others of the same age, sex, ethnicity and social class. Girls are likely to be exclusive in their friendships because they demand greater closeness than boys. Making good friends is a first step of individualizing and preparing for separation from the family. Peer groups share a sense of belonging, some unique values and standards of behavior, and a pecking order with leaders and followers. The leaders are usually the popular kids who have good communication skills and when they want to participate in an activity, know how to get with the program and try to fit in the flow of activity. Groups do a lot of things alike such as using their own vocabulary, dress code, and "hanging out" together. Some share rituals. Things tend to be black or white, right or wrong, great or disgusting, fun or boring to all members of the group. There is very little middle ground Peer culture is good because it allows kids to practice functioning in a group, develops their sense of identity and teaches them to develop a sense of loyalty to collective goals. Children who participate in-groups grow in social/moral understanding. But "in-groups," often do nasty things to "out-groups," often made up of kids who do not communicate well or don't seem to fit in.

Children who struggle with social and emotional development can be very vulnerable to feeling depressed, lonely and anxious during this time. Transracially adopted kids are easy to target for exclusion because of their obvious differences, that is being adopted and being of different races than their parents or the kids in the in-group. On the other hand, they may also be easier to relate to because they have characteristics from both groups that give other kids a way to feel familiar. Adopted kids in general may be cautious about intimacy because of their experiences with loss and not be as able to trust friends as kids who haven't shared their experiences of separation. Because of this and because in this stage kids feel increased sensitivity about belonging, you need to help your pride and joy have access to groups where he does fit in. Do this by identifying groups where tolerance for diversity is high or where your child will be of the same age, sex, ethnicity and social class as the others.

Special Issues for School-Agers
"Not" Talking About Adoption

> *Mother:* "When you talk about your birth mother as your 'real' mother, I wonder if it's hard to figure out how to think about having two mothers, a birth mother and a mommy?"
>
> *Child:* "Yeah, most kids just have one. And when I say I'm adopted, kids ask me about my real mother."
>
> *Mother:* "It is sort of confusing, when things are different for you than for some of your friends. But let's think of all the things that 'real' mothers do. Can you think of some?"
>
> *Child:* "They grow babies that come out of their bodies."
>
> *Mother:* "Yes, so one way of being a real mother is to be pregnant and give birth. And let's think of other things that 'real' mothers do. Can you think of some?"
>
> *Child:* Well, take care of babies, and make their lunches and their Halloween costumes, and work for money to buy them things.
>
> *Mother:* Yes, so your birth mother is a real mother because she gave birth to you, and I'm your real mother because I do all the other things real mothers do.
>
> *Child:* Can I have two real mothers?
>
> *Mother:* You can have a birth mother and a mommy, and both can be real. Neither one of us is a doll or a puppet or a storybook character or something that's not real."
>
> —Anne Bernstein *Flight of the Stork: What Children (and When) about Sex and Family Building*, Perspectives Press, 1994)

Between the ages of seven and twelve, children become much more concerned with accuracy; in fact it is often hard to get this stage child to speculate about things they don't understand. They are capable of a more accurate understanding of social relationships at this age, so this is a time when sadness and questions regarding permanence may arise in children who are adopted. At this age, children often stop asking questions, parents sometimes misinterpret to mean that they have stopped thinking about adoption or that they fully understand it now. Neither is likely to be true. Initiating conversations as the Mother in the example did becomes essential to remaining involved in how your child thinks about and processes her experience.

It's easy to imagine that since adoption has become a comfortable part of our own reality our children must be feeling the same. This is another reminder of how different the parent's experience is from that of the child. We have finally adjusted and become comfortable with our status as adoptive family; therefore we presume our child has too.

Children are in the moment. If we aren't speaking about it now, then there must be some reason. Coincidences don't exist. New feelings of sadness and connection to birth family are beginning to be felt—how safe is it for your latency age child to express feelings of confusion or pain with you? She is not going to risk it if you don't. Many a nine-year-old has claimed no knowledge of information that has been part of the family lore for years, much to the chagrin of his parents. How can this be? Because if you haven't talked about it lately you might as well never have bothered. This is now and if you aren't with the program then you will be left behind.

I Know I Made it Happen

"I was adopted because I cried too much."
"People like me are bad."
"Bad things don't happen by accident."

The awareness that it's different to be adopted deepens in middle childhood. When children first begin to understand how things work, they imagine themselves at the center of all of life. If something good happens, it's because they have been good. If something bad happens, it's their fault. Claiming responsibility for a negative outcome can feel less threatening than admitting the scary reality that the grownup world is largely out of their control.

Children of color often decide that their skin color is the reason that their birth family did not parent them. A child with medical problems or learning disabilities will often think that their birth parents couldn't take care of her because of her special needs. Even little ones who suffer the worst forms of abuse at the hands of the parents who are supposed to take care of them often believe that they get hurt because they are bad children.

Any sign of being different from other family members—regardless of whether the difference is positive or negative—is often understood by the child as "bad." In their eyes, it serves as proof that they are "bad" and that what has happened to them is their own fault. Young children believe that being like their parents is being "good." They are often deeply distressed about the ways they are not alike, focusing on things they cannot do or characteristics they don't share. Not being with the family that birthed you is very often seen as proof of low worth, reinforcing the messages received, through such negative actions as abuse or abandonment, that you are no good.

According to Joan McNamara (*Adopting the Sexually Abused Child*, Belews Creek, NC : Family Resources 1990), belonging to an ethnic or racial minority, especially when abuse or neglect has been part of their lives, seems to some children to be a logical explanation for why bad things happen to them. For some children who move into foster or adoptive families with different racial or ethnic backgrounds, the safety of the new family may unintentionally reinforce the child's own negative view of her own ethnic heritage, community and herself. Three Latino siblings who had been moved into a loving African American foster home together came to the conclusion that "Black people are okay," but that their own Mexican American heritage and community were not. Their experiences in a substance-abusing family within a poor community, in a neighborhood in which other families had similar problems and violence was prevalent had led them to discount a whole group and therefore their own worth.

When one of her birth children lost his hearing at age seven, McNamara realized that the children who had joined the family through adoption were confused, even stunned. In their minds, bad things happen only to foster and adopted kids (i.e. "bad kids" like them.) In their minds, bad things don't happen to birth kids (i.e. the kids who deserve to belong, the "good kids") in a family. The fact that bad things could happen randomly, rather than according to whether you were good or bad, was too disruptive, too scary to accept. They had made sense of their life histories by constructing a false sense of power based on their ability to "be bad" and then "cause" their rejection. The idea that abusive and neglectful parents' own problems might be the source of parental inability to give care and love to children would mean that their birth parents were the ones who, for whatever reasons, ultimately chose to have their children live away from them. For the children, to accept that this event was in fact not within their control meant that they had to face the pain of abandonment, surrendering the false armor of their own power, the control they imagined could be found by defining themselves as in some way bad or defective—but powerful.

The importance of birth parents

I (Beth) was talking with Sofia yet again about the struggles she was having with the girls in her class. Every day, coming home with another hurt feeling another proof that nobody likes her and everyone else is better friends than she. She explained yet again why it wasn't her fault and what a mean teacher she had and how unfair life was. We had explored seemingly endless possibilities about what and why she might be feeling insecure or sad. In one of those mystical moments of ideas being born outside of oneself, it suddenly dawned on me that it had been ages since she had talked about Ana. When I wondered aloud why it had been such a long time since she had talked about her birth mother she literally took a step back. "I wonder, if you think that I might feel bad if you talk about her?" Her eyes got wider. "I wonder if you worry about hurting my feelings if you say you love her?" As the tears began to flow, I knew we had made more progress on her growing relationships with her peers in that one moment than in the days and weeks of focus we had just completed. As is so often true with children, her behavior with her friends was the language with which she was demonstrating emotional turmoil. Her lack of verbal conversation about Ana didn't mean she wasn't thinking about her. I had forgotten but she had not. And it was my job to remember.

During middle childhood, children begin to have the ability to think about their birth parents in new ways. The ways that your child views her birth family and the reasons for adoption become extremely important to intellectual and emotional development at this stage, and are indicators of how your child will adjust to life in general. Encouraging honest talk about birth parents, race, and ethnic heritage helps children explore their feelings and untangle a common misperception among transracially adopted children: "Not only did my birth parents not want me, but no one of my race wanted me, either."

According to Rutgers-based adoption researcher and therapist Dr. David Brodzinsky (*Being Adopted: The Lifelong Search for Self*, co-authored with Marshall Schechter and Robin Marantz Henig, NY: Doubleday, 1993) "When adopted children have a more positive view of their birth parents and feel more connected to them, emotional adjustment is enhanced. When birth parents are viewed in a negative light, or the child has difficulty in accepting his connection to them, emotional well-being is undermined." Dr. Brodzinsky emphasizes the importance of helping children take comfort in their heritage during the middle years, saying, "Because of the importance of the birth family to school-age adopted children, it is extremely important to help them to find supportive views of their origins and, especially, the circumstances of their relinquishment." In families where there is little or no information about the child's background, or the child has a history or comes from a group about which the adoptive parent has negative feelings, this need is harder to address.

"Did my birth mom know you? "

"If not, how could she trust you with me?"

"Will she come back for me and take me away?"

A youngster who was adopted from Korea cried when she said she didn't know her age, her birthday or her race, because there were no records. "I was found on the street," she says. "My mother threw me away."

Make a priority of gathering as much background information as possible and sharing it with your child. Challenge the claim that there is no information available by asking more questions. If the child was found abandoned, exactly where was she found? On what street? Was it in a safe place where it was highly likely that someone would find her immediately? Instead of abandoning the child, perhaps your child's birth mother had waited in hiding to be sure a kind stranger would find her child and take her in, as Miriam did for Moses in the Bible. Often children are found outside of police stations or hospitals, where they are likely to be found safely. Perhaps the child was found in an area dominated by people of a certain ethnicity, which might be a clue to identity.

Many times it is an act of great courage to save a child by separating from her. A child with no paper trail can be helped to reframe the circumstances of her relinquishment in order to see her and her racial/ethnic community in a positive light. Children who feel emotionally connected to and proud of both their adoptive and biological families will be in the best position to embrace the fullness of their dual racial/ethnic heritage and to take pride in being themselves.

School Issues
Choosing a school

> *"Education is a ladder"*
> —Manuelito of the Navajos (speech given to Congress, 1865)

Expanding on the material provided in the section on pre-school aged children, here are some issues to consider and questions to ask to help you choose the right situation for your school-age child...

The child-to-child climate School age children are extremely peer conscious, so who else is in your child's classroom and school is much more significant than during the preschool years. Understanding whether or not your child will have peers with whom they share values as well as experience is critical.

- Do the children seem comfortable? Who plays with whom? Who is most popular? Who has the most status? Who succeeds in this school? What attributes or skills are valued here?
- Do students and teachers act as if what they are doing is important? Are the classrooms diverse? Welcoming? Are there children of your child's racial or ethnic background enrolled? Are there positive reflections of children of color in the environment?

- Do children have to deny their ethnic/racial background in order to fit in?

Questions for and about teachers and administrators Understanding the difference between teachers and administrators who have good intentions and those who have examined themselves and their teaching assumptions to be sure that children are being taught to question bias and succeed through strength is the first step. Parents can begin by assessing their child's school (or potential school) by noticing the people who populate the school. Are there people of color in the school community? Are they adults or children or both? Are they in positions of relative power or status? If the school's student population is diverse, how do children of color fare? Are they successful? Who are the top students in the graduating classes? Who tends to transfer out or drop out? If the student population is not diverse, why not? What about staff? Is the school a place where people of color feel comfortable and are invited to participate and succeed? Is race and culture something the school administrators and staff are comfortable talking about? If they are not, how will they talk about these matters when issues come up for your child? Have they given thought to how they handle racial slurs or at school or in their community? Exploring these kinds of questions will begin to tell you whether the school is committed to creating an environment that is truly multicultural, or whether the school's administration is simply paying lip service to the PC terminology of "multiculturalism." Teachers and administrators who are uncomfortable talking about differences with you cannot be doing so successfully with children. If they "treat every child the same" then they are certainly teaching from the mistaken supposition that children are the same and they are very unlikely to be able to meet or understand the unique issues your child and other's like her face. Don't be afraid to explore your options before your commit and both you and your child invest in becoming members of the community.

- How many children of color are on the school? How diverse is the administration? How many staff members of color work at the school? Are the staff members of color in positions of prestige? Do you particularly recruit for staff of color? How successful is that recruitment and what is your rate of retention?
- How important is diversity as a school value? How is it supported? How would you prioritize the values of the school? What race/ethnicity are children who succeed? What gender? Do you particularly recruit children of color? How do you make them feel comfortable once they are there? What holidays do you celebrate at the school? What rituals?
- What are your expectations: academic, social, disciplinary? What elective activities are offered? Does this school have any traditions? How are

they preserved? Do you think my child will be able to learn in your classes?

- Have there been any negative racial issues that came up at the school? How were they handled? When racial slurs occur, how are they handled? How do you approach the issues of slavery? Racism? Adoption? Do you speak out if racial issues occur? Are you willing to confront both subtle and pervasive issues?

- Do you have personal relationships with adults of color? Under what circumstances? Have you taken any training on racial awareness?

Questions for other parents of children of color Ally yourself with those with whom you have the most in common, the parents of other children of color, before your child even begins to attend his new school. When your child sees you trusting the antennae of other people of color you will be modeling your knowledge of their positive experience in their world. During these years, much of your time and community involvement will be with parents at your child's school. Finding great parents of color to work with will increase your family's opportunities to find role models and friends among people of your child's heritage.

- What are the strengths of the school? The weaknesses? Do your kids enjoy school and want to be there? What do you wish you had known before your child started? Any differences between what you expected and what happened?

- How does the school deal with parents? Expectations? Involvement? Any discomforts with teachers, administrators or support staff?

- Any differences between treatment of white and non-white children?

Curriculum issues

Multicultural education....

It's a "politically correct" term that sounds straightforward but that has multiple interpretations. Though most people agree that we all live in the same world, we may not agree how we value or establish priorities regarding learning about one another's history, lifestyles, contributions, traditions and attitudes and how (or how much) our schools should reflect the world's diversity. Though parents raising children of color, whether adopted domestically or internationally, want school experiences to enhance their children's cultural pride and their ability to value differences, they may be unsure how to go about making these changes happen.

Multicultural education means more than just a curriculum or environment in which different cultures are occasionally represented as special or unusual. For an educational environment to become truly multicultural, it must not take a tourist approach but must incorporate diversity and acceptance of difference into the core curriculum. In a truly multicultural educational environment, attention is given not only to the community's identity and the books and materials being used but also to the degree to which bias and anti-bias attitudes are being actively pursued. In her landmark books, *Anti-Bias Curriculum* and *Teaching/Learning Anti-Racism*, Louise Derman-Sparks offers insight into helping children examine both their own worlds and the larger world with acceptance and tolerance. Her work suggests that if children are to learn to recognize social bias and to develop strategies to create changes, they must be taught how to do so. And if teachers and administrators are to accomplish this important teaching task, they must be comfortable talking about differences of all sorts, including racial tolerance (and intolerance), gender bias, adoptism and other forms of societal preference or bias. For many, learning to discuss differences frankly is a difficult process which involves confronting their own prejudices and "isms" while learning how to address such issues in constructive and non-oppressive ways.

In the absence of a proactive approach, education will appear to support the status quo. Ours is neither a color-blind nor a difference-blind society. The only antidote to bias is acknowledgment, confrontation and change. Unless schools give children the tools to talk about bias, they will assume that their schools approve of the biases children perceive in the world. For children who are of color or who were adopted internationally, the school's failure to discuss differences will imply that their school, in some sense, "approves" of bias against them. It is difficult for a child to succeed in an environment that is not supportive.

Sometimes, when asked about their attitudes towards diversity, educators will point to particular holidays or "ethnic" study units that happen once a year or for a special occasion. If your child is Latino, for example, and the only element of curriculum offering information about a Latino tradition is a "cultural" festival on Cinco De Mayo (May 5th) acknowledging Mexican Independence Day, the school's implicit message to its students is that there is no other meaningful history, literature or cultural celebration in Latino culture. To create a curriculum that is more truly diverse does not mean that a school must celebrate all holidays for all cultures. In stead, it means that multicultural awareness must not be pushed to the periphery of the curriculum. To be relegated to limited sections and "special" occasions marginalizes race and reflects only a token sampling of the wonderful array of educational activities necessary both for those who embrace these issues at the center of our lives and for those who simply need to be prepared to live in a diverse world. Children will understand that what's "important" is reflected in the books they are assigned to read (are the characters all European in background, Christian, born to their families, etc.?) and the history they are required to know and understand. Do the historical and social attitudes reflect a white American point of view about complicated issues such as slavery, World War II and Indian reservations? Or does the curriculum include at its center the views of all the people affected and involved, such as African American, Japanese and Native American people?

At a minimum school age children (no matter their race) need to be taught the following:

- **That heroes come from every race, gender and ethnicity**. Help make sure your child's school includes literature, images and real life examples that embody this principle. Your internationally or transracially-adopted child needs heroic role models that reflect him- or herself;

- **That white middle-class America is not the measure against which all other lifestyles must be compared**. Don't tolerate an environment in which mainstream or "normal" means "white." Don't allow your child, or any other child, to be held out as the one "example" of their race. It's only with exposure that tolerance and understanding can develop;

- **That things happen in life without regard to race and ethnicity, yet race and ethnicity are a part of every situation**. Race matters. Period. We are a race-conscious society and our children deserve and need guidance to learn how to negotiate that reality. Our children also deserve to create their own dreams and should have the opportunity to become who they want to be based on what is inside them, not what is outside. This freedom of opportunity will emerge only when we teach the broader truth and expand everyone's point of view, enabling tolerance and inclusion rather than judgment and exclusion. Supporting our children means holding both viewpoints together without over- or under-emphasizing either one.

Adoption Savvy

School curriculums are often insensitive to topics or assignments that adopted children are likely to be sensitive to. "Bring in your baby pictures and let's guess which picture is you" doesn't work for a child has no baby pictures or a child who is the only one of his race in the class. Teachers are often completely unprepared for the powerful emotional issues that arise in adopted children confronted with certain units of study. Geography may bring up questions about the child's birth country. The famous family tree assignment is inappropriate for a child with both a birth family and an adoptive family. Adopted kids have complex personal histories and may find the study of history something they are passionately excited about or just as strongly want to avoid. School curriculum is likely to look at history exclusively from a white perspective, excluding contributions of people of color and events of importance. This can raise emotional questions about belonging and suggest to children of color that they are not important. In her book *The Family of Adoption,* Joyce Maguire Pavao tells the story of an adopted boy so sensitized to issues of loss that he burst into tears when asked about his difficulties with math and said, "I can't do subtraction. As soon as they say 'take away,' it makes me feel really sad."

Assume that your child's teacher wants to do what's best for him. Schedule a face-to-face meeting. Say you are coming with information about adopted children and questions about the curriculum and that you hope you can be a resource for her class. Prepare for the meeting by discussing the situation with your child to get his views. If the teacher becomes interested and would like you to make a presentation to the class to help the children understand adoption, be very sure your child thinks that's a good idea before your agree. For children who don't want to be the center of attention, it can be helpful to have such a presentation made by some other adoptive parent, anyone but theirs. Other kids are delighted to be the star of the moment and love it when their parents present to their class.

Home-Schooling and Transracial Adoption

Many children learn well in home-schooling and some parents are good at home-schooling their children. On the other hand, school is about more than academics. Children learn how to deal with peers, work on teams, resolve problems with other children and share, and they often learn faster in groups. Though some schools do not meet the standards parents would wish for, ask yourself three questions before deciding that home-schooling would solve your transracially adopted child's school issues:

1. What is the most important thing that my child needs at this stage of his or her development?
2. Who is best qualified to give this to my child?
3. Where does my child have opportunities to make friends with children of her birth racial/cultural heritage?

If your local school has teachers and families of color, be careful to fully consider how much the chance to attend school with other kids who look like her will mean in the long run. The decision to home-school takes away opportunities to make essential racial connections for transracially-adopted kids in a school context. You will have to work much harder to ensure your child has strong connections to same-race peers. Some home-schoolers are looking to protect their children from some of the negative aspects of the classroom, whether in curriculum or environment. For transracially-adopted people, this can be a lost opportunity to have access, in a relatively safe environment, to other children (and their families) who are of the same race as they. Parents need to ask themselves some very hard questions. Yes, there will be influences or treatment at school that you may not be comfortable with, but is it better to use those issues as opportunities to educate your children in your family values or to deprive them of the opportunity to connect with children and adults who live and understand their racial experience in the world?

In the see-saw struggle between providing your child with the type of education you always wished you had and providing access to other children and adults of the child's birth race/ethnicity, real effort must be made to strike a winning balance. Your family is built of diversity, commitment and choice. Make it work for all of you. No one knows your child better than you. When you examine her needs, make sure you give high priority to her need to build racial identity, something you as a white parent cannot provide directly but only by providing connections and permission to explore them.

Sleep-away camp

Many kids are away from home for the first time when they go to sleep away camp. It's normal for adopted kids to be more sensitive to this kind of separation than kids who have not shared their experience. Talk with your child in advance about how he will handle it if he feels homesick. Help him to understand that he has areas of strength and areas where his skills are average, just as every person in the world does. Talk with him about the possibility that he is like many other adopted children who have special vulnerabilities to separation that children who are raised by their birth families don't share. Assure him that he doesn't have to be ashamed of them. By opening the door, you will enable him to take better care of himself should he experience sadness or anxiety while away. If being separated from his family for the first time might make him worry about rejection, that he has been sent to camp because he has done something wrong. If that happens, you will be glad to help him remember that going to camp was *his* idea and that he picked out this camp out of many choices. Sometimes when you're having a bad moment it's hard to remember things like that. What if being with all new people makes him worry about being welcome and worthy? Then you can help him remember how happy the camp was when he applied, how excited his counselor was to meet him, and how many activities he's really good at. You can also help him know that all the kids feel weird at first and are scared that no one will like them, but he is good at getting along with people. Look how many friends he has at home. Though he needs to be prepared for hurtful things the other kids might say about adoption or people of his race and him as an adoptee or his heritage, it may not come up at all. If it does, you will help him remember that if kids are mean it's not about him, but about them. A good offense is the best defense. Reminding our children of ways to be strong when we are not with them can really help.

Racial Issues for School-Agers

> *"Failing to prepare children for racism is like deciding not to teach a child how to cross the street safely because there is a law giving pedestrians the right of way. It doesn't matter how right you are if the person failing to recognize your right has more power."*
>
> —Lois Melina

Ten Ways to Help School-Agers Handle Racism

- Admit that race will be a factor in the way a child of color is treated.
- Agree that this is unfair, and be absolute that you will not tolerate such behavior within your sphere of influence.
- Kids develop new problem-solving skills in middle childhood. When your child says she has been teased or excluded because of race, help her to use these skills. Help her to express her feelings and explore the short-term and long-term consequences of her possible response. Calmly ask her to tell what happened, how she feels, what she did, what else she might have done, and if other responses would have been more or less successful.
- Ask what she would do if it happened again. Would it be better to back off or to take a stand?
- Ask if you should do anything. It's important for kids to feel capable of handling their own problems—especially as they are learning about being treated unfairly because of race. Racial makeup affects them negatively. If possible, help her feel able to handle it without adult protection, especially if the adult is white.
- Elementary school kids are information gatherers. This is an ideal time to provide her with opportunities to gather realistic images of her racial heritage. Otherwise, she might be defenseless against stereotyped images of her race and feel bad about herself.
- Your child's growing ability to categorize and understand increasingly abstract concepts can help her to integrate seemingly contradictory ideas. Help her to learn that all racial groups have both good and bad historical figures and have made both positive and negative contributions to the world. She will arrive at a deeper understanding of how she can be both Mexican and American or both black and white.
- Make sure that she is able to talk with other people of color who have had similar experiences and can provide new ideas on how to react. Without this exposure the only role models for children adopted

transracially will be the narrow, generally negative stereotypical models from television and the movies.

- Kids usually choose friends by similar interests, not race. If your child resists getting to know other people of color because she has not had enough experience outside of an all white group to feel comfortable, insist that she participate anyway. She needs to break her isolation to develop skills to cope with racism as much as she needs food and water.
- Model an attitude that accepts diversity of all kinds—religious, economic, political, and social. Notice messages you send when you walk past a homeless person, when a fundraiser rings your doorbell, or when a person with physical differences serves you. Since none of us is bias-free, it's useful to discuss with our kids responses that may have been inappropriate or confusing. Soon your child will let you know when your bias is showing.

Positive Reflections

The door to the world outside the family is opening wider. Celebrate the world's diversity with your child. Your child will likely begin to have more significant contact with peers and adults beyond family connections during elementary school years. After school activities with teachers and children of your child's race will become more important. Language, sports, arts and crafts, drama, music, cooking and other classes are all elements with rich cultural connections and will enrich your child's connection to birth heritage as well as building links to other children interested in the same activities. Ongoing connection with the child's birth family, where possible, will be a continuing source of positive self-esteem and racial reflections for your child and hopefully lead to relationships with others of the same racial/ethnic origin.

Attending culture camps is another way to deepen connections to other children of the same race or ethnic background while learning some things about their cultures. Be sure to provide your child with opportunities to build familiarity with professionals of color, helping to convey the message that people of color play important roles in our culture. This is also the time to expand your child's visits to the theater, music and dance performances and museum or art exhibits where his culture of origin is highlighted. Now that your child is old enough to make his or her own friends, provide lots of opportunities to meet other children of his or her race/ethnicity. Don't allow your child to feel isolated or be the only person in his world who comes from his birth culture.

Elementary school children are old enough to learn a second language well even if they have not had the opportunity to learn from birth. Encourage the development of language fluency. It will be worth every effort. If your child is Latino, the mastery of Spanish will be a unifying bridge to those who share his or her ethnicity beyond national differences. If your child is of Asian origins, learning an appropriate dialect of Chinese, Japanese, Korean, Filipino, Vietnamese, Pakistani, or other language of his birth culture will allow him to feel a greater sense of belonging. The process of learning will also connect him to others of his group.

Opportunities to learn more about the music of her culture of origin and to participate in making music, either by studying a particular instrument or by singing in a group are perfectly suited to this age group. Many say music is the gateway to the soul. Do everything you can to bring the soul of your child's culture into your home through the richness of sound. Books, toys, magazines, art, household artifacts, clothes and other things that reflect images of your child's birth cultures should now have a strong presence in your home. Every time you purchase an object, bring books home from the library, or go to the grocery store, take a moment to focus on the messages inherent in the new items you are bringing. Do they present a positive image of your child's culture, a negative image, or are they absent altogether? When making choices, retain the goal of supporting your child's strong racial/ethnic identity. Don't settle for white bread all the time when there are so many other delicious choices!

Pursuing Social Justice

> *Last week I (Beth) was in the car with my daughter and two of her friends—preteens all. As we were driving, the other Mom in the car and I were talking about who drives in each of our families The three girls wondered aloud if men really do drive more than women when both are in the car; they were already prepared to jump out of the car and stand up for their future right to drive when they please. It wasn't long before we had a survey going—one counting cars with men & women where the women were driving, one counting the ones with men driving and the third keeping track of the numbers. When the girls determined that men drove 80%, they were up for the fight. This innocent conversation soon resulted in the subject of a newspaper column in the school newspaper project they were working on in class. Future plans are even now being waged to fight the injustices of men driving more than women in mixed gender cars!*

Because of the deep inner life enjoyed by children this age, they are very open to discussions and even actions which promote social justice. Nothing can compare to the wrath of a fourth, fifth or sixth grade class who has determined something "is not fair" and made it their job to do something about it. Kids this age are eager learners who are well equipped to look at material with a critical eye. They can be easily engaged to become the "isms" police if only given opportunities and voice.

Projects can be set up with their teacher if he is open and interested. Clubs hold great interest at this age, so Girl Scout troops, service groups or church groups can take on a task or "fight" and run with it. Kids this age also love to spend time with their parents doing "adult" activities. Mom & daughter groups, father & son, mom & son gatherings can be ideal settings for discussions about rites of passage, growing up and making change. These can be launching pads for kids eager to make a difference to grab hold of an issue and fly. Provide your child with opportunities to have discussions which focus on current events and situations in the world where they may want to make a difference. Be ready to give them support for actions that are about change or the good fight. Encourage them to work in groups, identifying allies for their beliefs and taking action against wrong. These are powerful lessons of standing up against oppression and finding ways to create support for oneself. These actions are the model for our children to find ways to stand up to the racism that is directed toward them and not only survive but triumph in a world they deserve to tame.

Teens

> "The seventh and eighth grades were for me, and for every single good and interesting person I've ever known, what the writers of the Bible meant when they used the words hell and the pit. Seventh and eighth grades were a place into which one descended. One descended from the relative safety and wildness and bigness one felt in sixth grade, eleven years old. Then the worm turned, and it was all over for any small feeling that one was essentially all right. One wasn't. One was no longer just some kid. One was suddenly a Diane Arbus character. It was springtime, for Hitler, and Germany."
> —Anne Lamott, *Operating Instructions.*

Perspective on Teens

> *Your children are not your children.*
> *They are the sons and daughters of Life's longing for itself.*
> *They come through you but not from you.*
> *And though they are with you, yet they belong not to you.*
> *You may give them your love but not your thoughts.*

For they have their own thoughts.
You may house their bodies but not their souls.
For their souls dwell in the house of tomorrow, which you cannot
visit, even in your dreams.
You may strive to be like them, but seek not to make them like
you.
For life goes not backward nor tarries with yesterday
—excerpted from Kahlil Gibran's "On Children" in *The Prophet*

The teen years, which can start as young as ten or eleven (and continue through age forty-seven) have often been compared with the preschool years because of the myriad of changes that occur. On the physical level, your child's body and general look may be so transformed that people perceive of her as an adult—not your baby. Teens develop a new ability to be introspective and analytical which plays out in new views of the world, some of which may be challenging to you. Emotionally their job is to separate from the family and begin to find ways to function independently, as a responsible adult. This is the time period when young people's job is to figure out who they are in the world. For our adopted kids, this will embrace adoption and racial issues perhaps on a deeper level than has ever been possible before. Thunder is common. "Seek not to make them like you."

Physical development

There is an enormous numbers of physical changes that generally occur during the teen years. For most transracially adopted teens, most of these changes lead logically to new or more intense questions about who his birth parents are. what they look like, and what their health issues and growth patterns are, Substantial changes in height, weight, and body proportion lead to new questions about birth family and genetic history; gender intensification through the emergence of adult male or female characteristics leads to questions about resemblance. The onset of puberty and sexual development often triggers tremendous interest in and identification with birth parents who may have been teens themselves when their child was born. Development of muscle and fat in a weight-conscious society may lead to an understanding of different racial and ethnic concepts of beauty. Due to lack of information, adopted teens who do not have access to their health history may be afraid that every new physical challenge or illness is potentially fatal. Boys and girls are faced with looking like full-grown adults while not always feeling like adults on the inside. Boys face people who fear them as they walk down the street. Girls are responded to with sexual appetite. Physical changes require new sophistication in the responses teens must manage. Depending on the circumstances and the way the adoptive family communicates, these questions may be addressed directly to the birth parents, asked of the adoptive parent, or never voiced aloud and remain worrisome inside the teen's head.

Intellectual development

Teens are often introspective, and many, but not all, teens may have a new ability to be analytical. They may have new interest in identifying with birth culture, greater compassion for birth parents and may be more critical of adoptive parents. If your teen is of higher or lower educational capacity than his adoptive parents a balance between expectations and potential must be negotiated. An increased sense of the future leads to consideration of factors based on racial and ethnic barriers. The teen's primary task is to establish a secure sense of identity and prepare for the new responsibility of finding his place in the world. The future looms large and the escape from such pressure can sometimes lie in a rejection of the values and concerns of childhood. Teens who do not see an optimistic future often see no benefit in being good students or pursuing their dream. "What's the point?" and "Why should I?" often become mantras of the child in adult "clothing" who is struggling to feel safe as she anticipates negotiating the world on her own.

Emotional development

Adolescents' behavior is in transition; their feelings about the world and their place in it are tentative and changeable. Physical growth changes the body from child to adult, in preparation for procreation, but mental and emotional development may take years to catch up with the body. Being able to live and work on one's own, to maintain a comfortable position in one's family and to become a contributing citizen in one's community are the goals. Adolescents need to *take* their independence rather than to be *given* it. A parent's most difficult task is to create a delicate balance of "to love and let go."

If normal adolescence involves a crisis in identity, it stands to reason that adopted teenagers will face additional complications. Adolescents often express their reactions to loss by rebelling against parental standards. Knowing that they have a different origin contributes to their need to define themselves autonomously. Sexual identity is an issue to all adolescents. Adopted children often have conflicting views of parenthood and sexuality. On the one hand, there is the perhaps infertile adoptive parent; and on the other hand, there is the fact of the birth parents' fertility and decision—whether voluntary or otherwise—not to parent the baby. By conforming to others' behavior, beliefs, or expectation, adopted adolescents may be inhibiting a part of themselves for the sake of basic security or out of a sense of guilt or responsibility to their adopter(s). Adoptive parents may be particularly rejection-sensitive and have difficulty with a teen's process of individuation.

It is normal for adopted teens to strive to define themselves autonomously, exploring such questions as "Who am I?" and "Who would I have been if I had been raised in my birth family?" Peer group membership becomes of ultimate importance. Since membership is signified by "being the same as," transracially adopted teens, who are different from the norm, may experience some or all of the following:

- Challenges to a sense of belonging;
- Difficulty identifying with appropriate role models;
- A feeling of never being fully understood by parents who don't "get" the issues of race/ethnicity present in the teen's life and by peers who don't "get" his/her connection to family;
- Sensitivity to and criticism of her changing self and sexual identity
- New interest in thoughts and feelings about others. Teen rebellion is often about comparing the actual with the possible and discovering that the actual is found wanting;
- Deepening attitudes about racism and increased willingness to take action against it.

Unmet expectations

"We want to be accepted just as we are, but at the same time we want to the other person to win the right to our acceptance of him."
—Howard Thurman

During our children's teen years, many of us go back to the beginning. All the choices we made at the beginning are now being played out in the bodies of young adolescents with no sensitivity to the fact that we tried our best or sympathy for our feelings. Fears are relived from those earliest moments when you held your tiniest treasure and prayed it would somehow all work out. Where we are and where we began have somehow come full circle but the ride is wilder and the fears more concrete. This isn't turning out exactly according to the plan.

Reality lesson 1:

You may come to fear that your child will not grow up to be like you in ways that you unconsciously thought that she would.

Reality lesson 2:

You may feel disappointment in the ways that your child is different from you, then guilty because you feel disappointment. You need to relieve that guilt. It's more common that you would imagine.

You want to be a terrific parent, but...

Most people start with idealized visions of what they will be like as parents and what their child will be like as a result. Issues *will* surface when a child begins to be an independent personality whose job is to individuate from his family. Parents need to set aside their expectations in accommodation to reality.

Your job is far from over, but instead of being in charge …

Who would have thought that after all you have learned and done, your growth and wisdom are not what's called for? It is your child who must find and harness his own wisdom and identity now. You will need to optimize your precious few opportunities to cheer and advise—letting go more than latching on. Another truism becomes reality. It's in the letting go that our children find their wings and come back to their roots—by birth and by nurture—but only in the letting go.

Special Issues for Teens (and their parents!)

"I only want to reclaim myself. I even want you to reclaim yourself."
—Nikki Giovanni

According to psychoanalyst Erik Erikson, adolescence is the period in which young people unconsciously work for a feeling of connection between their past, present and future; seek recognition from those who count; and push toward autonomy. A great reliance on peer support helps young people to separate from parents without feeling alone.

Humans experience a faster growth rate during adolescence than at any time except the neonatal period. For many adopted teens, this can foster moody, clingy, manipulative behavior, since the changes feel unpredictable and often beyond their control. A new mental ability to understand abstract concepts leads to preoccupation with values. Because of concerns with justice, equality and honor, many peace and human rights movements are led by teens. It is also the time just before most people's first step toward real independence: living away from parents and making one's own decisions about the future.

All teens look at themselves in new ways, but because of the way the world judges race, teens of color actively examine their racial identities in a way that most white kids do not.

Who should I have been? Who will I become?

Transracially adopted teens have two sets of parents and two cultures against which to measure samenesses and differences. If they have no way of knowing their past or the characteristics they may pass on to the next generation, they may experience "geneological bewilderment"— the sense that they have lost not only their history and birth parents but also a part of themselves. In the absence of biological relatives who can provide insight to future physical and personal development the growth spurts, mood swings, and hormonal changes of the teen years can increase self-consciousness and worry. As the clearest points of distinction between adoptive and birth parents may be based on race, culture, or class differences, it seems natural for teens to focus their movement toward independence in these areas. Adoptive parents also have to guard against resisting their adolescent's separation process, because of their own sensitivity to issues of attachment and loss.

> *(Gail): When Jeremy was thirteen years old, he stood in a line of unbroken tradition whose beginning we do not know. His life was about to change forever. Vigilant to every cue, all nerves and sweat, he sat taut, waiting to be called, at once terrified and proud. Because his father and his grandfathers and all the grandfathers before them had done so, on this first Sabbath after his thirteenth birthday he was about to undertake his coming of age ceremony. He was scared to admit he was scared. As in many cultures, the ritual encompassed sacrifice, the necessity for bravery, and perhaps a mystical experience. In the presence of loved ones, the elders and young ones of the community, more than one hundred people watching him, his test would be to sing out a portion of the Torah and lead certain important prayers. By this route he would formally make his transition from child to adult in the eyes of Judaism, changing forever his privileges and responsibilities. His voice was still changing. He was afraid he would sound like a dork…or not carry the tune…or worse, his friends would laugh. He had not been born a Jew. He had brown skin. What if he opened his mouth and nothing came out?*
>
> *It is said that the Torah must be handed down in the form in which God gave it to Moses. Since ancient Hebrew had no vowels or punctuation, it became necessary to write the Torah scroll without them. As a result, the Torah is not easy to read, not even by people with a lot of experience. He had memorized his portion. He prayed to remember.*
>
> *The congregation was curious. His friends were curious. Who was this child growing up to be and did he belong? To his own surprise Jeremy sang loud enough to be heard in the back of the room. And when a moment came that he lost the tune, the others sang along with him until in a sweet and husky voice he picked up the traditional melody. He did well and he felt it. When it was time for his speech which tradition- ally begins with the phrase "today I am a man," he talked about the toys he would leave behind as symbols of childhood—and those he was taking into teenage life—his modem, his skateboard and his music. Reading a poem he had written himself, he ended with the line "It's up to me. From now one I will be there, when someone needs my help," to*

emphasize that he now accepted a new level of responsibility. After that, friends and family made their individual wishes to him and his friends gave him big high fives. Someone mentioned how much more self assured he seemed these days—how he had a new bounce about him. Then everyone ate a little seven-course snack.

The process of defining oneself involves choosing between alternative behaviors and beliefs. Because there are so many different aspects of self to integrate, resolution may occur at different times for different areas of concern. Perhaps you can recognize your child in some of these patterns, as defined by Brodzinsky et al.

1. **Identity foreclosure**: premature commitment to values before the person has had a chance to experiment with alternatives. For example going into the family business. A young person in this mode may feel fearful or guilty about curiosity regarding adoption or birth family, preferring to focus on the life he lives now rather than exploring a potentially difficult past.

2. **Identity diffusion**: an inability to make a commitment to a career, sexual orientation, or set of moral values. Unsure of what she wants, unwilling to confront the options, unable to identify with a nurturing figure. Appears to be floundering with no sense of direction and an unrealistic view of the world.

3. **Identity moratorium**: thinking about making decisions without taking action. Exploring options but not making commitments.

4. **Identity achievement**: facing a crisis and resolving it by exploring alternative options to discover personal beliefs and values and then making a commitment to a particular set of values and identity.

What Teens Want to Know

"The important thing in putting talk into the air is not whether the teenager responds or agrees, but that he or she hears the talk. The psyche is such an extraordinary 'continuous learner' that it cannot help but assimilate every new datum of information in its lifelong quest for truth."

—Randolph W. Severson

Think out loud occasionally while driving to the store or working in the garage, watching TV or sharing a snack in the kitchen. Mention a shared encounter and recount the ideas it depicted or emotions that were stirred or the memories it evoked. The object is not necessarily mutual conversation but to communicate information that teens may need or from which they might benefit.

A young person's adoptive status will at times give a particular twist to the normal range of teenage concerns. Adopted teens hope for answer to three fundamental questions—which they rarely ask and often do not even completely admit to themselves: If my birth parents had irresponsible sex, will I? What did my birth parents look like? Who will be my friends?

Questions about sexual destiny.

> When Sarah was two weeks shy of her eighteenth birthday she let it be known that she wanted to go out with her parents for dinner and ice cream (an activity usually reserved for special occasions but one they were delighted to accept.) As they were enjoying the last of their sundaes, Dad asked her what had prompted her idea. "Don't you know what day it is?" she demanded. "Don't you realize how old I am?" Her parents sensed danger, once again proving themselves to be totally clueless but they sucked it up and asked her anyway. "No, why don't you explain it for us?" Barbara [her birth mother] had been two weeks shy of her eighteenth birthday when she had given birth to Sarah. Sarah had been holding her breath for who knows how long to see if she could make it past this anniversary without falling into the same pattern as her mother. It was as if the world was now full of new possibilities that hadn't even existed yesterday—now she could get on with her life and be who she wanted to be instead of who she might be destined to become.

What does it say about adopted teens that their birth parents had "irresponsible" sex? Most young people who are sexually active want to believe that they matter to someone else, that someone else cares. Sex can feel like caring and relationship even when it is only an event. Let your child hear you say, "Your birth parents were human and so are you; to be human is to be at times vulnerable, needy, impulsive; but to be human is always to be worthy of love and respect." Many cultural critics portray unwed mothers "who have babies to get welfare" as women of color. Adopted teens of color must hear that there are more whites than non-whites receiving welfare and having babies without being married.

Questions about body image.

> I (Beth) was thrilled when one of the mothers in my daughter's class held a "rite of passage" seminar—a chance for mothers and daughters to talk among women about our girls changing bodies, getting their periods, and all the feelings and expectations that they will undergo. "Our time," we agreed to call it. The girls were remark-

ably candid with their questions and refreshingly open to discussing the changes they were experiencing. At one point we went around the circle, each mother describing the age and way in which her own period had come, whom she had gone to, talked to. As many of the moms had grown up in different cultures, we talked about those differences and the meaning the event had had in our lives. When each daughter spoke we saw how the girls were developing according to the traditions of their family and culture and the genetic timeline begun in their mother's body and passed to them through the magic of birth. When were home later, I asked Sofia how she felt about not knowing exactly when she might start based on her birth mother Ana's biological clock. She looked at me in that way only a pre-teen can manage, half-baby in her almost grown body and said, "I know she had me and my sisters. We are beautiful and we are strong. She had six children so she must have been all right. I think I will be too even though I want to finish college before I have a baby. I might have one or two, then adopt a couple too. Really mom, sometimes you worry too much. We are going to be fine." The wisdom of the young! A few days later, she said she was ready to plan the search for her birth family. "It's our time," she said. I will never believe it was coincidence that she used this body language to indicate her readiness.

The development of body image and the successful assimilation of that body image into the psyche are essential elements of adolescent identity formation. It is critical for the development of positive body image that teens of color have role models that reflect body styles similar to their own. If a teen has no such personal experience, he will be at the mercy of the media's representations of people of the child's race or ethnicity.

What did their birth parents look like? If photographs of birth parents exist, an adoptive parent can "bless" and foster a positive body image by noting the attractiveness of the birth parents and the resemblance between the adopted person and the birth parents. When there are no pictures, adoptive parents can comment favorably on the child's appearance while also suggesting that this probably means that the birth parents, too share these features. Be as specific as possible—identifying eyes, hair color, complexion, build and so on—as especially attractive. "Your hair is really beautiful. I'll bet you got that from your birth mother." Pay particular attention to characteristics that are associated with members of your child's racial or ethnic group rather than your own. These affirmations can also serve as acknowledgement that you see and value her for who she is in a racial/ethnic context.

Questions about "finding one's own kind"

Few adopted people ever consciously wonder how their current relationship might reflect their feelings about their birth parents, but a phenomenon called "searching for their own kind" is familiar to therapists who work with teens. At some point in their lives, many adopted people develop an overwhelming attraction for "outlaw" relationships with people or peer groups that are of their own race. Parents complain about not knowing "where these people came from" but they do understand the attraction.

With adopted people of color, this search is often especially intense and is made more complex by our society's confusion or race and class. Teens in closed adoptions or without racial or ethnic mentors in their lives, may be compelled to actively seek people of their own race from a lower class system that that of their adoptive families because of unspoken assumptions about their birth families and cultural group. It is never too late to talk about these issues and change the patterns in your life so that more access can be offered. Make sure you and your child learn the difference between people of their race and socio-economic distinctions of class. This is best learned through real experiences with real people, personal demonstration of the inaccuracies of stereotypes.

Build an adoption and race library which is easily and privately accessible to your son or daughter. Don't limit it only to books with positive views. Make sure you have books for adults that are now accessible to your teen. In the absence of personal connections some of us are saved by the worlds and feelings we discover and recognize in books.

Stop Treating Me Like a Baby!

Who's in charge? Who should be?

To have been moved from one family to another without any say in the matter tends to facilitate a particular sensitivity to issues of control and difficulties with transitions. Added to that legacy is the transracially adopted child's experience of feeling different from family and community, an experience which tends to create individuals with a heightened need to find ways to fit in. It's logical to imagine that with this history, there will be extra complications in the adolescent quest for adult autonomy and identity.

Transitions are tough. For teens, everything is in transition. As with Alice, after she swallowed that bit of cake, it's easy to imagine the confusion and distress that result from waking up one morning to discover that your favorite pants no longer fit and that your skin—so smooth just yesterday!—is now plagued with problems. Making the change from grade school to junior high and high school means losing the comfort of having one teacher for every class and surrendering the security of that sort of familiar connection. Operating within an expanded world means encountering more pressure to figure out who you are and where you fit in.

And since you are older now, everywhere you turn you are expected to shoulder more responsibility with less supervision. Sometimes that's fun, but often scary (and what adolescent wants to admit that?) And who can one blame? Hey, that's what Mom and Dad are for! When the world isn't right, what safer place to lash out than at parents who have loved you this far, no matter how naughty you were?

Disrespect and rebellion are normal. Tantrums, verbal abuse and testing limits often come with the territory. Even some adults throw things through closed windows or swear at their partners when they find out that they've been transferred at work or that their favorite clothes shrank in the dryer or that the toilet has overflowed. Parents who can patiently confront the challenge of metamorphosis will be in a better position to offer compassion and to respond with humor and good nature. No matter what your kid yells, don't yell back. When the puppy piddles on the floor, after all, all you have to do is firmly and gently put him back on the newspaper, even if he nips at you. You don't give up because you know that—eventually—he'll get it. So will your kid.

As he did when he was two, your teen is taking on the task of separation from what feels safe and finding ways to become "grown-up" in a confusing and uncertain world. Invigorated by new abilities, he is biting off more (or less) than he can possibly chew and sometimes that hurts or makes him mad. You never caged your two-year-old despite her biting the neighbor's finger or pounding her head on the wall—your teenager needs the same understanding and help to get through a period that provokes great rage and melancholy while being exhilarating and frightening all at once.

Keep the boundaries in place, but understand that your adolescent needs to keep more things to himself in his effort to learn how to meet his challenges on his own. Instead of trying to control his life, take control of your need to know and to fix everything. Stay close to your child; let him know that you can talk any time, about anything, but let him solve his own problems and learn from his own mistakes. Help her build feelings of competence by trying on adult roles, whether that be by taking on an after-school job, survival training, joining a team, or taking a trip by herself.

Loyalty Tests

Transracially adopted teens have complex issues of loyalty to resolve. Can they be loyal to their white families and their same-race peer groups at the same time?

Adolescence is a time when loyalty testing comes with the territory. It's easier for teens to figure out who they are if they can measure themselves against a peer group. Peer groups often have some form of a fairly rigid pledge of allegiance that every member is expected to make and which determines who's in and who's out. For transracially adopted adolescents, a newly developing racial awareness causes new conflicts surrounding the question of belonging. Try to understand what your son or daughter is going through. Ask yourself:

- In what manner does he understand that his parents belong to a racial group that oppresses members of his racial group? How does she accept that her parents have privileges she will never have? How will she come to terms with this without either feeling rage all the time or giving up?
- If he believes people of his racial/ethnic group must trust only one another, how does he feel if he is injured by someone from his own group? How does she make sense of her relationship with white parents in the context of finding white people untrustworthy? How does he understand having loving feelings toward people who resemble those who create hurt?

Why friends come first

Why does she want to be with her friends all the time, instead of with the family? Being part of a group is a way of narrowing down the overwhelming range of options in deciding who one is and what one stands for. As young people try to determine who they are in relation to other people, a transfer of emotional attachments from the family to peers and adults in the outside world begins. One way to feel comfortable with body changes, hormonal urgencies, new responsibilities and the challenges of figuring our life is to belong to a group comprising others who are struggling with the same challenges. The easiest way to feel secure is not to feel alone.

Is it any wonder that most teens become super-attentive to their peers and want to spend as much time as possible hanging out with the people who "understand" the way no one else seems able to understand? Everyone does better when we have an arena to share with others experiencing the same issues, a place to talk about racial encounters and feelings of isolation. Think of peers as providing a support group for your kids.

Adopted adolescents in multiracial families commonly hold a strong feeling of being different simply on the basis of being adopted. For transracially adopted children, the adoption is always visible when they're with family members, adding to the complication. As one boy put it, "As soon as I walk out the door with my parents, everyone knows I'm adopted. Kids think I'm weird because I have white parents." Teens who begin with this sense of difference may feel an increased desire to find security by fitting in with peers through style of dress, music, the walk and the talk.

Teens tend to be rigid about their choices in these areas because they provide solid ground, an arena in which they know what to expect when so many other things are unpredictable. Parents who are able to understand these needs may avoid getting into power struggles over things like hair styles, clothes, loud music or slang, and may be able to create a more peaceful family life that those parents who are intent on making their children confirm to their limited sense of the acceptable.

What if he picks the wrong friends?

"No person is your friend who demands your silence or denies your right to grow and be as fully blossomed as you were intended."
—Alice Walker

We all want to pick our own friends. Once your child starts high school, you are unlikely to know all of her friends any longer. You may worry because the group he picks seems to belong to an "underclass." Parents who enjoy the benefits of middle-class life may worry if they sense that their teen's friends have different values or expectations for the future. In such cases, parents and their children may be confusing race and class, thinking that there is only one way to be acceptable as an African American or Korean or Mexican. The best way to expand that vision is to build significant relationships with families of your same class who share your child's racial/ethnic heritage and your values.

If the group your child aligns with disparages academic success, it is probably due to fear of peer pressure. Black teens who do well at school are often accused of "acting white" or of not being black enough. Remind yourself and your teen that by that measure, Martin Luther King must not have been black enough, since he earned a Ph.D., and Malcolm X as well, since he educated himself while in prison. Empathize with the deeper emotion of hopelessness that is being expressed in rejecting education as a way to make a better life. Find examples and activities for your teen which demonstrate the way an education has made a difference to people they consider "cool."

If your child's group is one that gets into trouble with the police or is into drugs or other bad stuff, the best advice is to remove yourself as a point of conflict. In doing so, you may create new space for your child to take responsibility for herself and to take a fresh look at personal values. This is neither an easy time nor an easy journey, but it is one many parents travel. You are not alone. Do find support.

What Do I Do Now? My Child Is a Teen!
Rejection-Sensitive Families

> *"It is the family that gives us a deep private sense of belonging. Here we first begin to have our self defined for us."*
> —Howard Thurman

Adopted teens who are afraid of rejection may reject others as a preemptive strike again being rejected themselves. You may notice that your child is pursuing friendships only to end them abruptly; he may provoke rejecting responses from you and other family members; she may avoid intimacy; he may resist growing up, behaving in age-inappropriate, dependent ways.

Pay special attention to periods of separation between yourself and your child. If your business travel or vacations without kids seem to correspond with increased anxiety and rejection-related behaviors for your teen, attempt to find some creative ways to give more comfort. Can you bring him along? Can you send someone else in your place?

Teen years are the time when children prepare for leaving home for the first time. If you notice your child's grades are suddenly falling, maybe she is unconsciously trying to fail so that she doesn't have to go off to college or move out of the family home. Perhaps she would prefer to commute to a local community college for the first year or two, continuing to live at home with the family while easing into this significant transition.

Vulnerable parents

> *"You do not solve problems by drifting backwards. You solve them by tearing down barriers so you can get at them."*
> —Benjamin Mays

According to Freud, at some point in childhood all kids think, "I must have been adopted; these jerks can't be my real parents," as they try to reconcile the problem of both loving and hating their parents, of desiring to emulate them but struggling to define themselves as separate. This process, called the family romance fantasy, is more complicated for adopted kids, because they actually *were* adopted! If they lash out, they are likely to use transracial adoption as a weapon. They may accuse their parents of stealing them from their real people, or they may find their parents to blame for their own feelings of uncertainly about their racial identity.

When our children idealize their birth parents and their racial heritage, it's a double-whammy for adoptive parents, who can in turn begin to feel intensely rejected. This pattern is enhanced as teens struggle for autonomy. Attempting to break away from family rules and restrictions, feeling misunderstood by Mom and Dad, who, after all, "don't know anything," may lead teens to idealize their birth parents. Fantasizing that their birth parents, of course, would surely understand, teens can create powerful models of injustice and unfairness all based on what is wrong with you—their adoptive parents. Peers, teachers, coaches, rock starts, sports idols, other family members and family friends all seem to have more credibility and receive greater respect than do Mom and Dad.

In addition, in late adolescence parents in general and adoptive parents in particular may feel unready to separate from the child who has been the center of their lives. They may wonder whether the ties between them are really strong enough to ensure their connection once the child has left home., Whether they have influenced their child's values in any way or how they themselves will survive a life with less focus on and time with their child. Adoptive parents may be especially vulnerable to teen rejection because society at large continues to questions the strength of the "bond" forged across racial and genetic lines.

Try to keep perspective. If you are like many adults, you swore to yourself that when you became parents you would not repeat any of your own parents' mistakes. Later, when you hear your mother's words spilling out of your mouth as you yell at your own child, you may realize with something of a shock that you share many of your parents' values after all. Most of us have come to understand that our own parents did the best they could, within the limits of their own capacity, our children will eventually realize this too. The important thing to remember is that teens need to question authority in order to figure out who they are. Since parents represent authority, in healthy families parents will be challenged and apparently rejected, at times, and questioned and questioned and questioned. It's called testing—and both you and your child can get through it.

Strategies for surviving the teen years

Though many of the strategies that follow apply to children of other ages as well, all are particularly appropriate during the teen years, when adolescents push toward independence and struggle to establish sexual, emotional, intellectual and physical identity.

- Trust that your family will survive and grow stronger by surviving this time period.
- Make sure that your child remains surrounded by non-European standards of beauty and attractiveness and is able to treat them seriously. Your child needs adult role models of his or her body type and racial/ethnic origin to help build positive sexual identity.
- Consider the effects on your teen of separation from you and make a priority of her need for your presence when you must travel.

- Understand that Mom may take more heat than Dad does when teens lash out. This is because often there is a transfer of anger from birth mother who did not parent to adoptive mom who did.
- Support your child's increased need to know about or connect with birth parents and racial or ethnic communities at this time. Seek cultural guides for age-appropriate interests such as rite of passage ceremonies, dating and marriage conventions.

Racial Issues and Teens
Extra challenges for transracially-adopted teens

- discomfort with interracial dating
- discomfort with same race dating
- internalized white standards of beauty
- feelings about birth parents' sexual history
- feelings about society
- society's challenges to the family

> *Natalie Reed has just turned sixteen. She is Latina (born in Guatemala,) was adopted at birth by white parents, and grew up in a primarily white community. She couldn't have been more thrilled and scared when Adam, a boy she had known since kindergarten, invited her to be his date for the junior prom. Nat thinks she is ugly and has difficulty thinking of herself as an attractive young woman. Her voluptuous curves, dark skin and large features make her look exactly the opposite from her best friend, JJ, who has long blond hair and a Twiggy body. When the girls return from their shopping trip having decided to wear the same dress in different colors to the prom, Nat's Mom is surprised but knows better that to comment. It was that very night that Adam's dad calls to say, "Sorry, folks, Adam can't take Natalie to the prom. Interracial dating is just too hard. The kids don't understand what they are getting into. I don't want them to start down a path that as adults we know will be filled with pain and frustrations just because it sounds like fun for now. This isn't about begin racist it's just about reality. Please tell your daughter that it's really for her own good."*

Sexual development issues are highly charged during the teen years. Add in the Adam's fathers of the world, and the teen of color is faced with many confusing and painful messages. Natalie's sexual self-image has been formed in the context of an adoptive mother who is as different in body type from Nat as is her friend JJ. Without similar models of womanhood (let alone beauty), she has difficulty thinking of herself as female. A child of a white school system and white community, her personal definitions of beauty have been shaped by European standards rather than Latino ones, even though her family has tried to provide her with positive reflections of Latinas through books, magazines and the like.

Nat does not realize that she is beautiful just as she is, but her consciousness of her own sexuality has increased her interest in her birth parents. She knows very little about them except that her mother was sixteen when she was born. When her adoptive mother suggest that Nat could ask as her date for the prom Andre, a young Guatemala teen who lives in a nearby city and for whom Natalie seems to have a crush, Nat says angrily, "Yeah, but how do I know he's not my brother? Maybe I like him too much. Maybe I take after my birthmom and I need to be careful I don't have a baby."

For Natalie, a lack of knowledge about her own genetic history has made her fearful of dating Guatemalans in case people she goes out with turn out to be relatives. The "bad seed" myth has made her afraid of sexual activity for fear of repeating her birth mother's teen pregnancy. The opposite reaction, becoming pregnant on purpose "to do for my baby what my birth mother didn't do for me" or "to finally see someone who really looks like me" can also come up during the teen years.

Nat and her family are also experiencing another challenge directly related to transracial adoption. When Nat's dad, a college professor, was invited to lecture in a distant state, he invited Nat to come along. Since the two do not look alike, simple things, like gestures of affection in public or sharing a hotel room, raised eyebrows and left little question in their minds that people perceived full-figured Natalie as a whore or a lover and her father as her customer. The public does not quite believe that parents and children in adoptive families have the same boundaries around sexual interactions between them as do families related by blood. Remember how few people seemed outraged when Woody Allen had sex with Mia Farrow's adopted daughter? The explanation seemed to be, well, she was not *really* his daughter. This is an adoption issue that can be made more dramatic by racial difference because stereotypes by which many people judge those of other races get thrown into the mix.

If you find yourself feeling this story is too complex to be real, get ready for the reality that will make this look simple. Coping with the complexities of teen issues in a transracial context is challenging. There are no easy answers. Nat is dealing with a myriad of cultural problems neither she nor her parents can easily fix: being a Latina in a country that elevates white standards of beauty above all others, Adam's father's bias, assumptions of strangers about her family not being a family. She also is distressed because she doesn't know her own history and has fantasies about her birth parents but no facts.

First and foremost, Natalie needs support and understanding from her family about how really hard and painful this is as well as opportunities to bury her head in the sand for a few moments of relief in between strategy session about what to do next. Affirmation and reflection of her own feelings of anger, pain, confusion and sorrow need to be offered without judgement or suggestions of "positive spins." These moments are dark days whose only comfort lies in being allowed to "feel like #*! #**," at least for a while. Later the time will come for ideas about what to do and special gestures of love and inclusion. In the moment, being present is the only option.

Perhaps reconnecting with her birth parents would relieve many of her inner anxieties. Search and reunion may be appropriate for Nat at this time. If that is her desire, her parents need to offer her as much support as possible but if she does not want to find her birth family it will not be useful for her parents to force her in that direction. It may also be a good idea for Nat to spend some time in communities or even countries where Latinos are in the majority. Since she is sixteen, there may be possibilities for exchange programs or teen travel that would allow her to spend time with others who look like her and where standards of beauty come from a Latin perspective.

Parents who can acknowledge their own regrets about what they wish they had done in terms of connecting their children to friends and adults of color or living in a more diverse area will also help their children understand that even adults can make bad choices or mistakes they regret and still move forward and change. If you will acknowledge your "failures" and be willing to make some changes, perhaps so will your teen. Taking some of the responsibility or "reason" for racial incidents off of them and onto you by virtue of your choices or simple lack of knowledge may help them when they are ready to dust themselves off and go back into the fray.

Smashing Stereotypes

> "It's a curious way to find your identity, labeling yourself by
> labeling all the things that you are not."
> —James Baldwin

There is more than one way to be African American, Asian, American Indian, Latino or white. The sooner each young person grasps this idea, the more options he has to explore his own identity.

We all are influenced by stereotypes, even when we make conscious efforts not to be. Teens—and transracially adopted adolescents perhaps more so—are particularly vulnerable to this influence; they have an increased need to figure out how to be accepted by their peers. Adoption issues may make them believe that they were placed for adoption due to some intrinsic flaw;

that the reason for their placement was something negative about themselves, especially if desirable role models are limited. In the United States, being poor is often imagined to be synonymous with involvement with crime and drugs; being black with being poor; being Asian with being good at math and music; being Latino with being an illegal immigrant; being Native American with being an alcoholic and a gambler; and so on and so on.

To resist these cultural claims, teens must come to understand that there is more than one way to behave and be seen as acceptably black or brown or tan. According to Drs. Darlene and Derek Hopson, authors of *Different and Wonderful* (NY: Simon & Schuster, 1990) within high school populations there are often two subgroups of each racial or ethnic group. Each group reflects a particular orientation and stands in contrast with the other. The group that has academic status and administrative support tends to be conservative and non-controversial; the other group, which often establishes ethnic loyalty as its first priority, is generally held in low esteem and is considered to be composed of trouble-makers. Often, class conflicts are embedded in the relationship between the two groups. Generally, the kids in these groups conflict with one another, establishing themselves in counterpoint to the behavior and attitudes of the other.

If your transracially-adopted teen is lucky enough to attend a school with a student population sufficiently diverse to support two groups, they will also be faced with choices that may feel more conflictual for them than most. They have the enormous advantage of experience with people who shatter the stereotypes of the media but they must also contend with their own strong desires to "fit" and "belong." In schools with only one or two students of color, the pool may be so limited that it will hamper your child's discovery of the variety of ways to be a person of color. To enable their child's ability to encounter diverse behaviors, parents can be most helpful if they work to provide regular and repeated social access to a broad range of role models and groups. The importance of such access can be amplified when it is combined with books, music, films, foods, and the like that also represent a broad range of ways of being. The goal is for your child to understand that there is an expansive range of options to choose among in developing the pieces of identity. Help your teen be creative in using all of her options; direct access to people and groups that may not be available immediately. Use local colleges. Use parent support groups. Use Pact. The goal is to find as many ways as possible to connect to role models and ideas so that your child can break through the stereotypes of generalizing to direct experience with individuals. No matter where you live, if you work hard enough, you can provide some level of access.

This message is for families in crisis

If you live with a happy, responsible, healthy, high-achieving teenager who fills your day with sunshine, skip this section.

If you do not, let's begin with a bit of reassurance: It is highly possible that things will improve within your lifetime. Incredible thought, isn't it?

Remarkable numbers of teens somehow do manage to turn into mature adults even before their own children put them into nursing homes. If your family, like one or two others we can think of, has hit turbulence during the stretching years and things are so bad that you are seriously thinking of running away from home, take heart.

The facts are these: You probably have not ruined your kid. Humans are remarkably resilient. Your family will survive and be stronger because of this. These statements are more likely to be true than false.

Our Children Are Our Children Forever

When Will Your Teen Grow Up?

What if your child has reached young adulthood but is still not ready to take on the responsibilities of being independent? What if you have no control of her life but she is not able to make healthy decisions or to work toward healthy goals? Parents often think that they have failed if their children "age out" of adolescence before resolving childhood issues. But some people don't begin to address their particular challenges until they become adults, no matter how much their parents attempt to help them or how their parents blame themselves.

The ability to learn and develop doesn't end with the teen years. For many, that's just the beginning. Many people begin to make commitments to careers and to building families of their own when they are in their twenties and thirties. Because they are thinking in fresh ways about their futures, transracially adopted people often become newly invested in understanding their own genetic/ethnic/racial heritage at this time. Wanting to be able to live intimately with a loving partner is a good motivation for taking stock of one's difficult behavior. If trouble brews with friends, career, or significant other, one may want to change behavior that just doesn't work in these new contexts. A door to healing that leads to maturity may open at this time.

When children leave home and move on to lives of their own, parents may also see them with new eyes. If we no longer feel responsible for making them strong and healthy, we may be able to see more clearly the strength and health they possess. Because life is long, there may even be enough time for them to meet their unique challenges.

Marriage and Significant Others

(*Gail*) *Our youngest daughter Liza had always said she would only marry a black man and so she did. Corey, her sweet husband, is fantastic, caring and real, an amazing guy to be around. He comes from a proud southern family with a history and daily life as different from ours as matzoh balls from sweet potato pie. Their wedding plans focused on respect for the tremendous diversity among their guests. Both a minister and a rabbi led the service. Liza and Corey had thought through every detail, their priority for everyone to feel comfortable, to create a balance, to be inclusive.*

At the wedding dinner, when the band started playing the hora, the Jewish guests formed the first circle but in moments it seemed like everyone in the room joined in. Those who didn't know the steps somehow felt comfortable moving with the lively circle, picking up on the simple rhythm, arm in arm, moving together to the klezmer sounds. And then, when everyone was good and sweaty, and definitely into it, the band started up the electric slide. The bride and groom's black friends taught the rest of us how to do the steps. It was like that mirror game where you find yourself making moves you never could have imagined for yourself, freer and more full of life than a puppy just off his leash, we were dancing, really dancing. The music was up, the laughter was up, and then they played the hora again. It went on like that all night—race mattered, but in a positive way. We were all so thrilled with ourselves for being part of a truly mixed group—perhaps for the first time in every person's life—that we danced with abandon, like fools, we were the stars in an all for fun ballet and by the time we were done, we were shiny and easy, like after a deep, cleansing workout. It was wonderful. For me, what was most wonderful was that nobody had to lose what he or she had to be able to embrace something more. It made me understand in my relaxed old bones that we really were not losing a daughter—we were gaining a son.

When two families of entirely different cultures are connected through the marriage of their children, finding the balance isn't trivial. Four of our four children have married. Four times out of four, the challenges of finding ways to build relationship with our child's spouse's world has been something like being tied between two objects moving in opposite directions and stretched beyond our own capacities. Is that what they call, "it hurts so good?" I guess it's what we'll work on forever, knowing we have no control, knowing our children must make their own decisions about their own lives, but hoping, secretly, deep inside, that nothing will ever take them away.

When your child is old enough to choose a life partner, your inner most feelings about race and parenting will get tested again. So what else is new? You'll be so used to it by then you'll have your own script; not to worry. For example, if your Latina daughter marries another Latino, will you pride yourself on having helped her build a positive racial identity and making the right choice or will you feel abandoned because she didn't choose a partner of your race? If she chooses a white partner like her mom or dad, will you feel embarrassed because you didn't help her feel connected enough with her heritage to build an intimate relationship with someone of her own race or will you be relieved because she chose someone more like you? If she chooses an Asian, African American or American Indian will you see her choice as continuing your family's pattern of celebrating diversity or worry that she only feels comfortable feeling different and wonder where you went wrong? The only way you can possibly feel safe is to remember that you're not in charge of any of it. There will be your child's plan, and your plan, and your plan won't matter. Give as much as you can. The more flexible you are, the more easily you can bend with joy.

When Our Children Have Children

I (Gail) was in the delivery room when my granddaughter Kai was born. Andy, her father, her sister Leah and I were there. Who was it that said, "If you are hear a child's first cry of 'I am', you will be connected to him through eternity?" In those first moments of wonderment, no one spoke, just looked. There are some events so sacred that the only possible response is to pay full attention in silence. Immersed in that rare cocoon, Shira's first words when they came were piercing. "She looks just like Andy," she said with tears streaming down her cheeks. "She doesn't look anything like me."

We had never seen a baby picture of Shira. She came to us when she was three. Kai, like her sister Leah before her, was born with a full head of her mother's thick black curls, her mother's almond shaped eyes, dimples on both cheeks like her mom, and white skin like her dads. She recognized her mother. The way she nestled in Shira's arms showed that. I held my breath praying Shira would recognize her.

"Mommy, the baby looks just like you," Leah, who was five years old, remarked innocently.

Sometimes, if you are lucky, you can watch as your grown daughter folds up the irrational fear which pops up from time to time unbidden—that as an adopted child, she's unacceptable—and watch her adjust her mantle of motherhood more comfortably on her shoulders, and start to nurse her baby.

When your grandchildren are born, of course you will be delighted. All those truisms you anticipated about how your family would be racially changed forever by adoption will turn real and you will marvel at the beauty of your children's children who look like them but not like you. We hope you don't find yourself in the middle of the night fighting off questions you don't want to have from your most guarded secret places like some of us. Where is my family going? How will I be remembered in the family portrait of the generations to come? Even though you knew what was coming, your future has suddenly arrived and you have to live it by yourself. Take heart. Many of us share these questions but rarely talk about them. The simple answer is, what is most essential is invisible to the eye. The links between our hearts, how we touch each other, that is the mortar that will hold and mold our families and we are part of that. With luck, we always will be.

When your grandchildren are born, of course you will be thrilled. Who could imagine revisiting the losses of infertility and feeling jealous of your own child for being able to give birth when you could not at a time like this? In the midst of your joy to feel jealous of your own child? How crazy is that? Or normal, for families like ours. If it comes up, it's a passing thought, one we rarely share with others because it holds shame even though we'd guess it's common. We are more alike than different. The bad news is, our stuff is our stuff. The good news is, we get used to it because it keeps coming back.

When your children have children, it will open whole new wonderful worlds for you. Grandparents are supposed to spoil their grandkids and if you go crazy and buy as many irresistibles as you can afford at Baby Gap, no one will blame you. As a grandparent, you can be overindulgent and still be considered "normal." This is a lovely relief from the scrutiny wrong race adoptive parent's endure. If you are lucky, you will also get to baby-sit frequently. People in the grocery store will still feel entitled to ask personal questions about your grandchild's race but this time around, you will answer or not answer with glee, you will be so comfortable. Your children will have their own ideas about parenting which may not agree with yours (imagine!) and you will have the opportunity to learn new lessons that they will generously not hesitate to teach you. So much gladness comes from a bronze-skinned child holding your hand, into tomorrow.

Search and Reunion

Search and reunion can happen for adopted people of any age but often takes place during young adulthood. Though the process of reconnecting with birth family is intense for any adopted person, when racial and cultural differences are present, as always, they often take center stage.

Here are three examples:

(Gail) When my Korean daughter's birth mother found her, their first give and take was wrapped up around Korean food and how foreign it was for Shira. From home made kimchee to bean cake and a special family recipe for squid. Linda had spent untold hours preparing an all Korean welcome home feast. Shira reported with true joy her deep appreciation of her mother's efforts and her nervousness about whether she had been disrespectful by only politely nibbling the dishes that didn't suit her palate. Their time together by her description was filled with smells and tastes and talk about the kinds of food Shira had lost in her upbringing and how to cook them. Smells and tastes that were intimate and pickled, salty, and pungent, hot and sweet— pathways to a distant land that was not spoken of directly where they had shared the best and the worst of times.

Soon after reunion, Liza attended the funeral of her birth grandmother whom she had never met. She described being counted in as one of the family as a wonderful experience, one that filled her with joy in a moment that her birth family was deep in grief. Because the African American funeral was very different from the Jewish ceremony she had been part of when her Nana died, she was self conscious about whether she was behaving appropriately, fearing her newfound family might not approve of her.

When a young man who was adopted in a closed adoption found his birth mother and she refused to speak with him or provide any family information, he couldn't help but wonder bitterly if it was because he was biracial and she was white and if that had been the reason for his placement.

Supporting your child's need to find him- or herself in a family other than our own can feel threatening. As parents, it's our job to handle our own feelings so our children can pursue their new relationships free of concern about us. Give all you can, because your child deserves it.

Where Do We Fit?

In the video *Struggle for Identity, Issues in Transracial Adoption* (New York State Citizens' Coalition for Children, Inc., Ithaca, NY: PhotoSynthesis Productions, 1998) John Raibel, a proud black man of biracial heritage and a transracial adoptee talks about feeling most comfortable in diverse situations with other people who are considered by society in some way marginal. We interpret his meaning to be that his experience of being transracially adopted leads him to form his most intimate relationships with others who whether they share his racial heritage or not, share his experience of not being mainstream, being different and being sensitive to issues of belonging. We hope that our children will not grow up thinking less of themselves because they do not have the same experience and fluency with their birth culture as children who were raised within it. If transracially adopted adults feel positive about being able to claim all of their unique history, their adoptive heritage as well as their birth heritage, and value their unique double inheritance—what a gift might have emerged. So many people in America feel a sense of their own "otherness," perhaps classifying oneself in this way is more mainstream than not.

Useful books

Bernstein, Anne C.; *Flight of the Stork: What Children Think (and When) about Sex and Family Building* (Indianapolis: Perspectives Press: 1994.)

The best book about how children understand sex and family creation (including adoption). 1994 Pact Praise book award-winner. Books in Print writes, "Bernstein examines how children think differently from adults concerning sex and birth. Page after page of enlightening interviews take us deep into the minds of children three to 12 years old. The interviews demonstrate each child's level of mental development and also show how a child's thinking changes with age. This understanding of child development will help adults communicate better with children about the origin of families as well as the origin of babies. Also deals with assisted reproductive technology, donor insemination, and surrogacy. These valuable additions make the book essential even for libraries already owning the first edition."

Davis, Laura & Keyser, Janis; *Becoming the Parent You Want to Be* (NY: Broadway Books: 1997.)

This book offers a developmental approach for both children and parents. Provides parents with energy to explore, experiment and grow along with their kids. Thought-provoking, challenging and enriching

Derman-Sparks, Louise; *Teaching / Learning Anti Racism* (NY: Teachers College Press: 1998.)

This new book is a guide for teachers, trainers, and anyone interested in fighting racism by Louise Derman-Sparks, who also wrote *Anti-Bias Curriculum* for young children. This book is full of excellent ideas but the presentation is formal and academic. Thus, it can be a challenging read. Contents include: The Dynamics of Racism; The Individual, Racism, and Anti-Racism; Beginning Explorations of Racism; Exposing the Contradictions; Transformation to an Understanding of Self and Society; Anti-Racism as a New Beginning; Making the Course Your Own

Greenspan, Stanley; *First Feelings* (NY: Penguin: 1994.)

A long look at the six stages of emotional development of infants, provides help in observing your baby, and offers strategies to support your child's emotional development. You will learn how to take inventory of your own parenting style and how to develop positive patterns of interaction with your baby; how to stimulate your baby; what to do when baby is nasty (temper tantrums, aggressiveness, attacks on siblings), how to encourage curiosity and independence, and more. Easy to read and useful.

Hopson Darlene & Derek; *Different & Wonderful* (NY: Simon & Schuster, 1992.)

This direct and clear book offers a positive and realistic approach toward preparing African American children to become positive, productive and self-respecting. Chapters focus on modeling, racial identification, sexuality, daycare and family relations.

Ito, Susan; *A Ghost At Heart's Edge* (Berkeley, CA: North Atlantic Books, 1999.)

A thoughtful and moving collect of poems and stories that dismantles adoption myths by showing people touched by adoption in all their complexity.

Karen, Robert; *Becoming Attached*, (NY: Oxford University Press, 1997.)

Fresh views about attachment theory and how contemporary thinking about bonding applies to the lives of children.

Kurcinka, Mary Sheedy; *Raising Your Spirited Child* **(NY: Harper Row, 1998.)**

Children who are more intense, perceptive and persistent may also be less adaptable, have more energy, and exhibit more difficult behavior. This optimistic book offers support and practical advice to parents raising spirited children. The author advises "progress, not perfection." The engaging writing clearly presents practical skills for parenting. Highly recommended to parents of adopted children, many of whom act out their feelings about their core experiences by having difficulty with transitions, testing authority, fighting bedtime, and a range of behaviors discussed by the author. A Pact bestseller.

Loewen, James; *Lies My Teacher Told Me* **(NY: Simon & Schuster: 1996.)**

A critique of the blind patriotism and misinformation of high school history texts. Loewen suggests a more honest approach to US history, complete with information most of us never learned in school. Of particular interest to parents of children of color. Winner of the 1996 American Book Award and the Oliver Cromwell Cox Award for Distinguished Anti-Racist Scholarship. Publisher's Weekly: "Sure to please liberals and infuriate conservatives. In condemning the way history is taught, he indicts everyone involved in the enterprise: authors, publishers, adoption committees, parents and teachers."

Rodriguez, Gloria; *Raising Nuestro Ninos* **(NY: Fireside Books:1999.)**

Rodriguez shares her experiences of raising Latino children from infancy through preadolescence. She encourages parents to strengthen the foundations of family, marriage, and the community. Valuable for parents of Latino infants.

Strauss, Jean A.; *Birthright* **(NY: Viking: 1993)**

This book is filled with stories…direct quotes from adoptive parents, birth parents, and adopted people who have experienced search and reunion. Includes guidelines for beginning a search.

Section Five
❖ ❖ ❖ ❖ ❖
Cultural Specifics
in Focus

Belonging or Be-Longing?

By Gail Steinberg

How many times do you go back and think about some certain afternoon, maybe one of five that changed your life, when whatever happened still eats at you because you still don't get it?

We were on sabbatical and had rented a little house in Greece, sight unseen. Life without electricity with four children under ten—including a baby who cried when she crawled on the kuklachia floors (mosaics of black and white stones standing vertically)—meant rising and setting with the sun, washing diapers by stomping on them in a metal bucket, heating huge kettles of water for everything, and feeding McDonald's-loving children on yogurt and sardines. Figuring out how to approach that pioneer life we had not ordered and were pitifully unprepared for was... let's just say our kids learned mournful whining and the plaintive question ("what will become of us?") from pros.

Unfortunately, venting, no matter how masterful, is amusing only for a millisecond. Once we got over ourselves and decided to offer praise instead, a new rhythm evolved. In the mornings we worked hard at meeting daily needs, but every afternoon we played on the most beautiful beach in the universe. Liza first learned to walk right there. We gave ourselves up to a life outside the confines of time, directed by the sun, accomplishing absolutely nothing—a profound sense of belonging to the universe and to each other. The stark colors of Lindos provided the fullness of the world to us—the bluest sea and sky, the whitest light, the black dresses of the older women of the village, the sharp yellow scent of wild chamomile in every breath.... And our sun-glazed children bleached golden blond or to the darkest ebony holding our hands and laughing into the waves. By the time we had to leave to go home, I felt more deeply connected to Lindos than to anywhere that I had ever been. I wanted to stay there forever. I had to wonder if I'd lived there before in some previous life. It felt like my true home.

I guess I was in a daze that last day as we hauled our belongings up to the car. When we came back from the last trip, we found out the landlord had locked us out of the house. He demanded money, claiming we had stolen some of his sheets.

"Oh, you've made a mistake," we told him. "We didn't! Why would we want to? We already have too much to carry." But he persisted. We were dumbfounded. We tried reasoning with him and when he didn't care, we were indignant and said we knew he was lying. He ran out of the house and came back with the chief of police.

The police chief said, Oh well, it was the custom to pay some small baksheesh upon leaving. Oh well, we said, what can we do, and gave the landlord the amount of money the police chief suggested. We all shook hands and our family proceeded to leave, hiking up the hill, packing the kids into the car with all the stuff, driving down to the main square via the dirt road that didn't go through the town so we could pick up our last mail at the post office before leaving Greece forever, a sad procession.

But in the time it took us to get to the square at the bottom, the landlord had run down through the streets and was waiting with a different policeman who didn't know we had already delivered some cash. A year's worth of overstuffed suitcases, strollers, diapers, boxes were jammed in with the kids and strapped to the top of the car. It was excruciatingly hot and dusty and we were running late to catch the ferry. The policeman wanted us to take all our stuff off the top of the car so he could search for the phantom sheets. Some of our friends had gathered to wave goodbye, but they didn't seem to understand what was going on. It wasn't the way we expected our friends—with whom we had shared endless discussions about living in utopia—to behave at all. I expected them to be harumphing and defending, not kibutzing on the kuklachia, for heaven's sake. As the policeman's hand gripped the open window, my husband suddenly sped off down the road—he had had enough.

I'm almost sure that what happened next was not anyone's plan, not even the landlord's. In the back seat of the station wagon Shira, Jeremy, Seth and Liza were screaming out the windows, "Two-four-six-eight, who should we assassinate, the landlord, the landlord, the landlord, yayyyy! No sheets, beware! Stupid mouth, yucky hair! No sheets, no care! No roots, no care! Yayyy."

"No roots, no care?" There was a roadblock set up for us in the next village. Two big policeman pulled my husband out of the car. Strangely, the kids and I were motioned to leave, but my husband was held prisoner in a one-room police station. Only I could get him free. What were we doing there? How could this be happening?

Behind the wheel, I drove frantically. Someone sent me to the office of the tourist police but landlord beat me there and told them his story dramatically, in Greek, while I waited, feeling helpless. I couldn't speak Greek. The tourist police yawned and looked out the window as I begged them for help. They were automatically on his side; truth had nothing to do with anything. Then someone spotted our kids.

"You are kidnapping children?" They seemed incredulous.

"They are my children."

"Not possible, madam! One is Chinese. One is from Africa. One is white. One looks Greek. Do you have four husbands? Do you have any husband? Show your passport."

"My husband has the passports. Look!" I shouted in desperation, "You are the tourist police. I am a tourist. You are supposed to help me, not him. If you won't listen, I'll call the American Embassy in Athens and the Greek Consulate in Washington. There will be an international incident. Tourists will stop coming here. Without tourists, no one will need any tourist police! You will lose your jobs. Ring the police chief in Lindos. He knows who we are." I don't know why, but they did what we wanted. My husband was released. The landlord went back under his rock. We missed the ferry.

Almost thirty years have passed now. I still think about that deep sense of belonging and not knowing what I didn't know until I got hurt. I hadn't understood that falling in love with Lindos and feeling I fully belonged to it did not make me belong. Becoming accepted is not that easy. I believe our children know that. No matter how much they connect with their birth cultures, they may always have more questions than answers. Here's to changing that to more answers than questions.

The Experts Speak Out

*"I was born in Korea and adopted in America. I used to feel
uncomfortable when I was around other Koreans because I didn't know
how to fin in, but not anymore. I don't feel like an outside because I
have reunited with my birth family and now I know in my guts that I
really am both Korean and American, all at once. My friends understand because they are mostly people who have two cultures, recent
immigrants, and other people of color in America, and adopted people
with experiences like mine. I guess I finally feel like I get to decide for
myself what I am, not wait for anybody else to accept me. What am I?
A proud Korean American adoptee."*

—Kevin

*"I wanted their hair. Dudes at school hid spit balls in my Afro mop
and laughed."*

—David French

*"Every black person knows in their soul that life is deeply unfair,
while a remarkable number of white people skate through most of their
lives unscathed, unmarked, unaware of the stacked hand they've been
dealt."*

—Joan Walsh

*"The woman said, 'You're so articulate. If I hadn't seen you, I'd
never have guessed you were black.' I said, 'This is what a black man
sounds like.'"*

—James

"In my dreams, I saw myself as being white."

—Chinese woman

*"If my kids are with a group of little white boys and there is rough
playing or anything bad happens, my kids will be the ones remembered
because they are black, whether they had anything to do with it or
not."*

—Aida LaChaux

*"Black is not black and white. White is not black and white. To be
black and white, or Latino and Anglo, or Native American and
Japanese, is to be both and neither simultaneously. A world divided
into boxes encourages us to choose one and let the other half rest in its*

*shadow. But if we comply with that system, we find ourselves dimin-
ished, divided against our wholeness, not fully who we are."*
—Lynda Marin

*"I really wish I could speak Spanish. I'm Mexican and I think that
I should know how. I wouldn't feel so dumb around the other Mexican
kids if I could talk like them. Maybe then they wouldn't get mad at me
and think I was stuck-up because I can only talk in English. Sometimes a bunch of the kids are talking to each other and using Spanish
words and laughing. I'm always afraid they are making fun of me."*
—Margarite, age 13

*"I'd like to line up the people who hate Native Americans and
wave my magic feather and turn them into Indians same as us. I'd take
away their money and credit cards and make them live on a reservation
in the middle of no place, on land the white people didn't want so bad
they gave it to us. They would have to make pottery, or get the hang of
dancing, or make silver jewelry. They'd have to learn some Indian skills
to get by. Then they'd see. They'd know why racism sucks."*
—Natanya

*"Referring to myself as biracial is not an attempt to distance myself
from my blackness or my whiteness, but an affirmation of all that I
am."*
—an adopted teen

Cultural Specifics in Focus

"Knowing is not enough; we must apply. Willing is not enough; we must do."

—Goethe

Building a Foundation

When my kids (Gail's) were small, they always seemed to know what I had in my pockets, my purse and in the drawer next to my bed even though I can't remember a single time when I showed them. They just knew. As family members, they absorbed the most intimate aspects of our everyday life, culture and values by osmosis, because they held full access to our stuff and to what we kept in our heads and hearts. Coming to understand "the way things are" on as deep and intimate a plane with people of their own races was a challenge, because they didn't live with them and so have had to work much harder to find it.

Intimacy with a culture and a sense of indisputable belonging comes from knowing the cues. Understanding what behavior is expected when; what is considered sacred, important or taboo; being able to interpret body language and subtle verbal communication; and feeling comfortable knowing where things are, what things mean, and what comes next are necessary. If you've ever been a tourist in another country, you undoubtedly have experienced the large gap between what one feels as a stranger observing another culture and as an insider, one who just knows the way things are. No matter how well-educated we make ourselves as tourists, we are still outsiders, sifting our observations through our internal sense of "normal." Because our children were separated from their birth cultures by virtue of being adopted by us, they cannot have the same kind of experience as children who grow in their native soils. No amount of exposure or cultural immersion will change the fact that their primary experiences are shaped by osmosis within our families where they grow up.

Experiences will start within the family but must not be limited to the family. This is a truism, not a deficit, the starting point from which we must build links to their birth heritage. Our children cannot have the same experience as children raised in same race households *and neither they nor we can waste time apologizing for that fact*. They don't deserve to feel less than others born to their heritage. They must acquire a deep enough connection to be able to fully identify as members while equally valuing their own experiences within the culture to which they are transplants. There is strength in biculturalism; the key is being able to be comfortable within both cultures and not to feel inadequate in either. For our children's psychological well-being, having strong ties with both their adoptive family culture and their birth family culture will afford them the opportunity to become a "biculturally competent' person (who) has a strong sense of ethnic identity and is able to function adequately within both cultures without feeling forced to choose between them." (T. Coleman La Fromboise in his article on "Bicultural Identity" in the *Psychological Bulletin*, 114 (1993) 395-412.)

A significant part of our jobs as good parents is to help our children first to understand cultural differences between what seems normal within our families and what is common for others of their heritage and then to know how to negotiate those differences. We need to find within ourselves full confidence that we deserve to be our children's parents and that we are sufficiently competent and responsible to guide them to adulthood. Without this sense of confidence, we will fail. Being alert to cultural differences, we can expect that helping them to know how to navigate will lead to rewarding personal connections. The rub lies in the fact that our own attitudes and ways of being usually become so natural to us that they remain unconscious. Though we often understand that what we experience as normal may be quite different from what is normal for people who are part of our child's birth culture, it's hard to keep that knowledge conscious as we find our way through daily events. Being able to sort this out is crucial when the core values our family lives by appear to be in conflict with the values of our child's racial or ethnic community. Harder still is the task of teaching our children behaviors and sensibilities appropriate to both settings.

Countering Racial Stereotypes

Spotting stereotypes is often difficult for children. To them, the black basketball wizard in cartoons and the bad guy in a turban or the Asian karate expert are familiar and often funny characters. When you watch a program with your kids, voice your disapproval of stereotyped characters and explain why. Ask your child to compare the images of race they see on television with people they know in real life. How are they different? If a popular movie is based on history, find a book or video that presents a true version of the event and have a discussion, comparing the real-life story to the popular movie. Look for shows where cultures and talents of individuals from different races are emphasized in a positive way, and talk with your child about them as well.

If your child is into sports, point it out if you notice that different adjectives are used to describe white players than black players. According to a *Boston Globe* reporter Derrick Jackson's 1989 content analysis of televised sports, stereotypes run rampant when sports broadcasters describe athletes. Jackson found that while 77% of comments made about white players pertained to intelligence, only 22.5% of comments about black athletes concerned intelligence, relying more upon athletic ability than intelligence during the game.

Talk about the ads in magazines. Why are certain ethnic groups linked to certain products? Take a look at running-shoe ads, for example. Why are Black athletes often portrayed "shooting hoops" and goofing around the gym, while white athletes are shown doing serious training. Notice with your children when Asian people are portrayed as quiet, compliant and hard-working rather than athletic, energetic or forceful. And don't forget that noticing stereotypes means noticing white ones as well—like the white man being portrayed as fair and unbiased or the white woman as professional and hard-working.

Cultural Competence

How much do you really know about your child's heritage? Most of us learn little about the history or contributions of people of color in America; consequently, we generally don't know much. Schools teach us mostly European-based history and knowledge. Society teaches us to view the world from the point of view of white America, a point of view that sometimes includes immigrant- or minority-bashing to justify our history and current actions. We must understand the limitations to such "official" versions and go beyond what is easily available in order to learn more and to provide access to more knowledge for our child. Without positive history and a realistic understanding of current race-based realities in society, children will think that white is better and that people of color have accomplished little in their world. Such limited understanding cannot help but undermine their own self-esteem and sense of ability and possibility. As a parent, you will have to safeguard and promote your child's cultural legacy in order to offer him or her the opportunity to thrive.

There are two necessary dimensions to building new skills: self awareness and competence. We can never attain true competence regarding matters not "native" to our experience. As our awareness expands, we realize anew what we do not know.

Don't get discouraged here—get energized. There are whole new worlds you can learn about and help your child to discover. The path to future growth can be lit by recognizing what you know and don't know. Knowledge is something you can acquire by reading, watching films, talking with and listening to experts, just to name a few. If you choose to do so, you can learn about anything you want to, at your own pace and in your own space.

This chapter will provide a brief look at some common values among African Americans, Asians, Latinos, Native Americans and people of multiracial origin as well as the stereotypes and bias that targets them. Despite the great diversity of thought and values among individuals of color in the United States, as parents we need to be aware of general attitudes passed along by those who share our child's roots. Understanding how attitudes within each birth culture may conflict with values of the dominant society will help us prepare our children to find their places in our larger society, a more complex job for them than for most.

Who Defines Normal?—White Identity

Definitions and Population Data

"If the world were a village with 1000 inhabitants, its population would be made up of 60 North Americans, 80 South Americans, 564 Asians, 86 Africans and 210 Europeans. 700 of them would be nonwhite, 300 would be white; 300 would be Christians; 60 people would own half the wealth and 500 would not have enough to eat. 600 would live in slums and 700 would be illiterate. If this village were our village, we would want it to change. But, in fact, this village is our village, since it is the world."

— anonymous

According to the U.S. Bureau of the Census's Current Population Survey, in 1990, the white population was estimated at 225.3 million and constituted 82.3% of the total population. Projections estimate that the white population will not grow as quickly as populations of color in the coming years.

"I have come to realize the irony of the possibility that all 'whites' may in fact be passing for 'white' (according to the racial laws still on the books in certain states that adhere to the one-drop theory.) Thus

there may be few 'Caucasians' in the great republic who can trace their ancestry back ten generations and confidently assert that there are no black leaves, twigs or branches on the family trees." (George Schuyler, Black no More, New York, Modern Library:1999)

Our Children

It is important for those of us who care about kids to look at statistics about our nation's children to understand who they are and the circumstances they in which they live. In 1990, two-thirds of American children were white of non-Hispanic origin. 15% were of African descent, 12% were Latino (of those about two-thirds were Mexican), 3% were Asian Pacific Islander, 1% were American Indian and 0.2% were other races.

Eighty percent of non-Hispanic white children lived in two parent homes compared to 37%% for non-Hispanic blacks and 64% for Hispanics in 1990.

Income Level	White (non Hispanic)	Black (non Hispanic)	Hispanic (of any race)
High Income	25.9%	8.9%	8.7%
Comfortable or Prosperous	37.3%	25.0%	27.1%
Enough To Get By	15.3%	14.7%	18.9%
Low Income	17.5	50.3%	45.3%

39.7% of black children and 32.2% of Latino children lived in poverty in 1990 compared to only 11% of white children.

Stereotypes and Challenges

"The only real disadvantage to being white is that it so often prevents white people from understanding racial issues. My voice gets heard in large part because I am a white man with a doctorate who holds a professional job with status. I speak with the assumption that people not only will listen, but will take me seriously. I speak with the assumption that my motives will not be challenged; I can rely on the perception of me as a neutral authority, someone whose observations can be trusted. Every time I open my mouth, I draw on, and in some ways reinforce, my privilege, which is in large part tied to race."
—Dr. Robert Jensen, a professor in the Department of Journalism at The University of Texas at Austin

There are only two kinds of white people: racists and racists in recovery. We live in a racist society. White people are the beneficiaries. We are all infected by it.

"If you live next door to a cement factory, inevitably you inhale cement dust and the cement dust becomes a part of your body. If you live in a racist society, you inhale racism and that becomes a part of your soul," says Rafael Ezekiel, a racial awareness trainer. Racism operates in a system of cultural messages and institutional practices that bestow advantages based on race. As a white person, you did not ask for these privileges—and you may not notice how regularly you receive them. But if you're going to deal with American's racist practices, first you have to own your own share. Ask yourself this: What has surprised me most about my own racism? Give yourself some current examples. If you can't find any, you probably aren't paying close enough attention. It's like saying, "Good morning." You've got to say good morning to the racism in yourself so that you can understand where it can trip you up and trouble your child.

Who's a Racist?

- Racists are those other guys over there—not me.
- I am not a racist.
- There's no racism in me.
- I believe in equality.
- I am not seeking power and control.
- I follow the golden rule.
- I am not a white supremacist.
- I am not anti-Semitic, sexist, ageist or homophobic.
- I have never knowingly discriminated against anyone.
- I take responsibility for the sins of my forefathers.
- I think church-burnings stink.
- I did not vote for David Duke.
- I do not support the Ku Klux Klan.
- Is it my fault that I can take some things for granted that others can't?

Recognize White Privilege

> "I was taught to recognize racism only in individual acts of meanness by members of my group, never in an invisible system conferring unsought racial dominance on my group from birth."
> —Peggy McIntosh, Unpacking the Knapsack of White Privilege.

Most adoptive parents who are raising children across racial lines praise the benefits of a diverse and multicultural society. We celebrate difference and have built our families on it. But when it comes to everyday life, it's natural for each of us to view the world through the lenses of our own experience. For white parents, that usually means using white experience as the standard. But don't let normal really mean white. Privilege is a system based on the notion that all have equal opportunity and that reward is earned by merit. Most white people grow up believing in a just world. We figure that we have earned the good things we have and that other people get what they deserve as well. But the world is not fair, and throughout life your child of color will have more than her share of experiences which will painfully contradict any ideas that justice prevails. Feeling anger and guilt is appropriate but not useful unless you move beyond those feelings alone.

> *"I'm white, but I told the census I'm African American....I did it out of old-fashioned liberalism, a hard habit to break. Minorities get undercounted in the census, and are thus under-served in government outlays. So I thought I'd balance an uncounted black family with our family. Sure, this means fewer benefits for my race, but I figured, hey, white people had a good year."*
>
> —Michael Finley

Become conscious of your own race-based advantages and attitudes and take action within your own sphere of influence to stop the system. To heal our racist world, we tend to require that racism be somebody's fault, a white problem. But if you are white, you have to find pride in that heritage. You can't equate being anti-white as being pro-people of color despite the historical evidence that this has often been the case. Each of us has a rich cultural history to share with out children, no matter our race or ethnicity. Give them everything you are and be yourself so that they will grow up feeling comfortable letting loose and being themselves.

Don't Indict—Enlist

Labeling someone as the enemy pretty much guarantees a hostile response, even from those who are sympathetic to the issue. "It's hard to talk about racism, because every time the subject comes up, half of us think the other half is accusing them," William Raspberry points out in his essay "Enemies Won't Help You Solve Problems" (*Washington Post*, January 2, 1998.) If we insist that all white people are the enemies (racists, or at best, racists in recovery,) is it really surprising that so many walk on by when we demand that they take blame? Educating the white community requires all the sensitivity we can muster. Very few are actively hostile. Most are just asleep. Sounding the wake-up call takes lots of energy and must be done in a way that allows people to count themselves in. It can become a waste of energy simply identifying those who don't get it. We need to figure out how to enlist our friends' support, pushing ourselves to do more. Only the white community can change the white community. It's an insider's job.

No more "business as usual." "Business as usual" means being passive about unintentional exclusions and omissions of people of color throughout your world. "Business as usual" means tolerating blatant bigotry and discrimination by remaining silent about any overt acts of racism you become aware of. If you're going to begin the process of stopping racism on your own turf, take action wherever you can. Object to ethnic jokes. Take a public stand on race-related issues in the news. Ask yourself who has been excluded from activities of the broad range of institutions you interact with, and then do something about it. As privileged members of society, we have an obligation to work with others to eliminate the advantages of unearned privileges.

- Learn to share the pain, anger, sadness and frustration instead of blaming others for not getting it.
- When somebody does something you just hate, go out of earshot and rave, scream and beat rocks with large sticks for about 20 minutes before you take them on.
- As a group activity, teach your family members how to analyze cartoons, books, commercials and TV shows for racial content. Let them keep score of the discrepancies. Use this information to convince local outlets to make changes in their programming and inventory.
- Take folks with you on a shopping excursion. Look for greeting cards reflecting people of color in large department stores, discount stores, stationery stores, bookstores and boutiques. If there are no such cards, or there are just a few, strongly suggest to the buyers your recommendations for change.
- Visit your local schools and evaluate the curriculum for diversity. If only white history and culture is in evidence, express your pain, frustration, sadness and anger, and volunteer to help make changes. Perhaps you can assist with fund-raising to purchase additional materials.
- When you encounter racist jokes or comments in films, in the media, in meetings or conversation, take the time to respond. Write a letter to the editor. Speak up at public meetings. Develop a zero tolerance for this kind of overt racism. Leadership by example is a positive way to spread the word.
- Examine logos, mascots and other team or business paraphernalia for racist slurs. If they are there, let the powers that be know your response.

> *"We are here, charged with the task of completing... ourselves. The process is jazz. It requires improvisation, the daring to strike out on your own coupled with a sure grounding in and respect that the tune on which you are working changes."*
> —William Cook

Behaviors, Philosophies and Cultural Conflicts
Race Doesn't Matter

> *"I sometimes visualize the ongoing cycle of racism as a moving walkway at the airport. Active racist behavior is equivalent to walking fast on the conveyor belt. Passive racist behavior is equivalent to standing still. No overt effort is being made, but the conveyor belt moves the bystanders along to the same destination as those who are actively walking. Unless you are walking in the opposite direction at a speed faster than the conveyor belt—unless you are actively antiracist—you will find yourself carried along with the others."*
> —Beverly Daniel Tatum, *Why Are All the Black Kids Sitting Together in the Cafeteria?*

White prospective adoptive parents who would like to adopt a child of color often tell us that it's okay to do so because race doesn't matter to them. Our job becomes to help them understand why the idea that race doesn't matter is a white luxury, something a person of color is unlikely ever to imagine. Kwame Anthony Appiah in the article "Racisms" (Anatomy of Racism, ed. David Goldberg, University of Minnesota Press, 1990) describes this as "cognitive incapacity"—a failure to distinguish between the world as it is and how one would like it to be.

As Eugenia Collier said, "Nobody exists alone. We are each part of a specific collective past, to which we respond in a way in which no person outside the group can respond." **Race does matter** and will matter to and shape the life of every child of color. Imagine the effect on a child of color of having parents who deny racism or who acknowledge racism but who don't believe it touches their lives. It would be crazy-making, and a denial of their direct experience. It would imply that everything that happens to them is personal, their fault and unconnected to the attitudes of the perpetrator. "We live in a world where your color matters more than your character. Skin is the first thing people see, and along with hair texture, facial features determine options often more than our authentic selves do. It shouldn't, but it does," says Sister Souljah.

Individualism

What method do you use when you have to meet challenges? Most of our collective education has taught us to follow a series of orderly steps: Define the problem, gather information, consider the options, decide which option to pursue, take action and evaluate the outcome. We have also been taught that "if at first you don't succeed, try again," as well as that it is a virtue to "try harder." Through this training, we come to know that our focus must be on taking individual responsibility; each of us has the job of figuring out what to do and then doing it, with courage if courage is called for.

Those who are most successful at these individual efforts of energy and concentration are expected to rise to the top like fresh cream, clearly separated from the rest. Achievers are honored, granted power, respected and financially rewarded. They become our role models, whom we aspire to become ourselves. But what we have not been taught is how to try "softer." What white culture has generally not taught is a method of working with others to meet group challenges and transform our world.

For those of us who have been raised and rewarded by the white value system that glorifies individual achievement, it can be shocking to face the inherent contradiction between this and the value placed by many communities of color on group identity over individual identity and goals. If our children are to be able to connect fully to other people of color raised within their cultures of origin, they have to learn that sometimes the needs and goals of the group are put first. In our families, our children generally learn by osmosis that individual growth and achievement are important. In fact, they are well served to have acquired all the skills we have to teach them about doing well in a white-dominant society. But for them and for us, those skills are not enough. We have to work to retune the messages we are sending them in order to make room to integrate the values of their birth cultures.

Group-sensitive skills include patience, tolerance, cooperation and an ability to endure. They place being responsive to the needs of others over personal needs for privacy or respect for private property. It all boils down to sharing what we have and moving over to make room when someone else needs help. Within the family circle, it says, "We are the kind of family that takes care of each other." When Uncle Charley is sick, we double up and empty a bedroom so we can bring him to our house and nurse him back to health. When Grandma is too old to live alone, she moves in with us; she doesn't go to a nursing home. Not that we can rescue every stray puppy or support twenty people on a salary that can barely cover the needs of five. Putting the needs of the group in front of individual needs does not mean dismissing individual needs and priorities, only weighing them in differently.

Unless we have fully acquired these skills ourselves, we cannot easily teach them to our children. Trying to understand that we cannot throw away everything we bring to the table so that we may take on more cooperative approaches—finding a way to integrate the two—is not at easy process. But when we work to incorporate both ways into our family culture, our children gain the capacity to make informed decisions about which bag of tools is likely to be appropriate and effective in a given situation: the individual tool bag or the group tool bag—a gift they might not receive were they not members of a true multicultural family.

Claiming Identity

In the development of a positive white racial identity, we must begin to recognize others with whom we can sing a common song. This is not a trivial task for those of us who are more comfortable singing solo in our showers than joining a choir. For many who choose transracial adoption, non-conformity, a lack of dependence on other people, is a strongly ingrained trait. We chose transracial adoption in part because we can tolerate being different. Now, can we do the opposite, and identify ourselves as part of a collective and communal effort in which our individual rhythms and styles must yield to a larger community? Can we authentically affiliate? Can we honor commitments to common goals without putting our personal feelings before those of the group?

The principles of democracy in the United States and the development of our country have many components for which we can feel proud, despite the events of our shared history that bring us shame. Finding the positive values within our white heritage is not impossible. What we must learn is to own the positives in our legacy as our own. What we must also learn is new patience with others and endurance in our commitment to a cause. Patience and endurance—if we can incorporate them into our own lives, perhaps we can also include them among the values we teach to our kids.

Build Hope and Pride

> *"(Working for racial justice) I found myself surrounded by ambitious, accomplished peers, most of whom happened to be black. They liberated me to want more, do more, dress better and have more fun doing it. I was shielded from white-girl guilt because it was all in the service of a higher goal: civil rights, social justice, uplift of the poor. I got a lot of nuts and bolts survival skills: silence instead of talking all the time. Strategy. Looking behind the surface of things. Patience and perseverance. Perspective. The long view. It was my black friends, ironically, who focused me on how much my Irish family gave me, for instance, and jolted me out of my white self-pity and shame about what they didn't."*
>
> *—Joan Walsh, Salon Magazine, "Confessions of a former self-hating white person," Feb. 18, 2000*

The hope for all of our children is that race and culture can matter as a source of pride, that they can feel the power of their connection to a proud people who give them strength, and that they are the keepers of a legacy of great accomplishments. Sometimes those of us who have gone through a reawakening around racial inequity and white privilege find it difficult to find pride in our own legacy. Race or ethnicity cannot be allowed to matter only as an expression of either shameful history or what one can't do. We can all take pride in America's promise of "liberty and justice for all," and as white parents of children of color we must model ways to come to terms with our own history and move forward as conscious and proud survivors. In this way we begin to make the promise real.

What is normal in one culture may not be normal in another. We are all members of our families, our countries and of our racial and ethnic groups. Some people may not understand who we are. The important thing is that we each know for ourselves who we are and enjoy it. Don't trivialize the importance of birthright. We can't assign ourselves membership in a racial or ethnic group. No one can choose one's race or ethnicity. Support your child's journey into his culture without trying to take up space you cannot occupy there yourself. Learn all you can. Enjoy all you can. Celebrate all you can. Every person has as his or her birthright a heritage that cannot be chosen or discarded.

Many of us would wish to pass as racially unmarked or as exceptions to white norms, hoping to escape the responsibility that comes with association. We often hear white adoptive parents talk about how they now see white people as pale and pasty looking, unattractive, etc. They may think they are saying, "I'm not biased, I prefer people of color," but in fact their attitude reflects a bias against whites that is no healthier or better than any other bias against human beings. If whiteness seems a source of shame, not pride, then the individual may strive to deny the very existence of a white culture. Finding racial pride is not a simple project for either us or our children but it is the very task we must address.

Sometimes white parents become racial wannabes, overcompensating, and making every possible effort to act as if they were the same race as their child. Not only is this crazy-making, it is a distressing message for kids: that is, one should try to assume a false identity in order to fit into the world. In order to love themselves fully, our children must find a way to embrace both their culture by birth and that by adoption. Masquerading through life dishonestly is a hopeless approach. The best way to help our kids love themselves is to model what that looks like.

In distinguishing between valuing and respecting your child's birth heritage and becoming a racial wannabe, the key feature is that the person is so focused on the race they want to be that they exclude the race they are. A racial wannabe finds it difficult to recognize his or her own culture because she is making such strong efforts to identify fully with the race of her child.

- A racial wannabe wears only tribal or ethnic clothing or jewelry, cooks only native or ethnic foods, chooses only hairstyles clearly associated with the race with which he is trying to identify and listens only to music and reads only books written for or about people of the race of culture with which he wants to be identified.
- A racial wannabe talks only about things related to the culture she wants to be identified with to the exclusion of her own culture sometimes even speaking in the language or slang of the culture she wants to be identified with.
- A racial wannabe makes little distinction in her own mind between her connection to the race or culture she wants to be identified with and a person who is a member of the group by birth.

This overcompensation seems unnatural and contrived to others of their own race and often offends those of the race they are trying to be like.

Find Role Models

> *"There is no way to give up white privilege; our society confers it upon us, no matter what we want. So, I don't feel guilty about being white in a white supremacist society, but I feel an especially strong moral obligation to push for change because I benefit from the injustice. What matters is what we decide to do with the privilege."*
> —Dr. Robert Jensen is a professor in the Department of Journalism at The University of Texas.

Some white people have always worked to oppose racial injustice. As important as it is for children to understand that there have always been white people who have worked to stop racism, it may be even more important for us adults to have white role models and heroes. In the face of the horrible injustices white people have committed against people of color during the course of U.S. history, we need to be able to hold our heads up and remember the many wonderful uncelebrated heroes and sheroes who have made a difference. We all need support and inspiration.

All over America, blacks and whites who believed in racial equality were threatened, beaten, arrested and killed. But they remained nonviolent themselves, and they never let violence stop them. In the end, they forced America to abolish a system of segregation that violated the most basic principles of democracy. Within fifteen years, blacks had won the right to sit alongside whites on buses, in restaurants and in theaters. White schools, swimming pools, and libraries were open to them. And they had won the right to vote. The civil rights movement brought phenomenal changes to the South and to all the country. But the progress of three decades did not erase the legacy of centuries of racial oppression. Today, the struggle for equality in education, housing and employment continues. And it will go on as long as there are women, men and children who believe that together we can change the world. Acknowledging contributions is not a bid for gratitude, nor an attempt to make into centerpieces those who acted as supporting players. But it's refreshing simply to note them as examples of white allies in what often seems an unredeemable history.

- Elijah Lovejoy was a white preacher who lived in Alton, Illinois, during the Civil War. He was killed by an angry mob because he had printed pamphlets calling for the end of slavery.
- Carl Van Vechten was a New York arts critic who helped promote the Harlem Renaissance.
- Tony Bennett, the singer/artist, helped finance the work of the Reverend Martin Luther King, Jr.
- Rev. James Reeb, a Unitarian minister from Boston, was among many white clergyman who joined the Selma marchers after the attack by state troopers at the Edmund Pettus Bridge. Reeb was beaten to death by white men while he walked down a Selma street in March, 1965.
- Ansel Adams, photographer, recorded the atrocities and injustices that were dealt to Japanese Americans in the internment camps of World War II.

Identifying white allies is a useful exercise, helping our children of color to understand that not all white people are bad and inspiring us to do whatever we can to use our personal influences and power to end biased attitudes and behaviors. It can be stimulating and provocative to read accounts of civil rights workers or biographies of people dedicated to antiracist activities. It is essential to find like-minded white people for mutual support and re-energizing. We can value for each other what we have done, remind one another of why we must keep going, celebrate the things that we are doing that make a difference, and kick each other in the butt when we fall into a funk because things are not going well. People of color cannot help with this process. It's an inside job.

Time is short and work expands, but this focus feels like a fresh start, a clear direction to pursue. To help children find pride in themselves, parents must find pride in themselves. May you always have new questions. May you lovingly seek answers.

One Drop Rules—African American Identity Issues

Definitions and Population Data

"The average American thinks that America is 32% black, 21% Hispanic, and 18% Jewish—although the actual figures are 12% black, 8% Hispanic and less than 3% Jewish."
—From a 1990 Gallup Poll

According to the U.S. Bureau of the Census, Current Population Survey, in 1995, the black population was estimated at 33.9 million and constituted 12.8% of the total population. In 2010, the African American population is projected to be 40.1 million, representing 13.5 % of the total population.

According to the U.S. Census Bureau, Current Population Survey, March1999, Racial Statistics Branch, Population Division the US population is dispersed like this...

- 19.11% live in the Northeast Region which includes Connecticut, Maine, Massachusetts, New Hampshire, New Jersey, New York, Pennsylvania, Rhode Island, and Vermont;
- 23.3% live in the Midwest region which includes Illinois, Indiana, Iowa, Kansas, Michigan, Minnesota, Missouri, Nebraska, North Dakota, Ohio, South Dakota, and Wisconsin;
- 34.91% live in the South region which includes Alabama, Arkansas, Delaware, District of Columbia, Florida, Georgia, Kentucky, Louisiana, Maryland, Mississippi, North Carolina, Oklahoma, South Carolina, Tennessee, Texas, Virginia, and West Virginia;
- 22.71% lived in the Western region which includes Alaska, Arizona, California, Colorado, Hawaii, Idaho, Montana, Nevada, New Mexico, Oregon, Utah, Washington, and Wyoming.

Two-thirds of African American families are in the lower class, based on their median annual income. 8.12% of the population is upper class ($50,000 or more); 28.82% are middle class ($25,000 - $49.000); 35.93% are working class ($10,000 - $24,999); 18.12% are working poor (under $10,000) and 9.11% are non-working poor. Source: 1996 U.S. Bureau of the Census, Current Population Survey.

In 1996, 54% of all African American families were headed by a single parent with no spouse present. Of those, 87% were headed by women and 13% by men. In contrast, less than 20% of non-Hispanic white families were headed by single parents. Source: 1996 U.S. Bureau of the Census, Current Population Survey.

In 1996 74% of blacks 25 years and older had completed high school. 16% of African Americans had completed 4 years of college as compared to 30% of whites. Source: 1996 U.S. Bureau of the Census, Current Population Survey.

Stereotypes and Challenges

> *"The reason even well-heeled blacks are angry is that even if you live in an ivory tower, work in a glass-enclosed office with Picassos on the wall, carry a briefcase, and dine at '21, you're still never far from that old line: 'What do you call a black man with a Ph.D.? A nigger.'"*
> —Charlayne Hunter-Gault

University of Wisconsin psychologist Patricia G. Devine studied hundreds of white students to test the depth and prevalence of racial stereotypes. She found that all the students were familiar with at least some negative stereotypes of blacks—such as their supposed aggressiveness, criminality, low intelligence, laziness, sexual irresponsibility, ostentatiousness, and being dirty or smelly—and automatically associated these stereotypes with blacks. Those who appeared to harbor less prejudice also thought of these stereotypes but simply made a conscious effort to repress them. "Thus," she wrote, "even for subjects who honestly report having no negative prejudices against blacks, activation of stereotypes can have automatic effects that if not consciously monitored produce effects that resemble prejudiced responses." Leonard Steinhorn and Barbara Diggs-Brown, By the Color of Our Skin, New York, Dutton, 1999

Stereotypes of African Americans confront us in practically every newscast we see—there seems to be a murder a night. Perhaps Robert Entman in his article "Representation and Reality in the Portrayal of Blacks on Network Television News" (*Journalism Quarterly* 71, no.3: 509-520) nailed it best when he said the American public has been taught to see African Americans as either "threats to or noncontributing victims of American society" or "superstars; entertainers or athletes." Responsible, competent, high-functioning middle-class citizens receive little play in the media and thus seem barely visible, leading to the conclusion that they don't actually exist.

Confusion of Class and Race

> *We were five hours into the racial awareness training when the white sixth-grade teacher finally got up the nerve to speak her mind; "I know we are talking about valuing difference. I get what you are saying about children internalizing negative stereotypes and how that is bad for self-esteem. But why do they make such a mess of their lives?*

*Most of their girls are mothers by 18 and most of their boys are in
prison. When I ride on the bus they are so rude to me just because I
am white. White people don't act like that."*

*An African American young woman watching a newscast with her
friends lamented, "Why do they always interview black women with
their hair in curlers wearing a housecoat? As if that's the way we dress
or look in public."*

*She called with the earnest intent of trying to do right by her
African American son. They were planning to do a major remodeling
of their home in a fairly white suburb of San Francisco. She recognized that this investment would mean they were unlikely to move for
a good ten years. "I know we said we would do anything for him. But
how can I feel good about moving to Oakland (across the bay from San
Francisco with a 48% African American population); I mean surely
you didn't mean we should live in the ghetto?"*

When this woman uses the term ghetto, she typifies many white Americans who really mean poor and black. Race and class are often confused,
most especially about African Americans. The presumption that most black
people are lower class and struggling with poverty is limiting. There are larger
percentages of blacks than whites living below the poverty line, but there are
also many African Americans who are financially secure. We must be cautious about assumptions regarding poverty. Not all poor people are criminals.

Some of our assumptions about African Americans result from lack of
direct contact or experience with a wide variety of black people, but the media and images that we see and hear depicted daily also make a significant
contribution to our inaccurate views. We must challenge ourselves to look
deeper at what we read, what we hear, what we think we know and what we
say if we ever hope to parent our children with a positive sense of who they
can become and where they fit in the world.

A Different Approach to Adolescence

In the book *Pathways Through Adolescence: Individual Development in
Relation to Social Contexts,* edited by L.J. Crockett (1995, New Jersey:
Erlbaum) L.M. Burton suggests that adolescence may not be a clearly marked
developmental stage for some African Americans in the way that it more often
is for whites. Although black young people between thirteen and eighteen
may be viewed as teens by society in general, depending on their class and
family circumstances they may have assumed the roles and status of adults
within their own community. Perhaps they are growing up in an "age-con-
densed" family with parents only fourteen and sixteen years older then themselves and share financial and child-care responsibilities for younger siblings

with their parents. Teens in this position tend to think of themselves as adults and to resent having anyone treat them like children.

When a black teen who views himself as an adolescent connects with black teens who view themselves as adults, they have a hard time understanding and relating to one another. Their assumptions that they will be similar are erroneous in both directions. Individuals find meaning in daily life based on their personal histories of internal and external experiences, and the experiences are likely to be profoundly different. Black parents of black children are dealing with this issue as much as white ones. Do not be fooled into imagining this is exclusively a transracial issue. In fact, connection on this challenge can prove a great opportunity to get to know parents of your child's race as you struggle together to help your children live with these conflicts.

Fear the Sons, Demean the Daughters

> *Every day for a year, my friend Malcolm and I (Beth) would take the trolley to work in downtown San Francisco. We were both 23 and recent college grads. I was off to my job in a research lab, he to his in a law firm. We talked a lot about race during those trips, both of us wondering how we could possibly change the world fast enough to survive. During the month of October we decided to conduct our own survey. Each morning we hopped on in the east side of the city and rode to the west, Malcolm in his three-piece suit and I in my jeans, we would compete to see who would sit next to us—how long it would take for the seats next to us to be filled. By the time we arrived at our destinations, the trolley was always full with many left standing. And each and every day of October, someone sat beside me before anyone sat beside him. Often people stood while the seat next to him remained the only one empty. Malcolm still takes the trolley each day and although he is alone he still spends each October surveying, never forgetting how much work there is to be done. Malcolm is African American.*

Conditioned to associate blacks with violent crime, whites may feel ashamed when they lower their car locks while driving through an African American neighborhood, but fear overcomes shame along with the rationale that "no one wants to take needless risks." The stereotype associating blacks with crime is so ingrained that even Jesse Jackson said he would "feel relieved" if the footsteps he heard on the street behind him belonged to "somebody white." Conventional wisdom among whites is that blacks don't like them, don't want to interact with them ("It's a black thing, you wouldn't understand") and may seek payback for the resentment caused by racism. Black males are often perceived by whites as threatening—why make oneself a target?

The stereotype of the African American woman is that she is a single parent with too many kids who doesn't care much about anything except getting her next welfare check. She's not so smart, and if she has made something of herself, it's probably because of affirmative action. For most white Americans contact is minimal, we do not have personal relationships with African Americans outside the work setting, and so most of what we think we know about black life we saw on TV. We don't have enough personal experiences to demystify these stereotypes.

The obstacles of racism are real and will affect your beautiful African American son or daughter. Even though they grow up in a nice neighborhood and get a good education, they will not be immune to DWB (driving while black), being passed up by cabs, being followed by security guards in stores, getting lousy service in restaurants, or the effects of the glass ceiling at work. The sad truth is that the median net worth for black households was one-seventh of the median for white households in 1992, a figure that has not budged much since. Until white society learns to see a black person without first seeing his skin color, stereotyping will remain our burden.

We All Look Alike

In the US, we presume all people of African descent to be African American. In reality, many Latino people are of African descent, as well as people from Jamaica, Samoa, Africa and other Caribbean islands. Immigrants among these populations often do not identify as African Americans. Sometimes this is seen as racist or one-upsmanship. Africans may not see black Americans as African. African Americans may interpret the inability of black Latinos to speak English as a racist choice. These relationships are fraught with complications in an already complicated racial playing field.

Tensions between Koreans and African Americans or Africans and African Americans are often rooted in a sense of competition for the same piece of the American pie. If members of your family include any or all of these groups, it is essential that you educate and familiarize yourselves with all sides of these struggles as you help and support your child's negotiation of his or her relationships with people of color.

Behaviors, Philosophies and Cultural Conflicts

There is no single entity one can call "the black family." Black families are diverse in their individual backgrounds, their economic and social standings, their values, their life styles and their degree of acculturation. African Americans share a history in the United States shaped by slavery, racism and social and economic discrimination. They also share having had family origins in Africa, where relationships were based on patterns of kinship and individuals were defined by their tribal affiliation, family membership or geographical region rather than individual personalities or contributions. Each aspect of this shared history has contributed important ways of thinking that have been formed over many years and are ingrained in the values and behavior of many African Americans. As it is for many people of any ethnicity, individual black people may not always consciously recognize that their behaviors are rooted in their group identity and history. It is important to remember that these are generalized concepts. Not all African Americans hold the same values. The goal is for your child (and you) to be able to develop a sensitivity and appreciation for common values and to integrate knowledge of how to behave adequately and respectfully with black individuals. If your child has no knowledge of the core values operating within her culture of origin, her naïve behavior may make it impossible for her to find social acceptance.

This is not to say that your child should assimilate a sense of black family life or black values in exactly the same way as a child who is raised in his or her birth family. Because he was adopted, and even more so if he has white parents, your child's life story is bicultural. Intergenerational influences will be different for a black child with white parents than for a black child with black parents. What you must work to help him avoid is the stressful experience of double-consciousness, "the problem of marginal man which arises when one identifies with two cultures simultaneously but feels alienated from them both." (E.V. Stonequist (1935) *American Journal of Sociology*, p, 1-12.) The central goal for adoptive parents is to promote within their child feelings of identification with her culture of origin, fostering a sense of security rather than confusion, isolation or alienation. This is accomplished only if both parents and child resist trying to be something they cannot be and value themselves as worthy.

> *We (Beth and family) were rushing to get ready to leave for a party to which we were already late. Ted told the kids to get in the car while we gathered the last minute items. James couldn't have been more than five years old. He went onto the front porch and was still hesitating there when Ted and I arrived. "Why are you still here?" Ted asked. James looked nervous. "I was afraid. I didn't want to go by strangers." We looked up to see two African American boys, maybe fifteen or sixteen, wearing low-rider pants, one carrying a boom box, both minding their own business, sauntering down the street—cool but not dangerous. I was about to laud James for being careful around strangers when I saw Ted putting everything down and slowly crouching so he was eye-to-eye with our son. "Those boys look just like you will when you get to be their age. You are going to grow up to be them." As I watched my little baby's eyes widen, I knew we hadn't even come*

*close to doing enough to counteract the stereotypes of "scary black
men" for our little son who wasn't so far from becoming one himself.
For two or three weeks after, James never stopped asking questions.
"Will people be able to tell if I'm nice just when I walk down the
street?" "If I wear dress-up clothes, will they still be scared?" "If I tell
them my name, will they still be scared?" "If I stay with Daddy, will
they still be scared?" I think in some ways this one was the hardest,
because white father to black son, Ted said, "Some people will feel
more comfortable around you when you are with me, because they like
white people better than African Americans. They will be making a big
mistake. Because they will miss knowing a proud black man who is
going to be a great friend and a great person when he grows up. His
name is James." I pray each night that our son will not fear those boys
on the street, because I know that really that is just a form of self-hate.
And no one survives self-hate.*

Your black child cannot decide not to be black. She needs your help and
encouragement to develop a positive black identity to enhance her personal
sense of security. This means she has to come to terms with conflicts between cultures and with the painful truth that, in the United States, African
Americans have always been on the bottom of the status ladder in the eyes of
whites, the people she lives among.

Religion and African American Culture

Understanding the history and current cultural significance of the religion in the black community is important. African American churches and
their ministers have long served as mainstays of safety and community where
black people could gather and replenish themselves in the face of their
struggles, first against slavery and later around civil rights. Many of the great
civil rights leaders have been and continue to be Christian ministers, much of
the language of change, pride and power calls on God and Jesus in a Christian context for solidarity and political movements. The Black Muslim na-
tionalist movement has been significant in addressing the needs of African
Americans through the Million-Man March, its focus on afrocentric thinking
and its positive models for helping black children feel good about themselves
as strong African Americans. The Jewish community has long played a significant role as allies to the civil rights leaders and movement.

Whether you as a family subscribe to the beliefs of any of these religious
groups or fundamentally oppose them will certainly dictate whether and where
you and your children participate in a spiritual community. The inherent conflict between the problematic dogma of racial separatism embodied by the
anti Semitic remarks of Louis Farrakhan, current leader of the American Black

Muslim splinter group, stirs controversy and often makes it impossible for transracial parents to embrace this particular group While it may be challenging to be appreciative of the great leaders that this movement has produced, particularly to acknowledge the value the current leadership has added to black political presence in the last decades given a fundamental disagreement with the tenets of monoracism, helping our children understand the full picture and positive side of the presence of it members within the community is essential to their larger sense of belonging.

Whatever our beliefs, it is important for all transracial parents to recognize the importance of the spiritual and religious community in the lives of African Americans. We must strive to teach our children to understand that it represents a significant cultural support that they deserve to understand and consider a part of their cultural legacy and heritage.

We Take Care of Our Own

> *"Hambone, hambone, where's that gone, Round the world and home again."*

From the days of slavery, African Americans have found the spirit and strength to stay alive and together by understanding that they must act as a group, not as individuals. The stolen hambone from the white man's kitchen was passed from family to family among the plantation slaves as each shared from one to another the good stock that kept them alive.

Interdependency holds a positive value. Kin and friends have an obligation to give as needed, sharing resources, housing, and household tasks through a lifelong network of resource exchanges. The famous African proverb "it takes a village to raise a child" indicates a sense of shared responsibility for the well-being of all members of the community.

This value is in conflict with the concept of the independent individual whose mission is to take care of himself first, a view prevalent in white American culture. African Americans tend to develop strong kinship systems, making fewer boundaries between nuclear families and extended families than do whites. Adopted black children interacting with black families in the community need to understand that uncles, aunts, cousins and grandparents may have a different presence and status than the child may be used to.

> *When we (Gail's family) first moved to our new neighborhood, old Mrs. Johnson, the African American widow who lived down the block, shocked our oldest son. He couldn't avoid walking past her house on the way home from school, and Mrs. Johnson would always be waiting on her front porch with a lot more to say than hello. A feisty woman who'd lived a long life, she never hesitated to scold him harshly if she*

thought he was too loud or his hair wasn't neat or if he used words Mrs. Johnson didn't approve of, words which seemed to pop out all the time, "on accident." Mrs. Johnson would ask him to run to the corner store and bring her back a nice cold drink. She insisted on teaching him how to pick the greens in her yard and "ham bone," which he loved.

"She thinks she's my mother," he'd complain with a twinkle in his eye. "She's got no right. She's picking on me 'cause I'm black." Mrs. Johnson taught him lots of things in our first years in the neighborhood—more than he wanted to know. That's how he discovered that having a stranger take some responsibility for helping you out was not so bad. "She thinks she's s'posed to help me," he told us. "That's just how some black folks are." He cried his heart out when she passed on.

Concepts of Time

Concepts and approaches to time differ between cultures. In their article "The Mental Health of Black Americans; Psychiatric Diagnosis and Treatment" (*Ethnic Psychiatry*, New York: Plenum, 1986) C. Wilkinson and J. Spurlock noted that black clients at a mental health center were consistently fifteen to thirty minutes late for appointments, despite the scheduling difficulties this created for their sessions. Black friends sometimes joke about being on "CP (colored people's) time" which is just another way of recognizing that some African Americans are likely to operate on a separate system of time than that of white people. White families, schools, and public institutions sometimes teach children that being on time is a virtue and that it is rude to keep others waiting. But in African (and Latino) cultures, being punctual around arrival and departure times can be interpreted as acting as if you and your time are more important than that of the people around you—an insult that could result in a cultural disconnect for your child. You can see the confusion that might arise for a black child raised by white parents with the idea that being late is not okay who might feel resentful if other black people kept her waiting. If she understood the cultural difference, she would not take it as a sign of personal rejection if she were the one kept waiting.

Eye Contact

According to E. Smith's study, "Cultural and Historical Perspectives in Counseling Blacks," in D.W. Sue's *Counseling the Culturally Different: Theory and Practice* (New York: Wiley, 1981), African Americans often converse among themselves while engaging in another activity. It is understood within the group that one can participate in the conversation without needing to maintain constant eye contact. White parents often admonish their children to "look at me when I'm talking to you" and to maintain eye contact as an indicator of their interest whenever they are speaking with another person. The black child growing up in a white family may perceive a lack of eye contact between herself and other blacks as a sign of disrespect or disinterest. She needs to understand that body language may have different uses within the two cultures and to learn how those differences work.

On the other hand, African American strangers often greet one another and make eye contact on the street or in passing. This familiar form of acknowledgment probably originated from the need for blacks to stick together and take care of one another in the presence of white society. Although we do not currently have to fear extremes such as lynching, it is still wise and reasonable for African Americans to stick together and be aware of who and what is going on around them in a racial context. Black people stick together and value the importance of taking care of each other. This form of greeting and eye contact is one way of expressing solidarity.

Being Seen More than Heard–Staying Safe

In some African American families, approaches to child care may include expressing conflict less openly, placing more emphasis on achievement and morality (religion,) and they may be based on more organization and control than is common in many white families. A greater reliance on physical punishment may also be present. The story of being black in America is of struggle, of rising from slavery, of overcoming obstacles with faith and humility. Being threatened creates a stronger need to train for survival. Obedience can be a prerequisite for safety, particularly when a parent needs to protect children who are unable to recognize danger for themselves. It may be difficult for white parents to accept, but the fact is that every day spent living among whites requires racial coping skills for blacks. The strategies used in some black families of teaching children to control their anger at unfairness, to master the skills needed to become upwardly mobile, to build a strong spiritual foundation for support, and to expect stricter parental control over their actions and progress are logical.

White parents, lacking personal experience with the double consciousness of racial stress, sometimes want to embrace an exclusively child-centered approach and emphasize different values, such as expressiveness, self direction, independence and creativity, building their family with a looser organizational structure and less parental control. A black child from a family choosing this style of parenting is likely to behave differently in public than the black child of parents with different values. Likely her "entitled" behavior will cause problems. Blacks may see her as rude, spoiled and unacceptable, whites as cocky and aggressive, kids of all backgrounds as different and therefore weird. Is there a way to help your children grow up valuing individualism and at the same time not estrange them from the black community by that very approach? We think there is, that just as our children come to understand the ways in which they are bicultural in other arenas, they can also understand that there is a different culture and mode of appropriate behavior inside their home and out the front door.

Kids easily learn at very young ages to modify their behavior based on the requirements of where they are. When we go to the library we walk softly and speak in whispers because it must be kept a quiet place. When we go to the park it's fine to run around and be noisy. Coming to understand that the rules inside your house are different from the rules for what you do in public is possible. That duality is part of everyday life; for our children knowledge that's necessary both for their survival and for their psychological health.

To support behavior that is contrary to your values is an extreme stretch. What we would invite you to do is to use a juncture like this to revisit your ideas about the issues and to talk honestly with your child about the different pressures which will be placed on him or her to conform to peer-group behavior. When you're not around, your child will be making his own decisions about how to behave.

The key for any child being raised biculturally is to be able to be comfortable within both cultures and not feel inadequate in either.

A matter of life and death

> "My biggest struggle is with the advice of my AA friends that my son needs to be 'toughened up' to survive. They say he is too 'soft.' He is extremely gentle and sensitive. Some peers appreciate this but some take advantage of it. So, here's the conflict for me—my bias has always been to value men who are NOT tough but who are down-to-earth, view themselves as equal partners with women, and treat ALL people with respect. How do I reconcile that view with one saying he is going to need to toughen up? Am I doing him a disservice by not teaching him 'survival skills'? Sigh!"
>
> —Signed "Just a mom"

Remember Rodney King? These issues can be matters of life and death for African Americans. To encourage your child to behave in ways that will alienate him from the black community at a minimum will cause a disconnect he will resent and at a maximum could cost his life. For African Americans, driving down the freeway or walking down the street can become very dangerous activity.

We must warn our children about how to behave when stopped by the police. They must be careful to keep their hands visible and be respectful even when they know that there is nothing they have done to deserve this treatment except be born into their own skin. Our children must talk with adults of color who can help them to strategize how to shop without being accused of shoplifting. Similarly parents must learn how to discipline our children in public without being accused of child abuse. We cannot operate within the dream that our children will somehow be immune and we cannot let them end up on the pavement hurt or dead because we were too afraid or too ashamed to talk about it.

Be the first to tell your kids about slavery

The first time black children hear about slavery is a stressful event for them and for you, particularly if you are white. We all have to own this sordid period of history. Your African American child deserves to be introduced to this powerful information in a setting where you can provide support. Here are some tips to help you know when and how to begin.

How old should your child be?

African American kids growing up in African American families tend to hear stories of slavery and segregation along with civil rights victories at home, when they are still tots, where they have a chance to absorb as much or as little of it as they choose. This is often part of Grandpa telling about walking to Selma or Mom remembering a trip to visit Auntie where the signs were still intact—"Whites only." Perhaps it begins with the story of her first day of school which involved bussing and crowds of grown-ups who didn't want her kind at their school. Or maybe it is the story of Grandma whose husband was lynched while she fled town with Papa and his brothers to escape the mobs or Big Mama describing how she felt when she visited the plantation where her own daddy had died as a slave. These stories are part of the natural flow of family history that gets passed down in all families. So how do transracial adoptive parents tell their own stories of family and still make sure their kids know that African American history is also theirs?

African American kids growing up with white parents will be more shocked when they hear about slavery because they will be confronted with the perpetrators of the evil being the same race as their parents. This cannot help but raise questions about their parents. Are white parents like white slave owners? Did Grandpa or Great Grandpa own slaves? Acknowledging slavery as our own legacy, directly or indirectly, as well as our black children's legacy is essential.

> When Sofia and James were only three and four, we (Beth) had an
> evening conversation over the book Follow The Drinking Gourd.
> "How could the black people tell which white people were safe?"

"I don't think they could. Since most of the white people in the south owned slaves or at least liked to feel more important than black people, they had to assume that no one was safe unless someone they really trusted told them that a certain white person was OK."

"I wish you and Daddy and Grandma and Grandpa had been alive then because you would have helped and been safe white people."

"Well… it's true if I was there right now I would help African American slaves get away on the underground railroad and be safe. But, my great, great Grandfather and his family were not safe people. They owned a plantation and they owned slaves. It was called Rosewood and we have a book about it."

"Did they hurt black people?"

"Yes, they did."

"Would they have hurt James?"

"Yes, I think they probably would have."

"Would they have hurt Sofia?"

"They might have because she has brown skin and they might have seen her as more like an African American than a white person."

"Sometimes I feel really ashamed that my ancestors did such bad things. They were wrong and I wish I could have been there and tried to make them different."

"I wish your family had been different, Mommy."

"I do, too."

If your family has a history of slave ownership or collaboration, you need to acknowledge it with your children. For those of you who do not have that specific history, talking about the way all white people benefited from slavery in this country is important, although your conversation may not be so personal in terms of family legacy.

These conversations happen over and over again. They can't always be planned but they must be expected. They aren't always easy but they mustn't be avoided. Conversations like this will provoke thoughtful questions for days afterwards even in very young children. Sometimes there will be times of silence on the topic but always it must be re-addressed so that permission is felt by our children to experience the pain and find their strength in the face of this American tragedy.

Elementary school texts tend to introduce this topic in third grade, but African American specialists on slavery studies suggest that you can help your child understand before that, as long as you do so thoughtfully. Your child may be in the minority in his school setting or even be the only African American child in his class. His presence may bring the story of slavery to life for his classmates, but at what cost to him? Do not let the classroom be the first place he hears about this legacy. Prepare him. You can't protect him. Preschools and kindergartens are filled with picture books about slavery. If your child identifies as an African American, he needs to be comfortable with this information before he has to deal with other children's responses.

Sharing difficult information— before you start

How is everyone feeling? Is your child too tired or too fidgety to listen? Are you? It's best to introduce this story when you are both rested. Don't wait until the end of a tiring day. Make sure that his or her attention span is long enough to take this on and that nothing distracting is going on. Settle down in a comfortable spot where you can hold your child as you talk. A hug can be reassuring and say more than words. Before you begin the story, let your child know that it is important for him to know the truth about something painful, and that this will be a serious story you want him to understand.

What your child needs to know:

When the Europeans came to America they needed workers but didn't want to pay them, so they kidnapped people from Africa and brought them here as slaves. That was long ago. You were never a slave and will never be a slave. The Africans who were kidnapped tried to escape, but the white people had guns. Other white people tried to help the slaves escape and worked to bring an end to slavery. Now it is against the law to have slaves. Some freed African Americans did go back to Africa, but others wanted to say here because they had family and friends here.

African American children are entitled to understand that:

- It is wrong to own another human being.
- African Americans survived slavery because they took care of each other, even if they weren't family members. Their own strength, faith and courage saved them.
- White slave owners in the South were not able to survive after their slaves were freed. They could not make their plantations work without the free labor and strong spirits of the African Americans.
- You should be proud to be an African American.
- We can change things that are bad. Slavery was very bad.

This history is more than just slavery

When the slave owners couldn't have slaves anymore there were still lots of white people who didn't want African Americans to have the same things that they had. They wanted to make sure that they got to have the most money, and they were worried that if they made the same rules for black people as for white they would end up with less.

Be sure that you talk to your children not just about slavery as an experience of the far distant past, but also about the legacy of slavery and the ways it still affects us today. This means that eventually you will want to educate yourself about and discuss with your children:

- Carpetbaggers
- The 3/5ths rule
- Segregation: Separate but Equal
- Brown vs. Board of Education
- The Civil Rights Movement
- ...and the list goes on.

Physical Appearance

Many folks who decide to adopt transracially are also likely to be highly self-directed, not dependent on other people's approval and not "slaves to fashion," believing that it is "what's inside that counts, not the outer packaging." In some cases this may show up in choices that disdain the glamour industries or consumer culture. It logically follows from these core attitudes that spending time or money on hairstyles for children might seem unimportant or even morally wrong. On the other hand, the phrase "your hair is your crowning glory" is especially true in the black community. It is more common than not for black families to place a high premium on good grooming, styling, and hair products as a way of expressing black pride and sometimes, as well, as a way of illustrating their concern for cleanliness and success to a dominant culture which stereotypes being black as "dirty" and "underclass." For the black child of white parents who leaves his or her home looking unkempt, the consequences are that he will look unkempt in a way that sets him apart from the other black children. Perhaps he will be told that if his parents didn't even care enough to learn how to take care of his hair properly, what could they be doing about the other needs that don't show as clearly?

> *"My black son has enough things to face in his life without being teased for dressing like a 'geek.' I am not about to go out and buy him the most expensive Tommy and FUBU clothes, but I do make sure his clothes do not provoke ridicule in school. If he wants those expensive $150 running shoes, he will have to earn the difference between those and the $30 shoes I would have bought him. Nonetheless, we talk often about the superficiality of appearances and the importance of respecting himself first and foremost for his values and actions rather than for how 'cool' he is."*
>
> —An adoptive mother.

Transracial parents may have to resign themselves that their idea of proper dress may be in conflict with what their child's black peer group wears and they may have to go beyond their own taste to accommodate their child's need to fit in enough so that he won't get teased.

Why hair is an adoption issue

> *When Liza was ten, her best friend in the entire world, Melanie, looked like Farrah Fawcett Majors in "Charlie's Angels." Melanie, had—as you would guess—long blond hair and all the cool clothes. In contrast, Liza's hair wouldn't grow past the tips of her ears, no matter what we rubbed on it. Mel and I (Gail) took turns chasing her around the house every morning to pick her Afro with the plastic pick, an activity she hated even more than we did. Nobody ever told us what we were going to have to do to get her out the door for school every morning, and if they had, we wouldn't have believed them. No wonder she found another way to have long hair. For years, she covered her head with a bath towel (solid color only—no stripes or flowers) or even better (because it was longer,) a beach towel if she could find one. The towel was held on with bobby pins, and Liza tried to get it to drape gracefully down her back, as long as the hem of her dress, twisting and bobbing it, whipping it sharply from side to side as only long, straight hair can go—until it all fell off. Which it always did. We always imagined it was from our Liza that Whoopi Goldberg got the idea for her routine about the little girl pretending a towel was her long hair. Whether she was playing in the backyard or riding her bike with her brothers and sister to the Tastee Freeze, Liza could be found with the towel drooping down her back. It used to both break my heart and make me proud to see her do it: proud, because it was a solution, ingenious if slipshod; and broken-hearted because I knew that she'd never have long blond curls and there was nothing I could do either to make her not want them or to give them to her.*

> *I (Beth) want to share two pictures of my children with you. They are beautiful, yes, but I need to tell you that it is with some difficulty and shame that I show the first. Not shame of them…never! But of myself, because when I look at James' hair, I see now what I did not know then. I see that I didn't know how to care for his hair and I see that it shows on him. James had to carry the demonstration of my lack of knowledge. I didn't know how to care for his hair. I tried; I combed it every day, but I didn't know all the other things I needed to do and not do. I didn't know what the length, dryness and disarray said to the world. I do not say this to shame myself. But we cannot know what we do not know. I used to be proud of that picture. Now I am proud*

because I know more. My life has changed in the four years since this picture was taken. Now I have many more friends of African descent. Now I am around them and their children, doing their hair, going to the salon every two weeks, all the time. I have found that the more I become connected to people of my children's races, the more I learn. My fear of feeling stupid and being judged to be incompetent is not as important as is helping my kids. Now, it is easy, because the connection has bred my own need and intense desire to connect more.

"I take my daughters' hair very seriously.... In the black community, the care and maintenance of hair means more than just barrettes and ponytails; hair reflects pride and care, and neglected heads display a serious lack of mother's love.... Years ago, I met a woman whose mother refused to style her hair. I remember the hurt in her voice when she described it, and I thought about a mother's rejection reflected in tangles and neglect...I'm just grateful for conditioner... Rosette is tender-headed, and the slightest tugging at her scalp makes her cry. I'm willing to be patient, because this is what we do... Most white women do not know the kitchen, the snarls at the nape of the neck. Many white women I know express shock that I spend this much time on my girls' hair...The women who don't have to do this miss out on hours of touching, talking and closeness... My fingers weave and weave, and I know what is braided into each minute we spend there. ...don't think it doesn't matter. Because it does."

—Susan Straight, *Salon Magazine*

"I am the white mother of a black daughter whom I adopted when she was age eight. She was in sixteen homes from ages three to eight, and I don't think anyone groomed her hair. Hairdressers say that she has three times the hair of a grown woman and hair that tangles especially easily. Hair is a huge issue with her, and consequently for me, the groomer, incorporating different emotional issues in our five years together."

—Judith

"I don't like to, but I wash and comb my daughter's hair once a week and rebraid it in the middle of the week. I say her hair is her crowning glory, that it is beautiful and I'm going to make sure that it stays nice. She complains the whole way through and grabs the nape of her neck when I get to that part (there is just no way to avoid pulling those little tiny hairs back there) but we get it done."

—Esther

"I plan to call a hair salon. I have called them before, but all I ever got was an answering machine. I don't like waiting for people to return calls. But I'll leave a message if I have to. If they don't do kids' hair, maybe they can refer me to someone who does. There aren't a lot of African American beauty salons around here. I guess I could go to the city, but that's sure a scary thought"

—Kim

"If I put my daughter's hair in cornrows, she would stick out like a sore thumb. There are no black families in our town. Next year we intend to send her to preschool in the next town. They had a black teacher last year and I hope they still do, but we don't live close by— fifteen minutes. I believe God gave our child to us, and I'm sure that He will guide us in raising her to be what He wants her to be."

—Jane

I have formed some instant bonds with older African American women when they learn that I braid my daughter's hair myself.

—Becca

Learning how to groom black children's hair for the first time is not an easy matter. It does not come intuitively and usually requires hands-on help from someone with great familiarity about what is needed. Many children are tender-headed and will cry when parents first try to comb out the knots and gnarls. In black families, this is taken for granted, and the hair is groomed anyway, because there is no tolerance in the community for not taking care of a child's hair. White parents may have great difficulty and feel they cannot bear to inflict pain on their kids, having little idea of the importance of looking good. The end results of your efforts will be judged by the high standards of the black community and not the laissez-faire white model.

"Those parents just don't love their kids."

Pact was delighted recently when a group of black teenagers volunteered to provide a series of hair care workshops to help white parents learn how to take care of their children's hair. The workshops covered the importance of looking good in public, the how-to's, and some special styling tips for each child given by the hair-stylists the teens brought into the program. At the end of the six-week session, to celebrate the positive outcomes of this series, the teens invited the parents along with their children to a grand party. Each family was delighted to attend and show off the children's hair, fixed as best they could—they were decked out in their best.

Though a good time seemed to be had by all, when the adoptive families went home and the teen volunteers were relaxing with our staff we began to talk about how the kids had looked. "Those parents just don't love their kids. We told them why they needed to do it. We told them how to do it. We showed them exactly what to do, and look at how those poor little kids looked at the party. Those parents just don't care. I'd never let my kid out the door looking like that." "Did you see the one whose head was practically shaved?" "What about the one with the bun, she looked like she had a halo she had so many broken hairs." "How about those dreadlocks on a two-year-old? Who do they think they are?"

We knew that parents had tried. The results seemed fine to them, but not at all fine to their teachers. Those teenagers are representative, not exceptions. Our children will be scrutinized more than their peers with black families. But listening in to their conversation makes it clear that the stakes are high. Not one of those parents understood that they were being judged as having *failed to love* their child. Nothing could have been further from the truth. Our challenge was to continue to teach the parents without losing the teachers in the process.

Hair-care basics for African American children
How hair-educated are you?

For white parents of black children, doing your child's hair is totally different from doing your own. Most white people never had a chance to learn how. Young children need to feel beautiful and handsome to take pride in themselves. If their hair is a source of frustration not just for them, but for you, they may begin to develop low self-esteem. There are no absolute rules, any more than with white hair-care. The following ideas are commonly, though not universally, accepted within the African American community.

- Growth: My child's hair is not growing. What should I do? Each child's hair and texture is different. If your child's hair is not growing as fast or in the direction you'd like, have a professional decide if there is a problem. Likely you are not seeing length due to curl.

- Combing: How often should I comb or brush my child's hair? What kind of comb should I use? Are there special techniques for combing? How do I comb out tangles? What styles minimize tangling? It depends on the hair type. With daily (or more frequent) brushing, the hair will have fewer mats and thus hurt less with time. A very fine-toothed comb removes scalp build-up. A wide-toothed comb or pick is best for combing through the hair to minimize breakage. Natural bristle brushes are often softer and easier to use than synthetic brushes. Always comb the ends first. Spray with detangler and then massage in moisturizer. The hair will be easier to comb. Don't try to comb through the roots until the ends are tangle-free. Braiding will minimize tangling.

- Can my child and I use the same products? Probably not. Products designed for African American hair add moisture to the hair. It is also necessary to use some kind of hair moisturizer (crème or oil) at least once a day and after every washing. Make sure you use enough so the hair looks shiny but not greasy.

- Shampooing: How often should hair be washed? Which shampoo should I use? Only wash once or twice a week. Water is a drying agent. Most African Americans have to be very careful about keeping enough moisture and oil in their hair. Frequent washing may dry out the hair, preventing the natural oils from moisturizing. There is no single shampoo that suits every hair type. Try several kinds that are made just for African Americans to find the one that works best for your child. Alternate shampoo brands during the year. Hair condition changes with the seasons and the environment, so what works well in the summer may not work as well in the winter. Scrub the scalp to remove build-up of dead skin cells. Use the pads of your fingers or a scalp brush. (You can find one in the baby department of stores.) A mixture of two well-beaten egg yolks and 1/4 tsp. sea salt can be massaged into the scalp, then shampooed out for deep cleaning.

- Dry Hair: Moisturize, Moisturize, Moisturize! Dry hair feels hard, brittle and looks dull. It is caused by under-active oil glands. A dry scalp is often flaky or looks as if it is cracking. Find a moisturizing product or conditioner for extra-dry hair. The leave-in type is better. Leave-in conditioner usually has humectants, which help bring moisture to the hair. Avoid using too much leave-in conditioner because it will make the hair sticky, flat and difficult to style. Too much grease will attract dirt and dust. Deep conditioner is a heavier cosmetic such as cholesterol or mayonnaise that is enhanced by body heat or an electric heat cap. The heat dilates the cuticles. causing the conditioner to penetrate the cuticle layer of the hair shaft. Hair oil has been used in Africa for centuries to lubricate, stimulate and keep moisture in the scalp. Massage hair oils into a clean scalp once or twice weekly using circular motions to help stimulate the blood flow. A moisturizing treatment should be done once or twice a week; a leave-in conditioner can be used. Follow the instructions on the label about how much of the product to use. Check your intuitive assumption carefully, which is probably based on your own hair type, not your child's. Use enough so the hair looks shiny but not greasy. Conditioners provide a protective coating to the hair, make the scalp and hair supple, and give luster to the hair shaft.

- Tender-Headed: What if my child hates to be groomed? Your child may not like being groomed, but if you don't do it consistently, her hair will begin to mat and can reach a point where it can't be untangled. In fact, this is how dreadlocks (a style that is controversial within the African American community, particularly when considered as a hair style for children) are formed. Very often, parents tell us they feel bad because their children cry, but many children cry, even when they have same-race parents. Don't use this as an excuse. Your child will get used to it and their scalp will become less sensitive over time. Grooming must be done daily. There is zero tolerance in the African American community for an unkempt transracially adopted black child.

- How do I talk about my child's hair? Avoid negative terms such as good-hair, bad-hair, knotty head, even if you hear them from African American friends. As you are grooming, comment on specifics that he or she can see, smell, or touch such as "Your hair is so shiny today!" "Just smell your hair. I love that smell when it's first oiled, don't you?"

- Techniques for braiding: Use lotion or oil while braiding. If you don't like grease, use lanolin and lighter products. Some people prefer the smells of coconut, olive or jojoba oils. Braiding is done by sectioning the hair, paying care to make straight parts. Braid one section at a time. When you take the braids out, comb the hair out thoroughly before you wash it. It will be easy to handle because the braids will have kept it from getting tangled. Wash, condition and rebraid. Don't make really small children sit for long periods of time to have their hair elaborately braided. The younger the child, the simpler the braiding style should be. Work to avoid breakage. Don't pull the hair too tight with rubber bands, braids or barrettes. Use cloth bands, bobby pins or clips.

- Frizzies: How do I control frizzy hair? Use a styling gel to help control the frizzles but be sure also to moisturize because the styling product can dry out the hair. Frizzies also means breakage.

- Sleeping care: How should my child be sent to bed? Have your child sleep in a satin scarf or sleep cap. Satin is soft and stops the ends from breaking. The "do" will last longer and hair won't break as much.

- Cradle cap. How can we get rid of severe scalp build-up? Children of any race can have cradle cap, which is a thick, scaly build-up of dead skin cells on the scalp. Cradle cap is especially an issue for children who have full heads of hair when born and especially children whose hair is very tight and curly. Hair-care products are culprits when used incorrectly, but mostly it's just a function of how the scalp is taken care of. Treat by combing oil through the hair to soften the build-up. A really fine-toothed comb helps. Pure vitamin E can be used instead of oil. When the build-up has softened, wash it out.

- Lint: What is that white stuff in my child's hair? The "stuff" in your child's hair is lint or dust. Too much grease will attract it. Some types of hair can be like Velcro and will pick up lint no matter what you do. There is no preventive technique. You simply must pick it out. Sometimes parents confuse cradle cap with lint.

- What about straightening and relaxers? Relaxers are chemicals which straighten hair. These should not be tried without professional consultation and are rarely suggested for children under nine years old. To press hair means to heat it, making it straight. Straightening is done with a hot comb and can make the hair easier to manage but should also be done only by an experienced professional. Again, very young children do not usually have the patience for this kind of procedure. The chemical used for straightening is sodium hydroxide which is lye. It changes the molecular structure of the hair by breaking down the bond which creates the "S-shaped" curl. Once this bond is broken, the hair loses much of its natural resiliency. Children's scalps are more sensitive and prone to irritation, burns, and hair loss. Avoid putting chemicals on a child's scalp before age nine and never do it at home. Let an experienced professional handle it. The percentage of chemical is adjusted for the texture of the hair. Assessment of how much is honed by experience.

- Should I give my child a curly perm? Kiddy perms chemically straighten the hair and then use other chemicals to produce a "loose" curl. They are no different from the chemical products for adults, even though they are marketed for kids. Some consider it advisable to hold off on perms until young adulthood. Unskilled parents have produced second-degree burns. Braids, twists and cornrows are far safer to manage.

- Professional care: Where can I get help? It is a very good idea to go to a professional salon that specializes in serving African Americans to learn how and what to do with your child's hair. We recommend asking African American friends or others who would know to recommend salons open to helping white parents of black kids. A wonderful side benefit of this activity is the experience it gives you of being the only one of your race present in the salon or barber shop while your child is in the majority. Nothing is as nice as to see your children leaving the salon with an extra strut in their step because of the fuss and attention they have just received. It's easy to feel great about yourself when you look great! Find a black hair stylist who is good with kids!!! Drive as far as you need to. Get your child's hair professionally washed, conditioned and styled. You'll learn a lot, it will look great, and everyone will have time to relax about hair issues. Once you locate a stylist that you like, go regularly and stick with it. Help your child look great and feel part of the community of the barber shop or salon.

- Styling: What styles should we consider? The younger the child, the simpler the hair style. Your child needs to look like other African American children. She needs to be able to look at pictures of African Americans and be able to see herself reflected. Make sure your child's hairstyle is similar to other black kids. Study photos in magazines for continuous inspiration. Be careful about trying to have young children look too hip. Be very careful about choosing styles reflecting your personal preferences over what is common for black children in your community. Generally, sectioned braids for girls and close-cropped hair styles for boys are safe bets.

- What about hair care for boys? Be careful about trying to have young boys look too hip. Boys need oils and conditioners too, even if their hair is kept short. The first time a barber cuts your son's hair with a razor may be scary. It may help to practice at home first, teaching your child how to sit still and not be afraid of the razor or the buzz. Brush hair forward, toward the face instead of back, going against the grain. Use a light pomade for daily use. Many African Americans do not cut their children's hair, even boys, until they are one year old. Braiding your son's hair along the back of his head can help manage it at night (or even during the day) if it is long.

Hair politics—Who makes the rules?

Beauty trend-setters can't help but trade hairstyles back and forth between black and white cultures, imitating one another, incorporating ideas from each other, and creating new ideas from shared images. What looks fresh and cool or new and exciting is transformed on a monthly basis by people who earn their living creating new styles and starting trends. There is no more one "right" way for African Americans to style their hair than for people of any other racial background. The rules change all the time and different norms exist in different communities. In the '60s, the natural or counter-culture look was important in certain circles. Wearing makeup in these groups was unacceptable. In the '90s, there appears to be more tolerance for individual choices—a woman can wear cosmetics or not without aligning herself with any particular class or political group.

Let your child make choices. How our children want to style their hair is something we need to let them tell us. Our children's choices will often be based on their desire to fit it, not feel special or different. They are happy to tell us what hairstyles "all" the boys or girls in their school think are cool. It's helpful to talk about who "all" includes: white kids or children of color or both.

The mother of a ten-year-old said she had her daughter's hair relaxed because it was important to her child that she be able to do her own hair and because "all" the girls her age had either straightened hair or extensions. This child would have stood out as being very different if she wore braids, and she was different enough, having white parents. On the other hand, if that same child had been comparing herself to only white or Asian girls it might have made more sense to wait and find ways to help the child feel more connected to the looks of people of African descent.

Spend time reminding your son or daughter that he is handsome and she is beautiful. Express pride and love for her hair, acknowledging it as "her crowning glory." Be careful about the idea that for African Americans hair straightening or relaxing is simply a way of trying to have "almost like white" looks.

Don't make value judgements concerning hairstyles. Isn't it presumptuous for white parents to pass judgment on what kinds of hairstyles are legitimately black? Do African American women with straight hair feel less black because their hair is straight? Be supportive and cautious. Recognize there is much to learn and begin today. Your children will thank you.

Racism and Rice—Asian Identity Issues

Population Characteristics

In 1990, three percent of the population of the United State was composed of people of Asian heritage, roughly seven million people. People of Asian/Pacific Islander descent include people from six regions and forty-three ethnic groups

- East Asia: Chinese, Japanese, Korean
- Southeast Asia: Vietnamese, Laotian, Burmese, Thai
- The Pacific Islands: Samoan, Guamanian, Fijian, Marshalese
- South Asia: Indian, Pakistani, Nepali
- West Asia: Iranian, Afghan, Turkish
- Middle East: Iraqi, Jordanian, Palestinian

Between 1970 and 1980, the number of Asian Americans grew by 141%, and between 1980 and 1990 the number of Asian American continued to increase by another 99%, reaching a total of 7,273,662 people. In the year 2000, it is projected that the Asian American population will reach ten million, about 4% of the U.S. population.

Asian Groups	**Percent of Total**
Asian Population	
Chinese	23.8%
Filipino	20.4%
Japanese	12.3%
Asian Indian	11.8%
Korean	11.6%
Vietnamese	8.9%
Laotian	2.2%
Cambodian	2.1%
Thai	1.3%
Hmong	1.3%
All other Asian groups	4.4%
including Burmese, Sri Lankan,	
Bangladeshi, Malayan,	
Indonesian and Pakistani.	

Pacific Islander Groups	**Percent of Total**
Asian Population	
Hawaiian	57.8%
Samoan	17.2%
Guamanian	13.5%
Tongan	4.8%
Fijian	1.9%
All other Pacific Islander groups	4.8%
including Palauan, Mariana Islander and Tahitian.	

Each region of Asia is home to people of varied ethnic differences, many of which may not be easily visible to outsiders but which represent essential cultural differences among Asians themselves. The religious beliefs of Asians include Buddhism, Islam, Protestantism, Catholicism, Hinduism, Shintoism, Judaism, ancestor worship and animism. The Asian American population is diverse in terms of geographic and linguistic, religious and class backgrounds.

- Asian Pacific Americans have grown in population by 99% for Asians and 58% for Pacific Islanders between 1980 and1990.
- Most Pacific Islanders are born in the US (87%) while 66% of Asians residing in the US in 1990 were born elsewhere.
- 54% of Asians and 86% of Pacific Islanders make their homes in the West, with 66% of Asians living in California, New York, Hawaii, Texas and Illinois and 75% of Pacific Islanders in California and Hawaii.
- The average Pacific Islander family had 4.1 persons in 1990, larger than the average number for Asians of (3.8 persons) and all American families (3.2 persons).

- In 1990, a higher percentage of Asians and Pacific Islanders graduated from high school and particularly college than is true for the total U.S. population as a whole. 74.8% females and 75.7% males within the total population are high school graduates while 73.9% females and 81.7% males in the Asian/Pacific Islander population graduate. 23.3% males and 17.6% females of the total population are college graduates and 43.2% males and 32.7% females of Asian/Pacific Islanders are college graduates.

The major countries of origin (ranked by number of children adopted in the U.S. in 1999) for Asian international adoptees were China, Korea, and India.

Stereotypes and Challenges
May Your Child Never Have Surgery to Change the Shape of her Eyes

Asians suffer from positive stereotyping. This means expectations that all Asian people share certain "desirable" tendencies rather than allowing for individual differences. I (Gail) remember the day my Korean-born daughter came home from school steaming, slamming her books to the floor, refusing her favorite snack and kicking her brother each time she passed him. "Why should I try?" she said. "Miss Peters told our class today that Asians are the model minority, because they are 'good, quiet, smart, hard working and good at math.' She said some of the best students she's ever had have been Chinese. Then she made me stand up in front of the room for being good in math. I wish I wasn't good in math. It makes me sick. She used to be my favorite teacher but now I know she doesn't see ME, she sees an Asian, a model minority. She thinks all Asians are Chinese. I'm never going to school again."

My daughter had a look on her face that I'll never forget. It was one of complete despair and horror, for being betrayed by her favorite teacher, for being so foolish as to think her individuality would be noticed in the way it was for the white children in the class, for believing that she would not be seen as a stereotype. And it made me angry that she was so hurt and that I not only hadn't found a way to protect her but wouldn't be able to keep her from future acts of bias any better. Positive stereotyping made the process of finding her personal voice harder for my child. She seems to have felt challenged to resist internalizing these stereotypes and to resist identifying as Asian until she could define a more honest meaning of ethnicity on her own terms.

Stereotypes are harmful because they plant negative images in the people they attempt to describe and create perceptions of limits that may feel like barriers. Stereotyping of Asians can be confusing because stereotyping often appears on the surface to be positive, leading many to think that it isn't a serious problem. Since the 1950s, educational achievement, occupational status and income have measured the "success" of Asians in achieving "total assimilation," but this standard of measurement must be challenged. Asians have been labeled the "model minority" because superficially they appear to embody the Protestant work ethic and the morals of the American middle class; they seem "just like whites." On the other hand, Asians are also portrayed as "the yellow peril," foreigners who are a mix of threatening, dark and sinister traits as reflected in Hollywood films such as *Raiders of the Lost Ark* and *Year of the Dragon*. This mix of the yellow peril (a stereotype that became especially widespread during WWII and then was easily extended through the Korean and Vietnam war eras, especially among veterans of these wars and their kin) and the model minority can be seen in fears of Japanese "economic imperialism" and the large numbers of Asian Americans in the United States' higher education system. Such stereotyping not only divides people of color—pitting Asians against blacks and Latinos—but it also divides Asians amongst themselves—those who think it is an insult and those who perceive it as a compliment. Transracially adopted children will absorb and be confused about the stereotypes of Asian identity along with everyone else in our culture.

Behaviors, Philosophies and Cultural Conflicts

The best way to help transracially adopted children make sense of history and clashing values is to tell the truth, discussing the question of where ideas come from and "who benefits" by the situation. On an age appropriate level, all children must learn to deal with difficult history such as the Japanese internment camps, slavery, or the holocaust, but white parents of Asian children have a responsibility to be especially resourceful. Though it is not commonly acknowledged in Western civilization, Asians have contributed many of the most important aspects of our global civilization. Helping your child to find the positive images she can embrace will strengthen self-pride and esteem

Philosophies

The main philosophies in Asia are Confucianism, Taoism, Hinduism, Islam and Buddhism. Each has contributed important principles that have been incorporated over many centuries and are ingrained in the values and behavior of many Asians who may not even consciously recognize them or where they have come from. These are generalized concepts. Not all Asians hold these values. The goal is for your child (and you) to be able to develop a sensitivity and appreciation for traditional values and to integrate that knowledge so that your child will feel comfortable and know how to behave adequately and respectfully when needed.

Confucianism
Defined family roles

Right relationships in personal life and in society are based on the idea that each role in the family—father, mother, sister, brother—has a true and specific nature. Each person's job is to create order by conforming with and maintaining his or her proper role. Males dominate. Between Man and Wife, there shall be distinction: Man calls; Wife follows. Between Parents and Children, there shall be love. Children should respect parents and be filially pious. Certainly adoption supports love and respect between parents and their children but the emphasis in contemporary western families may be more reciprocal and democratic in nature than in the more traditional, hierarchical approach of Asian family life. These roles and especially roles for women are extremely different from Western-based American values.

Traditions of hierarchy require respect for elders

Western society tends to value youth and is child focused in ways that are quite different from Eastern tradition. Our society tends to worship youth and denigrate the aged. An adopted Asian child needs to know how to gain acceptance from other Asians by adhering to cultural norms regarding social rules of conduct and showing respect for family hierarchies.

Individual needs, feelings, or goals have a lower priority than the welfare of the family as a whole

Interdependency is highly valued. Family members have a lifelong obligation to support and maintain the family and to bring honor, not shame, to the family by their actions. People are born into the world carrying pre-ordained obligations to others, ranging from the family to the state. Between the Rulers and the Governed, there shall be justice. The Rulers will be just; the Ruled must be loyal. Loyalty to authority for a child raised to question authority, then, can present an inherent challenge. The tradition of relational trusts relies on a sense of mutual obligations to one's family members and working partners and is the basis for "crony capitalism" and "personalism."

Problems must be solved within the family, never shared with outsiders

The need for privacy and confidentiality may be higher in Asian communities than your child is used to. If your child shares what other Asians view as private family business with them, for example complaining about mommy or daddy or a sibling, it may be seen as a sign that yours is not a "real" family or that the proper family loyalty has not developed. Similarly, if your child were to share some information she had about an Asian friend or family in public, that would be considered disloyal. Your child's ability to understand that she may have a different sense of boundaries than many Asians she comes to know will help her decide on appropriate behavior.

Emphasis on education and meritocratic advancement

The emphasis on education unfortunately has resulted in a new kind of racial backlash. Widespread acceptance of the model minority success story hints at discrimination, an attitude that there is no need to worry about Asians because they are "doing better" than everyone else. This is divisive and destructive, resulting in reverse discrimination at educational institutions, welfare agencies, etc. As a result, your child's individual learning needs may not be taken as seriously as the needs of a child of a different race or ethnicity.

Taoism

The goal of Taoism is to maintain harmony with nature and in social relationships. Behaving in ways that avoid conflict, confrontation, disagreement, or taking the initiative stems from this goal. As Westerners we often teach our children to stand up for themselves and their own ideas and, when appropriate, to take the initiative to solve problems or make things happen. We tend to advocate direct methods, calling things what they are and communicating as clearly as possible to get our points across, being willing to discuss or debate items of disagreement with others. This can look like conflict or non-harmonious interaction to someone influenced by Taoist thinking. Adopted Asian children will benefit from learning indirect methods of communication and ways of avoiding conflict or confrontations when interacting with people influenced by Taoism.

Taoism is a religion based upon the idea that certain energies contribute to your body's natural balance and health. Illness, therefore, is attributed to a lack of balance in energies. Taoist patients may prefer to treat illnesses with medicinal herbs as opposed to surgery or other Western medical procedures.

Buddhism

Buddhists believe in Karma—that what you do in this life is shaped by what happened to you in past lives, and your actions in this life will shape what will happen to you in your next life. This belief leads to an acceptance of what fate hands out and sometimes leads non-Asians to assume that Asians have limited motivation to work for change.

The concept of *ahimsa* (i.e. equal respect for all life forms) seems to have been first associated with Buddhism. This dichotomy is often hard for many Westerners to grasp. How can a philosophy from which the roots of non-violent protest emerged be consistent with the belief that outcomes and destiny are pre-ordained? Yet the roots of passive resistance come from both Buddhism and Hinduism. During India's freedom struggle, Mohandes K. "Mahatma" Gandhi forged passive resistance into a political weapon to peacefully push out British imperialism. A principle of passive resistance is that the conquest of another person is not to be had by defeating him but by winning him over.

Many martial arts, most of which originated in Asian cultures, incorporate the philosophy that "violent" actions are only appropriate in response to inappropriate actions of aggression rather than acts of aggression themselves. Acts of direct aggression can be viewed as impolite or shameful. These attitudes can contrast starkly with some Western approaches.

The process of adoption itself may be brought into question, in that it appears to be a rearrangement of the "natural order of things." Transracial adoptive parents have a tendency to believe that change is possible. The creation and preservation of our families is built on the notion of working toward a new form of family structure with an increased tolerance for difference among its members. By osmosis, we tend to inspire our children with the belief that change and choice are possible. We are not suggesting that the Buddhist concept of "natural order" needs to be discarded, only that you and your children recognize that some Asians may not share it.

Buddhism is a religion that incorporates reincarnation; in suffering, a patient may feel that he or she will gain benefit in the next life. This may result in members' refusal to vocalize discomfort and demonstrations of stoicism with health care professionals.

Hinduism

Hinduism has very few set dogmas and allows great latitude for believers to decide for themselves which ideas and practices are important to them. The character of Hinduism is conducive to pluralism and religious tolerance. Important principles of Hinduism include the following

- A formal recognition of the Vedas as revealed wisdom is all that is required for a Hindu to be known as such. But a Hindu may even be an atheist and still be accepted as a Hindu.
- From birth to death, a Hindu can involve him- or herself in rituals which are considered to be prayers or barter for prosperity in this life and the next.
- The association of gods with animals is one of the reasons many Hindus choose to be vegetarians.

- Hindus worship the cow as the divine mother. Therefore, beef is forbidden.
- Water is considered sacred. Most temples have a pond for washing hands and feet.
- The concepts of Karma and the caste system are elements of Hindu belief.
- Hinduism contains human sacrifice, nature worship, ancestor worship, animal worship, idol worship, demon worship, symbol worship, self worship, and the highest-god worship.
- Duty (dharma), material prosperity (artha), enjoyment (kama) and salvation (moksha) are the general objectives.
- The Hindu Philosophy of Advaita-Vedanta looks upon the material world as an illusion and considers the supreme reality to lie beyond it, not visible to humans.
- The idea of renunciation (i.e. using meditation to retire to an environment which is devoid of material considerations) is a contribution of Hinduism.

The ability to pick and choose aspects of this religion seems likely to decrease potential conflicts for transracially adopted children who have a cultural connection to Hinduism. On the other hand, the message that people of different races must not interact freely as designated by the caste system (designated to keep the distinct, hereditary Hindu social classes—Brahman, Kshatriya, Vaisya, and Sudro—separated from each other) is in total conflict with the construction of the racially-mixed transracial adoptive family of which your child is a member.

Islam

The followers of Islam, the second largest religion in the world, are called Muslims. The largest numbers of Muslims are in Asia and Africa. The founder of Islam, Muhammad, was born in about A.D. 570 in Mecca. The five principle beliefs of Islam are

- There is no God but Allah, and Muhammed is His prophet.
- The faithful pray to Allah five times daily.
- The faithful help the poor and provide for upkeep of places of prayer.
- The faithful fast, and they never drink alcohol or eat pork and certain other foods.
- A Muslim must make a pilgrimage to Mecca at least once in his or her lifetime.

    It is the duty of the ruler of an Islamic state to maintain five basic universal rights among the people:

- Life: The right that your body as an individual or any one of your bodies as a group is safe from harm.

- Property: The right to own property safe from any attempts to force it away from you or to defraud you.
- Freedom of conscience: The right that no one can try to force you into having any opinion or belief you do not choose yourself.
- Freedom of religion: This is a lot more than freedom of conscience. It implies that you are able to follow the teachings of your religion so long as it doesn't infringe on the freedom of others to do likewise. An Islamic state would try to ensure that each religious group could have its own laws and own legal system for matters of distinctive religious laws (e.g. marriage, divorce, inheritance, etc.)
- Honor: This is the right not to be defamed and libeled in public.

    Islam is a religion with an absolute prescription for how to behave and what to believe that goes against the more Western philosophies of "each to his own" or "live and let live." Many Muslim states have rigid rules about women's place in society, ownership of children as property, and a willingness to wage violence in the name of their beliefs that are hard for Americans to understand. Finding the virtues of Islam, of which there are many, will be important to giving your child a balanced view that will allow him or her to appreciate the strengths of this aspect of their heritage.

Sikhism

The Sikh religion emerged during the early 16th century in Punjab in North India. Guru Nanak was the founder. Born a Hindu, but also inspired by the teachings of Islam, Nanak tried to unite humanity through the message of universal brotherhood and communal harmony and to launch a new movement for the establishment of an egalitarian society and a joint social order. Sikhism propounds worship of one God but embraces the idea of Karma. It also opposes the caste system and believes that all men are equal. Guru Nanak advocated man's direct link with the Ultimate Reality. He denounced asceticism, monasticism, formalism and image worship and all rites and rituals connected with religious service.

Family Values

The interdependent view of families common to most Asian cultures and religions described above is in conflict with the concept of the autonomous individual as the ground of all rights and duties, a view that is prevalent in the West, where we have made "co-dependency" or "enmeshment" symptoms of emotional malfunctioning. Asians also tend not to draw the rigid lines between nuclear families and extended families that Westerners are more prone to draw. Adopted Asian children interacting with Asian families in the community need to understand that uncles, aunts, cousins, and grandparents may have a different presence and status than is "normal" in the child's home experiences.

When she was about four years old, my (Gail's) granddaughter made friends with Jennifer Kim, a new little girl who had recently joined her preschool. Her mom, Shira, had invited the Kim family for an informal Sunday lunch so the girls could play and their parents could get to know each other. She hadn't imagined that the Kims would assume that the invitation included Jennifer's mother and father, his grown son by a previous marriage who lived at home, his son's girlfriend, Jennifer's mother's parents, who also lived with them, and their daughter, Helen, who had never married and also lived at home. That made a total of eleven people for lunch instead of the six that had been expected. Shira said she felt lucky to be able to stretch the food to feed the larger group but she was embarrassed and not sure that the Kims felt properly honored.

The Kims seemed to expect that the focus of the afternoon would be on the grownups while my daughter had thought it would be for the kids. She complained to me later that the conversation between the grownups had been stiff, more focused on what was different between the two families than what was similar. They seemed to suggest that Korean thinking was better about most things. This didn't make her angry, only regretful that she didn't know what Korean thinking on most things was and that once again she was an outsider, even in her own home.

Gender Issues: Views of Women (and, by Extension, Men)

Asian children who are adopted by white families may have difficulty with the history of subjugation of women in male-dominated hierarchies in traditional Asian cultures. To a much greater extent than in the West, women in Asian societies continue to be treated differently from men both in social custom and in law. In many countries, women suffer from severe discrimination. This is the case in India, where wife-burning still occurs and a predominance of female adoptees, which (as with China) can be viewed as another expression of the "expendability" of the girl child. While female labor-force participation can be high, girls generally work only until they are married, and then drop out to raise families. Women across Asia are also less able to control their own reproductive cycles. In the more socially conservative parts of Asia, in one way or another women are prevented from earning enough to support themselves and their children without a husband. This value conflict and its contrast with mainstream American support of feminism and individualism may make identifying positively with birth culture even more sensitive for transracially adopted Asians, particularly girls. Many Americans consider the subjugation of women as wrong, plain and simple. It is challenging to help Asian American children raised to believe in equal rights and opportunities find a way to take pride in their cultural history and traditions when basic values seem so different from the ones with which they are being raised.

To further complicate the issue, mainstream America's stereotypes about Asian men and women also contribute to a drive toward acculturation (for women) and a movement away from their heritage. Whereas white men are glamorized in movies, sports, books, etc., Asian males are seldom put in leading roles or in a sexy light. Some teens tell us that for a white female to date an Asian male is considered "dating down," whereas an Asian female who dates a white male is considered to be "dating up" or "marrying up." "Many Chinese males were brought over with the coolie trade and were viewed as subhuman units of production." Marlon Villa, a Filipino, says, "Black guys are studs, white guys have all the power and Asian guys are the nerdy little wimps that women wouldn't glance at."

There is evidence that this is changing. Money talks and Asian men are becoming immensely visible. It's no coincidence that sexy new images of Asian men are popping up on movie screens at a time when Asian-Pacific Islanders have the highest median household income in America and role models like Yahoo's cofounder Jerry Yang have come on the scene. A new wave of Asian actors and action heroes—Chow Yun Fat, Rick Yune and Jet Li—are showing that Asian stars can be objects of lust as well as the next guy. Stanford history professor Gordon Chang says the image of Asian American men has progressed from "laundryman's son" to "future Internet millionaire." How this change will relate to the idea of male dominance is an interesting question.

Gender differences also contribute to patterns in the adoption of Asian children, as evidenced by the fact that more girl children have been adopted from China, India, Korea and Pakistan than are boys and that in some of these Asian countries, advanced reproductive technology that allows for sex determination before birth is being demanded and used by even very poor women so that girls can be aborted. The reasons for these gender preferences need to be explained to girls who are adopted from Asian countries so that they can understand them in the broader context of history, culture and circumstance rather than imagining that they were disliked or abandonned by their country and people simply because they were born girls. Though political and historical explanations must be tailored specifically to your child's birth country, the following can be used as a model.

Explaining being adopted from China. Do Asian people hate girls?

Only when a child has the ability to think abstractly can she begin to appreciate that all people don't share the same perspective and are sometimes driven by painful choices for reasons beyond the child's own experience. The ability to fully understand being adopted requires a child to be able to think about life from their birth parents' points of view. Children are not usually able to understand the economic, political, religious or social pressures that precipitate international adoption, though they will undoubtedly have questions at younger ages. After adolescence, children may develop the capacity to understand the pressures that their birth parents faced.

For a daughter still in the stage of concrete thinking and not yet able to understand the complexities of the situation, parents can tell a simplified version of the truth without overloading her with details she can't process. Reframe the fact that she was found in the street and brought to a police station or adoption agency by a stranger by pointing out that her birth parents must have wanted very much for her to be found and taken care of. How do we know? Because she was not left in a deserted place where no one would find her, but in a busy public place where she would be sure to be found quickly. Parents in China do not have the luxury of "making an adoption plan because that's against the law. But they do the best they can under unimaginably difficult circumstances."

Reassure your daughter that there was nothing wrong with her. There was nothing she did to cause her Asian parents not to keep her. Most likely they were not able to keep her with them because of the rules. Most kids understand that sometimes we must do things because of the rules. China does not let parents choose how many children they want to have. The government has rules that say that most parents can have only one or two children. If they have more they have to pay a lot of money, more money than everyone except the very, very rich could ever have. Some parents have lost their homes because they had more children than they were supposed to. Some people in this situation think the only thing they can do if they have another child they weren't supposed to have, is to leave that child in a safe place where she will be sure to be taken care of. They usually stay out of sight themselves so they won't get in trouble but they might watch the baby until they see someone has taken her so they know she will be safe and brought to an orphanage.

Another reason Asian parents sometimes have to send their baby to an orphanage is because medical care in certain parts of the country is very expensive and people who live on farms or small towns often cannot afford it. They believe that their baby will get better medical help in the orphanage than if they keep them at home with them. Once they give them to the orphanage they cannot come to get them back without getting into a lot of trouble with the government.

Why do they have such dumb rules: What kind of a place is China?

China is a country going through many changes. It is neither a rich country nor a very poor country, but a country that is trying to be sure that all its people have enough to eat or drink by making firm rules about how large the population can grow. China has the largest number of people of any country in the world. The rules, though very difficult, were made to be sure all of the people would have enough resources to survive. You are not the only child who was adopted from China. Many girls have been adopted during these times because their birth parents believed they had no choice but to follow the rules. China is an ancient country with a very rich culture. Many of the greatest contributions to our civilization have come from China. As a Chinese person, you can take pride in these achievements.

Do Asian people hate girls?

Chinese people like girls as much as boys. The reason girls get placed for adoption instead of boys is because of the way people in China are taken care of when they are too old to take care of themselves. According to Chinese tradition and the rules of modern China, sons take care of their parents in their old age. When daughters grow up and get married, they help take care of their husband's parents instead of their own. Many Chinese parents feel that their future depends on having a healthy son who will take care of them with his wife when they get old. In most cities families can only have one child. In the countryside, where most Chinese families live they can often have two children before they must stop or pay a fine. Sometimes they can afford to have three or maybe four, depending on how expensive the fine for extra children is where they live. Since they want to have at least one son to take care of them later, if they get to the highest number they can afford then some of them decide to place the newest girl in a safe place to go to the orphanage a later be adopted so they can try again for a son

China has a long tradition of "informal" adoption. That means that instead of going to a judge or an orphanage, a family who wanted to adopt would simply ask around their community to find out about a baby whose family could not take care of them and then take that baby and make them their son or daughter without signing any legal papers. Because of the governments new rules, there are more children now than families who can afford to adopt them the old fashioned way, so they have to be adopted using orphanages and judges. Many Chinese girls get adopted by parents from other countries because it is not easy to adopt this new way if a person is a Chinese citizen. Only infertile or childless families were allowed to adopt and families who did adopt often worried about their future economic security and decided to add only boys to their family, leaving more Chinese girls than boys available for international adoption. Even though it was hard, there were still many more Chinese babies who have been adopted by Chinese families than by families from other countries. In 1999, the Chinese government made it a little bit easier for Chinese families to adopt. Before the rule was only one child for each family, after 1999 families who already had a child could adopt another one.

Education

Schools are regarded as an extended family in many Asian cultures. The family is often regarded as an inseparable social unit with collective duties and responsibilities. In more traditional families children may be seen as reflections of their parents. "Losing face," "family disgrace," and shame are all strong incentives for doing one's best. The goal of education is to become human. Becoming a moral being is central to education. Respect for and trust of teachers is reciprocated by teacher's "love" of students, a parallel to parental love of children. Parents are expected to display all-out support for children's education, often sacrificing their own comfort. Parents are the "teachers" of morals; teachers provide intellectual nurturing and social learning. "Studenting" is regarded as full-time work, as one's "occupation." Children are expected to study hard. Much homework is expected, especially by parents.

- Public criticism and disagreement are avoided. Being "spotlighted" in a negative sense in a group situation, particularly at the secondary school level, may bring about an overwhelming sense of shame. It is best to counsel individually after class.
- Symbolic difference of "head-down" when scolded or disciplined. "Head-down" is generally a sign of regret, remorse, or accepting the consequences, while looking straight into the speaker's face is interpreted as a sign of defiance. Smiling or laughing may conceal embarrassment.
- Students tend to be less verbal or "spontaneous," which is not necessarily a sign of non-study, ignorance or uncooperativeness. It is partly due to an emphasized value of humility and partly due to less emphasis on "independent" thinking.
- Structured group approaches with clear directions, expectations and demands are considered the best educational approaches. "Free time," "free school," or "Summerhill ideas" would not be widely appreciated.

Reflections in the Mirror, Countering Invisibility

From an early age, kids form lifetime attitudes that form the basis for making critical personal decisions. Those attitudes are shaped each day by an array of message not only from home, school and friends, but also from popular culture and from an increasingly bewildering technological society. Whose voices will break through? Whose should? None is more important than yours.

According to a study by the Children's Defense Fund, Asian children are less likely than are white or black children to see people who look like them on TV, in books, or in the movies. Mostly they see only white and black characters. That means that they are more likely to associate having lots of money, being well educated, being a leader, and being intelligent with white characters; while associating lawlessness, financial inability, laziness, or silliness with black characters (even though they are also likely to choose black characters as their favorites.) You may not be disturbed by the notion that your child sees whites as superior since you are white. But think about what it means to be invisible while you try to fit into another culture.

Because of this absence of media images and the greater availability of good books that reflect Asian children, we suggest that you bend over backwards to make sure that your child has access to the wonderful books that are available. Asian cultures have a great reverence for tradition and history that your child needs to learn about. If your local library does not stock them, suggest that it gets them. When you purchase a book for your child, make sure that Asian children are represented in it. If you can tune in to an Asian TV station or radio program, do so, and ask the stations when they have children's programming or how you can access stations that do. Err on the side of abundance in making connections that will bring cultural guidance to your child.

Are Asian contributions and history included in the curriculum at your child's school? It is your responsibility to make sure that they are. Education contributes to bias against Asians by omission, overlooking the presence and contributions of Asian Americans, rendering them invisible. Talk with the teachers and administration about ways of integrating this important material into the existing curriculum and reflecting Asian culture in the classroom. This means providing a balanced number of books, videos, posters, art projects, games, music, etc. that stem from Asian roots or reflect Asian pride, not just one or two. Good materials exist and new ones are being created all the time. They can all be there for your child. It is a crime if she is denied access to them.

Mi Familia, Mi Corazon—Latino Identity Issues

Population size and characteristics:

According to the U.S. Bureau of the Census, Current Population Survey, March, 1999, one in nine people in the United States is of Latino origin. The 1999 estimate of the Latino-origin population in the United States was 31.7 million or 11.7 % of the total population. Between 1980 and 1990, the Latino population grew by 53%, seven times the rate the rest of the population grew during the same period. It is anticipated that, due to immigration and patterns of high birth rates, Latinos will become the largest ethnic group in the U.S. by the 21st century with one in four people being of Latino origin. The majority is Roman Catholic. Nearly two-thirds of all Latinos were of Mexican origin (65.2%). Latinos of Central or South American heritage made up 14.3%, Puerto Rican 9.6%, Other Latino 6.6% and Cuban 4.3%. The median age of the Latino population (25.6%) is 1996 was about eleven years younger than the median age of the non-Latino white population (36.5). Despite significant progress, 27.8% of Latinos 25 years and older has less than a 9th grade education. Latinos were also more likely to be unemployed, less likely to be married, more likely to earn less, to live in large households and live in poverty than the white non-Hispanic population.

Of the Central Americans 42.7% are Salvadoran, 20.3% Guatemalan, 15.3% Nicaraguan, 9.9% Honduran, 7.0% Panamanian, 4.3% Costa Rican and 2.1% are other ethnicities. Of the South Americans 36.6% are Columbian, 18.5% Ecuadorian, 16.9% Peruvian, 9.7% Argentinean, 6.6% Chilean and 11.7% are other ethnicities.

Latinos? Hispanics? What's the Right Label?

Mexican Americans, Puerto Ricans, Cuban Americans and others with Latin American origins who live in the U.S. use the umbrella terms Latino or Hispanic when referring to cultural group identity. Until the mid-1990s, *Hispanic* was the dominant term for referring to Spanish-speaking people in the U.S., or descendents of Spanish-speaking countries. The term came about in the 1970s as a result of the U.S. Census' attempt to quantify Spanish-speaking people. Today, *Latino* and *Hispanic* are used interchangeably, yet *Strangers in a Native Land*, a report of the Latino Ethnic Attitude Survey (LEAS), conducted by Daniel L. Roy of the University of Kansas, 1999, found that though "there is no single, preferred term. The term *Hispanic* is uniformly disliked, and the term *Latino* ranked higher than any other." Some prefer the name *Latino* because it does not reflect the imperialist history of South and Latin America's conquest by Spain, instead describing the people themselves. Some embrace the term "Hispanic" as a means to bolster solidarity among the various groups and gain political power.

Eighty-five percent of Roy's referents preferred a national origin label to either of the umbrella terms. An individual may use different labels at different times. Labels are not static and consistent but tend to change depending on the context and differ depending on age, country of origin, education and geographic region. Often more specific labels are used within the ethnic community and more general terms in the broader society when the use of more descriptive terms may not be correctly understood. For example, individuals of Mexican heritage may use *Mexicano* or *Chicano* among their social group but refer to themselves as *Mexican American* or *Latino* at work or in other public environments.

There are distinct regional preferences. According to the LEAS report, individuals of Mexican decent in California, Arizona, New Mexico and Colorado prefer the term *Chicano*, which may be traced to the 1930s, when rural Mexicans (often native Americans) were imported to the U.S. for field labor. Because they had difficulty pronouncing the word *Mexicanos*, it became instead *Mesheecanos* in part because it is common for Mexicans to use the "CH" blend in place of certain consonants to create a term of endearment. So *Mesheecano* became *Mecheecano*, which led to *Chicano*. Whatever its origin, the term *Chicano* was first insulting. But Mexican American activists reclaimed the term during the Civil Rights movement. It has since come into widespread usage. In Texas, the terms *Mexican American* and *Mexicano* are preferred. In Florida, *Latin American* followed by *American* and *American of Mexican descent* are common. In New York, terms of choice are *American*, *Chicano*, or *Central American*. In Illinois, *Mexican* is preferred in the first and second generations and *Mexican American* in the later, more assimilated generations. A sub-population of Mexican Americans located primarily in New Mexico prefer the term *Hispano*. An interesting subgroup called the *Marranos*, descendants of persecuted Jews who fled Spain and Portugal during the 16th and 17th centuries and survived by hiding their cultural identities, may be of particular interest to Jewish parents of Latino children.

In the end, terms of choice depend on the individual. The easiest and most respectful way to find out someone's preference is to ask in a direct way. "What terms do you prefer that I use when I refer to your ethnicity? Latino, Hispanic, Mexican American, etc?"

Latino Is Note a Race, It's a Culture

"Why am I so brown? God made you brown, mija color broce—
color of your raza connecting you to your raices, your story/histori as
you begin moving toward your future."
—Trinidad Sanchez, Jr.

Latinos may be white, black, indigenous people, or any combination. While Latinos tend to identify first by national origin, they also feel an affinity with other Latinos based on language and cultural similarities and sharing the experience of being treated as outsiders by the European Americans they refer to as Anglos. A transracially adopted child of Latino heritage should be helped to feel part of his national group—Columbia, Chilean, Guatemalan, Mexican, etc.—but will benefit most by feeling part of the larger group of Latinos who have lived for the last 150 years in America. Cultural values and shared experience—not a common history or shared origin—help Latinos identify as one ethnic group. In the U.S., people of Latin American heritage find commonalties among the different groups, paying less regard to national origin than do those who remain in their countries of origin.

One result of the mixed racial and cultural heritage within almost all Latino communities is that they bring to North American society a differing perspective on racial issues. A tradition of social fluidity among cultures and races in Latin America allows for greater flexibility in relations among Latinos of different racial mixes. This is illustrated in Oscar Hijuelos' Pulitzer Prize-winning novel *Mambo Kings Play Songs of Love* (New York, Farrar-Strauss-Giroux, 1989), in which light- and dark-skinned Cubans interact regularly in Spanish Harlem during the 1950s. Despite the tense U.S. racial climate, Cuban immigrants of all races interacted freely as they had in Cuba. In her book *Puerto Ricans: Born in the U.S.A.* (New York, Westview Press, 1989), Clara Rodriguez makes a similar observation of the Puerto Rican community in New York. She points out that Puerto Ricans of all races interacted socially, and she offers music as an example: the "new Latin sound incorporates Afro-Cuban, White rock, Black soul, and the Latin rhythms.."

Stereotypes and Challenges

"Dinky is a negative image because representing Latinos as a dog is
negative and because the context of Dinky's activities includes low-
riders, brothels, and entering people's homes without invitation."
—Amelia Mesa-Bains, Director for Visual and Public
Art, California State University at Monterey

Stereotypes are often created or reinforced by the media which, as always, devotes more attention to "sexy" stories than those that might promote positive identity for Latinos. In recent years the image of the "Cholo," a Latino gang member with shaved head, tattoo, and baggy pants, has emerged, adding another less than positive character to a list that is dominated by illegal aliens, drug dealers, hoodlums, Don Juans, "greasers," "spics," "beaners," "wetbacks," and "low-riders." Job opportunities for Latinos seem limited to maids, nannies, fast-food servers and gardeners.

Because even negative portrayals on TV are so few and far between, advertising images have also become large influences on associations the general public assimilates about Latinos. Taco Bell's $60 million ad campaign featuring Dinky, a hairless Chihuahua who loves Mexican food and is always asking, "Yo quiero Taco Bell," underlines the point. Various Latino groups threatened to boycott Taco Bell, claiming the ads were racist, and there has been similar outrage about characters like Speedy Gonzalez, Chiquita Banana, Juan Valdez and Frito-Bandito, the image of a sleepy bandit in a large sombrero. Biased as such images are, they most likely were created by people who were trying to capture the 350 billion dollar Latino market rather than offend the community. But negative images hurt every Latino person in America—including our children. Encourage your children to discuss what's wrong with ads that portray Latinos using stereotypes; take the opportunity to encourage them to write letters or set up boycotts as a way of fighting back.

Where Are You From?

One of the experiences that unites Latinos of different origins in the United States is the shared experience of being seen as "outsiders" by Anglos, including being often stereotyped as "illegal aliens." Non-Latinos often presume that all Latinos are bilingual (speaking Spanish and English) and that all Latinos share the same traditions and foods. Like Latino American citizens who were born in the United States and whose families have lived here for generations, Latino children who are transracially adopted are commonly and repeatedly asked where they come from. They need to be prepared for these inevitable questions and to have a range of responses that they feel very comfortable delivering. You can help your child to develop a strong sense of authority if you role-play or plan at home the kinds of responses he might choose, ranging from a simple, "I've got to go now," "Why do you ask?" or "My family came from Guatemala" or "I've been an American all my life, how about you?" Help your child understand why these kinds of assumptions make it seem as if Americans are white Anglo-Saxon rather than people of all cultures and ethnicity.

Having been designated as *aliens*, the ultimate outsider, Latinos are targeted by Anglo culture as the "reason" for lack of jobs, good educational and health care systems and almost any other available ill that society can concoct, making Latinos automatically suspect as to whether they are honest or upright people. While Latinos are now recognized by the elite of Wall Street as an important target for sales, the working and middle classes of America often see them as the culprit that keeps them from climbing higher up the economic or status ladder by stealing their jobs or undercutting their earning power. This imagery will be especially challenging for Latino children who are in fact immigrants themselves and may find themselves feeling very fearful about being "caught" or "identified."

The Dirty Secret of Racism within the Community

Latinos also struggle with internalized racism. In fact, many Latino cultures are extremely mixed, with people of all descents ranging from African to European, Asian and indigenous all making up the varied group. In many South American, Central American and Caribbean countries, the people in power are lighter-skinned with more visible roots to the European Spaniards who ruled their lands for many years. This has led to internal racial strife which is not easily talked about or dealt with by the Latino community. In fact, many immigrants who may have been part of the more privileged classes in their native country come here to find themselves members of the less privileged sector of society inhabited by people of color in North America. This has created confusion and sometimes a tendency for Latinos to verbally deny the importance of racial designation out of their own attempt to find success in America. On the other hand, some have retreated into barrios (Latino ghettos) where they can replicate the world of their homeland and as much as possible resist the assimilation into a culture that devalues their status.

Whites must be very careful and cautious in approaching this complexity. This is an internal struggle within the community that our adopted children will have the right to speak out about and try to change but about which we must keep a respectful distance. If we are critical, we are likely to be seen as hypocrites, given the state of our own country and culture. On the other hand, we must help our children negotiate a world filled with its own inequities and injustice without leaving them blindsided in the face of racism that may be directed towards them or their friends. These complexities are never easy but cannot be ignored.

Behaviors, Philosophies and Cultural Conflicts

To assist transracially adopted Latino children, it is necessary to take a look at common attitudes of Latino adults and children in the U.S. Ethnic identity is important to Latinos in defining who they are, although there is considerable variation in how it is expressed. Among some more educated Latinos ethnicity becomes less important to their identity, while others maintain a very strong identity and express their cultural values on an every day basis. Certain values of Latino culture cross ethnic lines and can be summarized below.

El Matrimonio and La Familia (Marriage and Family)

Family is everything for Latinos. They often conceptualize family differently than do Anglos, including extended family members, compadres (godparents) and close friends among those they call familia. More than any other racial group in the United States, Latinos are likely to form conventional family units of a married couple with children in which the husband assumes the instrumental role of provider and protector and the wife the expressive role of homemaker and caretaker. These values reflect a lifelong commitment to parenting and permanence which match the values of most adoptive parents.

Motherly love is considered the greatest form of love, even taking precedence of that of a wife for her husband. During early family years, most Latinos are very child-centered, tending to be permissive and indulgent with younger children. In spite of an emphasis on good behavior as children get older, parents tend to give a lot of nurturing to young children and have a somewhat relaxed attitude toward achievement milestones, particularly those related to self-reliance. As children approach latency and adolescence, they are given more tasks and expected to take on more responsibilities.

> *Spending Christmas in Oaxaca (Mexico) with our children (Beth's) when they were seven and nine was a great way to relieve ourselves of the normal holiday hubbub and enjoy quality family time together. We knew that Sofia would enjoy looking like so many of the people in the region and we had prepared both children to be open to the cultural differences and enjoy Christmas according to the Oaxacan way rather than trying to recreate our own. What we had forgotten was how loving and generous the Mexican people are to children. In the hotel, in the village square, on the buses, wherever we went, the people would greet our children and welcome them by moving them to the front of the line, opening doors and helping to entertain them as we would wait in a line or to cross a street. "Children first" was the attitude throughout. For Christmas, the children got a bouncing ball for play in the hotel pool and at the beach town in which we spent some days. Later in the trip, when we were in Mexico City we had the opportunity to stay in one of the city's finest hotels, five star. As the kids were waiting for me to exchange money at the front desk on our way to the pool (with the ball,) they began to play a form of basketball in which the clerks behind the desk would hold their arms in front of them to make a basket and the children would shoot. I was touched by*

this display of willingness to cater to my children, and when they had made a few baskets I shushed them along, telling them we should let the people get back to their work. Claudia spoke for them all, saying, "No please, we love your children. Let them play until they tire. It is our pleasure to love them." And yes there was a line waiting for the clerks, mostly other Mexicans who seemed to enjoy the game as much as the staff. But none enjoyed this more than Sofia. She has decided she will attend college in Mexico City. "The nicest people I ever met," she says. I think she secretly hopes that Claudia will still be there when she returns, inspiring my daughter to college and her wider connection to Latino people. Amazing what can be accomplished with a simple game of hoops when it includes valuing children and family above all else!

Differences in sex-role socialization are thought to be strong in Latino culture because of the history of patriarchal domination. Throughout history, the role of Latina mothers was to be self-sacrificing and submissive to the father who played out a machismo model with total authority and power, although there is considerable variation in how gender roles are expressed and maintained in Latino families. Moreover, these patterns have changed some as Latinas have become more education and entered the work force. The concept of machismo has led to stereotypes of Latino men as wife beaters and Latino women as doormats. Latino community leaders would call these negative spins on a positive value of Latino men valuing women and family above all else, and Latina women being committed to the importance of family connection and nurturing above all else.

La Comunidad (Community)

Latino culture is collectively oriented and focused on ways in which individuals can experience harmony with their social environment. Many Latin cultures place high regard for community as a reference group and source of support. There is a sense of responsibility for the group, with community needs often being considered before individualism. Working within groups often comes quite naturally. As in African American communities, there is a sense that all children belong to the community and everyone in it has a responsibility to care for them and look after their well- being. Latino adopted children raised with white parents may not be used to having people outside of their own family members offer them guidance, and may feel that members of the Latino community are being intrusive when they feel entitled to do so.

Sense of time

In Latin fashion, observance of the *hora latina* is an attitude toward schedule and punctuality which places higher importance on relationship and attention to people than being on time for appointments, visits, parties, etc. The notion of *siesta* is rooted in the belief that relationships and community involvement are of high importance compared to business success and accomplishments. It can be considered bad manners to act as if "business is business" or "competition is healthy," just two of many common virtues in European-based value systems. Conflict is never a goal, rather the priority is to work things out through personal charisma and charm.

Personalismo

A core cultural concept for Latinos is *personalismo*: developing a personal relationship and understanding before beginning interactions with others. Good personal relationships are more important than accomplishments or ability. The individual is more important than ideology or society consequently, personal needs or desires take precedence over responsibilities. The exception to this notion is responsibility to family.

A person facing difficulties turns to her family rather than the government or agencies for help. Latinos would care for elderly relatives on their own rather than place them in a nursing home. Cultural beliefs often keep the Latino community from utilizing the services already available, especially when community services lack "personalismo." If a Latino approaches an agency for help and has to provide private information, he would need to feel he had a relationship with the agency employee before providing the information. Latinos need to develop a personal relationship before engaging in business.

Jesús has been a good friend to our family (Beth's) for many years. We were delighted to make him Sofia's godfather and pleased that he was willing to remain her friend and family member for life. Not so long ago, when he got married he had a very small ceremony with family only. We were honored to be included. I had not seen his mother for many years, as she was living out of state. As they fussed over Sofia and we reacquainted ourselves, I was reminded of the first time I met her so many years ago.

We were in college and Jesús had warned me that bringing a Gringa home might cause some stir, especially for his mom. They had emigrated while she was pregnant, in order to offer their children opportunities they believed they could only get here. Indeed Jesús, as the oldest, had accomplished the dream, attending a private college known for academic success. But behind the pride must also have lurked some fear that she would lose him to my world.

The plan was to come and visit for a short while and then take his sisters on a shopping trip. They were in high school and I had visions of taking them to new fashion heights. When we arrived she showed me around their small home and we lingered long in front of the pictures of the family, commenting on each one. Then we went into the kitchen where a feast had been prepared. (Jesús and I had eaten on the way over so we were certainly not hungry.) As I began to sputter our apologies, Jesús touched my arm and exclaimed that we hadn't eaten in what sounded like a week! As we sat down to the meal, I was antsy and uncertain how to proceed. I was offered everything first, many foods I had never experienced before. Some were wonderful, others more frightening. But each time Jesús answered that yes, I would love just a little bit more. I probably suggested eight or ten times that we really should get going. I sensed it probably wasn't the right thing to do, but I was stuffed to the gills and feeling sick and frustrated that our plan was being shanghaied. It was early evening before we left, long past the time for me.

When I asked Jesús later if his fears had come true, had his mother been critical of this first Anglo visitor, he took a long time to answer. The answer was yes. I rolled my eyes. "I guess it was predictable, even after all that we did, staying for too long, eating when we didn't want to, missing our shopping trip." And he rolled his eyes back and began a conversation that took years to penetrate my thick skull. His mother was showing me the highest respect and offering me chances in every way to be included within the circle of her family, and at every turn I had placed a higher emphasis on my own comfort and sense of priority. I hadn't gotten it. I had rejected her and not even known it.

And so those many years later, at her son's wedding, she and I spent a great deal of time together and she commented later that she was glad we were part of the family. I felt as if I had learned my lesson and what a beautiful lesson to learn. People and relationships trump appointments and acquisitions. Every day of the week.

Respeto (Respect)

Latino culture is structured around hierarchies and based on notions of giving proper respect to the elderly or those with more power. In many Latino families, you will find a grandparent living with one or more generations of kin. Latinos are usually very polite. When meeting someone for the first time, it is custom to use their formal title. When meeting a smaller group of people, one must greet each person individually and say good bye to each one as well. Friends will often hug. Men shake hands with other men. Men greet women with a kiss on the cheek. Women greet one another in the same manner. A transracially adopted child may need to learn new forms of showing respect that are different from what her own family practices in order to know how to behave appropriately within the Latino community. Recognition of the significance of how one treats others in all circumstances can be the difference between being included or rejected as rude. Young children will always be given the benefit of the doubt, but as children grow into young men and women the expectations for meeting social obligations will be higher.

Language

Whereas disparity of language is one of the things that separates the in other culturally linked Asian societies discussed earlier, the Spanish language is a dominant link among nationally-diverse Latinos. For many Latinos bilingualism is necessary to meet the social and work requirements for moving between mainstream and Latino cultures. For transracially adopted Latino children growing up in white families, the benefits of being able to speak and communicate directly in Spanish include being able to communicate with more people and to be understood in different settings. Latino culture is rooted in Spanish; many of the words and meanings central to one's outlook on life do not even exist in English. Being able to speak Spanish will be a source of self-esteem and enhance their sense of belonging. Language development research indicates that bilingual children do better than others on tests of analytical reasoning, concept formation and cognitive flexibility. Because the Latino population is growing so rapidly, there will be an ever-increasing number of people for your child to speak Spanish with and being bilingual is likely to become an important asset in the work place. "When I was little, my parents asked me if I wanted to learn Spanish," one woman said. "I told them no, but I didn't realize how important it was at the time." Your child may find studying Spanish to be exciting or a burden in their younger years, but because of the desire to feel confident about their birth culture, they will probably have a higher interest than most Latinos in eventually becoming fluent.

Spirituality

An overwhelming majority of Latinos are Christian, primarily Catholic. The church plays a pivotal role in Latino culture. Major functions in the community almost all center around the church. Catholicism in many Latino cultures has come to take on an almost pagan aspect, as characterized by the often more pedantic doctrines of Protestantism. Latinos often believe in elaborate folklore involving saints and other spirit visits from those who are passed on. Many of their traditions have grown out of the merging of Catholic rituals with the tribal beliefs of the indigenous peoples who originally populated Central and South America. This connection to the land, the world of spirits and the church offers many Latinos a way to enjoy life in the face of painful circumstances. It can also be connected to their high degree of comfort with demonstrative emotions.

The strong sense of family legacy and connection to ancestors can be a problem for some adoptive families in that it presumes a "blood" or family connection that is beyond personal choice or control. On the one hand, this speaks volumes for each child's connection to culture, something that cannot be denied. On the other hand, it would seem to place the connections formed by adoption lower than those of blood and birth. This challenge is often mitigated with Latinos who have a deep strong relationship with one's adoptive family. In this intimacy, they get to experience the strong familial relationships typified by adoptive families and valued so highly in their own culture. But for strangers or acquaintances, the "adoptism" can pose a problem.

Latino culture is frequently typified by a sense of fatalism, which rather than making the people hopeless allows them to enjoy the good in life, while largely ignoring what is bad. This attitude has proven extremely helpful in the face of the hard lives of many of the people but can also be used to hold Latinos back if translated into a sense of having no control over ones circumstances. This has also made Latinos a people with a strong zest for life, able to enjoy the moment and relish the here and now. Celebrations and gatherings are often boisterous reflections of this love of life.

Being Seen—Native American Identity Issues

Definitions and Population Data

Population size

In 1998, U.S. Census Bureau, Current Population Survey data stated that an estimated 2.4 million Native Americans, Eskimos, and Aleuts resided in the United States, approximately one per cent of the total population. There was a 14% increase in population size between 1990 and 1998 compared to 8% growth for the US population as a whole. It is estimated that there will be 3.1 million Native people by the year 2020.

Geographic Distribution:

- 45.6% lived in the Western region, which includes Alaska, Arizona, California, Colorado, Hawaii, Idaho, Montana, Nevada, New Mexico, Oregon, Utah, Washington, and Wyoming.
- 30.2 % lived in the South region which includes Alabama, Arkansas,

Delaware, District of Columbia, Florida, Georgia, Kentucky, Louisiana, Maryland, Mississippi, North Carolina, Oklahoma, South Carolina, Tennessee, Texas, Virginia, and West Virginia.

- 17.9% lived in the Midwest, region which includes Illinois, Indiana, Iowa, Kansas, Michigan, Minnesota, Missouri, Nebraska, North Dakota, Ohio, South Dakota, and Wisconsin.
- 6.3% of Native people lived in the Northeast region, which includes Connecticut, Maine, Massachusetts, New Hampshire, New Jersey, New York, Pennsylvania, Rhode Island and Vermont.

Median income: 1995

Upper class	($50,000+)	3.00%
Middle Class	($25,000-49,999)	10.26%
Working Class	($10,000-24,999)	21.62%
Working Poor	(under $10,000)	42.12%
Non-working Poor		33.00%

In 1998, 74% of the nation's Native people households consisted of families. Of these families, married couples maintained 65%, women with no spouse present, men maintained 26% and an additional 9% with no spouse present. The typical family size was 3.6 people.

65.4% of Native people 25 years old and over had completed high school degrees in 1990; 7.6% completed 4 years of college or more.

Terminology

The terms *Native American, American Indian, Indian, Native people, First Nations people* (in Canada) and *indigenous people* are all used to describe members of the tribes that live in North America. Though there are regional differences in preferences, it is our understanding that members of these cultures generally prefer the terms *Native people* and *American Indian* at this time.

Tribes—Respect Diversity

In 1990, over 500 distinct American Indian Nations lived in the United States; 143 of them registered with the U.S. Government. Among Native people 16% reported themselves to be Cherokee, 12% Navajo and 6% Chippewa and Sioux, the four largest tribal groups.

Tribal Affiliation (in thousands)	**Members**
Cherokee	308
Navajo	219

Chippewa	104
Sioux	103
Choctaw	82
Pueblo	53
Apache	50
Iroquois	49
Lumbee	48
Creek	44

Each of the 500 tribes, however, has its own language and history, its own sacred places and rituals. Each is rooted in and part of the land out of which it grew. Do present Native peoples as separate from each other, with unique cultures, languages, spiritual beliefs, and dress. Show respect for, and understanding of, the sophistication and complexities of Native societies.

Stereotypes and Challenges

Beverly Daniel Tatum, in her book *Why Are All the Black Kids Sitting Together in the Cafeteria?* (New York: Basic Books, 1997,) describes a research project conducted by one of her students to find out how three-year-olds think about Native people. When children were asked to draw pictures of Native Americans, they couldn't because they did not know what the term meant. When they were asked to draw pictures of Indians, they could do so easily. Most of the children included feathers, a knife or tomahawk, and drew a warrior. Even though none of the children were living in a community with a Native population or had ever met an indigenous person, at the age of three they had already learned society's stereotypes about Native people. Most said that they had learned what Indians were like from the Disney movie *Peter Pan*.

Stereotypes are also transmitted to young children by ABC books that have "I is for Indian" or "E is for Eskimo," counting books that count "Indians," story books with characters like "Little Chief," and books that show Native peoples as savages. Insulting terms like "Indian givers" or "wild Indians," are still in common usage. Resist letting children dress up as "Indians," with paper-bag costumes or paper-feather "headdresses," singing "Ten Little Indians," or letting go "war whoops" and "Indian" dances or making "Indian crafts" unless you know authentic methods and have authentic materials. Native people are invisible in the media and reduced to a hobby or interest by members of the dominant culture who love to collect their art and handcrafts but who do not understand who they really are or what their lives are like.

The oral tradition of Native people is filled with rich, sophisticated and colorful images that often get lost in translation in books for young people. Far too frequently, the main characters in picture books do not represent the lives of Native people in the present but are pseudo-historical figures, speaking in a corny style that is supposed to sound like a "noble savage" but instead is disrespectful. Look for books written and illustrated by Native people. Seek out primary source songs and poems that show off Native skill with words and include good poetry, suitable for young people, by contemporary Native writers. Be aware also that women, children, and Elders play important roles in Native cultures that often do not get portrayed in books. Make sure to include some books where men and boys are not the dominant characters and when they are, which do not portray women and Elders as subservient to warriors.

New stereotypes are evolving of Native people as interested in get-rich-quick schemes and gambling because of their legal right to host gaming facilities on their reservation land. The high incidence of alcoholism among native populations has led to numerous stereotypes of the "drunken Indian" as a comic or sad-sack caricature with little humanity or charm. The religious beliefs are often seen as silly or naïve and Native people are too often portrayed as simple-minded or stupid. These are powerful images that must be counteracted with strong role models and positive interactions with Natives who value the strong traditions of their tribes.

White Americans Systematically Slaughtered Native People

Not unlike the African American history of slavery, the first time Native children hear about Native American history is a stressful event for them and for you, particularly if you are white. We all have to own this sordid period of history. Your Native child deserves to be introduced to this powerful information in a setting where you can provide support. Children deserve to understand both the stories of strong community belief and the ways in which white Americans waged unfair battles because of their own greed and desire to be in charge. Children respond eagerly to stories of fairness and good Vs evil. Begin by helping them understand the positive legacy of the Native people and what they stood for. Express admiration for the way the people were unwilling to sacrifice their beliefs or take advantage of others despite the white people who did just that to them. Give children room to feel angry for the bad choices that were made and the bad things that were done to their people.

You might begin something like this:

When the white people gave the Natives land, they tried to give them the land the white people cared the least about. They didn't care if Indian ancestors had been on land for many generations or if they needed a certain kind of land or place to do the jobs they knew how to do. They locked the people up unfairly and treated them as if they weren't as good as white people. This was wrong. There are still many Native people who are very poor or having troubles because of how discouraged they feel after being treated so badly and forced to live in places where they could not take care of their children or do the work they were trained to do.

Native kids growing up with white parents will be more shocked when they hear about the killing, banishing and enslavement of Native people because they will be confronted with the perpetrators of the evil being the same race as their parents. This cannot help but raise questions about their parents. Are white parents like white settlers? Did Grandpa or Great Grandpa kill Native people or take away their land? Acknowledging this atrocity as our own legacy as well as our Native children's is essential.

These conversations happen over and over again. They can't always be planned but they must be expected. They aren't always easy but they mustn't be avoided. Conversations like this will provoke thoughtful questions for days afterwards, even in very young children. Sometimes there will be times of silence on the topic but always it must be re-addressed so that permission is felt by our children to experience the pain and find their strength in the face of this American tragedy.

Do not let the classroom be the first place she hears about this legacy. Prepare him. You can't protect her. Preschools and kindergartens are filled with picture books about "Indians." If your child identifies as a Native American, he needs to be comfortable with information before he has to deal with other children's responses.

Behaviors, Philosophies and Cultural Conflicts

"We can only be, what we give ourselves the power to be!"
—Cherokee Feast of Days

Some cultural concepts are common to Native Americans across tribal lines. (Manuel Ramos in his book Multicultural/Multiracial Psychology (New Jersey, Jason Aronson, 1998.)

- "The universe is a mirror of the people and each person is a mirror to every other person."—Hyemeyohsts Storm, Seven Arrows (New York: Ballentine, 1985.) Each person is part of the environment and an open system, open to experience. What is learned from interactions with others and the surroundings helps the person to understand the meaning of life.
- Live with nature rather than conquer nature. This may conflict with a desire to tame nature to serve mankind, an idea more common to non-

native society. Nature and animals are often the teachers in Native lore and typically hold more wisdom that the common man or woman might. When the Sioux would kill the buffalo for food they first honor its pride and spirit. Native Americans would have been unlikely to have made such a travesty of our environment. This is something which Native children deserve to understand and feel proud of as part of the traditional Native appreciation for our natural environment.

- The spiritual world is a great source of power and knowledge. The spiritual beliefs of Native peoples often look like superstitions to Judeo-Christian thinkers. Finding a way to be respectful of the enormous amount of wisdom and truth that is contained in these traditions is essential to respecting the heritage of Native children. This may conflict with an idea that the spiritual world does not exist or can be understood via only one particular religion. There are many Christian Natives who have incorporated their religious beliefs together. These people can be great mentors for families facing this conflict.

- Generosity is emphasized in interpersonal relationships with more concern for those who are closely related (family, friends, business associates) than with privacy. Native people borrow and lend things often and easily. This may conflict with a concern about not disturbing others, respect for private property, and tendency to seldom borrow and lend approach, common in many white families. Community identity and responsibility to the group is of great importance. "I am the people."

- There is an emphasis on liberty, freedom, and respectful individualism in social institutions. For example, at a powwow no one is in control. Collective activity of all participants shapes the actions. Events are not mandated and controlled from the top. Each participant responds to the collective mentality and mood of the whole group, but not to a single, directing voice. This is very different from the hierarchical style of organization founded on top-down leadership and delegation of responsibilities familiar to many of us. Much current thinking about encouraging strong values and self-esteem in children suggests that non-competitive interaction is healthy. Teaching children that this is a strong value among Native people is one way to reinforce this positive characteristic of the culture.

- Full development of abilities and skills is achieved through self-challenge. This tradition of self-testing and expectation should warm the hearts of all parents who have concerns about whether their children will become the best they can be. Native children's cultural legacy means they should be given opportunities to take pride in this strong value. This is in direct conflict with the pleasure principle, an idea that being

happy is the most important thing in our consumer oriented society.
* Time commitments (deadlines, schedules) are objectives to be achieved, if possible, but are not as important as other values that may conflict.

More than a Box—Biracial and Multiracial Identity Issues

Definitions and Population Data

Population size

The Census Bureau estimated 1,937,496 children of a different race from one or both parents in 1990 or 4.1% of the population. In 1997 the Public Policy Institute of California stated that children of parents belonging to more than one race or ethnicity now make up the third-largest category of births in that state, behind Hispanics and non-Hispanic whites. This number continues to grow as more than 100,000 multiracial children have born annually over the last decade. In the year 2000, the U.S. Bureau of the Census allowed more than one racial or ethnic designation to be chosen for the first time. Census information is used as a basis for race-based representation in government, program funding and a variety of social services. Though organizations such as the NAACP and the National Asian Pacific American Legal Consortium are concerned that multiracial census categories could dilute estimates of racial populations, and cost some groups political clout, while others believe that data from the census provides the information necessary to support self-interested or partisan arguments and does not acknowledge multiracial people's need to self-define. The Federal Office of Management and Budget (OMB) is also mandating that by 2003 schools similarly amend their own forms, a change that will affect the way more than two million students report their race (Chiong, J.A., *Racial Categorization Of Multiracial Children In Schools*, Westport, CT, 1998). Many expect that we will find that there are substantially more multiracial people in the U.S. than previously thought, information that activists hope will encourage an increase in their acceptance and influence.

Geographic Distribution:

In his book *Understanding Diverse Families* (New York: Guilford, 1996,) B. F. Okun states that interracial families reside primarily in urban areas. It is not clear if this pattern is equally true for multiracial families formed by adoption.

Stereotypes and Challenges
Fitting In

> *"It is the combination of inquisitive looks, longer than passing*
> *glances to comprehend unfamiliar racial-ethnic features... along with*
> *disapproving comments and nonverbal communications that begin to*
> *convey to the child that this otherness is 'undesirable' or 'wrong.'"*
> —Maria Root, "Resolving 'Other' Status" in *The*
> *Multicultural Experience: Racial Borders As The New*
> *Frontier,* Thousand Oaks, CA: Sage, 1996)

An interracial couple decides to get married. At least one someone, but probably more than one, asks, "But what about the kids?" They may remind you of the derogatory terms: "Heinz 57," "half-breed," "neither fish nor fowl," "light, bright, damn near white." They express concern that "He'll think he's white. She'll think she's better than we are." Or they'll worry aloud, "How will they fit in?"

Though research shows that biracial individuals do not suffer from any more psychological problems than their so-called "monoracial" counterparts, family and friends still worry (Poussaint,1984; Brown, 1991; Cauce, et. al., 1992.) Conventional wisdom says that biracial kids are all mixed up. The word "mulatto" comes from the Spanish for "little mule," that is, mutt. Of course you could also say that it is the people who can claim only one racial origin who suffer impairment because of their limited experiences, narrow vision and lack of resiliency. Karl Oguss, an anthropologist, suggests that if the first anthropologists had been Masai (a culture where average height is seven feet tall), they most likely would have been disturbed to discover the "fact" that all the rest of the people in the world were deficient in height! (*In Between Cultures,* H. Ned Seelye and Jacqueline Howell Wasileski, Lincolnwood, Illinois, NTC Publishing Group, 1996.)

Society has a strong need to classify its members racially. Biracial folks challenge the boundaries. It is not unusual to find *them* and *us* groups in every pocket of life. A biracial person, by being a blend of *them* and *us*, is a potential challenge to everyone. Compared with being a person of color who is wholly of one race, developing racial identity as a biracial person has more issues, not fewer. Its reconciliation is a process that continually evolves from early childhood through adulthood, with different approaches and conclusions throughout the journey depending on an individual's temperament, environment and politics.

One thing is certain: biracial children are constantly asked to explain their racial identity. Even if they're not asked, they may feel that they are not being true to themselves unless they take a stand. Is there an answer that people who have roots in two or more distinct cultures can agree on? Here are some common choices: human or with no racial label, one race only or multiracial.

"Human"

Some parents oppose racial labeling altogether, teaching their kids to respond to the question "What are you?" by answering that they are human. They think that they've done something wonderful in putting together a family that defies racial convention and they are consciously choosing to live in this way. They argue that the acceptance of any labels tacitly supports racism. They dismiss the process of racial classification as nothing but a social construct and protest all race-based bias. They want their children to be judged by "the content of their character" and not the colors of their skin, and do not support the notion that when most people define themselves they include their racial heritage.

We'd argue back that when everybody else has a racial identity to take pride in, stripping your children of their racial identity is like sending them naked to the playing field. Just another way to feel less than. Labels are important vehicles for self-empowerment. In this case, less can't be more. In 1928, sociologist Robert Park coined the phrase "marginal man" to describe people who were "cultural hybrids" who live "in two worlds, but are more or less a stranger in both." Our goal is to build positive connections for our children, not to foster a feeling of being marginal.

Parents are sometimes not willing to support any strong racial identifications for their racially-mixed children, hoping instead for a raceless identity. "The parent's perspective is really different from the kids' perspective. That's what's most striking. They think it's the same for the kids as it is for them. And it's truly not. It's not the same set of tasks," writes Mindy Thompson Fullilove in *Black, White, Other,* edited by Lise Funderburg (New York, William Morrow, 1994)

Greg Wolley, an adopted biracial man raised in a black family recalls that when he was in the ninth grade "James Brown had this song, 'Say It Loud (I'm Black and I'm Proud),' and that got on my father's nerves. He was like, 'Why do you have to say I'm black and I'm proud, I'm black and I'm proud? Why can't you just be Greg? Why do you have to be black?" (*Black, White, Other,* edited by Lise Funderburg, New York, William Morrow, 1994)

Choose one only: Black, White, Latino, Asian, American Indian

Some parents foster their children's identification with only one race.

With her delicate features and mocha skin, Stephanie Campbell has been mistaken for Spanish, Egyptian and Thai. "Some people look at me and have no idea I'm part black, while others don't know I'm part Asian; it depends on if my hair is straight or curly that day," says Campbell, 24, the daughter of a Filipina mother and Jamaican father. "My parents used to argue about my identity, 'She is Asian.' 'She is Jamaican!' Back and forth, until my dad said: 'When the world looks at her they'll see black.' That was the end of it."

"I'm just as much white as I am black in the United States of America. But I tell you one thing, when I walk through Harlem and say, 'Hello brothers and sisters, what's happening?' I get a much different response than if I walk on the Upper East Side and say, 'Guess what, I belong here just as much as you do.' 'Get 9-1-1!! We got a crazy nigger out here!'"—Michael Mayson, a biracial man adopted by black parents

> *Amy is half white. Her white parents accentuate their racial similarities and deny the differences, teaching her that she is white, not Latina. Her parents want the best for her. They think this means ensuring a place for her in white society. The child wonders What's wrong with being Latina? What's wrong with me? Like the emperor who wears invisible clothes, she is asked to believe the opposite of what her eyes (and society's eyes) tell her. In spite of the fact that her skin is brown, she is led to believe that she will be treated the same as if she were white. Reality and self-image have to split. The child must hide half of herself behind a white mask. Can she wear a mask all the time and feel good about herself? If, because her parents taught her to identify as white, Amy is surprised when identified by others as Latina, her ability to trust her parents will be compromised. She will wonder what other things her parents were wrong about. If Amy doesn't know how to relate to Latinos, those who feel she is not Latina enough may reject her. She may also be rejected by white society.*

White parents, especially, may emphasize their own ethnicity with their child because they know it best. They may think that if their children can "pass" as white, they can avoid experiencing racism.

Some parents of children with African ancestry raise them as black to prepare them for racism. Dr. Larry E. Davis, a professor of social work and psychology in the George Warren Brown School of Social Work at Washington University in St. Louis, believes it's a terrific mistake if kids who are partially black don't identify as black, because they can never be non-black. "To deny being black when everyone else who looks like them is considered black will cause the children to lose out on what is a rich heritage and a positive sense of who they are. Biracial children will be subjected to all the liabilities of being black, Latino, Asian or American Indian in America. Yet failing to acknowledge themselves as members will result in their denying themselves a wealth of benefits, an outpouring of friendship and support from black society." Pam Austin, a biracial woman, adds that "When the shit hits the fan the vast majority of white America is not going to deal with you as being white. That's the bottom line. That's just the reality of this country. The country was founded on racism, and it's been working on it very well ever since."

You will remember from Section 2 that there are steps in the development of a positive racial identity. For biracial kids, choosing a monoracial identification may be a particular stage in their development process, or the conclusion of it. In either case, it represents the child's effort to connect. A parent's attempt to cause a disconnection is likely to be resented and/or rejected.

200% People

Some parents help their children bring together and integrate a biracial or multiracial identity based on the two or more cultural components of their background. They believe that it is important for the children to take equal pride in all their heritages. Some of these families also recognize that their children's appearance reflects their dual heritage, and they want the family's culture to embody that.

The increase in numbers of individuals who are multiracial has led some to predict the end of distinctions based on racial appearance. That seems unlikely. Even in Brazil, the Dominican Republic and South Africa, where racial mixing has been common for a very long time, color-coding has not lost its sting. Status and privilege are still connected to lighter skin and people of mixed race carry an intermediate status between the dominant ("white") group and the subordinate ("black") group. From this point of view, it's easy to understand why a black person might resent a multiracial person who chooses not to be associated with the subordinate group ("blacks")because it may seem as if he is looking to raise his status by identifying with the dominant group.

When Tiger Woods said he thought of himself as "Cablinasian"—a mixture of Caucasian, black, Indian and Asian—he was greeted with bemusement, even hostility. From a black perspective, identifying oneself as multiracial can seem the same as passing, attempting to discount black heritage to appear as not black. Identifying as multiracial rather than black can be a magnet for hostile responses from the black community.

If this were a perfect world, descendants of more than one race could easily claim their full racial identity, but in the United States, white is still an exclusive club. Although a child may in fact possess multiple ethnic heritages, she will likely be identified in many public contexts not as biracial, but as a person of color, and she may well choose to identify herself that way. To do so is not to deny the reality of her multiple heritages, but to find strength and power in embracing elements that have such significance in this race-conscious society.

On the other hand, a transracially adopted biracial teen who feels pressured by peers or parents to choose one racial group over another may feel not quite "enough"—whether black, Asian, Latina, Native American—and may feel caught between the rock of anger expressed toward whites by her peer group and the hard place of her white parents who feel threatened by her peers. Only when she can embrace the notion that different is just different and not bad can she feel that her heritage is acceptable.

There are additional compelling reasons why adopted children must be taught to identify with the racial group society will identify them with. To feel confident, they need to feel ownership of the beauty, strength, worth and rich heritages that are their birth right. Lise Funderberg, editor of *Black, White Other* (New York, William Morrow and Co., 1994,) says that biracial children who are in part black "should be taught to claim their black side first, because that's the part that needs sticking up for most." We agree that priority should always be given to the non-white components of each child's particular background, because in our current white-dominated society, those are the parts that need sticking up for.

If *multiracial* or *biracial* are labels understood as racial shorthand for an individual's combination of backgrounds, then for those lucky enough to have plural heritages to draw from, racial identification can also remain fluid. We have watched young adopted adults identify as black the majority of the time and as biracial once in awhile, without for a moment being untrue to themselves. It's something like that TV commercial where a car morphs into a tiger in front of our eyes. We can see it happening, observing the adjustments she makes, the changes in her tone, style, attitude and attire, then —Shazam, she "acts" more white than black. Shazam, she is a strong black woman. Her uncanny ability to locate herself between identities and make a seamless transformation at will, somehow continuing to be herself is something she shares with others with more than one racial heritage. Like that cover of *Time* (Fall, 1993) which displayed a series of faces that merged to create an image of the "New Face of America," the various components are visible as she goes between her boundaries to others she might become. This switching in which part of her identity takes the spotlight at a given moment seems to increase her understanding of role subtleties and both accentuates cultural differences and illuminates similarities. People like her, with a foot in more than one race, get to shift back and forth between parallel identities, public and private. This seems to have the same abundant benefits of being truly bilingual, an ability to be at home with two distinct cultures.

The Strength of the Hybrid

> *"We who have two cultures from birth are not half but double,"*
> —Daburu no Kai

People with meaningful cultural opportunities to be balanced and integrated spend their lives in a rich dance of being part of and apart from all the portions of themselves. In the end, coming to appreciate having the best of two or more worlds can mean identifying strongly with a single group, shifting between groups, and/or embracing multiculturalism as a unique identity in itself. The idea that a multiracial or biracial person has the opportunity to feel 100% connected to each aspect of his or her ancestry—and is therefore a 200% or 500% person—demonstrates the unique strength of this birthright. Hybrids in any species are stronger than single species or a single race, being more resistant to disease and genetic defects and having the strength of both genetic lines. Growing up feeling part of two cultures provides a larger knowledge base, a more well-rounded sense of the world, and an increased ability to see all sides of a situation. Be careful, however. Even though a biracial person can identify with two or more racial or ethnic groups and would therefore seem to have the potential to be a cultural bridge bringing separate communities together and increasing understanding, it's unfair to make that his or her job. Creating racial harmony can not be a responsibility of biracial people, especially children. We all have a great deal of work to do.

Ambiguous Identity

> *"White-appearing multiracial children pose a special challenge and an opportunity. Carrying both white skin and the legacy of the oppressed, they can suffer from white guilt and minority rage. Even before they can articulate what they feel about race, their identities are forming. It is essential that parents give their multiracial children an environment that honors all of their parts and allows them room to talk about the tensions they are discovering inside."*
> —Jennifer Morales

A child of ambiguous racial identity may be in the hardest position of all to find a comfortable and strong self-identity. Ambiguous identity usually translates to one of two things; the child is of color but looks (at least to white people) as if she is white or looks of color but perhaps of a different ethnicity or even race than he actually is. Either situation creates conflicts for the child. She will be questioned regarding her exact racial makeup, but she will not likely be mistaken for white. Encourage her identification with people of color; they are the group with whom she is most likely to have shared experiences. Encourage her to trust that she will find positive support from them.

While encouraging self-determination regarding racial identity, it will be important for you to offer opportunities for realistic feedback regarding his choices and how likely the world is to accept those choices. If he says, for instance, "I think I will tell people I am white now," although he has no shared look with people of this descent, he will need to be given feedback that the world is highly likely to question him if he insists on this designation. He must be given the opportunity in the safe haven of your family, and with the help of trusted advisors and friends, to come up with cover stories or answers to outsiders' questions about who or what he is. The fact that you help him anticipate these questions, rather than being surprised or appalled by people's inappropriate curiosity will help him see you as an understanding ally rather than an out-of-touch adult who doesn't understand. When planning responses, be sure that your child feels entitled to make her own choices about how she wants to respond, which may be different each time. There will be times when sharing personal information with others feels good and creates a connection to someone else. In other circumstances, short snappy answers which are not the whole truth or even any of the truth can be very appropriate in response to people's need to classify her by race. Neither she nor you owe the outside world positive responses to those kind of intrusions. Most important is that the child—not the parent—should be the one to determine how to tell his own life's stories. This child's needs are always more important than the needs of the person asking the questions. Politeness is not as important as the support family members show each other in the face of even polite challenge.

What ARE you?—Unknown Racial Identity

Sometimes we just don't know our child's racial heritage. First of all, leave no stone unturned. Situations like this often do not have to remain as unclear as they begin. Go back to the birth mother or agency to see if more information can be gotten. Often this is possible, especially if you work hard at it and become the squeaky wheel. The sooner this is done the better, before the trail grows cold. Use the Internet and get the help of professional searchers if need be. Don't give up simply by taking one person's word that there is no information. You would be surprised how many times that one person has been wrong.

For those circumstances when there is no clear information about the races of birth parents, please consider the following issues...

Tell the truth—even when it hurts

Sometimes parents with children of unknown heritage are tempted to consider naming a likely heritage because of their eagerness to allow their to have a clear racial identity. Although tempting from the point of view of protecting an already vulnerable child (having been adopted by parents of another race and perhaps another country) from another potentially painful reality, it is nevertheless dangerous to the long-term stability of the adopted child's self esteem.

Adopted children are often unusually sensitive to having access to their own truth. This is a logical consequence of having had adults make decisions that changed their history without their permission. Thus the way adoptive parents talk with their children about their history very important. Keeping secrets or changing the truth can lead to extreme distrust and anger later, when the adopted person finds out. It leads to a sense of false self, something adopted people are already struggling with. Despite your good intentions, it is important to be absolutely honest with your son. Tell him you do not know his racial heritage for sure. You and he can make guesses based on the way he looks and, if you know his personal history, the characteristics of people specifically from his region of birth. Involving him will be critical, as the exploration of these questions will allow him the opportunity to bemoan his frustration at what is not known as well as come to his own positive conclusions about who he is. This process is the one piece of control left to him under his particular circumstances of birth and will be best served by his self-directed exploration in the safe and supportive environment you can provide.

If your daughter was born in another country, she deserves to understand her cultural connection in the fullest way possible. Her racial composition does not affect this heritage. She is and always will be of that heritage by birth, so connecting to people as well as learning the history, language(s) and culture of her homeland will be greatly to her benefit. If you do not know even that much, then it will be extremely important to connect your child to others of Latino, African American, Asian, American Indian and multiracial heritages who will share the experience of being people of color in the US.

Behaviors, Philosophies and Cultural Conflicts

> "As a person of multiracial descent (white/European and Chinese), I noticed …that The New York Times rarely printed news stories about people who were racially mixed…. Rarely did I encounter a picture of someone multiracial, or find an article that did more than point out the 'difficult struggle' mixed-race individuals face.
> Multicultural people play a special role in combating stereotypes. They are a visible reminder that everyone deserves to be treated as a multifaceted individual."
>
> —Emilie Schlegel

Is Transracial Adoption Easier for Multiracial Kids?

No, it is not easier. It is filled with more challenges. The family structure is the same whether the child is of a single race or multiracial, a child of color looking around at white parents. From the child's perspective, what's the difference? White adoptive parents of either a mixed-race or single-race child have the same responsibility: to connect their child to her roots. Feelings of belonging do not come in halves; one either feels part of or separate from. Parenting a multiracial child across racial lines is one more complexity in an already complex family. To imagine that it is easier is a denial of the difficulties of each, which added together certainly become more and not less.

At a support group meeting, a white adoptive mom of a biracial child expressed the hope that when her child grew up, he would feel comfortable in both white and black cultures and would be able to choose how others would classify him. Another adoptive parent, this one African American, said, "You know, all my life, I've never heard anyone except adoptive parents refer to someone as 'biracial.' In the black community, if you are one drop black, you're black. We're all mixed and we're all black."

Our society is lazy about subtle matters. We tent to oversimplify rather than appreciate complexities and confusing dualities. When we look at race, individuals are generally perceived to be part of the racial group they resemble the most, no matter what the truth of their origins. People of mixed heritage do not have half the experience of being one race and half the experience of the other, any more than children of a mother and a father have half the experience of being their mother's child and half the experience of being their father's. They are all that they are all the time, always.

Name ten famous African Americans. Are any of the people you named of mixed racial heritage? Are you sure? How do you know? If you are like most white people you thought of people you presumed to be black because they "look" black, and you may have included some who were born of parents of different races. People are generally perceived to be part of the racial group they resemble the most. A white person's image of biracial people sometimes conforms to the narrow range of "looks" presented by models in advertising. The full presentation of multiracial people is much larger.

Individuals who are half white but look to be of color do not participate in the experience of being white, do not inherit the white privilege of their European American parent, because society does not see them as white. Whether we like it or not, one cannot be white and have "black blood," though, paradoxically, one can be black and have a white parent. Our kids cannot help but be surrounded by white culture; by osmosis, they become familiarized with it and come to appreciate it as an important part of their birthright. In contrast, it is usually harder to provide equal access to the rest of their heritage.

Some parents have identified with the movement among multiracial people to identify themselves as multiracial rather than one race or another. This movement is led almost exclusively by families where children grow up with racial role models within their families. The vast majority of multiracial and biracial people identify as people of color.

Mirrors and Windows

> *"Once you see yourself truthfully depicted, you have a sense of your right to be in the world."*
>
> —Paul Miller

An ability to empathize and communicate with people from cultures different from their own is likely to become a positive byproduct of having multiple origins themselves. Learning about the history of biracial people in the United States will help your child see himself as a member of a group that relates in unequal ways with others. The legacy of slavery and miscegenation laws mandating that races not mix and the arguments that caused them to be struck down by the Supreme Court (Loving v. Virginia, 1967) are harsh issues but especially influential since knowing about them aids in understanding the racism of today. In addition, once your child has developed the cognitive skills of analysis, coaching her in the skills of media literacy will provide both mirrors and windows, helping her to critically analyze what we all take in endlessly and often mindlessly. Talking about the target audience for particular ads, or the assumptions driving a news story, or responses to a movie through different racial lenses will help her to be able to understand the stories of our times and perhaps the storytellers.

We want biracial and multiracial children to feel confident about their personal answers to the question, Why do I think what I think about race? The answer must rest on an acceptance that not everyone shares their point of view and that's OK.

It was only a generation ago that the 1967 case of Loving vs. Virginia addressed the illegality of outlawing interracial marriage. This legacy means that even very recently the biracial person was seen as the product of both an immoral and illegal union. The implications for positive self image cannot be overstated. The recent movement of multiracial individuals to define themselves is filled with stories of individuals who have experienced the constant tug of "choosing." Many refuse to identify as any one race out of a sense of loyalty to their parents in the literal sense and a need to self-define beyond the too simplistic system society continues to try to impose.

Communities of color fear that a multiethnic or multiracial classification will diminish the visibility of their own communities needs and realities. The white community is uncomfortable with the notion of a growing group of color. Either way, the individuals living the experience are complaining of being squeezed and their new voice is raising up to create a new community of their own.

> "Ultimately, the official classification of people by 'race' is abhorrent to many of us. Nevertheless, it would be fair to say that many of us believe there may be some temporary utility in obtaining ethnic data for purposes of providing programs aimed at addressing the special needs of historically mistreated ethnic groups, which include, we would maintain, interracial families and individuals. Arguably, there may also be a real societal interest in knowing the degree to which our nation's demography is changing interracially, not a small matter given the gravity of race relations generally.
>
> "Without a doubt, as time goes on, the interracial, multiethnic community will grow and become more visible. Indeed, it may already be larger than is acknowledged. We cannot know with any real degree of certainty because of existing racial categorization schemes on government forms. Be that as it may, it's a safe guess that a majority of Americans are already multiethnic, if not interracial in the popular sense of the term.
>
> "At the very least, we feel we deserve, no less than anyone else, the respect of recognition for who we really are. Ideally, many of us also believe our community has the potential of becoming a stable core around which the ethnic pluralism of this country is unified, and perhaps, the core for promoting understanding and peace among the nations of the world. Let us be recognized."
>
> —Carlos A. Fernandez, Association of Multiethnic Americans (and a leader in the movement to change the one check box rule for the 2000 census.)

Claiming Identity...Whatever the Culture

For children of color, claiming identity is in part about making visible that which so often is not—culture and role models, culture and role models culture and role models....Writing this chapter about specific differences between African American, Asian, Latino, Native American, white and multicultural heritage was without question the greatest challenge of this book for us. It began in that frantic sort of way, fueled by a sense of overwhelm, almost panic. There was so much that needed to be known, so much we didn't know. We spent several centuries industriously reviewing the literature, looking at web sites, talking with people and accumulating information. One of our goals was to provide pride-building information parents could share with their children regarding the unique history, holidays, special events, music, art, literature, inventions, science, cuisine, folkways and everything else that seemed interesting, amusing, or useful about each culture. The process continued, both of us (Gail and Beth) looking for information about famous African Americans, Chinese history, Native powwow ceremonies, El Dia de los Muertos, Quinceañera and more. We created a section called "Claiming Identity" to encompass this abundance of material. Working vigilantly, we tried to be consistent in formatting it into a series of simple lists which we weighed against each other on a page-by-page basis, trying to make sure we had created a positive balance between cultures. God forbid that anyone reading our work should feel disrespected if there were fewer pages about their group than some other. Inequality on the basis of page count alone sent us back for more information, seeking still more experts, creating still more pages, like obsessed little squirrels collecting nuts for the winter. We were so intent on adding to our lists that we completely lost sight of the meaning or value of what we were doing. Filled with information, ever growing, we finally stopped at 150 pages crammed with important facts and lessons, satisfied that most of you wouldn't have to gather them for yourselves because we had provided them.

Then a profound thing happened. A Latina reader asked us a series of simple questions about why we had chosen to include certain information about her culture but omitted other important items she would have emphasized instead. That queasy feeling that begins in the pit of your spine and works its way through your stomach and into your throat started moving in full force, trying to say something. It zapped us. She said this right before the book was ready to go to the printer, when it was twice the size of a heavy dictionary, apologizing because she couldn't say our work was good, speaking almost in a whisper, but very sincere, very for real. We were on the telephone. One of us was jabbering about a list of traditional foods we were recommending that we thought she would approve of: *pan dulce, arroz con pollo, cado de res,* …. But then we asked if we had missed any important items and she said, as clearly and kindly as a critic can, "Missed anything? You really don't have any idea." We both just "got" that we were way off base. It reverberated deeply. And as we tried to make sense of it later, the slam came hard. Her words rang through our ears again: "You really don't have any idea."

The next day two more readers, both of whom were Korean, called asking similar questions but about different particulars. And then it seemed to erupt all at once, the moment when we both knew. *We had undermined the very core of our own message.*

Because of the many times throughout this book that we have dogmatically said to you, "You can't transmit a culture you are not a part of," we couldn't believe we had tried to do just that. Stand aside, we had said to one and all, and embrace who you are. Acknowledge that your child is different. Don't be a racial wannabe. Don't imagine that you can become the first duck mother who actually will be able to teach the swan how to be authentically a swan. This lesson that can't stay learned, like the story that never ends, goes on forever in our walk of life. It's harder to stay conscious of our own misassumptions than it is to understand that we have them. If sharing this story has any merit, it is to demonstrate how easy it was for true believers like the two of us to completely lose sight of the meaning of what we were doing and stay busily engaged, page after page, in trying to represent a series of cultures we had no business trying to represent.

Who was it who said, "I dreamed a thousand new dreams. I woke and walked my old path?" Here we were, speaking to you from a hard-earned base of expertise we had then disregarded entirely—somehow imagining ourselves to be entitled and able to pick through the jewels of many cultures and come up with consistent lists that would make a difference in your children's lives. Lists? Consistent? As if we could transmit the essence and importance of a culture through lists and facts, as if… Hey our advance readers agreed our lists were good. We learned a lot of new information from them ourselves. But in the end, we slashed more than fifty pages, In the end, we had to come face-to-face with knowing that we had not questioned our own assumptions and had instead moved forward in a way that imagined that we could make choices there was no way we had the sensibilities to make.

In the light of day it felt diminishing for us to have imagined that we could be direct providers of information. Better you should go find a book about Kwanza and how to celebrate it rather than read our many times removed compressed version of the holiday or any other piece of information. You owe it to your kids to let them learn about their culture from people as clear and direct as our readers, not from you, and not from secondary resources like us. Real people in real time who are living the culture are alive and well and you can and must find them.

Even then, you must know that no one person within any culture can solely represent or transmit the fullness of their culture. It is only in the sum of each individuals practice and experience that the group culture and identity emerges. Don't ever forget how much you need them—all of them—to help your child understand the priorities and emphasis her culture puts on its own experience—priorities and emphasis even our well intentioned selves can never properly teach. The goal for us as parents is not of getting the information right or knowing enough. That misses the point and is inherently off the mark because the goal lies in the journey itself. The experience of being who we are alongside our children who are someone else. A profound reality of accepting and acknowledging difference that is harder than hell to live with because of all the temptations and ego needs to feel in control.

Our success is in the journey, not the knowledge. No one of you, not any, oh so gentle readers, can possibly be so slow or dense as we. So take heart as we continue to stumble, you can only do better. Just hold onto your stomach and remember when you stumble that we have stumbled further so that you may get up faster to stumble further yet again. For truly it is this journey of realization that gives our children the freedom and wisdom to find their own paths and the strength we all know they possess and deserve.

All of the following are true:

> *"Keep your words soft and sweet, just in case you have to eat them."*   —unknown

> *"Experience: that most brutal of teachers. But you learn, my God do you learn."*   —C S. Lewis

> *"You miss 100 percent of the shots you never take."*
> —Wayne Gretzky

Useful Books

White Identity issues

Fine, Michelle; *Off White: Readings on Race, Power and Society* (NY: Routhledge, 1996.)
Essays on white identity, challenging racism. Includes discussion of politics, education, is white a race?, loss of privilege, media representations, double binds of whiteness and more.

Latino Identity Issues

Aparicio Francis; *Latino Voices* (Brookfield, CT :Millbrook Press, 1994.)
Booklist calls it "a thoughtful collection of Latino poetry, fiction, and excerpts from actual accounts of immigrants and settlers that offers a broad view of the Latino experience in the U.S. Chapter introductions provide insight into the authors' lives and their writings, which explore the themes of immigration, home and family, work, language, love, religion, and racial discrimination. Twenty-four writers from various backgrounds and countries are included. The selections are enjoyable as well as provocative. A glossary of Spanish terms follows each selection, and a list of sources and a bibliography are provided."

Bernal, Marta E. and. Knight, George P; *Ethnic Identity* (NY: State University of NY Press, 1993.)
Formation and transmission among Hispanics. Covers acculturation and the development and socialization of Mexican Americans. One of the few books to review the development of racial identity in Latino children.

Darder, Antonio & Torres, Rodolfo: *Latino Studies Reader* (MASS: Blackwell, 1998.)
Growing faster than any other ethnic group, Latinos are predicted to become the largest ethnic-minority group by the year 2009. Conventional theories of 'race' and 'race relations,' with its exclusive Black/White focus, present serious theoretical problems as applied to Latinos. Instead, Darder and Torres use class analyses employing social, scientific and theoretical concepts to explore issues addressed by Latinos in America.

Kanellos, Nicholas; *Thirty Million Strong* (Golden, CO: Fulcrum, 1998.)
In this controversial and lively book, Nicolás Kanellos chronicles and analyzes the changing images of Hispanics in the United States from the age

of exploration and conquest to the present, reclaiming the Hispanic role in American history and culture. Part history, part manifesto, this book challenges our notions of the Hispanic peoples, giving us a perspective into the great contributions this group has made to American society.

Johnson, Kevin; *How Did You Get To Be Mexican?* **(Philadelphia; Temple University Press, 1999.)**

This is the first book to focus on the experiences of being mixed race Anglo/Latino in America. Johnson's mother denied her Mexican ancestry and claimed to be Spanish. Johnson's candid view of his own life on the color line and his development of racial identity addresses issues of assimilation for minority groups, anti-immigration policies, and being of mixed race in a time of identity politics. Though dryly written, the issues ring true; this is an important read for anyone interested in identity issues

Asian Identity Issues

Bumiller, Elizabeth, ed., *May You Be The Mother of A Hundred Sons* **(NY: Fawcett, 1991.)**

Acclaimed journalist Elisabeth Bumiller presents a revealing look at the women of India. From horrific practices such as "bride burnings," sterilization camps and arranged marriages to vital women, struggling to succeed, Bumiller "zeros in on women and ends up illuminating a whole world," as *Newsweek* explained.

Caon Lan & Novas, Himiliee; *Everything You Ever Needed to Know About Asian American History* **(NY: Plume Books, 1996.)**

How did the U.S. get involved in Vietnam? Why do Filipinos have Spanish names? What is the origin of the fortune cookie? Most Americans are woefully uninformed about their country's history, and most standard history books provide very little information on the rich history of Asian American peoples. This text helps fill that void, with a lively question-and-answer format that documents the dramatic impact of Chinese, Japanese, Vietnamese, Korean, Indian, and Pacific Island cultures on American society.

Hagedorn Jessica; *Charlie Chan is Dead* **(NY: Penguin, 1993.)**

As Hagedorn wrote in her introduction, for too long White America has seen Asian Americans as Charlie Chan. Her anthology shatters myths of the "model minority," featuring selections from some of the most talented Asian American writers today, including Meena Alexander, Hisaye Yamamoto, Peter Bacho, Cynthia Kadohata, Amy Tan, Gish Jen, Maxine Hong Kingston, Bharati Mukherjee, and others. "A generous and varied sampling here...usually focused on personal life rather than on culture and history," said Kirkus Reviews.

Lee, Marie; *Finding My Voice* **(NY: Laurel Leaf, 1994.)**

The only Asian in a small American high school, Ellen Sung must contend with the subtle kind of day to day racism that doesn't make the evening news

Kingston Maxine Hong; *Woman Warrior: Memories of a Girlhood Among Ghosts* **(NY: Vintage, 1989.)**

Kingston's account of the conflict between the two worlds she grew up in, (the China of her mother's stories and her own life running a Laundromat in a small California town), is particularly important to people who are not Chinese who want to understand how some Chinese people view them. This book provides a peek through the barrier of race that is as unsettling as it is informative. White parents of Chinese children will be afforded a mirror to help them see themselves as many members of their child's cultural community view them.

Bishoff, Tonya and Rankin, Jo; *Seeds From A Silent Tree* **(1998: Minnesota, Pandal Press.)**

Explores issues of adoption, identity, race and sexuality. Born in Korea and raised in the United States, assigned new names and families, thirty men and women write of their complex experiences.

African American Identity Issues

Beal, Ann C. *The Black Parenting Book,* **(NY: Broadway Books, 1998.)**

Written expressly for the parents of America's 3.6 million Black children under six, this book includes information on health, development and cultural issues to help parents provide their children with racial pride and a sense of their heritage. Black kids are more at-risk than White kids in matters such as obesity, asthma and loss of self-esteem. The authors raise and answer questions such as "How can I find a pediatrician who shares my values?" "Are all-Black preschools best?" and "Should I straighten my child's hair?" Advice about handling racist incidents, selecting a preschool, and support for spirituality and family traditions is included.

Edwards, Audrey & Polite, Craig; *Children of the Dream* **(NY: Mass Market Paperback, 1993.)**

Black readers who are tired of depictions of African Americans as lacking ambition and ability can take heart in these stories of self-made successes who realized their dreams in spite of racism's challenges, and other readers should be encouraged to consider and discuss this upbeat and realistic collection of complex personal stories of people overcoming obstacles, including politics, power plays and their own self-doubts. Contents include: Black success in America: a progress report; From separate to equal; To be young, gifted, and qualified; Getting mad, getting even; Success and the Black woman; Success and the Black man. Inspiring reading, highly recommended.

Feagin Joe and Mel Sikes; *Living With Racism* (Boston: Beacon Press, 1994.)

This study exposes the prevalence of racism that middle-class Black Americans face. A man is refused service in a restaurant; a woman is harassed while shopping; white children taunt a little girl in a public pool. The authors argue that in the cumulative effect, these episodes are experienced not as separate incidents, but as a process demanding their constant vigilance and shaping their personal, professional and psychological lives.

Johnson, Charles R.; *Middle Passage* (NY: Scribner, 1998.)

Rutherford Calhoun becomes the captain's cabin boy on a slave clipper bound for Africa, and he's able to help the African slaves taken aboard to stage a revolt. Middle Passage won the 1990 National Book Award.

Josleen Wilson & Barbara Dixon; *Good Health for African American Kids* (NY: Crown Books, 1996.)

Addressing the sometimes unique health concerns of African American children, this book includes up-to-date information on diseases that significantly affect them. Covers allergies and handling milk intolerance, food and environmental sensitivities, and stress. HIV and AIDS, asthma, diabetes, heart disease, high blood pressure, sickle-cell disease, and common childhood ailments are discussed. The bad news is that Black Americans are more likely than any other group to die sooner and of a more major disease. The positive message of this self help book is that by incorporating healthy diet and lifestyle, African American kids can improve their chances to live long and healthy lives. $10.00

Books about African American Hair Care

Barrie-Laven, Gwendolyn; *The Barber's Cutting Edge* (NY: Children's Book Press, 1994.)

The first book about hair for African American boys. Hooray! The story of a young boy's first trip to the barber shop.

Bonner, Lonice; *Good Hair* (NY: Crown, 1994.)

Good Hair challenges black women not to succumb to white ideas of beauty for themselves. A combination of "how-to" beauty book and hilarious autobiography.

Ferrell, Pamela, *Kids Talk Hair* (Washington, DC: Cornrows & Co., 1999.)

A wonderful book about hair care for African American children filled with practical techniques and easy to use information.

Ferrell, Pamela, *Let's Talk Hair* (Washington, D.C.: Cornrows & Co., 1996.)

Hair care and positive self image for African Americans. Information about history and cultural values concerning hair.

***hooks, bell Happy to Be Nappy* (NY: Hyperion, 1999.)**

Acclaimed author and poet bell hooks joins forces with illustrator Chris Rashchka to celebrate the joy and beauty of "nappy hair" in an exuberant, rhythmic, read aloud book.

Tarpley, Natasha; I *Love My Hair* (NY: Little Brown, 1998.)

Kenyana doesn't feel very lucky about her hair until her Mama shows her the many wonderful ways she can style it. Soon she is filled with pride over its versatility.

Yarbrough, Camille, *Cornrows* (NY: Putnam, 1997.)

As Great Grandmaw braids the children's hair, she tells them stories they love to hear about the symbolism of braided hair.

Biracial and Multiracial Identity Issues

Funderburg, Lise, ed.; *Black, White, Other* (NY: Wm. Morrow,1994.)

Biracial Americans talk about race and identity. This book, the first to explore the lives of adults with Black-white heritage and to present their unique view on race in America, presents a series of interviews with biracial adults.

O'Hearn, Claudine, ed; *Half and Half* (NY: Pantheon, 1998.)

This work presents personal essays from seventeen writers, including Julia Alvarez, Indira Ganesan, James McBride, David Mura and Lori Tsang, on the experience of being biracial and bicultural in the United States today. Through its range of distinctive voices, this anthology reveals the constancy of the human concern to find the place that feels right, and the challenge of addressing and incorporating dual ethnic identities in the context of America's social and racial climate. This outstanding work offers food for thought for all readers, but in particular for those interested in transracial families or multiethnic identity

Root, Maria; *The Multiracial Experience* (Thousand Oaks, CA: Sage, 1996.)

A rare collection of 24 stimulating essays on multiracial issues. Booknews writes, "For the first time in U.S. history, according to the Census, the number of biracial babies is increasing at a faster rate than the number of single-race babies. Practical ideas for incorporating multiracial thinking into human rights, identity, blending and flexibility, gender, education, and the future." Includes "Transracial Adoptions: In Whose Best Interest?" by Ruth G. McRoy; "LatiNegra: Mental Health Issues of African Latinas," by Lilian Comas-Diaz; "Race as Process," by Teresa Kay Williams; "Without a Template: The Biracial Korean/White Experience," by Brian Chol Soo Standen; "Multicultural Education," by Francis Wardle and more.

Senna, Darcy; *Caucasia* (NY: Putnam, 1998.)

The *New York Times Book Review* says that "Senna superbly illustrates the emotional toll that politics and race take on one especially gutsy young girl's development as she makes her way through the parallel limbos between black and white and between girl and young woman." When their family breaks up, Birdie's father and sister move to Brazil to find racial equality, while Birdie and her mother take on new identities and move to a small New Hampshire town. Birdie tries to fit in but she wants both her white and black heritage to count. Her search for her sister leads to a search for her own identity."

Native American Identity Issues

Allen, Paula Gunn; *Off the Reservation* (NY: Beacon, 1998.)

Off the Reservation gives us the best of Allen's political essays, literary criticism, and personal reflections. Section One explores the boundary between Native American cultures and Western civilization, contrasting proprietorship, literacy, individualism, and "rape culture" with the communal and spiritual connection to the earth that characterizes native societies. Section Two reviews contemporary Native American literature, including the work of N. Scott Momaday, Leslie Marmon Silko, and Mary Tallmountain

Campbell. Maria; *Halfbreed* (Nebraska: University of Nebraska Press, 1982.)

Maria Campbell is Scottish, French, Cree, English, and Irish. This is her story. "I write this for all of you, to tell you what it is like to be a Halfbreed woman in our country. I want to tell you about the joys and sorrows, the oppressing poverty, the frustration and the dreams.... I am not bitter.... I only want to say: this is what it was like, this is what it is still like." —Maria Campbell. This book, which has become a classic, speaks directly to the heart about challenges of racism.

Erdoes, Richard; *American Indian Myths and Legends* (NY: Pantheon, 1985.)

This book combines unpublished tales related by living storytellers with the best of folklore sources, creating a collection of myths and legends representing native American tribes across the country. This collection of tales preserved through oral history—either from the mouths of storytellers or from documents which first recorded their words—presents a comprehensive overview of Native spiritual philosophy. Though each chapter opens with an overview provided by Erdoes and Ortiz, the stories themselves are untrammeled by editorial revision

Silko, Leslie Marmon; *Gardens in the Dunes* (NY: Simon & Schuster, 1999.)

This novel begins at a hidden garden on the California-Arizona border. But Silko covers ground that moves between two opposed worlds—the timeless, "traditional" world of Native American peoples and the elaborate, stylized world of White upper-class culture. Indigo is an Indian girl orphaned by an act of White brutality and adopted by a proper Victorian family. Her fascination with the world of privilege never eclipses her faith in the culture of her own people or her desire to return home to what remains of her tribe and her family. A major novel by perhaps the best-known of Native American writers today.

Silko, Leslie Marmon; *Yellow Woman and a Beauty of the Spirit* (NY: Simon & Schuster, 1996.)

"There is no one writing in America who more deserves our attention and respect."—Larry McMurtry. From *Booklist*: "

Silko's essays are like songs; their harmonies are autobiographical, their melodies topical. The source is a controlled blend of pride in Pueblo heritage and anger over the perpetuation of injustice against Native Americans." And Kirkus Reviews writes, "Silko is best when recounting stories that demonstrate the strong spiritual relationship of the people to the land, as in the tale of Yellow Woman, who agrees to go away with a buffalo spirit so that her tribe will always have food."

Slapin, Beverly; *How To Tell The Difference* (Oakland, CA., Oyate Books, 1995.)

A guide to evaluating children's books for anti-Indian bias. This important guide provides assessment questions to ask about children's books about children of color. Though focused for Native Americans, the questions are adaptable to books for children of any race: Is this book truthful? respectful? Would anything embarrass or hurt a child? Would anything foster stereotypic thinking? Is attention paid to accurate design and color and is the language respectful? Do people look all alike or just like whites with brown faces? Do characters use language skillfully? Are they portrayed as successful by their own standards? Is the history distorted?

Section Six
Parting Thoughts

And so it goes...

By Beth Hall

Today I went to pick up a baby girl. She is a little one who is currently between families while her birth mother considers whether adoption is really the right choice or on to a new family as yet unknown and unchosen, no doubt desperate and anxious, wondering if they will ever succeed in adoption. And while I was in the nursery, seeing her alone in an empty room for babies who aren't with their parents, I knew that no one would be adequate to the task of parenting her, only blessed with the opportunity to try. I was flooded with memories and struck by the incredible magic and mystery that is life, with paths unknown and sometimes un-chosen which turn out to make our journey the one it turns out to be.

Perhaps it began when my parents brought home my sister. I thought they must have gone to the baby store, my grandmother and I waiting with our paper bag hats and celebration ready. Or maybe when Gail and Mel came over for dinner and talked to us about adopting children of color. In truth their generosity of spirit and experience, their family's willingness to welcome us into the circle enough to see that they were real, opened the door for our own path into multiracial family-hood that forgave our doubts and allowed us to imagine that we could become adequate enough to deserve the children we were so desperately hoping for. Perhaps there never really was a beginning, just moments, and life waiting to happen.

And so Gail and I began our kitchen-table dreams, in which my road to parenthood was inextricably mixed with Pact's birth and evolution. As we came to understand that women carrying children of color did not have the same level of adoption opportunities available to them in California as did women hoping to place white children for adoption, so too did Sofia come to be Ted's and my daughter. Gail's and my need to see that equal access to equal services for those in need be made available brought James' birth parents into our lives and so my family added a son. With a start-up budget of zero, Pact installed a telephone and began the process of creating a non-profit organization dedicated to connecting children of color in need of adoption with prospective parents and then serving them in their journey for all time. It became clear immediately, from the sheer number of calls received from expectant parents throughout the United States, that the need was huge and not simply a local situation. That was the beginning...

I saw today, in this child's eyes, my own children's experience of muddling through with parents always late to catch on but desperate not to fail. I saw the trust, the acceptance of comfort and remembered the truth that one door closing is another opening. And so the journey goes on… one baby in a nursery waiting for her fate to be announced… one baby between two families waiting to make her mark on the world… one baby crying out to say—love me, I am ready. And so it goes…

A Transracially-Adopted Child's Bill of Rights

By Liza Steinberg Triggs (Pact Press, Fall 1996)

- Every child is entitled to love and full membership in her family.
- Every child is entitled to have his culture embraced and valued.
- Every child is entitled to parents who know that this is a race-conscious society.
- Every child is entitled to parents who know that she will experience life differently than they do.
- Every child is entitled to parents who are not adopted to "save" him or to improve the world.
- Every child is entitled to parents who know that being in a family doesn't depend on "matching."
- Every child is entitled to parents who know that transracial adoption changes the family forever.
- Every child is entitled to be accepted by extended family members.
- Every child is entitled to parents who know that if they are white, they benefit from racism.
- Every child is entitled to parents who known that they can't transmit the child's birth culture if it is not their own.
- Every child is entitled to have items in his home that are made for and by people of his culture.
- Every child is entitled to opportunities to make friends with people of her race or ethnicity.
- Every child is entitled to daily opportunities to have positive experiences with his birth cultures.
- Every child is entitled to build racial pride within her own home, family, school, and neighborhood.
- Every child is entitled to have constant opportunities to connect with adults of the child's race.
- Every child is entitled to learn survival, problem solving, and coping skills in a context of racial pride.
- Every child is entitled to parents who accept, understand and empathize with her race and culture.
- Every child is entitled to take pride in the development of a dual iden-

tity and a multicultural/multiracial perspective on life.

- Every child is entitled to find his multiculturalism to be an asset and to conclude, "I've got the best of both worlds."

A Transracial Adoptive Parent's Wish List

It would be so nice if…

- Everybody didn't think they were experts on my family.
- Nobody ever wondered whether I was the best parent for my child.
- Nobody ever wondered whether I was a good enough parent to my child.
- Nobody in the grocery store checkout line ever asked if my child belonged to me.
- Nobody ever asked at the playground, the emergency room, or the barbershop where my child's parents were when I was right there.
- My extended family supported my decisions to adopt across racial lines 100%!
- I was able to see beyond my experience and anticipate every time racial issues would affect my child.
- I could protect my child from all pain.
- I was always effective in building bridges to my child's culture.
- I had more energy and was able to go the extra mile every time to connect my child to her culture without sometimes making choices that were easier for me.
- I could give my child my white privilege
- I could participate with my child in aspects of his birth culture without by my very presence making the point that he is different.
- It were easier and more natural for me to seek out friends of my child's birth culture
- I didn't feel that outsiders through their attitudes about race judged most things I did.
- Nobody ever questioned whether we were their "real" parents or they our "real" children.
- We always "got" it before it happened, anticipated every hurt or affront and were somehow able to protect our children from pain while still giving them the opportunity to become deep and incredible human beings with full capacity to love, care and be happy.
- Everybody could be viewed and valued for who they are on the inside, not just the outside.

Conclusions

"There are only two ways to live your life. One is as though
nothing is a miracle. The other is as though everything is a miracle."

—e.e. cummings

Transracial adoptive families rest on the capacity to love one another without the common markers of "sameness." We don't look alike; the world doesn't treat us like other families; each member in our family comes with a different history. But when we ask, "Who is on my side? Who?" (II.Kings 9:32) the answer is "Our family members."

Wrapped together under a splendid quilt that holds us warm, holds us up and tucks us into our daily lives, we act like a tribe, because that's what we are. We serve as allies for one another, because we must. We pool our resources because that's what families do. Together, we are greater than the sum of our parts; all we ask is to be.

Transracial families are pioneers. Our lives are miracles. We share a respect for difference and an appreciation for diversity that are models for all people and all communities. Life provides us with more opportunities every day than most people get in a lifetime to:

1. Face hurts and celebrate blessings together
2. Address our differences and celebrate our sameness
3. Marvel when we are stupid and repair the mistakes we make with each other.
4. Interact even when it feels overwhelming.
5. Live with the pain of our losses.
6. Yell, laugh, shout, scream, and praise our funny, crazy, totally cool adventures.

All of this builds our sense of common identity and common purpose, a heightened ability to perceive each of our members as the unique person he or she is. We must not allow ourselves or our children ever to believe that our families are marginal. Though we may rarely acknowledge it, the truth is just the opposite. We are trailblazers.

Racial and cultural issues present difficult questions. We can be their victims or we can rise to their challenges. As families and as individuals, we can reap great benefits, becoming adept and flexible, well-equipped to respond to the ever-increasing complexities of our world.

In the end, our task is like that proverbial jigsaw puzzle. There are many pieces, and each is necessary. Nothing can be either overlooked or overemphasized if we are to complete the full picture. Let's pledge our vigilance and honesty regarding all of the issues. Let's not abandon our children to facing the issues on their own.

Positive Outcomes

"Adoption is a metaphor for the human condition, setting us forth on that mythic quest that will prove we are connected to each other and to all the creatures of this world—and in the process reveal to us who we really are."

—Betty Jean Lifton

What Doesn't Kill You Makes You Strong

Being a member of a multiracial family through adoption is a great way to build character. Not only do we get more opportunities than most people to face new challenges and develop the ability to value differences within our families; we also have more occasions than most to practice these skills in the world beyond our doors.

We Can:

- Take apparent contradictions in stride
- Accept our shifts in position without getting defensive
- Look at situations from more than one point of view
- Be more creative in developing solutions to problems
- Be more effective in working cooperatively
- Put more effort into the construction of self than the presentation of self
- Personalize and customize meanings rather than accept somebody else's scripts
- Judge oneself by measuring the overall self rather than by assessing a particular ability
- Value flexibility
- Be guided more by self-evaluation than buy the opinions of others
- Make choices that require negotiation and cooperative agreements
- Act effectively within a group setting.

Kid Power

As Martin Luther King, Jr. said, "Let us move on in these powerful days, these days of challenge to make things what they ought to be. We have an opportunity to make a difference."

> *One of the things I (Gail) have learned, now that my babies are adults, is that the most valued connections are the ones they've made for themselves. Contrary to my modest hopes—that (because of the terrific job my husband and I would do to prepare them) our children would move out into the world ready for anything, they weren't. But they have built and continue to build the real connections with their cultural heritages for themselves. What we did was useful, but it was only a small piece. As adults with complex identity components in a race-conscious society, they themselves deserve the full credit for integrating all that they become.*

Parents raising children across racial lines cannot sit back and wait for their kids to take care of these issues by themselves—not on your life. But their growth does not stop when they reach eighteen. In fact, some of the more profound comforts may be found only beyond childhood, in a more mature realm of development.

It's true, deeply true, that as a first priority, parents are obligated to

S — T — R — E — T — C — H

as much as they can in order to include their child's birth heritage into the family's everyday life, but as you finish reading this book, we'd like to pass along the experienced and hoped for relief and pride we feel when we see grown sons and daughters accomplishing things for themselves in adulthood that we were not able to accomplish for them when they were little ones. May your children do the same for themselves. May you expect that their leaving the nest will be only their beginning.

> *"Be what you are. Give what is yours to give. Have style. Dare."*
> — Stanley Kunitz, "Journal for My Daughter,"
> *Poems of Stanley Kunitz,* Boston: 1979, Little Brown

Test Your Knowledge

How much have you learned from working through *Inside Transracial Adoption?*

Instructions:

1. Read each section carefully.
2. Answer all questions.
3. Time is limited to four hours.
4. Begin immediately.

History: Describe the history of African American people in the United States from its origins to the present day, concentrating especially, but not exclusively on its social, political, economic, religious, and philosophical impact. Be brief, concise, complete and specific.

Music: Write a race-awareness hymn. Orchestrate and perform it with flute and drum. You will find a gospel choir under your seat.

Public Speaking: 2500 riot-crazed white supremacists are storming your living room. Calm them. You may use any language except English.

Political Science: There is a red telephone on your desk. Let the President know how to end the war on racism. Report at length on the sociopolitical efforts, if any.

Biology: Create life. Estimate the differences in subsequent human culture if this form of life had developed 500 million years earlier, paying special attention to its probable effect on the American democratic system. Prove your thesis.

Psychology: Based on your knowledge of their works, evaluate the emotional stability, degree of adjustment and repressed frustrations of the following: Dr. Martin Luther King, Jr., Miriam Santos, Woody Allen, and Amy Tan. Support your evaluation with quotations from each person's work, making appropriate references. It is not necessary to translate.

Ethics: Take a position for or against brotherhood. Prove the validity of your stand.

Sociology: Estimate the sociological problems that might accompany the end of the world. Construct an experiment to test your theory.

Philosophy: Sketch the development of human thought, estimate its significance. Compare with the development of any other kind of thought.

General Knowledge: Describe in detail. Be objective and specific.

The more we learn, the more we understand how much more there is to learn.

Acknowledgments

This book represents a significant step forward in Pact's mission to provide families, educators and adoption professionals with information to support transracially adopted children. On behalf of the children, and all who love and care for them, we offer our deepest appreciation to those who have contributed to this effort. This book could not exist without the extraordinary efforts, patience, and inspiration of many individuals. Each contribution represents an essential link in the chain that helped us bring this work to you. There is no beginning and no end; in the circle of support, everyone came first.

Together, we would first like to thank:

Sofia Hall Gallagher, James Hall Gallagher, Liza Triggs, Seth Steinberg, Jeremy Steinberg, Shira Gale, our children, for loving us when we were busy and for taking seriously their responsibility to teach us new lessons every day.

Mel Steinberg and Ted Gallagher, our husbands. Were it not for their amazing patience, good humor, support, and absolute commitment we could not be who we are or do what we do.

Hundreds of transracial adoptive parents, in Pact's workshops, support groups, and one-on-one, who have shared their challenges and joys with us. Their honesty, courage, commitment and wisdom have helped make this book what it is.

Marta Barton and the rest of Pact's staff, board and volunteers throughout the years, for their clarity, insight, stimulating ideas and thoughtful suggestions. Special thanks to Rebecca Weller for her remarkable passion for making language transparent and easily accessible to readers which she has generously donated for past Pact Press publications as well as her last minute help with editing on this manuscript.

Annette Baran, Anne Bernstein, David Brodzinsky, Susan Soon-Keum Cox, Joseph Crumbley, Louise Derman-Sparks, Marion Wright Edelman, Erik Erikson, David S. Kirk, Mary Sheedy Kurcinka, R.D. Laing, Jane Lazarre, B.J. Lifton, Peggy McIntosh, Lois Melina, Joyce Maguire Pavao, Sharon Kaplan Roszia, Randolph Severson, Gail Sheehy, Beverly Daniel Tatum, Michael Trout, Holly van Gulden, and Kenneth Watson, for "lighting the lamps" for us through their work, informing, influencing and expanding our insight. Special thanks to our editor and friend, Patricia Irwin Johnston, another of the lamplighters, but more than that too, as she has enhanced our work. On behalf of their contributions to all families, we offer our deep appreciation.

Gail would also like to thank Beth Hall, my co-author and partner, for a wonderful collaboration. I love your vision and the passion you bring to it. Knowing you, too, are working at your computer in the middle of the night makes everything more possible. Your "can do" way of being, and your absolute willingness to give 100% of yourself, day after day to the dreams we share, move Pact forward.

To my grandchildren, Leah Gale and Kai Gale; my son and daughter through marriage Corey Triggs, Patty Steinberg; my family—the Zaleskis, the Ralskes, the Jacksons, and Rose Freedman, my mother—thank you for sharing your wisdom and joy as the arm of adoption drew us closer.

Beth would like to acknowledge the tireless drive with which Gail Steinberg moved this project forward. You, in fact, often are the engine which pumps both of us forward in all of our work. Your non-stop effort made this book possible, as you shouldered far more than your equal share of the work.

To Barbara Hall Harbaugh , my sister, and to the first adoptive parents we ever knew, our parents Margaret and John, my family the Gallaghers, the Halls and the McNarys for introducing me to life and love without boundaries of blood or genetics.

Index

Index

Adams, Ansel, 300
ADD, 178, 181-82. *See also* ADHD
ADHD, 175, 180-82. *See also* ADD
adolescence, 303. *See also*
    development, teenage
Adopting the Sexually Abused Child,
    241
adoption
    and abuse/neglect, 241
    awareness about, 109-119, 240-41
    and children's literature, 82-84
    communication about, 82-84,
        213, 239-44
    international, 159-67
        from China, 326, 335-37
        from Korea, 2-3, 93
    issues concerning, 12, 106, 225
    of multiracial children, 364-65
    and schools, 240, 247-48
    and sexuality, 221
    of special needs children, 171,
        177
    and teen-agers, 254
    transracial, 8-9
        Bill of Rights, 379-80
        and learning disabilities, 179
        open, 140-42
        and pre-natal substance abuse,
            182-85
        suitability for, 12-13
Adoption Day rituals, 126-27
adoption groups, 69-70
adoptism, 91, 106-09, 115
    acknowledgement of, 40
    definition of, 108-09
    examples of, 107-09
affirmative action, 43-44

African Americans. *See also* Black;
    multiracial
    culture of, 301-19
    definition of, 21
    and eye contact, 309-10
    and family, 101-02, 305-08
    and hair, 72, 115, 117, 315-24
    history of, 312-15
    interdependency among, 308-09
    and other persons of color, 305
    physical appearance, 315-16
    and religion, 173, 307-08
    safety issues, 310-12
    and skin color, 50-51
    slavery, 312-15
    time perception, 309
Amazing Grace, 46
Amerasian, definition of, 21
American Black Muslims, 307-08
American Indian. *See* Native
    American
Anti-Bias Curriculum, 246
Appiah, Kwame Anthony, 295
artificial twinning, 154
Asian Americans. *See also* Chinese
    Americans; multiracial
    culture of, 327-38
    ethnic specifics, 324-26
    notable persons, 81, 334
Asian/Pacific Islander, definition
    of, 21
asthma, 178
"A Transracially-adopted Child's
    Bill of Rights", 379-80
attachment, 128-31
    in early childhood, 219
    in infancy, 207-10

and pre-natal substance abuse,
    183-84
Austin, Pam, 359

Bastard Nation, 21
*Being Adopted: the Lifelong Search
    for Self*, 242
Ben-Zeev, Sandra, 162
Bennett, Tony, 300
Berkeley, California, 61
bicultural, 21, 288. *See also*
    biracial; multiracial
"Bicultural Identity", 288
bilingualism, 93, 161-63, 251. *See
    also* language
biological relatives. *See* birth family
biracial, 21, 355-66. *See
    also* bicultural,
    multiracial
birth country, travel to, 163-66
birth culture, 15-16, 115. *See also*
    culture (specific sub-headings);
    racial heritage; racial identity
    education about, 73-79, 93-94,
        289-90
    and food, 77-78, 127
    identification with, 54, 67,
        277, 306
    importance of, 45, 167, 252,
        289-90
    loss of, 11
    and music, 78, 81
    and names, 211-12
    negative images of, 166-67
    pride in, 163
    and religion, 173
    and smell, 78
    and style, 77
birth family. *See also* birth
        parents; birth mother
    absence of, 257
    connection with, 141-42, 251
    messages about, 138-39
    significance of, 139
birth father. *See* birth family; birth
    parents

birth mother. *See also* birth family;
        birth parents
    experience of, 107
    and racial identity, 54, 362
birth parents, 115. *See also* birth
        family; birth mother
    and adoption awareness, 166-17
    feelings about, 261-62, 268
    and genetic disorders, 175
    idealization of, 139-40, 266
    importance of, 142, 241-43
    loss of, 257
    questions about, 260
    and racial identity, 54, 362
    search and reunion, 262, 276
    and substance abuse, 182-85
birth relatives. *See* birth family;
        birth parents; birth mother
*Black and White Racial Identity
        Development: Theory,
        Research, and Practice*, 36
Black Muslims, 307-08.
Black.*See also* African Americans
    definition of, 21
    non-African American, 305
Black, White, Other, 357
body image, 260. *See also* self-image
bonding, 128
Brodzinsky, David, Dr., 93, 221,
    242, 259
Buddhism, 327, 329-30
Burton, L. M., 303
By the Color of Our Skin, 302

camp, 249. *See also* culture camp
Catholicism, 348-49. *See also*
    Christianity
Central American. *See* Latinos
Chicano/Chicana. *See* Latinos
child care, choice of, 226-27
China
    adoption from, 326, 335-37
Chinese New Year, 65-66, 121
Chiong, J. A., 390
Christianity, 307, 348-49. *See also*
    Catholicism; Protestantism

Christmas, 95
　and rituals, 126
Cinco de Mayo, 67, 95, 246
civil rights. *See* social justice
class, confusion with race, 302-03
Collier, Eugenia, 295
communication
　about adoption, 47-48, 120-21
　and infants, 202-03, 206-07
　about racism, 47
　with teen-agers, 259-60
community, and Latino culture, 345
Concrete Operational Stage, 233-34
Confucianism, 327-29
consciousness, racial. *See* racial
　consciousness
Counseling the Culturally Different:
　Theory and Practice, 309
Cox, Susan Soon Keum, 161
Crosby, Faye, 42
Cross, William, 34-35, 106
Cuban American. *See* Latino
"Cultural and Historical
　　Perspectives in
　　Counseling Blacks", 309
cultural competence, 289-90
culture
　African American, 301-19
　Asian, 327-38
　conflicts in, 295
　definition of, 21-22
　differences in, 288
　and identity, 366-69
　Latino, 339-49
　multicultural, 355-66
　Native American, 350-55
　and parenting, 15-16
　pride in, 297-99
　and self-awareness, 289-90,
　　366-69
culture camps, 70-71
Cummings, Rhoda, 181

Davis, Larry E., Dr., 358
death, of parent(s), 169, 176

depression, post-placement, 129
Derman-Sparks, Louise, 246
desegregation, 299
development
　and adoption, 197-99
　in early childhood, 216-31
　emotional, 205-07, 218-19, 235-
　　36, 255
　of infants, 199-207
　intellectual, 203-05, 217-18,
　　233-34, 255
　moral, 237-38
　physical, 200-02, 217, 232-33,
254
　of school-age children, 232-41
　of teen-agers, 253-72, 303-04
Devine, Patricia G., 302
diabetes, 178
Different and Wonderful, 41, 271
Diggs-Brown, Barbara, 302
discrimination. *See* racism
diversity, 60-69
divorce, 170

education
　and adoption issues, 247-48
　home-schooling, 248-49
　about minorities, 41
　multicultural, 95, 245-47
　view of by Asians, 337
"Enemies Won't Help You Solve
　　Problems", 293
Entman, Robert, 302
Erichsen, Heino R., 160
Erikson, Erik H., 237, 257
ethnic, definition of, 22
ethnic connections, 167, 269
ethnic groups, Asian, 324-26
ethnic heritage, 269
ethnicity, definition of, 22
European American, definition of, 22
Ezekiel, Raphael, 42, 292

family
　and African Americans, 101-02,

305-08
and Asians, 332-33
birth plus adoption, 157-59
extended, 143-48
gay and lesbian, 170-72
importance of, 16-17, 101-02
and Latinos, 344-45
multiracial, 33-34, 150-53, 355,
    364-65
rituals in, 122-27, 154
single-child, 155-57
single parent, 168-70
fantasy parents, 139-40
Farrakhan, Louis, 307
FAS. *See* Fetal Alcohol Syndrome
Father's Day, 127
Feagin, Joe R., 40
fertility, 255
Fetal Alcohol Syndrome, 182-85
First Feelings, 205
First Nations People. *See* Native
    Americans
Fisher, Gary, 181
food, 77-78, 127
Fourth of July, 95
Freud, Sigmund, 266
Fullilove, Mindy Thompson, 357
Funderburg, Lise, 357

Gardner, Howard, 234
Gay and Lesbian movement, 21,
    170-72
genetic privilege, 106
graduation, and rituals, 126
grandchildren, 274-75
Greenspan, Nancy Thorndike, 205
Greenspan, Sidney, M. D., 205,
    222-23

hair care for African Americans,
    319-24
Halloween, and rituals, 126
Hart, Louise, Dr., 131
hate groups. *See* racism, organized
Helms, Janet, 36

Henig, Robin Marantz, 242
heritage, definition of, 22
Hijuelo, Oscar, 341
Hinduism, 327, 330-31
Hispanic, definition of, 22. *See
    also* Latinos
Hoffman, Mary, 46
holidays, 94-95.

home-schooling, 248-49
homophobia, 171-72
Hopson, Darlene Powell, Dr., 41,
    146, 271
Hopson, Derek S., Dr., 41, 146, 271
How to Adopt Internationally, 160
human, as racial designation, 357
hypersensitivity, 208-09

identity
    African American, 301-02, 304-05
    Asian, 324-27
    cultural. *See* identity, racial
    development of, 34-36
    family, 105-06
    Jewish, 174-76
    Latino, 339-43
    multiracial, 355-66
    Native American, 349-53
    racial, 10, 34-36
    sexual, 255, 345
    and stereotypes, 270-71
    and teen-agers, 262
    white, 297-99
Identity, Youth and Crisis, 237
IEP, 180
In Between Cultures, 356
Indian, definition of, 22. *See also*
    Native American
indigenous people. *See* Native
American
individualism, 295-97
infants, development of, 199-216
infertility, 255, 275
intelligence, multiple, 234-35
interracial, definition of, 22

interracial marriage, 365
Islam, 327, 331-32

Jackson, Derrick, 289
Jackson, Jesse, 304
Jewish community, 126, 307
Jewish identity, 174-76
Johnston, Patricia Irwin, 106
Jusczyk, Peter, 212

Kennel, J. H., 129
King, Martin Luther, Jr., Dr., 300
Kirk, H. David, 106, 109
Klaus, M. H., 129
Korea, adoption from, 2-3, 93

La Framboise, T. Coleman, 288
language, 251. *See also* bilingualism
   Latino, 162, 348
   learning, 93
   of birth culture, 161-63
Latin American. *See* Latinos
Latinos. *See also* Hispanic; multiracial
   and birth language, 162
   black, 305, 341
   and community, 345
   culture, 339-49
      and religion, 348-49
   definition of, 22-23, 341
   population, 339
   and racism, 343
   self-image, 339-40, 343-44
   and skin color, 50-51, 305, 341
   stereotypes of, 341-42
   and time, 345-46
learning disabilities, 175, 178-82
Living with Racism, 40
loss, coping with, 224-25
Love You Forever, 83
Lovejoy, Elijah, 300
Loving v. Virginia, 365
loyalty, and teen-agers, 263-64
Lunar New Year. *See* Chinese New
   Year

MacIntosh, Peggy, 106
mainstreaming, 71-72
Malouf, David, 45
Mambo Kings Play Songs of Love, 341
Mahoney, Jim, 42
marriage, 273-74
   interracial, 365
   and Latinos, 344-45
Maternal Infant Bonding, 129
McNamara, Joan, 119, 241
mental illness, 178
Mexican American. *See* Latinos
Mexicano. *See* Latinos
Mongolian Blue Spots, 213-14
Mother's Day, 127
moving, 61-66
mulatto, 356
   definition of, 23
*Multicultural/Multiracial
      Psychology*, 353
multiple intelligence, 234-35
multiracial. *See also* bicultural;
biracial
   definition of, 23
   identity, 355-66
music and culture, 252

names
   re-naming, 212
   significance of, 192-94, 210-12
Nation of Islam. *See* Black Muslims
Native American, definition of, 23
Native Americans
   culture, 350-55
   history of, 352-53
   philosophy, 353-55
   stereotypes of, 351-53
   tribes, 350-51
Native people. *See* Native American

Naturalization Day, 127
neglect, and adoption, 241
Nelson-Erichsen, Jean, 160
Njeri, Itaberi, 40

Oguss, Karl, 356
Okun, B. F., 355
only children. *See* families, single child
Oriental, definition of, 23

Pact, 131, 271, 318, 378
parent(s), death of, 169, 176
parenting
  foster, 7, 33, 128
  patterns of, 131-35
  of teen-agers, 256-57
parents
  adoptive, 380
  and divorce, 170
Park, Robert, 357
Passover, 126
Pathways Through Adolescence: Individual Development in Relation to Social Contexts, 303
Pavao, Joyce Maguire, 248
peer groups, 55, 238, 255-56, 264-65
  support from, 257
people of color, definition of, 23
personalismo, 346-47
Peters, Arno, 41
philosophy, Asian, 327-32
physical development, 200-02, 217, 232-33, 254
Piaget, Jean, 233
Playground Politics: Understanding the Emotional Life of Your School Age Child, 222
Pocho. *See* Latinos
population data, 290-91
  African American, 301-02
  Asian, 324-26
  Latino, 339
  multiracial, 355
  Native American, 349-51
Post-traumatic stress disorder, 186-87
preschoolers, development of, 216-31
Projection Equal Area Representa-
tion Map, 41
Protestantism, 348. *See also* Christianity
psychological disorders, 177-78
PTSD. *See* Post-traumatic stress disorder
Puerto Ricans. *See* Latinos
Puerto Ricans: Born in the U.S.A., 341

race. *See also* racism
  and adoption, 11-12
  confusion with class, 302-03
  definition of, 23
  feelings about, 59
  and growth charts, 201
  pride in, 297-99
  significance of, 295
Racial Categorization of Multiracial Children in Schools, 355
racial heritage. *See also* racial identity; birth culture
  connection with, 63-64, 167, 268
  consciousness of, 36-38
  and teen-agers, 266
  and young adults, 272-74
racial hierarchy, 44-45
racial identity, 53-54. *See also* racial heritage; birth culture
  multiracial, 355-66
  positive, 52-53, 359
  unknown, 362-63
racial issues
  in early childhood, 227
  and infants, 214-16
  and school-age children, 250-53
  and teen-agers, 254, 268-72
  and toddlers, 229-30
racism, 34-35, 39. *See also* race; social justice
  acknowledgement of, 40, 51-52, 291-92
  dealing with, 85-93, 95-96, 112-13, 146-48, 293-94

definition of, 108
as disease, 145-46
effects of, 40-41
in extended family, 144-48
feelings about, 59
identification of, 292
institutionalized, 40, 42, 60
internalized, 41-42
and Latinos, 343
in the media, 52, 60
as obstacle, 305
organized, 42-43
preparation for, 45-47, 146-47
and religion, 173
and school-age children, 250-53
and toddlers, 227-28
"Racisms", 295
Raibel, John, 277
Raising the Rainbow Generation,
146
Ramos, Manuel, 353
Raspberry, William, 293
Reeb, James, Rev., 300
rejection, and teen-agers, 266
religion
    in African American culture,
        307-08
    in Asian culture, 327-32
    choice of, 173-74
    conflict involving, 173
    and Jewish identity, 174-76
    in Latino culture, 348-49
    role of, 172-73
"Representation and Reality in the
        Portrayal of Blacks in
        Network Television News", 302
respect, and Latino culture, 347-48
rituals, 122-27
Rodriguez, Clara, 341
role models, 170
Roszia, Sharon Kaplan, 12
Roy, Daniel L., 339-40

Schechter, Marshall, 242
schizophrenia, 175

school-age children, development
of,   232-53
schools, selection of, 226-27, 243-
45
Seelye, H. Ned, 356
self awareness, 289-90
self-concept, 36. *See also* self-image
    changes in, 236-37
    definition of, 23
self-esteem
    and birth family, 251
    changes in 236-67
    definition of, 24
    and failure, 57-58
    and praise, 58
    and race, 53-59, 79-80
self-expression, 84-85
self-image. *See also* body image;
        self-concept
    definition of, 24
    multiracial, 357-59
    and pre-natal substance abuse,
184
    and teen-agers, 267-68
    white, 36
self-regulation, 205-06
self-respect, 51
Seven Arrows, 353
sexism, 252-53
    definition of, 108
sexual destiny, 260
sexuality, and adoption, 221
Shades of Black, 34
Shared Fate theory, 106
siblings, 148-54
    rivalry between, 149, 154
Sikes, Melvin P., 40
Sikhism, 332
Silverstein, Deborah N., 12
skin color, 50-51, 305, 341
slavery, 312-15, 365
Smith, E., 309
Smith, Jerome, 106
social justice, 252-53, 297-99, 307.
        See also racism

role models for, 299-300
Souljah, Sister, 295
Spurlock, J., 309
Steinhorn, Leonard, 302
stereotypes, 270-71, 288-89
  of African Americans, 302, 304-05
  of Asians, 326-27
  in media, 288-89
  of multiracial persons, 356-57
  of Native Americans, 351-53
  and racism, 291-92
Stonequist, E. V., 306
Storm, Hyemeyohsts, 353
Strangers in a Native Land, 339
stress, in infants, 200
*Struggle for Identity, Issues in
    Transracial Adoption*, 277
substance abuse, pre-natal, 182-85
Sue, D. W., 309
Suomi, Stephen, 128
*Survival Guide for Kids with LD
    (Learning Differences)*, 181

Taoism, 327, 329
Tatum, Beverly Daniel, 351
Teaching/Learning Anti-Racism, 246
teenagers
  development of, 253-70
  difficulty with, 272
  and loyalty, 263-64
terminology, 8, 21-24
  and skin color, 50-51
Thanksgiving, 94, 126
The Conversations at Curlow Creek,
45
The Family of Adoption, 248
"The Mental Health of Black
    Americans; Psychiatric
    Diagnosis and Treatment", 309
The Racist Mind, 42
The Winning Family, 131

time
  and African American culture,
309
  and Latino culture, 345-46
  and Native American culture, 355
transitions
  preparation for, 135-38
  and teen-agers, 262-63
transracial, definition of, 24
Two Birthdays for Beth, 82

Understanding Affirmative Action, 42
Understanding Diverse Families, 355

Van Vechten, Carl, 300

Wasileski, Jacqueline Howell, 356
Watson, Kenneth, Dr., 57-59
white
  child's desire to be, 231
  definition of, 24
  and skin color, 50-51
white identity, 290-93, 297-98
white privilege, 36, 106, 291-93,
296, 299
  definition of, 24
"White Privilege: Unpacking the
    Invisible Knapsack", 106
*Why Are All the Black Kids Sitting
    Together in the
    Cafeteria?*, 351
Wilkinson, C., 309
Wolley, Greg, 357
women
  view of by Asians, 333-34
  view of by Chinese, 335-37
Woods, Tiger, 359
"Words to Live or Die by", 40

Zilla Sasparilla and the Mud Baby,
90-91

About Pact

Pact, An Adoption Alliance, provides the highest quality adoption services to children of color. Our primary client is the child. To serve the child, we address the needs of all the child's parents, by advising families facing a crisis pregnancy and by offering lifelong education to adoptive and birth families on matters of race and adoption. Our goal is for every child to feel wanted, honored and loved, a cherished member of a strong family with proud connections to the rich cultural heritage that is his or her birthright. Pact was incorporated in 1991 as a non-profit 501(c)(3) charitable organization.

Adoption Services

Pact helps find permanent adoptive families for African American, Latino, Asian and multiracial children born in the US whose birth families are seeking to make adoption plans. We believe every child deserves to grow up in a permanent, nurturing home. We work with families from all over the country, and we are always seeking potential adoptive families, whether same-race adoptive parents or potential transracial adoptive parents who are willing to make special strides to help provide their children with positive racial identity.

Pact Programs for Children and Families of Color

Pact is the largest national organization serving adoptive parents, birth parents, adopted people, foster parents, adoption professionals and friends devoted to a better understanding of and support for adopted children of color.

As a result of increased federal interest in transracial adoption, Pact was the only organization in the United States to have been awarded a Federal Grant in 1998 to support transracial adoptive families and in 1999 to begin a pilot research project to determine the predictable developmental milestones of adopted children of color. Pact has created 13 programs for these families, each one designed to help build or strengthen connections between transracial adoptive families and people who share the racial heritage of the children in these families.

At the same time that we strive to provide exemplary services for children in transracial adoptive families, we retain a primary commitment to provide support and education for same-race adoptive families; we believe all Pact families will benefit from these new programs.

Pact Membership

Adoptive families—whether parents are the same race as their children or of a different race; formed through domestic or international adoption; led by two parents or a single parent—are invited to join. At Pact, you will find support, new resources, services, information and advocacy addressing your special issues. Membership includes a subscription to *Pact Press* and discounts on books and other Pact materials. You will also receive regular mailings containing new information important to your family, along with invitations to special events. Some programs are open to Pact members only.

Program Title	*Program Purpose*
My Friend	A program linking transracially-adopted kids to same-race mentors.
Hand In Hand	A cross-cultural program to build enduring Friendships through family-to-family social interaction programs.
Good Times!	A series of multicultural child-focused entertainment events.
Transcultural Mini-Grants	Sub-grants to support groups to strengthen their services to transracial adoptive families.
TAPS (888) 448-8277	Transracial Adoptive Parent Support A toll-free telephone line to provide referrals and support.
Multicultural Reading Groups	A small group reading program focused on racial issues.
Camp Just Like Us	A summer day camp to strengthen cultural identity.
Virtual Village	Internet access to experts, peers & mentors.
Moving A Mountain	Connects families to projects which interrupt racism.
National Conference	*Interracial Families, Interwoven Cultures* will be an annual national conference for transracial and international adoptive families. Innaugural date: July, 2001
Multicultural Resource Guide	Yellow pages format.

Pact Resources
Pact's Multicultural BookSource–2ⁿᵈ Edition

A comprehensive reference guide to over 1200 books for children and adults containing current, concise and informative referrals to the widest possible range of books related to adoption, race and family life. Each description includes reviews, ratings, a keyword guide and a brief synopsis. The first edition sold out quickly. The 2nd edition includes 400 new reviews and books as well as updated information on all books.

Best of Pact Press

Forty-eight-page collections of the best articles Pact's magazine addressing issues of race, adoption and foster care. Provocative and thoughtful articles written by experts of national acclaim. Our readers tell us they read every issue from cover to cover.
- *Attachment* Practical in-depth exploration.
- *Being Adopted* From those who are living it!
- *Biracial Identity* Dual heritage, dual loyalties.
- *Birth Parents* Personal stories and perspectives.
- *Open Adoption* The joys and challenges.
- *Racial Identity* Building pride and connection.
- *Talking with Kids about Adoption* For parents of children of all ages.

Below the Surface

Below the Surface is designed to provide feedback to anyone considering adoption across racial or cultural lines, offering insight into the kinds of adjustments they may want to incorporate into their lives to support a child of a racial or ethnic heritage different from their own. *Below the Surface* gives pre-adoptive families the chance to quiz themselves in four areas pertinent to transracial parenting and to determine their Transracial Adoption Suitability Index. Designed as a user-friendly learning tool, this pamphlet does not debate transracial adoption; instead, it gives potential parents real tools to decide whether this choice suits them.

Pact Manuals

- *Is Adoption The Right Choice for You?* A thoughtful collection of articles to help you consider whether adoptive parenting is right for you. Gives information and suggestions for how to think about and investigate the kind of adoption you want to pursue. (31 pages)
- *Parenting After Adoption* A lively collection of articles on strategies for parents of infants through teens. Treats adoption as an issue - not a

problem. Focuses on children's needs and ways parents can meet them. (76 pages)

- *Transracial Adoption ... Being A Family of Color* A collection of articles which take a hard look at the issues, going beyond the debate to provide important information for families who have adopted either domestically or internationally. (138 pages)

Interracial Families, Interwoven Cultures

A six-hour audiotape looking at the challenges of transracial adoption. Recorded at a day-long training program led by Beth Hall and Gail Steinberg, it concentrates on the child's experience in the world.

Trainer's Kit For Transracial Adoption

A training curriculum for professionals working with pre- and post-adoptive families considering transracial placements. This kit offers step-by-step outlines and instructions for planning workshops using Pact materials and two instructional videotapes exploring transracial adoption issues. The trainer's guide includes advice on how to use the materials, how to establish topic priorities and suggested exercises for pre- and post- placement families. Instructions include goals, trainer preparation, agendas and handouts. Modules for twelve individual workshops as well as all-day sessions are described.

Contact Pact

Pact, An Adoption Alliance
3450 Sacramento Street Suite 239
San Francisco, CA 94118
Voice: 415.221.6957
Fax: 510.482.2089
Email: info@pactadopt.org
Website: www.pactadopt.org
TAPS [Transracial Adoptive Parent Support] 888.448.8277
Birthparent Line: 800.750.7590
(include logo on this page)

Perspectives Press: The Infertility and Adoption Publisher

http://www.perspectivespress.com
Since 1982 Perspectives Press has focused exclusively on infertility, adoption, and related reproductive health and child welfare issues. Our purpose is to promote understanding of these issues and to educate and sensitize those personally experiencing these life situations, professionals who work in these fields, and the public at large. Our titles are never duplicative or competitive with material already available through other publishers. We seek to find and to fill niches which are empty.

Currently in print titles include:
For Adults

Perspectives on a Grafted Tree
Understanding Infertility: Insights for Family and Friends
Sweet Grapes: How to Stop Being Infertile and Start
        Living Again
A Child's Journey through Placement
Adopting after Infertility
Flight of the Stork: What Children Think (and When)
        about Sex and Family Building
Taking Charge of Infertility
Looking Back, Looking Forward
Launching a Baby's Adoption
Toddler Adoption: The Weaver's Craft
Choosing Assisted Reproduction
PCOS: The Hidden Epidemic
Inside Transracial Adoption

For Children

The Mulberry Bird
Filling in the Blanks
Lucy's Feet
Two Birthdays for Beth
Let Me Explain

Authors Beth Hall and Gail Steinberg

About the Authors

Gail Steinberg is the adoptive mom of four grown daughters and sons; Shira Beth Gale is Korean and American Indian and arrived from Korea when she was three, Liza Anya Triggs is African American and joined the family when she was three weeks old, Jeremy Ben Steinberg is African American and white and joined the family when he was three and a half and Seth Ari Steinberg is white and was adopted at ten months. Gail is also the grandmother of Leah Rachel Gale and Kai Rebecca Gale. She lives in San Anselmo, California, with her husband.

Beth Hall is the adoptive mom of two school-aged children: Sofia Hall Gallagher who is Latina and and James Hall Gallagher who is African American. She grew up a member of an adoptive family—her sister, Barbara, adopted by (and Beth having been born to) their parents. She lives in Oakland, California, with her family.

Together Beth and Gail are founders and co-directors of Pact, An Adoption Alliance. The author of numerous articles, they lecture across the country and are committed to serving children first.

Advance Buzz about *Inside Transracial Adoption*

Eloquent, interesting and intensely practical, you can't read this book without thinking differently about your own life as a child, a parent, and a member of our diverse society.

> —**Lois Melina, author of** *Raising Adopted Children* **and** *The Open Adoption Experience*

As a first generation Korean adoptee, I carry in my bones the longing for clarity about identity and peace with my Korean and adopted nationality that *Inside Transracial Adoption* is all about. The authors' insights, compassion, and willingness to tackle both the joys and challenges of these pioneer families makes this a must read.

> —**Susan Soon-Keum Cox, transracial adoptee and Vice President of Public Policy & External Affairs, Holt International Services**

This is an honest and insightful book that is at once very personal and universal to all transracial adoptive parents. The authors tackle the very real issues; emotions, responsibilities and joys transracial adoption asks us to take on. As a transracial parent of grown children myself I wished I had had this book when they were young. insights. As a professional anti-bias educator I appreciate the authors' insistence that parents face the realities of racism in the US. Through a stimulating combination of enlightening anecdotes and wise analysis, *Inside Transracial Adoption* is an indispensable resource for people planning to adopt, for parents currently in transracial families and for professionals working with transracial families.

> —**Louise Derman Sparks, transracial adoptive parent and author of** *Anti-bias Curriculum* **and** *Teaching/Learning Anti Racism*

With remarkable insight, admirable honesty, and gentle humor, Gail Steinberg and Beth Hall expertly guide readers through the complexities of transracial adoption—clarifying the issues and offering critical tools to help transracial families navigate the challenges they confront on a day to day basis.

> —**Madelyn Freundlich, Executive Director, Evan B. Donaldson Adoption Institute**

This book will provide adoptive parents practical and useful information for parenting a child of a different race or culture from authors eminently qualified as both professionals in the field of adoption and as parents who have adopted transracially themselves.

> —**Joseph Crumbley, LCSW, author of** *Transracial Adoption and Foster Care*

Steinberg and Hall candidly and eloquently bare their souls about their transracial adoption journey. They share prescriptive insights based on well-documented research and personal experience. Their children provide a unique filter through which the parents learn to appreciate the child's birth culture and the child matures to embrace a multicultural world view.

> —**Gloria King, M.S., Executive Director, Black Adoption Placement and Research Center**

Meaty must reading for parents and professionals involved in transracial placements.

> —**Joseph Kroll, Executive Director, North American Council for Adoptable Children**